THE AVIATION FACTFILE
HELICOPTERS

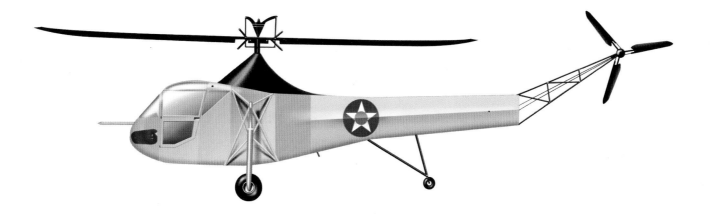

THE AVIATION FACTFILE

HELICOPTERS
Military, Civilian, and Rescue Rotorcraft

GENERAL EDITOR: ROBERT JACKSON

THUNDER BAY
P·R·E·S·S

San Diego, California

Thunder Bay Press
An imprint of the Advantage Publishers Group
5880 Oberlin Drive, San Diego, CA 92121-4794
www.thunderbaybooks.com

ISBN-13: 978-1-59223-504-9
ISBN-10: 1-59223-504-2

Library of Congress Cataloging-in-Publication Data available upon request.

Printed in Singapore

1 2 3 4 5 09 08 07 06 05

Contents

INTRODUCTION

Left: Paul Cornu's 1907 'Flying Bicycle', the first machine to take off vertically with a pilot and make a controlled free flight.

Above: The European-manufactured EH.101 Merlin is one of the new generation of large multi-role helicopters.

Right: The CH-53E is currently the West's most powerful helicopter.

Far right: The tandem-seat AH-64 Apache is one of the leading battlefield helicopters in the world, and packs a powerful punch.

As long ago as the fourth century BC, children in China were playing with a little toy whose principle would be used hundreds of years later to bring a new dimension to the science of flight. It was a simple round stick with feathers mounted on top, each feather twisted slightly so that it struck the air at an angle when the stick was spun, creating enough lift to enable the device to fly up into the air. Two hundred years later, Archimedes of Syracuse – the Greek physicist and inventor who was responsible for many scientific discoveries that laid the foundations of modern science – hit upon exactly the same principle for use in a different medium. He perfected a rotating screw which, when fitted inside a cylinder, made an excellent water-pump. Rotated continuously inside the cylinder, the screw pushed against the water and moved it along, and this in turn gave rise to a reaction: the water resisted by pushing back. Two thousand years were to elapse before the principle that governed the operation of Archimedes' screw in water was applied to another fluid – air – to produce a lifting force.

On 13 November, 1907, a Frenchman named Paul Cornu made the world's first free, untethered, manned helicopter flight at Coquainvilliers, near Lisieux. His primitive machine – known as the 'flying bicycle' – hovered 30 cm (1 ft) clear of the ground for 30 seconds. It would be

many years before the dream of vertical flight became a practical reality, but it was a beginning.

The early pioneers of rotary-wing flight faced a formidable challenge, because to make a helicopter (the name means, literally, 'flying screw') fly successfully, several different principles must be brought together. The first of these is lift.

The cross-section of a helicopter blade is of aerofoil shape, just like the wing section of a conventional aircraft. The top surface of this aerofoil section is more curved, or cambered, than the under-surface, so that when a stream of air flows over it the speed of the air increases and its pressure decreases. Under the wing the opposite happens; since the wing is

usually inclined at a small angle to the airflow, the air passing underneath it is slowed down by being obstructed and the pressure increases. The high pressure area below the wing tries to move towards the low pressure area above the wing, and a lifting force is created.

A conventional aircraft has to move forward through the air to reach the speed

where enough lift is obtained to take it off the ground, but with a helicopter, the wings – or rotor blades – are given motion through the air by rotation, even when the aircraft is not moving.

The amount of lift produced by a helicopter's rotor blades depends on three things: the shape and size of the blades, the speed at which they rotate, and their

Left: The Eurocopter Panther is one of a number of highly successful multi-role helicopters built by Aérospatiale and then Eurocopter.

Above: Mil Mi-26s have been used on United Nations humanitarian relief operations in recent years.

Right: Igor Sikorsky pictured piloting his first successful helicopter, the VS300, in 1939.

Far right: A Wallis autogyro in the colours of the Royal Air Force.

angle of attack – the angle at which they bite into the air. One or more of these factors must be increased if the lift is to be increased. The first two possibilities are both ruled out; there is nothing the pilot can do to alter the size of the blades, nor has he the reserves of engine power at his disposal very quickly when he needs extra lift.

He can, however, alter the angle of attack, for the main rotor blades of a helicopter can be automatically 'feathered' – in other words, made to twist in the rotor hub. If the angle of attack of all the blades is increased at the same time, there is a sudden increase in total lift, and when the lift becomes greater than the weight, the helicopter rises off the ground. Once airborne, the pilot can make the aircraft hover by slightly reducing the angle of attack of the blades so the total lift of the rotor now balances the weight of the helicopter. To alter the angle of attack of all blades at the same moment the pilot uses a lever known as the collective pitch control.

The helicopter is now off the ground and hovering, but to make it move forward through the air some form of horizontal thrust is needed. A conventional aircraft achieves this by means of its propeller or jet exhaust; in a helicopter, the lift force is tilted slightly to produce a horizontal thrust component. This can be achieved by tilting the whole rotor assembly slightly forward, but in practice it was found more effective to

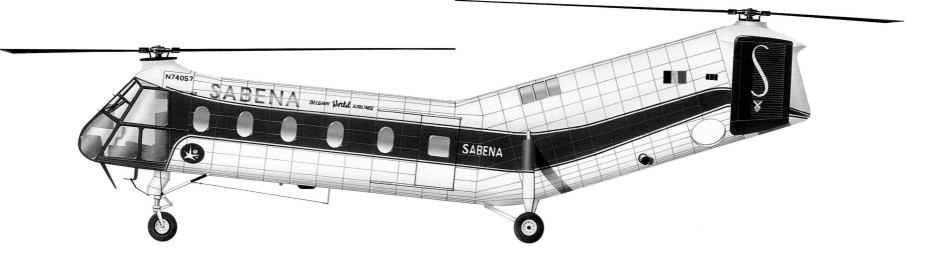

Above: The Piasecki/Vertol H-21 was flown in Sabena colours at the 1958 World's Fair.

Right: The Flettner FL 282 Kolibri appeared towards the end of World War II and was one of the world's first successful military helicopters.

hinge each blade to the rotor hub so that it can 'flap' up and down. When the helicopter is motionless on the ground, its rotor blades have a noticeable 'droop' because of this hinge arrangement; a stop is fitted below each blade to prevent it drooping too far. When the main rotor starts to revolve at increasing speed, centripetal force (the force that is exerted when you swing a weight around on a piece of string) tends to lift the blades back to a horizontal position.

As each blade is feathered – its angle of attack increased to produce more lift – it rises slightly on its hinge. If the angle of attack is reduced slightly as it approaches the forward position on its way around the rotor disc, the lift is slightly reduced too; and if the angle of attack is increased again as the blade 'retreats' rearwards so the lift is increased – with the result that each blade flaps downwards as it revolves through the forward position under the influence of centripetal force and rises under the influence of lift as it passes around the rear of the disc.

The whole effect is of the rotor disc tilting forward to produce forward thrust, with each blade changing its pitch as it moves round. This change of pitch is automatic and is governed by the cyclic pitch control.

If the helicopter consisted only of a set of main rotor blades mounted on the fuselage, the reaction to the rotor as it

revolved would turn the fuselage in the opposite direction. This is known as torque effect, and is normally overcome by a small vertically-revolving rotor mounted at the tail to prevent the fuselage from swinging round.

To operate all the helicopter's mechanical devices, the pilot has four main controls: the collective pitch control, the throttle, the cyclic pitch control and the tail rotor control.

In the 1920s, while designers struggled to overcome the problems of helicopter design, a young Spanish aircraft designer named Juan de la Cierva y Cordonia came up with an alternative, which he named the autogiro. In this machine, lift was provided by a freely-windmilling rotor, and forward propulsion by a conventional aero-engine. Although the autogiro could never perform all the functions of a helicopter, it had practical applications in

both civilian and military fields, and was widely used in the years between the two world wars.

It was left to the inventive Germans to produce the world's first truly successful helicopter, the twin-rotor Focke-Wulf Fw 61. Designed by Professor Heinrich Focke, it first flew in 1936 and went on to establish a number of world records. For the next few years, the Germans enjoyed an undisputed lead in helicopter

development, the two companies at the forefront being Focke-Achgelis and Flettner. These firms pioneered the operational use of the helicopter in World War II, both as an air observation platform and a transport vehicle. On the Allied side, one name quickly came to the forefront of helicopter design: that of Igor Sikorsky. It is a name that still stands at the forefront of medium and heavy helicopter design today. Another American

Far left: The huge twin-rotor Mil V-12 shattered every record for helicopter payload.

Left: Pescara's No.3 helicopter, the first to incorporate collective and cyclic controls.

Right: The giant Mil Mi-6 pioneered the use of supplementary wings for extra lift.

Far right: The Sikorsky S-61 is one of the most common search and rescue helicopters.

Below: The Westland Lynx is a very successful light shipboard helicopter.

firm, Bell Helicopters, dominated the post-war market for lighter machines, ranging from utility to fast attack helicopters.

In the Soviet Union, Igor Sikorsky's opposite number was Artem I. Mil, whose design bureau was responsible for a range of massive heavy-lift helicopters. By the beginning of the 21st century, more than 30,000 Mil helicopters had been built, with many of these rugged machines remaining in service worldwide.

In western Europe, economics eventually compelled companies that specialised in helicopter production to join forces. Eurocopter is now the official manufacturer of all MBB and Aérospatiale helicopters, and Britain's Westland now operates under the name GKN Westland. In common with other types of aircraft, both civil and military, helicopters are now the subject of joint design and production on both sides of the Atlantic.

Today, helicopters are applied to so many different tasks that it is difficult to list them all. They are the most versatile flying machines in existence, and they enable the pilot to operate in three dimensions in a way that no fixed-wing aircraft can – except, of course, VSTOL machines like the Harrier, which are intended for a specific role and which are by no means as prolific.

The helicopter, for all that it is expensive to operate, has become an indispensable tool of modern aviation. New technology, in particular the use of advanced composite materials of far greater strength and lightness than anything previously available, has given designers the means to enter a new phase of development that combines greater speeds with lower operating costs. It is in the commercial world of tomorrow that the helicopter will make its greatest impact.

AÉROSPATIALE

ALOUETTE II

● High altitude ● Air ambulance ● Excellent handling

▲ Spacious and relatively well equipped for rescue work, the Alouette II has found a ready market in both civil and military services as a dependable rescue platform.

Sud-Est, one of the forerunners of Aérospatiale, combined Turboméca's new Artouste turbine with a gearbox adapted from the Sikorsky S-55 to produce power for the Alouette. It flew for the first time in March 1955, and within three months the machine had set a new helicopter altitude record of 8209 m (26,925 ft.). Two years later an Alouette raised the record to 10984 m (36,028 ft.). This altitude performance made the aircraft a natural candidate for mountain rescues.

AÉROSPATIALE ALOUETTE II

Oral warning ▶
Equipped with a large amplifier, this example is used to issue warnings of avalanches to climbers in the mountains.

◀ Saving lives
A French Air Force Alouette II hoists up another rescued skier. Despite their military role the Alouettes are often tasked with rescuing civilians in distress.

Airborne ambulance ▶
Once retrieved from the mountain, survivors are flown to hospital in special fuselage stretchers.

▲ The search is on
Pilots often look for the survivors themselves, exploiting the excellent visibility from the Alouette's cockpit.

Star performer ▶
Demonstrating the capabilities of the helicopter is this example, lifting a large balloon as part of a publicity stunt. Crews find the helicopter a delight to fly.

FACTS AND FIGURES

➤ The Alouette II first flew on 12 March 1955; French certification on 2 May 1956 cleared the way for production.

➤ Germany has used the helicopter for more than 25 years without any crashes.

➤ Because of the shape of the fuselage the helicopter is known as 'bug-eye.'

➤ Options available for the helicopter include skid landing gear, floats or a wheeled undercarriage.

➤ In the rescue role the Alouette has a 120-kg (264-lb.) capable hoist.

➤ Many civilian examples operating today are ex-military machines.

PROFILE

High mountain rescuer

Even before flight testing had been completed, the Alouette II was showing its abilities as a mountain rescue aircraft. The second prototype Alouette II was in the Alps for performance tests in July 1956 when the test team learned that a climber was dying after having a heart attack in the Vallot Mountain refuge, one of the highest in Europe at 4362 m (14,307 ft.).

The first attempt at a rescue was unsuccessful, but the second worked: within five minutes of landing the helicopter had transported the climber to hospital in Chamonix, thereby saving his life.

At the beginning of 1957 two Alouettes carried out a similar rescue, retrieving six mountain guides, and two pilots of an S-55 rescue helicopter which had crashed, from the same refuge.

Since then the Alouette II and its high-altitude version, the Lama, have carried out many mountain rescues, retrieving stranded climbers from places that would not have been reachable by any other means.

Above: Small and nimble, the Alouette looks very dated compared to modern helicopters.

Right: With the extra-high skids this Alouette derivative is known as the Lama. It combines features from both the Alouette II and III variants.

The Alouette's successor, the Aérospatiale Ecureuil, is now serving with the Nepalese Army. The type has already retrieved climbers from high on Everest.

SA 318C Alouette II

Type: trainer/utility/rescue helicopter

Powerplant: one 395-kW (530-hp.) Turboméca Astazou IIA turboshaft engine

Maximum speed: 205 km/h (127 m.p.h.) at sea level; cruising speed 180 km/h (122 m.p.h.)

Endurance: 5 hr 18 min

Initial climb rate: 396 m/min (1,300 f.p.m.)

Range: 720 km (446 mi.)

Service ceiling: 3300 m (10,824 ft.); hovering ceiling 1550 m (5,080 ft.)

Weights: empty 890 kg (1,958 lb.); maximum take-off, with full rescue equipment 1650 kg (3,630 lb.)

Dimensions: fuselage width 2.22 m (7 ft. 3 in.)
length 9.75 m (32 ft.)
height 2.75 m (9 ft. 1 in.)
main rotor disc area 81.71 m² (879 sq. ft.)

SA 318C ALOUETTE II

The German army has operated the Alouette II for more than 25 years for general duties including scouting and as a VIP transport. Now facing replacement, the helicopters are being sold on the civil market.

Despite reaching the end of its military service, numerous examples of the Alouette II have been purchased by civil operators to be used for liaison duties. Later designs have entered the market but the rescue performance of the Alouette is proving hard to beat.

The Alouette's turboshaft engine gives it excellent performance. Even when loaded with the equipment needed for with the rescue role, the Alouette II has been able to reach exceptional altitudes.

A single twin-bladed rotor is fitted to the Alouette II. Pilots have found that manoeuvring the helicopter is easy.

Visibility from the cockpit is excellent because of the extensive glazing.

Despite the dated look of the open tail boom, this network of metal tubes allows the helicopter to be extremely light. This is particularly useful because of the altitudes at which most rescue operations are undertaken in the mountains.

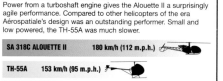

A range of options is available for the landing gear on the Alouette II. Apart from the traditional skids, floats, wheels and specially adapted extra-wide skids to land on snow are available.

Positioned at the rear of the fuselage boom is a large wire loop, designed to protect the tail rotor from striking the ground during landings.

ACTION DATA

MAXIMUM CRUISING SPEED

Power from a turboshaft engine gives the Alouette II a surprisingly agile performance. Compared to other helicopters of the era Aérospatiale's design was an outstanding performer. Small and low powered, the TH-55A was much slower.

SA 318C ALOUETTE II	180 km/h (112 m.p.h.)
TH-55A	153 km/h (95 m.p.h.)
SKEETER T.Mk 12	171 km/h (106 m.p.h.)

RANGE

Additional auxiliary fuel tanks added to the Alouette allowed the helicopter to ihave a range beyond that of any of its competitors. The outstanding range of the helicopter has seen it used for patrol duties in both civilian and military guises.

SA 318C ALOUETTE II 720 km (446 mi.)

SKEETER T.Mk 12 422 km (262 mi.)

TH-55A 370 km (229 mi.)

SERVICE CEILING

Although it is used as a mountain rescue helicopter, when compared to the British Skeeter and American TH-55A the basic Alouette had a relatively poor performance at high altitude. Despite this, specially adapted models were developed to allow the Alouettes to fulfil rescue duties.

SA 318C ALOUETTE II 3300 m (10,824 ft.)	TH-55A 3110 m (10,200 ft.)	SKEETER T.Mk 12 3901 m (12,800 ft.)

Help from above

■ **AÉROSPATIALE AS 352 COUGAR:** Derived from the earlier Puma, the Cougar is a far more capable rescue helicopter.

■ **BOEING CH-113 LABRADOR:** Operated by the Canadian Armed Forces, the large Labrador is able to land on water.

■ **WESTLAND SEA KING:** The primary rescue helicopter of the RAF, the Sea King is based at several UK locations.

AÉROSPATIALE

ALOUETTE III

● Alpine search and rescue ● Unrivalled high-altitude performance

High in the Alps, the Alouette is a guardian angel – risking fierce winds, snow, ice and treacherous terrain to rescue those in trouble on Europe's high mountains. The highly successful Alouette is found in dozens of nations performing hundreds of jobs. None have become better known than its dramatic mercy missions, which it carries out at great risk to the crew to save those in peril.

▲ *A roomy cabin*
allows the Alouette III to operate as an effective troop transporter. The Alouette has also been used in support of quick-reaction units to intercept terrorist forces.

AÉROSPATIALE ALOUETTE III

▲ **High performance**
Fitted with a more powerful Astazou XIV engine, the SA 319B has superb high-altitude performance. This example also carries floats for water-based operations.

▲ **Taking the load**
Where landing is impossible the exceptionally versatile Alouette can still provide vital supplies using an external sling.

▲ **Mountain rescue**
An Alouette of the French Sécurité Civil picks up an injured skier from a high mountain top. Alouettes have carried out hundreds of missions like this.

◄ **Vintage gunship** ▲
Using AS-11 rockets and heavy cannon, the Alouette was a pioneer in the development of helicopter gunships. The Alouette served in the war in Algeria with French forces, and also in the Rhodesian civil war.

FACTS AND FIGURES

➤ In June 1960 an Alouette III proved that it could operate at 4810 m (15,780 ft.) on Mont Blanc, Europe's highest mountain.

➤ The first flight of the Alouette III took place on 28 February 1959.

➤ On 21 June 1972, an SA 315B Lama (Alouette II airframe and III engine) set a height record of 12442 m (40,820 ft.).

➤ Alouettes also serve as light transports, agricultural, liaison, observation and photo-mapping aircraft.

➤ The Alouette III has an external sling for loads up to 750 kg (1,650 lb.) or a rescue hoist which can lift 175 kg (400 lb.).

➤ Indian Alouettes regularly operate in the Himalayas, the world's highest mountains.

Rotors to the rescue, Alpine style

The Aérospatiale SA 319A/C Alouette III, manufactured by the company known today as Eurocopter, has been a spectacular aircraft almost from its first flight in 1959. This fine helicopter exhibits many superb flying qualities, but none is more impressive than the Alouette's high-altitude performance. Part of the credit for the success of Europe's best-known helicopter is due to the Turboméca company, which was the first in the world to develop light turbine aero engines.

On the heels of the earlier Alouette II, 1,305 of which serve around the globe, the Alouette III has reached operators in numbers exceeding 1,500. In every climate, the Alouette is a versatile aircraft and military operators have used the Alouette III for light-attack and anti-submarine duties. However, it has become famous for flying life-saving missions in mountain ranges the world over.

French Alouettes have performed a variety of jobs. As a military light utility transport they have been replaced by the Gazelle and Puma, but the Gendarmerie continues to appreciate its superb high-altitude performance in the mountains.

Alouette III

Type: general-purpose helicopter

Powerplant: one 870-kW (870-shp.) Turboméca Artouste IIIB turboshaft derated to 425 kW/550 shp. (SA-316B); one 649-kW/870-shp. Turboméca Astazou XIV turboshaft derated to 448 kW/600 shp. (SA-319C)

Maximum speed: 210 km/h (137 m.p.h.) at sea level

Hovering ceiling in ground effect: 2880 m (8,400 ft.)

Hovering ceiling out of ground effect: 1520 m (5,000 ft.)

Range: 480 km (375 mi.)

Weights: empty 1143 kg (2,440 lb.); loaded 2200 kg (4,960 lb.)

Dimensions: rotor diameter 11.02 m (36 ft. 2 in.)
length (blades folded) 10.03 m (33 ft.)
height 3.00 m (9 ft. 10 in.)
wing area 95.38 m² (1,027 ft.)

ALOUETTE III

The Netherlands army operates weaponless Alouette IIIs in an observation and light transport role. It is shortly due to replace them with McDonnell Douglas AH-64D Apaches, but the Netherlands air force will retain some for search-and-rescue operations.

The Alouette has a traditional hinged rotor head with three rotor blades. Despite its old design, the Alouette is a nimble machine and is well liked by pilots.

Turboméca's Astazou has proved to be a reliable and powerful engine. The Astazou's light weight and high power output give the Alouette much of its famous performance at altitude.

Tail rotors are a vulnerable area of any helicopter, and even with this large guard below it the pilot is always concerned about the tail. The successors to the Alouette have an enclosed tail rotor in a 'fenestron' fin mounting, for protection and improved performance.

The roomy cabin is a useful feature for search and rescue. Six passengers can be carried, or two stretchers and two seated passengers in the casualty evacuation role.

The excellent view from the Alouette's cockpit is vital for crews in search-and-rescue work.

Many Alouettes have winches and spotlights fitted for light transport. The maximum 750-kg (1,650-lb.) payload can also be carried externally on a sling.

The six passenger seats in the standard Alouette III's roomy cabin can quickly be removed. The helicopter then becomes a light cargo transport, able to lift payloads of up to 750 kg (1,650 lb.).

The fins on the tailboom give added stability in forward flight, and also help the pilot keep a steady hover when performing delicate rescue manoeuvres in high wind conditions.

Alouettes in the mountains

■ **UNDERCARRIAGE:** The ski-equipped undercarriage of an Alouette in a high mountain valley shows that it operates here all year round. The warm summer weather in this picture makes the helicopter's performance lower than usual, as the air density is reduced even more.

■ **SNOW OPERATIONS:** The Alouette's small size, light weight, forgiving flying characteristics and ski undercarriage are essential when operating on snow. Heavy helicopters with normal wheels would probably get stuck in these conditions, as well as finding it hard to fly in the thin alpine air.

■ **RESCUE VETERAN:** Thousands of people owe their lives to the Alouette for saving them in daring winch rescues. This mission needs careful work between all three crew – the pilot, winch operator and the winchman. Long periods in the hover also demand the good performance given by the Alouette.

ACTION DATA

SERVICE CEILING

The key to the Alouette III's high-altitude performance is the use of the Turboméca Astazou XIV turboshaft. Light but powerful, the engine allows the Alouette to operate at heights most other helicopters cannot reach, making it ideal for mountain rescue. The Gazelle also has a respectable ceiling but rarely operates above 1000 m (3,280 ft.). The less powerful JetRanger struggles above 3000 m (9,850 ft.).

ALOUETTE III 6000 m (17,700 ft.)

GAZELLE 5000 m (16,400 ft.)

206 JETRANGER 4100 m (13,400 ft.)

AÉROSPATIALE

SA 321 SUPER FRELON

● Heavylift ● Anti-submarine warfare ● Assault transport

▲ Although the market in heavy helicopters was dominated by American and Soviet designs, the SA 321 achieved notable export success. The aircraft went to war with Israeli forces in 1973 in the assault transport role, and has also been used to rescue French navy pilots.

E urope's largest production helicopter, the Super Frelon was built with the assistance of Sikorsky. Used for assault transport, anti-submarine warfare and delivery to ships, the SA 321 was also converted to fire Exocet missiles for Iraq in the war against Iran. More than 35 years after its first flight, the Super Frelon is still in service with the forces of China, France, Israel and Libya, mainly as a utility and assault transport aircraft.

AÉROSPATIALE SA 321 SUPER FRELON

Submarine hunter ▶
Equipped with dipping sonar and surveillance radar, the Super Frelon was responsible for shipboard anti-submarine warfare.

▲ **Still in service**
In their fourth decade of service, Aéronavale Super Frelons now fly in a low-conspicuity dark grey colour scheme.

▲ **Floating Frelon**
Like many Sikorsky designs the Super Frelon could land on water, but only if the sea conditions were extremely calm.

▲ **Pick up**
The Super Frelon was used by the Aéronavale for air-sea rescue duties from carriers.

Pacific deployment ▶
A small number of Super Frelons were deployed to France's Pacific island nuclear test centres.

FACTS AND FIGURES

➤ Iraq used Super Frelons, equipped with Omera radar and AM39 Exocet missiles, in anti-shipping strikes against Iran.

➤ Production of the Frelon continues in China, where the type is called the Z-8.

➤ Israel re-engined eight of its Super Frelons and sold them to Argentina.

➤ In French naval service the Frelon equips three units: 33F and 20S at St Mandrier and 32F based at Lanveoc.

➤ The prototype troop-carrying Super Frelon first flew on 7 December 1962.

➤ French Aéronavale Sa 321s are used to refuel naval vessels from the air.

PROFILE

Biggest of the 'Eurocopters'

Bravely entering a competitive market dominated by Soviet and American designs, the Super Frelon was a derivative of the original Frelon (Hornet). This large, three-engined aircraft was designed to a French military requirement for a multi-role, medium-sized helicopter with the assistance of Sikorsky in the United States. Fiat in Italy were responsible for producing the main gearbox and transmission.

The first prototypes flew in 1962 and 1963, with the Aéronavale receiving the first Super Frelons, equipped with a podded Sylph surveillance radar, in 1966. Some were later modified with nose-mounted radar and Exocet missiles for anti-ship attack, and the SA 321Ga was delivered for utility transport duties. The 20 surviving Aéronavale Super Frelons carry out search-and-rescue, vertical replenishment and transport duties, having largely relinquished their

anti-submarine warfare role.

The Super Frelon was exported to Iraq, Israel, Libya and South Africa. A 27-seat civil heli-liner variant, the SA 321J was also produced but not widely used.

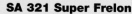

Below: A total of 99 French-built Super Frelons were produced. The type also flew as a fire-fighter and heli-liner.

Above: There is little externally, except for camouflage, to distinguish the transport Super Frelons from their maritime counterparts.

SA 321 Super Frelon

Type: three-engined medium-assault transport and naval helicopter

Powerplant: three 1099-kW (1,473 hp.) Turboméca Turmo tuboshaft engines

Maximum speed: 275 km/h (171 m.p.h.)

Initial climb rate: 300 m/min (984 f.p.m.)

Combat radius: 1020 km (634 miles) with 3050 kg (6,724 lb.) payload

Service ceiling: 3100 m (10,171 ft.)

Weights: empty 6863 kg (15,130 lb.); loaded 12500 kg (27,558 lb.)

Armament: four homing torpedoes or two AM.39 Exocet missiles

Dimensions:
span	18.90 m	(62 ft.)
length	23.03 m	(75 ft. 6 in.)
height	6.76 m	(22 ft. 2 in.)
rotor disc area	280.55 m²	(3020 sq. ft.)

SA 321 SUPER FRELON

The Super Frelon remains in limited use in the Aéronavale, although it has now given up its former roles of anti-submarine and anti-ship warfare.

Power is provided by three Turboméca Turmo IIIC engines. Fuel is stored in flexible tanks under the floor of the centre fuselage; these helps to lower the centre of gravity.

The rotor is a six-bladed, fully-articulated unit. The first few rotor units were ground tested in the United States. The blades are of all-metal construction.

The Super Frelon has a nose-mounted radar for anti-ship work.

The remaining Super Frelons in French service are painted all-blue. Previously, the fuselage was painted white above the cockpit and halfway up the tailboom.

MARINE 63

The main cabin houses up to 28 troops in the assault transport role. Exocet missiles can be carried on special mountings on the fuselage sides. The SA 321F does not have the stabilising floats which are fitted to the SA 321G.

The tail rotor is a five-bladed unit of similar construction to the main rotor, rotating at 990 revolutions per minute. The rotor is driven by gearing from the shaft linking the rear and port forward engines.

The boat-shaped hull was inspired by the Sikorsky SH-3.

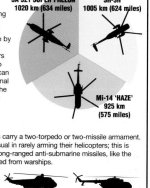

COMBAT DATA

MAXIMUM SPEED

Generally, the biggest helicopters are also the fastest. The Super Frelon is a powerful machine with a streamlined fuselage shape and a high top speed. The SA 321s purchased by Israel had new engines fitted, giving improved performance.

SA 321 SUPER FRELON 275 km/h (171 m.p.h.)

SH-3H 267 km/h (166 m.p.h.)

Mi-14 'HAZE' 230 km/h (143 m.p.h.)

RANGE

Naval and assault helicopters require long range to be effective. They can supplement their patrol endurance by carrying out hovering refuels from destroyers which are too small to actually land on and can often carry extra internal fuel for ferry flights. The naval Mi-14 is usually shore-based.

SA 321 SUPER FRELON 1020 km (634 miles)

SH-3H 1005 km (624 miles)

Mi-14 'HAZE' 925 km (575 miles)

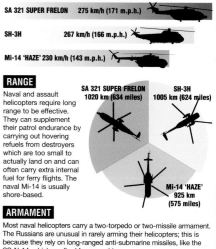

ARMAMENT

Most naval helicopters carry a two-torpedo or two-missile armament. The Russians are unusual in rarely arming their helicopters; this is because they rely on long-ranged anti-submarine missiles, like the SS-N-14, which are fired from warships.

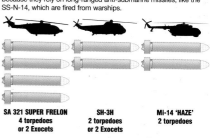

SA 321 SUPER FRELON	SH-3H	Mi-14 'HAZE'
4 torpedoes or 2 Exocets	2 torpedoes or 2 Exocets	2 torpedoes

Medium utility and naval assault helicopters

■ AÉROSPATIALE SA 330 PUMA: Built in collaboration with Westland, the Puma remains in service with the RAF and French air force, and many exports are used as assault transports.

■ BOEING-VERTOL CH-46 SEA KNIGHT: Derived from the larger Chinook, the CH-46 is in service with the US Marine Corps as the standard medium-lift helicopter based on assault ships.

■ MIL Mi-8 'HAZE': The most numerous helicopter ever built, the Mi-8 (and the newer, more powerful Mi-17) remain in service with navies, armies and in civilian roles around the world.

AÉROSPATIALE (WESTLAND)
SA 330 PUMA

● All-weather transport helicopter ● Gulf and Bosnia veteran

Building on its experience with the earlier, larger Super Frelon, Sud Aviation (later Aérospatiale) answered the French army's call for an all-weather medium transport helicopter with the Puma. France and later Britain ordered sizeable fleets. Civil operators, too, found uses for what was to be the first all-weather helicopter in the West. Military and civil exports have flourished and the Puma is still in production almost 30 years later.

▲ Despite their advancing years, Pumas are still widely used by the world's armed forces, including those of its original customers, France and the U.K. RAF examples took part in the First Gulf War.

AÉROSPATIALE (WESTLAND) SA 330 PUMA

◄ **Still in active service**
France deployed Pumas to the former Yugoslavia for use by the U.N. This example fires self-protection flares.

▼ **Civilian sales**
A Japanese civil SA 330 with flotation gear fitted to the nose and sponsons. This would inflate if the aircraft ditched.

◄ **Say aaah!**
A Puma will fit in the hold of a C-5 Galaxy—once its rotors have been removed. This RAF Puma is en route to the Persian Gulf in 1991.

◄ **Oilfield support**
Once the Puma had been equipped with radar for night/all-weather flying, operators in the oil industry became valued customers. Bristow Helicopters supports rigs in the North Sea.

◄ **Early prototype**
The SA 330A prototype first flew in 1965. This is the fifth of eight prototypes ordered in June 1963. In 1968 the last of this batch was delivered to the U.K. for evaluation.

FACTS AND FIGURES

➤ SA 330Js and Ls were the first Western helicopters certified for all-weather flight including operations in icing conditions.

➤ Aérospatiale replaced the Puma with the more powerful Super Puma from 1981.

➤ In the 1982 Falklands War Argentina used Pumas to move radars from site to site.

➤ The RAF's Pumas have given over 30 years' service.

➤ The Puma prototype had two 970-kW (1,300-hp.) engines; SA 330Ls have two with 1175kW (1,575 hp.) power.

➤ Romanian Pumas have been armed with 9M14 (AT-3) anti-tank missiles.

PROFILE

First all-weather Western chopper

To fill a French army requirement for an all-weather medium-lift transport helicopter, Sud Aviation (later to become part of Aérospatiale) designed the SA 330.

This, France's first attempt to build a medium helicopter without outside technical contributions, was a resounding success, though the all-weather capability did not come until after several years of development.

The first deliveries of SA 330Bs to the French army took place in 1969, the type becoming operational the following year.

Meanwhile, the last pre-production Puma was being modified by Westland for the RAF. After promising tests, a joint production agreement was reached and the British firm built 48 SA 330Es (Puma HC.Mk 1s).

Aérospatiale went on to build 686 SA 330s (before switching production to the Super Puma in 1981) in successively improved versions for numerous export customers. These included civil operators, especially those in the oilfield support industry once the all-weather capability was available in the SA 330J and L. Between 1970 and 1984, Aérospatiale sold 126 civil models in all.

Romanian company IAR began license production in 1977 and by 1994 had built over 200. Production of the IAR-330L continues and there are plans for an upgraded Puma 2000.

Left: The French Orchidée battlefield surveillance radar program was shelved in 1990, but was revived during Operation Desert Storm. The system was carried aboard a Puma.

Above: The U.K. Defence Research Agency at RAE Boscombe Down operated this Puma HC.Mk 1 for several years.

SA 330L Puma

Type: Medium transport helicopter.

Powerplant: Two 1175kW (1,575-hp.) Turboméca Turmo IVC turboshafts.

Maximum speed: 294 km/h (182 m.p.h.)

Service ceiling: 6000 m (19,700 ft.)

Range: 572 km (355 mi.) at cruising speed.

Accommodation: Up to 20 fully equipped troops or 3200 kg (7,000 lb.) of cargo.

Weapons: Optional provision for various combinations of weapons including cannons, machine guns, rockets and missiles.

Weights: Empty 3615 kg (7,953 lb.); max takeoff 7400 kg (16,280 lb.)

Dimensions:
Main rotor diameter	15 m (49 ft. 3 in.)
Length	18.15m (59 ft. 6 in.)
Height	5.14 m (16 ft. 10 in.)
Rotor disc area	176.7 m² (1,901 sq. ft.)

SA 330H PUMA

The SA 330H is known to the French air force as the SA 330Ba. 1515 was based in the French Caribbean with Overseas Transport Squadron No. 58 in 1983.

The fully articulated main rotor with four aluminum blades on the initial production SA 330s were replaced by a new rotor with composite blades in the SA 330J and L.

Turboméca's Turmo turboshaft engine was also used in the SA.321 Super Frelon heavy transport helicopter of the early 1960s.

The tail rotor has five blades to absorb the power of the two engines while maintaining low noise levels.

Dual flight controls are standard on the Puma, which flies with two flight deck crew. There are two independent hydraulic systems.

The Puma's tricycle landing gear is semi-retractable and there is provision for pop-out flotation gear.

The main cabin of the Puma was designed to hold 18 passengers. In the military transport role 3200 kg (7,000 lb.) can be carried (or 2500 kg/5,500 lb. on an internal hoist). RAF Pumas have a door-mounted rescue hoist with a 575 kg (1,265-lb.) capacity.

Though painted in a predominantly green camouflage color scheme, this Puma also carries large patches of Day-Glo paint work, indicating a search-and-rescue role.

ACTION DATA

SPEED

Late-production Pumas have a good top speed compared to other helicopters in a similar category. Both the Sea King and Mi-8 are, however, slightly larger aircraft.

SA 330L PUMA	294 km/h (182 m.p.h.)
SEA KING HC.Mk 4	241 km/h (149 m.p.h.)
Mi-8T 'HIP-C'	250 km/h (155 m.p.h.)

RANGE

Though smaller than the Sea King and Mi-8, the Puma has a good range with its maximum load aboard. With over 90 miles more range, Pumas can lift almost as much as larger types.

SA 330L PUMA	572 km (355 mi.)
SEA KING HC.Mk 4	396 km (246 mi.)
Mi-8T 'HIP-C'	400 km (248 mi.)

PAYLOAD

Its ability to lift over three tons combined with its relatively compact size makes the Puma ideal for the tactical transport role and also oil rig support sorties.

SA 330L PUMA 3200 kg (7,000 lb.)

SEA KING HC.Mk 4 3629 kg (7,985 lb.)

Mi-8T 'HIP-C' 4000 kg (8,800 lb.)

Military Pumas show their colors

■ **ROYAL AIR FORCE SA 330E (PUMA HC.MK 1):** XW229 was painted in tiger stripes for a NATO Tiger Meet while with No. 230 Squadron based in West Germany in the 1980s.

■ **IRISH AIR CORPS SA 330J:** The single SA 330J used by the Irish Air Corps is a converted civil example. It has the standard weather radar set and is used for troop and VIP transport.

■ **BELGIAN GENDARMERIE SA 330H:** Assigned to NATO in time of war are three civil-registered upgraded export model SA 330Hs, normally used for VIP transport and flown by army pilots.

AÉROSPATIALE (WESTLAND)

SA 342 GAZELLE

● Missile-armed tank-killer ● Helicopter trainer ● 'Fan-in-fin' design

Serving in attack, spotting or training duties, the Gazelle is a reliable and cost-effective helicopter. A natural successor to the Alouette, this trim five-seater has much greater performance, and no utility-class rotorcraft looks more pleasing or performs better. In addition to aesthetic appeal and superb handling for its pilot, the Gazelle is among the most versatile of helicopters, and has been widely embraced by civilian and military users.

▲ *The Gazelle is a superb performer despite being unarmoured and also a generation behind the latest combat helicopters. France used missile-armed Gazelles to great effect in the Gulf War.*

AÉROSPATIALE (WESTLAND) SA 342 GAZELLE

▼ Mountain Gazelle
Like its French-built predecessors, the Lama and Alouette, the Gazelle has a great reserve of power, giving excellent altitude ability and making it popular with users in mountainous areas. The Gazelle gained several helicopter speed records in the early 1970s, and is still one of the fastest in its class.

▲ Going to the Gulf
Gazelles served on both sides in the Gulf War, being used by French and British forces and by Iraq, whose Gazelles also saw combat against Iran in the 1980s.

▲ Staying low
In the anti-tank scout role, short, fast hops between cover are key tactics, and the Gazelle's agility and speed are vital.

With the Legion ▶
Gazelles supported the fast-moving light units in the Gulf, operating far to the west of Kuwait.

▲ Tank-buster
Both French and British Gazelles are fitted with roof-mounted sights. But whereas British machines are unarmed scouts used to locate targets for other weapons, French Gazelles can make their own attacks with HOT wire-guided missiles and 20-mm cannon.

FACTS AND FIGURES

➤ The SA 340 prototype flew on 12 April 1968 with the same engine and rotors as the Alouette.

➤ The glass-fibre rotor blades introduced by the Gazelle were first used in 1970.

➤ Manufacture of the Gazelle began with a civil-registered aircraft on 6 August 1971.

➤ Syrian Gazelles armed with HOT missiles destroyed several Israeli tanks in Lebanon's Bekaa Valley in 1982.

➤ The Gazelle can carry out loops and barrel rolls in capable hands.

➤ The Serbs used Yugoslav-built Gazelles in the Balkan civil war during the 1990s.

PROFILE

Fast moving in the Gazelle

The SA 341 Gazelle all-purpose lightweight helicopter began as a proposal for a new observation helicopter for the French army. It was re-named the SA 340 soon afterwards. The finished design looked like the well-known Alouette and initially used the same engine. Unlike the Alouette, the Gazelle features a fully enclosed fuselage structure and, while it can be flown by a single pilot,

has provision for two pilots with side-by-side seating.

In 1967, Britain joined a production-sharing agreement and began its long association with the Gazelle as a military helicopter. Westland performed final assembly of the first British military version in 1970.

The SA 341 designation reappeared in 1970, when the Gazelle established three world helicopter speed records. The upgraded SA 342 first flew in

1976. About a dozen versions of the Gazelle are in wide use, including military variants employed by 27 countries, and are performing with distinction. France has nearly 300 heavily-armed Gazelles.

As long as the Gazelle can stay out of range of enemy fire, it is an excellent light scout. It has fought in the Falklands, both Gulf Wars and in Bosnia. Its future in this role may be coming to an end as air defence against helicopters gets more deadly.

SA 342M Gazelle

Type: five-seat utility helicopter

Powerplant: one 640-kW (860-hp.) Turbomeca Astazou IIA turboshaft engine

Maximum speed: 310 km/h (192 m.p.h.) at sea level

Range: 670 km (415 mi.) with standard fuel

Weights: empty 908 kg (2,000 lb.) ; loaded 2100 kg (4,620 lb.)

Armament: 36-mm rockets, 20-mm cannon, AS.11, TOW, HOT, Mistrale or other missiles

Accommodation: pilot; four/five passengers or 700 kg (1,540 lb.) of cargo

Dimensions:
main rotor diameter	10.50 m	(34 ft. 5 in.)
length	11.97 m	(39 ft. 3 in.)
height	3.15 m	(10 ft. 4 in.)
rotor disc area	86.50 m²	(931 sq. ft.)

GAZELLE AH.MK 1

The Gazelle AH.Mk 1 is used by the British Army Air Corps as an anti-tank scout, spotting armoured targets for tank-killing TOW-armed Lynxes. Unlike their French counterparts, they are unarmed.

The Gazelle rotor head is of the conventional hinged type, but is sufficiently strong to withstand aerobatics in the hands of the Royal Navy display team.

The Astazou turboshaft was also used in the early BAe Jetstream business aircraft. It has a centrifugal compressor first stage and axial second stage.

The three rotor blades are glass fibre, wrapped around an aluminium 'D-spar' leading edge.

The Gazelle has an extremely small forward profile. This is vital in the anti-tank role, as it is the Gazelle's only defence against enemy fire.

Pilots share a single, central instrument console, but have separate dual-controls.

The Gazelle's cyclic pitch lever has an automatic throttle.

All Gazelles have a tubular metal skid-type undercarriage, which has provision for flotation equipment.

The tubular tail rotor drive-shaft runs down the spine of the tail boom.

The fenestron, or 'fan-in-fin' tail rotor, was designed to give increased performance in turbulent conditions as well as being less prone to damage.

ARMY XX457

COMBAT DATA

CRUISING SPEED

Although it has been in service for many years, the Gazelle remains one of the fastest helicopters in its class. This, together with its superb agility, means that it can perform at least as well as its more recent rivals.

SA 342M GAZELLE	264 km/h (164 m.p.h.)	
MODEL 406	235 km/h (146 m.p.h.)	
BO 105	242 km/h (150 m.p.h.)	

RANGE

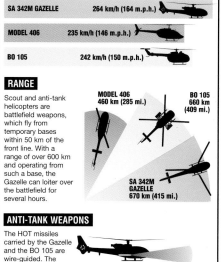

Scout and anti-tank helicopters are battlefield weapons, which fly from temporary bases within 50 km of the front line. With a range of over 600 km and operating from such a base, the Gazelle can loiter over the battlefield for several hours.

MODEL 406 460 km (285 mi.)
BO 105 660 km (409 mi.)
SA 342M GAZELLE 670 km (415 mi.)

ANTI-TANK WEAPONS

The HOT missiles carried by the Gazelle and the BO 105 are wire-guided. The launch helicopter must continue pointing towards the enemy until the missile hits. The American Bell 406 is smaller and lighter, but the latest versions carry the very powerful laser-guided Hellfire, which is a 'fire-and-forget' weapon.

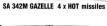
SA 342M GAZELLE 4 x HOT missiles

MODEL 406 4 x Hellfire missiles

BO 105 6 x HOT missiles

Multi-role civil and military machine

■ **COMBAT WEAPON:** Fitted with advanced sights and armed with heavy HOT wire-guided missiles, the Gazelles of the French army can destroy tanks at ranges of up to 4 km (2.5 miles).

■ **ADVANCED TRAINER:** While being relatively easy to fly, the Gazelle has enough performance and agility to train student pilots in the challenges of tactical rotary-winged flight.

■ **EXECUTIVE TRANSPORT:** Although most of the 1,200 or so Gazelles that have been built are military versions, its speed and economy have made it a popular civil transport.

AÉROSPATIALE

ALOUETTE II/LAMA

● World's first production turbine helicopter ● Worldwide success

▲ Despite their age,
the Alouette II and Lama soldier on.
While Alouette production ceased in 1975,
the Lama was built in France until 1991 and
continues to be produced in India.

Design work on the now famous
Alouette (Lark) aircraft began in
1947. Originally designated SE 3120
and powered by a piston engine, it was the
installation of a turboshaft engine which
produced the world-beating Alouette II.
As the first turboshaft-engined helicopter
to enter production anywhere in the world,
it was soon in great demand internationally.
The series has gone on to be France's
most successful helicopter.

AÉROSPATIALE ALOUETTE II/LAMA

Civil success story ▶
Although conceived as a military helicopter, the Alouette II and Lama
found a large numbers of civilian customers worldwide.

▲ Lama in the Alps
Both civilian and military customers take advantage of the
Lama's improved 'hot-and-high' performance.

▲ 'Blue Bees'
Belgium's 'Blue Bees' display team was
famously equipped with Alouette IIs.

▲ Strong, lightweight construction
An exposed tailboom structure was
typical of helicopters of the 1940s and
1950s. This is a Belgian military SE 313B.

Training with the Heeresflieger ▶
Germany took delivery of 247 Alouettes,
beginning in 1959. After more than
30 years of service, the army continues to
operate about 60 in the training role.

FACTS AND FIGURES

➤ On 21 June 1972 a Lama, with just a pilot
on board, set an absolute height record
for helicopters of 12442 m (40,800 ft.).

➤ Hindustan Aeronautics in India still produce
the Lama; it is known as the Cheetah.

➤ The Alouette II was the first foreign
helicopter to gain certification in the US.

➤ Licences to produce the Alouette II were
granted to Saab in Sweden and Republic
in the US; few were built, however.

➤ Alouette IIs and Lamas have served with
more than 120 users in nearly 50 countries.

➤ In Brazil, Helibras assembled Lamas, as
the Gavião, using French components.

PROFILE

Larks and Lamas from France

Three months after its first flight in March 1955 the Alouette II proved the potential of this great design by smashing the helicopter altitude record, taking it to 8209 metres (26,925 ft.). Orders followed quickly and mass production was initiated at Marseilles/Marignane, with the first deliveries going to the Armée de l'Air in May 1956.

Eclipsing its contemporaries in performance, payload and reliability, the type gained significant civilian and military sales, including to the armed

forces of Austria, Belgium Germany and Switzerland. Thanks to its exceptional performance at altitude, the British Army acquired 17 machines for use in Cyprus, Kenya and Uganda.

When production of the Alouette II ended, after more than 1,300 airframes had been completed, Sud (which later became part of Aérospatiale) concentrated on building the Lama. This married the airframe of the Alouette II with the Alouette III's engine and rotors. The Lama continues to be

produced in India, where the type is ideal for air force operations in the Himalayas.

Above: In the military role, Alouette IIs can be fitted with a variety of rockets, missiles and guns. This machine carries SS.11 anti-tank missiles.

SE 313B ALOUETTE II

This is one of 90 SE 313B and SE 318C Alouette IIs which was supplied to Belgium for training, liaison and observation duties. A few remain in army and Gendarmerie use.

Above: Here a Lama demonstrates its ability to lift the weight of an Alouette II (around 895 kg/1,970 lb. empty). The Lama can be distinguished from the earlier machine by its three-bladed tail rotor.

The 'bug-eyed' glazed cabin, which offers an excellent all-round view, seats up to five – a pilot and passenger in the front and three passengers abreast behind.

Powered in its original SE 3120 form by a 149-kW (200-hp.) Salmson radial piston engine, a redesign substituted the 269-kW (360-hp.) Artouste turboshaft. In this form the aircraft was known as the SE 3130 Alouette II, which entered production as the SE 313B. The Astazou IIA-engined SE 318C boasted an output of 395 kW, while the Lama, with a larger Artouste engine, was rated at 640 kW (860 hp.).

Listed roles for the versatile Alouette family include flying crane, liaison, observation, training, agricultural work, photographic survey and ambulance (with two stretchers).

The open fuselage structure carries a fuel tank immediately behind the cabin. The engine is above and to the rear of the tank and is, as in a number of European helicopter designs, exposed to the elements.

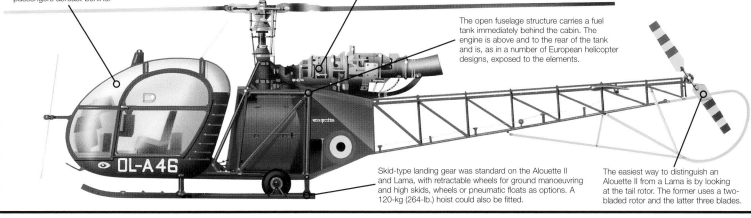

Skid-type landing gear was standard on the Alouette II and Lama, with retractable wheels for ground manoeuvring and high skids, wheels or pneumatic floats as options. A 120-kg (264-lb.) hoist could also be fitted.

The easiest way to distinguish an Alouette II from a Lama is by looking at the tail rotor. The former uses a two-bladed rotor and the latter three blades.

OL-A46

COMBAT DATA

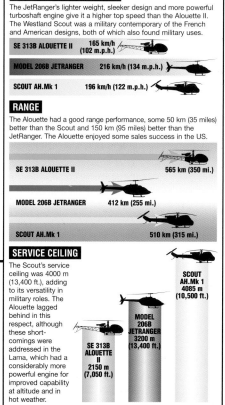

MAXIMUM CRUISING SPEED

The JetRanger's lighter weight, sleeker design and more powerful turboshaft engine give it a higher top speed than the Alouette II. The Westland Scout was a military contemporary of the French and American designs, both of which also found military uses.

SE 313B ALOUETTE II	165 km/h (102 m.p.h.)
MODEL 206B JETRANGER	216 km/h (134 m.p.h.)
SCOUT AH.Mk 1	196 km/h (122 m.p.h.)

RANGE

The Alouette had a good range performance, some 50 km (35 miles) better than the Scout and 150 km (95 miles) better than the JetRanger. The Alouette enjoyed some sales success in the US.

SE 313B ALOUETTE II	565 km (350 mi.)
MODEL 206B JETRANGER	412 km (255 mi.)
SCOUT AH.Mk 1	510 km (315 mi.)

SERVICE CEILING

The Scout's service ceiling was 4000 m (13,400 ft.), adding to its versatility in military roles. The Alouette lagged behind in this respect, although these short-comings were addressed in the Lama, which had a considerably more powerful engine for improved capability at altitude and in hot weather.

SE 313B ALOUETTE II 2150 m (7,050 ft.)
MODEL 206B JETRANGER 3200 m (13,400 ft.)
SCOUT AH.Mk 1 4085 m (10,500 ft.)

Alouette IIs and Lamas worldwide

■ **CHILE:** This SA.315B Lama is one of 19 still in service with the Chilean army and air force in the search-and-rescue and communications roles. Deliveries began in 1974.

■ **FRANCE:** Large numbers of Alouette IIs were ordered for the French armed forces and police. Around 80 remain in army service, as well as a handful with the Armée de l'Air.

■ **UNITED KINGDOM:** The Army Air Corps ordered 17 Alouette IIs, which saw service in such diverse locations as South America, Africa and the West Indies. All have been retired.

AÉROSPATIALE

AS 332 SUPER PUMA

● Airborne workhorse ● Increased power ● Civil operations

▼ Overseas service
To increase safety during long over-water flights, the Super Puma can be fitted with emergency flotation bags around the nose. This example operates from Ireland.

▲ Increased volume
The larger fuselage of the Super Puma is evident in this view of an AS 332C lifting off from a snowy landscape.

◄ Worthy successor
The AS 332 was developed from the successful SA 330. This French SA 330 is seen demonstrating fire-fighting equipment.

▼ Advanced design
Aérospatiale was able to utilise the latest advances in aviation technology in the design. One of these was the use of glass-fibre rotors.

◄ Added strength
An increase in power along with the larger fuselage has seen the Super Puma employed heavily in the construction industry. Extra nose mirrors are installed to allow the pilot to monitor the load.

A n established favourite with helicopter companies specialising in the support of offshore oil exploration and production, the Super Puma, along with its Cougar military variant, has also won orders from many other companies and agencies for a wide variety of applications. They range from VIP transport to the support of UN peace-keeping forces in the world's troublespots. The type is readily adaptable for a whole host of other tasks.

▲ Having already developed a highly capable transport helicopter with the Puma, Aérospatiale proposed a model with increased power and cabin volume.

FACTS AND FIGURES

➤ The first flight of the AS 332 Super Puma was on 13 September 1978. Service entry occurred in 1981.

➤ Civilian Super Pumas have the capacity to seat 24 passengers.

➤ Luxury variants have been developed to fill the VIP transport role.

➤ In the event of a mishap, the Super Puma is able to land on water because of the fitting of emergency flotation bags.

➤ One variant, the AS 332L, has more than 70 examples in civilian service.

➤ Super Pumas are widely used as transports for oil exploration support.

PROFILE

Aérospatiale's super workhorse

A cabin big enough to accommodate 24 passengers on standard seats is clearly big enough to carry smaller numbers in much greater comfort. Aérospatiale has exploited the possibility in a big way, and claims to have created the market for VIP helicopters by combining the versatility of rotary-wing flight with the all the comforts of a business jet.

The Prestige range of VIP interiors offers luxuriously upholstered seating in a single nine-seat cabin, or separate compartments with four seats forward and another eight aft,

along with such amenities as a bar, individual video screens and telephones.

Super Pumas and Cougars are used to transport no fewer than 25 heads of state, and more than 50 VIP versions are in service. Apart from the 8-m (26-ft.) long cabin, the type's attractions include low noise and vibration levels and large windows along with high performance and long range.

Other roles have included supporting the United Nations peace-keeping force in Mozambique. The Super Puma is well suited to operations in Africa, where it is able to take

off with full tanks even in temperatures of 30°C (86°F).

Above: Taking to the air is the prototype Super Puma; the helicopter is identifiable by its prominent ventral fin.

Right: An increase in the nose volume of the Super Puma has allowed the type to be fitted with a weather radar.

AS 332 SUPER PUMA

Proving to be a highly capable transport helicopter, the Super Puma is fast becoming the first choice for operators who require a dependable and safe helicopter. The exceptional power available coupled with long range will ensure sales success.

AS 332L-1 Super Puma

Type: twin-engined transport/support helicopter

Powerplant: two 1184-kW (1,590-hp.) (continuous rating) Turbomeca Makila 1A1 turboshafts

Cruising speed: 266 km/h (165 m.p.h.)

Initial climb rate: 486 m/min (1,600 f.p.m.) at sea level

Range: 870 km (539 mi.)

Service ceiling: 4600 m (15,100 ft.)

Weights: empty 4460 kg (9,812 lb.); maximum take-off 8600 kg (18,920 lb.)

Accommodation: two pilots plus 24 passengers

Dimensions: rotor diameter 15.60 m (51 ft. 2 in.)
length 16.29 m (53 ft. 5 in.)
height 4.92 m (16 ft. 2 in.)
main rotor disc area 191.10 m² (2,056 sq. ft.)

As a safety precaution the Super Puma can be fitted with emergency flotation bags around the cockpit. These inflate in the event of the helicopter landing on water.

The large cabin area of the Super Puma can accommodate 24 seated passengers or a sizeable cargo load. This particular version operates in the passenger configuration.

Aérospatiale was able to equip the Super Puma with the latest technology. Apart from the improved avionics and radar, the helicopter is fitted with glass-fibre rotor blades to increase its performance.

-LN-OLA

A-S LUFTTRANSPORT

F-WTNI

Positioned either side of the fuselage in streamlined fairings is the large single-wheel high-energy absorption landing gear. The landing gear can be retracted.

The increase in power of the engine required the addition of a large ventral fin. This is a distinguishing feature of the new Super Pumas now on operation.

HELICOPTERS AT WORK

CONSTRUCTION WORKER: Despite its small size, the Aérospatiale SA 315 Lama (pictured left) is a specially developed variant of the SA 318 Alouette II. The helicopter offers a better performance at high altitude and is equipped with raised skids to allow it to operate from any rough terrain.

OIL INDUSTRY: Offering an increase in range and capability, Bell's LongRanger (pictured above) was derived from the extremely successful JetRanger. With its long-range, the helicopter is used to explore potential sites for oil exploration. The helicopter can be equipped with a ski undercarriage, if required, during winter months.

Multi-purpose Pumas

■ BELGIAN POLICE: This Puma is one of three examples used by the Belgian Gendarmerie. They are based at Brasschaat in the north of the country and employed for patrol and VIP duties.

OL-GOI

■ VIP FLIGHTS: This SA 330C Puma serves with the Gabonese air force. Most are flown by mercenary pilots. The Pumas are used for VIP and support tasks.

TR-KCD

■ RESCUE ROLE: With its extended range and improved all-weather radar, Singapore's AS 332Bs operate with No. 125 Squadron at Sembawang. They are used for SAR and VIP flights.

RESCUE_21

AÉROSPATIALE

AS 350 ECUREUIL TV NEWS

● On-the-spot news ● Rapid response ● Economical and reliable

▲ With its ample cabin space, the Ecureuil makes a perfect camera platform. This was recognised by Aérospatiale, which offered a TV camera installation as standard equipment.

Helicopters are responsible for some of the most dramatic television news images. The use of these aircraft as TV camera platforms has mushroomed since the late 1970s, when the first microwave transmitters small enough to be carried by a light helicopter appeared. The helicopter usually carries a reporter and a camera operator, and the AS 350 Ecureuil, with its combination of affordability and reliability, has proved popular for the task.

PHOTO FILE

AÉROSPATIALE AS 350 ECUREUIL TV NEWS

▼ **Camera system**
When fully equipped, there is little space available inside the Ecureuil.

▲ **US TV**
Even in America, where Bell and McDonnell Douglas helicopters have traditionally been favoured, the AS 350 has been popular with TV news companies.

◀ **UK newscasting**
This much-modified, smartly painted Twin Squirrel is operated by ITN.

JetRanger on air ▶
Many other light helicopters are used for TV duties, including the Bell JetRanger.

Chicago ▶
bulletin
This JetRanger is operated by Chicago's WLS-TV. The helicopter also represents a high-profile publicity tool for the TV station.

FACTS AND FIGURES

➤ A Textron Lycoming-engined version of the Ecureuil is marketed in North America as the Astar.

➤ By 1 March 1989 Ecureuils and Astars were flying in 43 countries.

➤ Most of the AS 350's outer skin is made from thermo-formed plastic.

➤ An uprated electrical system on the Ecureuil 2 makes it particularly suited to the TV reporting role.

➤ Apart from its twin engines, the AS 355 Ecureuil 2 is similar to the AS 350.

➤ The Ecureuil is still in production, and is now built by Eurocopter.

PROFILE

Going live with the Ecureuil

Once it became possible to relay live pictures from helicopters, many broadcasters rushed to buy their own machines. Within 18 months there were more than 100 in use across the United States alone. But operating in this way was very expensive, and it became more common to charter an aircraft when it was needed to cover a specific story or event.

The AS 350's main advantages for news-gathering operations are reliability and performance. Good reserves of power, simple flight controls and rapid response mean that the pilot can concentrate on the subject and does not need to be concerned about the machine's limitations.

This is particularly important when the pilot is also the reporter. Keeping clear of other helicopters, respecting minimum height regulations and handling the controls, while selecting the right shot to illustrate the story and describing the scene to viewers, is a full-time job.

In spite of the expense, if a helicopter can get to the scene of a major event as it is happening, or to the aftermath of a natural disaster, there is no substitute for the sense of immediacy it can provide.

Above: Some TV broadcasters use their helicopters as relays for signals transmitted from the ground. This system is especially useful for live broadcasts from built-up areas.

Above: This is ITN's AS 355F-1 in action. A special seat is installed to allow the camera operator to work in safety from the open door.

AS 350B2

Type: general-purpose light helicopter

Powerplant: one 540-kW (724-hp.) Turboméca Arriel 1D1 turboshaft

Maximum cruising speed: 246 km/h (153 m.p.h.) at sea level

Climb rate: 546 m/min (1,790 f.p.m.) at sea level

Range: 690 km (428 mi.) with maximum fuel

Hover ceiling: 3200 m (10,500 ft.) in ground effect

Weights: empty 1132 kg (2,490 lb.); maximum take-off 2250 kg (4,950 lb.)

Accommodation: pilot plus up to five passengers

Dimensions:
main rotor diameter	10.69 m (35 ft)
fuselage length	10.93 m (35 ft. 10 in.)
height	3.14 m (10 ft. 4 in.)
rotor disc area	89.75 m² (966 sq. ft.)

The AS 355 and AS 350 share the same rotor system design. The blades are of glass fibre construction with stainless steel leading-edge sheaths. Glass fibre is also used in the rotor hub.

The Ecureuil 2 can be operated by a single crewmember, which makes the aircraft more economical.

Twin Allison turboshafts give the Twin Squirrel large reserves of power in most flight conditions, allowing the pilot to react to a developing situation.

A broader chord tail rotor is one modification which allows the AS 355F-1 to fly at increased weights.

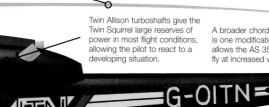

For night-time or low-light work, this aircraft carries a powerful spotlight which allows filming regardless of conditions.

A remotely-controlled sensor pod, containing a camera system, is mounted on a boom which runs through the forward part of the cabin.

When using heavy camera equipment, the camera operator must remain safely restrained at all times, regardless of flight attitude. There is a large footrest on the side of the cabin and comprehensive harnessing is also fitted.

AS 355F-1 TWIN SQUIRREL

This aircraft contains specialist camera and transmitting equipment. Belonging to Independent Television News Limited, it is appropriately registered G-OITN and has become a common sight across the UK.

ACTION DATA

CABIN HEIGHT

With its spacious cabin, the Ecureuil has plenty of room to accommodate bulky TV camera equipment. The AS 350B also has large sliding cabin doors, which allow good access and give a camera operator an excellent vantage point from which to film or take photographs.

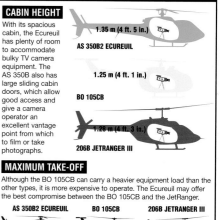

1.35 m (4 ft. 5 in.) — AS 350B2 ECUREUIL
1.25 m (4 ft. 1 in.) — BO 105CB
1.28 m (4 ft. 3 in.) — 206B JETRANGER III

MAXIMUM TAKE-OFF

Although the BO 105CB can carry a heavier equipment load than the other types, it is more expensive to operate. The Ecureuil may offer the best compromise between the BO 105CB and the JetRanger.

AS 350B2 ECUREUIL	BO 105CB	206B JETRANGER III
2250 kg (4,950 lb.)	2550 kg (5,610 lb.)	1451 kg (3,192 lb.)

RANGE

Range and endurance are important factors if the aircraft is to remain on station and avoid missing a major event. Again the Ecureuil comes out on top, which makes it popular around the world in this role.

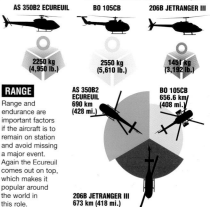

AS 350B2 ECUREUIL 690 km (428 mi.)
BO 105CB 656.6 km (408 mi.)
206B JETRANGER III 673 km (418 mi.)

Multi-purpose Ecureuil

■ **ARMED:** Several air arms use the Ecureuil in its armed form as a light battlefield helicopter. It is compatible with a range of gun pods and guided and unguided missiles.

■ **FIRE-BOMBING:** France's Sécurité Civile is one operator of the specially equipped fire-bombing Ecureuil. Other aircraft, often with local modifications, are flown in Canada.

■ **RIG SUPPORT:** A few AS 350 Ecureuils are flown on rig support missions in Japan and the US. The twin-engined AS 355, such as this Air Logistics aircraft, is more commonly used for this, however.

AGUSTA

A 109 HIRUNDO

● Air taxi ● Military transport ● Anti-tank attack

Widely recognised as one of the most graceful and attractive helicopters ever built, the Agusta A 109 Hirundo has sold well in both civil and military markets. Since 1971 the Hirundo has performed superbly as a light passenger transport, freighter, air ambulance, law-enforcement craft and search-and-rescue ship. In its military guise, the A 109A is employed for anti-tank attack, reconnaissance and electronic warfare.

▲ Agusta 109s are often seen nestling among New York's skyscrapers. Whether ferrying top executives or performing law-enforcement duties the aircraft performs with quiet efficiency.

AGUSTA A 109 HIRUNDO

◀ **Maritime missions**
Fitted with searchlights, floats and a 360° radar, the A 109 can fulfil a number of maritime roles such as search-and-rescue, coastal patrol and anti-ship duties.

▼ **Hot and high**
Designed for operations in arid, mountainous regions, the A 109K incorporates more powerful engines, dust filters and improved avionics, giving it the durability to survive in harsh conditions.

▲ **Spy launcher**
An unusual use of the A 109 is as a launch ship for unmanned reconnaissance drones. These can spy on enemy positions using conventional or infra-red cameras.

Alpine rescue ▶
The A 109 can be fitted with skis and is used in the Alps as an air ambulance, evacuating victims of avalanches or skiing accidents.

▲ **Flying ambulance**
The A 109's capacious cabin is ideal for casualty rescue. The versatile helicopter can ferry two stretcher cases plus three attendants to hospital.

FACTS AND FIGURES

➤ The first of three civil A 109 prototypes made its initial flight on 4 August 1971.

➤ Deliveries of the first production A 109A began in 1975.

➤ Two of Argentina's four A 109As were captured during the 1982 Falklands War and were used by the British.

➤ In 1981 the civil model was redesignated A 109A Mk II, reflecting changes in transmission and other features.

➤ The A 109C is a 'wide-body' version with more room and increased power.

➤ The Belgian army uses A 109s for scouting and anti-armour duties.

PROFILE

Agusta's best-selling machine

Although Agusta has a solid track record for making helicopters designed by other companies, the A 109 Hirundo (Swallow) was the first mass-produced helicopter actually designed by the Italian company.

The sleek A.109 was originally intended to have a single 551-kW (740-hp.) Turboméca Astazou XII turboshaft, but for additional safety it was redesigned in 1967 around two Allison 250-C14 engines.

Development of the A 109 was protracted, but the result has been satisfying. Large corporations, police departments and military users are pleased with its solid performance. For military and naval use, the Hirundo carries dozens of combinations of electronics gear, weapons and equipment. The hi-tech maritime A 109A ECM (electronic countermeasures) variant has a radar display, direction finder, electromagnetic emission analyser and jamming equipment.

A specialised military utility model, the A 109B, was proposed, but in 1969 this was abandoned in favour of the eight-seat A 109C civil version.

Above: The A 109 upholds the Italian tradition of producing aircraft with sleek, graceful lines and excellent performance. However, the Hirundo is also reliable and durable, making it ideal for both civil and military roles.

Above: A modified A 109 was used as Boeing's Advanced Rotorcraft Technology Integration (ARTI) testbed. The pilot was situated in the passenger cabin and had no external view; he used the cameras on the nose to fly the aircraft.

A 109A Hirundo

Type: light general-purpose helicopter

Powerplant: two Allison 250-C20B turboshaft engines each developing 313 kW (420 hp.) for take-off derated to 258 kW (346 hp.) for continuous twin-engine flight performance

Maximum cruising speed: 266 km/h (165 m.p.h.)

Endurance: 3 hours 18 minutes

Service ceiling: 4968 km (3,080 ft.)

Weights: empty 1415 kg (3,113 lb.); loaded 2450 kg (5,390 lb.)

Armament: (military version) two 7.62-mm machine-guns and two XM157 rocket launchers (seven 70-mm rockets), up to 866 kg (1,905 lb.) of alternate weapons including guns, rockets and missiles

Dimensions: main rotor diameter 11.00 m (36 ft.)
length 10.71 m (35 ft. 2 in.)
height 3.30 m (10 ft. 9 in.)
rotor disc area 95.00 m² (1,022 sq. ft.)

A 109A HIRUNDO

The Argentine army deployed several A 109s to the Falkland Islands in 1982. Some were destroyed in Harrier attacks, but two were captured by the British and are now used by the Special Air Service.

In the newer A 109K the Allison engines are replaced by a pair of Turboméca Arriel turboshafts.

The latest A 109s have composite rotor blades, but earlier versions had conventional aluminium alloy blades with a Nomex core. Blade-folding can be performed manually.

The A 109A has a two-bladed tail rotor. Some military versions have the ventral fin removed and alpine versions have a small tail-ski fitted under the tailboom.

Military A 109s can be fitted with a Saab Helios sight system and a laser rangefinder on the roof.

The A 109A Mk II featured a redesigned tailboom structure and a new tail rotor drive shaft.

The lower rear fuselage contains two bladder-type fuel tanks with a capacity of 560 litres (146 gallons). An auxiliary tank with a capacity of 170 litres (44 gallons) can also be fitted in the fuselage.

ACTION DATA

PASSENGER LOAD

The S-76 was designed more specifically with the civil helicopter market in mind, and therefore has a higher passenger capacity. The A 109 and Bell 222 are smaller all-rounders, with more versatile airframes but lower passenger capacity.

A 109A HIRUNDO
6-7 passengers

MODEL 222
8-9 passengers

S-76 SPIRIT
12 passengers

MAXIMUM CRUISING SPEED

Conventional helicopters have limited speeds due to the laws of aerodynamics. Even so, all these machines are well streamlined, giving them much higher cruising speeds than similar sized helicopters designed 10 or 20 years earlier.

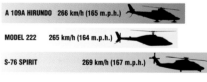

A 109A HIRUNDO   266 km/h (165 m.p.h.)

MODEL 222   265 km/h (164 m.p.h.)

S-76 SPIRIT   269 km/h (167 m.p.h.)

RANGE

The larger S-76 requires more fuel but has greater range than the A 109 or Bell 222. The range of any helicopter varies greatly according to its payload. At maximum all-up weight, the amount of fuel carried is often limited, and a large proportion of the force generated by the rotor is used to keep the aircraft flying rather than pushing it forward. Other factors such as ambient air temperature and 'density altitude' also affect range.

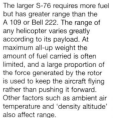

A 1094 HIRUNDO
565 km (350 mi.)

S-76 SPIRIT
748 km (464 mi.)

MODEL 222
523 km (324 mi.)

Multi-role middleweights

■ **AÉROSPATIALE SA 365 DAUPHIN:** This helicopter was designed to replace the Allouette II. The Dauphin II was the main version, featuring twin engines. China bought the production rights to the SA 365 and builds the type as the Z-9 Haitun; a military version armed with anti-tank missiles is also projected.

■ **BELL 222:** Another capable design, in fierce competition with the S-76 on the civil market, the Bell 222 has had little success in the military field. Its successor, the Bell 230, shows every sign of changing this, with trials on Chilean navy vessels proving very successful and many other nations showing signs of interest.

■ **SIKORSKY S-76:** The S-76 has been very successful, especially in America. It has also been developed as a military helicopter, but has had far more sales in the civil market. The latest versions have Arriel turboshafts like the A 109K and advanced 'glass' cockpit displays.

AGUSTA

A129 MANGUSTA

● European attack helicopter ● Advanced systems ● Highly versatile

▲ Fully integrated avionics, a comprehensive range of compatible weapons and a crash-survivable airframe make the Mangusta a highly capable attack and battlefield helicopter.

Although originally based on the A109A, the Mangusta eventually emerged as an all-new design. The result is Europe's first dedicated all-weather day/night combat helicopter – a machine that can carry a wide range of weapons, withstand hits from 12.7-mm (.50-calibre) or even 23-mm shells and operate for up to 90 minutes at a time over a battle area 100 km (60 miles) from base. The Italian army operates the Mangusta as its primary anti-tank system.

AGUSTA A129 MANGUSTA

▼ A129 International
Aimed at the export market, the International has T800 engines, which produce up to 40 per cent more power, and a five-bladed main rotor.

▲ Poised for attack
Agusta chose the classic attack helicopter layout of a slender fuselage and stub wings for carrying weapons.

Flying in primer ▶
Five prototypes were built, of which this is the third. This aircraft has the original nose profile and is not painted in the familiar green colour scheme.

▼ Anti-tank mission
For its primary anti-tank task the A129 carries eight TOW missiles in launchers on the outboard pylons, plus either seven- or 19-round rocket launchers on the inboard stations.

▲ Testing Mangustas
The first and second prototypes are seen in formation during a test sortie.

FACTS AND FIGURES

➤ Plans for the Mangusta were originally laid in the mid-1970s, but the first aircraft did not fly until 11 September 1983.

➤ Development was further delayed by funding problems for the HeliTOW sight.

➤ A joint European project, known as Tonal, was to have been based on the A129.

➤ A Lucas chin turret, with a 12.7-mm (.50 calibre) machine-gun, may be fitted, but it is not used by the Italian army.

➤ The British and Dutch armies bought the AH-64 in preference to the Mangusta.

➤ Iran has shown interest in ordering an export version.

Italian anti-armour system

For dealing with tanks and armoured vehicles, the Mangusta is equipped with a mast- or nose-mounted sight and TOW or Hellfire missiles. It can launch Stinger, Sidewinder, Mistral or Javelin air-to-air missiles against airborne targets and can carry a range of rocket and gun pods to provide fire support for ground troops.

The Mangusta (Mongoose) is also highly automated. A data management system records malfunctions and recommends how they should be repaired. It also controls the various flight and mission subsystems. The crew consists of co-pilot/gunner forward and pilot aft. They both use helmet-mounted displays which present targeting information and the imagery from infra-red sensors for operations at night. They also have fly-by-wire controls and multi-function displays showing all flight data.

Italian army A129s were deployed in the peace-keeping role in Somalia. To make the helicopter even more versatile, Agusta has developed the A129 International. This has T800 engines, plus a new drive system, and carries a three-barrelled 20-mm cannon under the nose.

Above: A production standard Mangusta demonstrates the helicopter's revised nose contours.

Right: Although fully armed, the second prototype did not represent the final production standard. Current aircraft carry a Saab/ESCO HeliTOW sight above the nose.

A129 Mangusta

Type: lightweight anti-armour helicopter

Powerplant: two 615-kW (825-hp.) Rolls-Royce Gem 2 Mk 1004D turboshafts

Maximum speed: 315 km/h (195 m.p.h.)

Endurance: 3 hours

Initial climb rate: 655 m/min (2,150 f.p.m.) at sea level

Weights: empty 2529 kg (5,564 lb.); maximum take-off 4100 kg (9,020 lb.)

Armament: eight TOW or HOT or six Hellfire anti-tank missiles on outer pylons, or two Sidewinder, Mistral, Javelin or Stinger air-to-air missiles in an air-to-air or escort role, plus two machine-gun or rocket pods on outer underwing pylons

Dimensions:
main rotor diameter	11.90 m (39 ft.)
length	14.29 m (46 ft. 10 in.)
height	3.35 m (11 ft.)
rotor disc area	111.22 m² (1,197 sq. ft.)

A129 MANGUSTA

Finished in full Italian army markings and wearing the standard green finish of service machines, the third prototype underwent extensive service trials. The green paint has infra-red suppressing characteristics.

Control linkages for each of the four main rotor blades run inside the driveshaft, reducing the rotor's radar signature. All gearboxes and associated systems are designed to run for at least 30 minutes after the loss of all lubricating oil.

Unusually for a modern attack helicopter, the Mangusta has a two-bladed tail rotor. Most designs use a multi-bladed unit in order to keep the noise signature to a minimum and to make the rotor less vulnerable to ground fire. The broad-chord blades of the A129's tail rotor can withstand 12.7-mm (.50 calibre) hits, however, and may even be able to tolerate strikes from 23-mm ammunition.

Gunner and pilot are seated in tandem in armoured cockpits. All glazing is flat plate, which keeps glare to a minimum. The Martin-Baker seats have composite armour.

Placing the engines on either side of the fuselage renders them less vulnerable to ground fire. It is also means that a single hit is less likely to disable both powerplants.

Special hydraulic struts in each main undercarriage leg are designed to withstand descent rates of up to 10 metres per second (30 f.p.s.).

While the standard weapon load consists of TOW missiles and rockets, the aircraft is also compatible with Hellfire anti-tank missiles and a range of air-to-air missiles.

COMBAT DATA

MAXIMUM CRUISING SPEED

Although the A129 has the lowest cruising speed, it is a smaller machine than the other two types. This makes it is less vulnerable to attack since it presents a more difficult target.

A129 MANGUSTA	250 km/h (155 m.p.h.)
AH-1W SUPERCOBRA	278 km/h (172 m.p.h.)
Mi-28 'HAVOC-A'	270 km/h (167 m.p.h.)

WEAPON LOAD

Although it has considerably more power than the A129, Bell's Supercobra carries a similar weapon load. This indicates the penalty of developing an older design for the modern battlefield.

A129 MANGUSTA 1200 kg (2,640 lb.)
AH-1W SUPERCOBRA 1119 kg (2,460 lb.)
Mi-28 'HAVOC-A' 1920 kg (4,220 lb.)

POWER

With its hugely powerful engines, the Mi-28 is in a different class to the A129. It is with such attack helicopters that the A129 must compete for export orders, however.

Mi-28 'HAVOC-A' 3280 kw (4,395 hp.)
AH-1W SUPERCOBRA 2570 kw (3,444 hp.)
A129 MANGUSTA 1230 kw (1,650 hp.)

Armed Agustas

A106: First flown in 1965, the A106 was a remarkable single-seat design capable of carrying two torpedoes over 740 km (460 miles).

A109: A number of armed variants of the A109, many with TOW missile launchers, are in service around the world.

AB204: In its anti-submarine warfare/anti-ship role, the Agusta-Bell AB204AS carries either two Mk 44 torpedoes or AS.12 missiles.

AB412 GRIFFON: Agusta has developed an attack variant of the AB412, which is suitable for attacking ships and tanks and for armed assault.

AGUSTA-BELL

AB.212ASW

● Licence-built Italian sub-hunter ● Ten operators worldwide

▲ With 60 examples, the AB.212ASW is Italy's principal naval helicopter. It serves aboard Italian frigates and destroyers and is tasked with both anti-submarine and anti-shipping roles.

Bell installed a Pratt & Whitney Turbo Twin-Pac engine into its 205 airframe to produce the AB.212 – the equivalent of a twin-engined helicopter. The Italian company Agusta was alone, however, in recognising the potential of the aircraft as a highly successful and effective anti-submarine and anti-surface vessel platform. Agusta went on to build in excess of 100 AB.212ASW helicopters.

PHOTO FILE

AGUSTA-BELL AB.212ASW

▼ **Early production**
Agusta built the first 12 of 60 AB.212ASWs for the Italian navy equipped with MEL ARI-5955 search radar carried in a distinctive domed radome.

▲ **Sub-hunting sensors**
Two sensors are used to detect and localise submarines: a Bendix dipping sonar and a search radar – the British Ferranti Sea Spray or Italian MEL APS-705.

▼ **Torpedo armament**
Italian AB.212ASWs carry a range of homing torpedoes, from the American Mk 44 and 46 to the Italian Motorfides 244AS (below).

▲ **Anti-ship missile armament**
The AB.212ASW also has an important anti-surface vessel role. The primary armament is the fire-and-forget' Marte Mk 2 missile. Alternative weapons include French AS.12s and British Sea Skuas.

◀ **Middle East combat**
The 20 AB.212ASWs sold to Iran in 1974 are now believed to be non-operational due to poor servicing and a lack of spare parts. Iraq's order for 10 machines was embargoed with the outbreak of the Gulf War.

FACTS AND FIGURES

➤ Comprehensive avionics allow the AB.212ASW to operate in all weathers, and at any time of day or night.

➤ Two torpedoes or depth charges are available for submarine attacks.

➤ For utility operations a 2270-kg (5,000-lb.) cargo sling may be fitted.

➤ The AB.212ASW is able to operate from decks previously used by the similarly sized AB.204AS.

➤ In the search and rescue role, the AB.212ASW can carry four stretchers.

➤ The engine is protected against salt water corrosion.

PROFILE

Italian maritime striker

Moving beyond the usual confines of merely building an aircraft under licence, Agusta used its experience with the earlier AB.204AS to produce the well-equipped AB.212ASW.

Agusta incorporated advanced systems from the outset and also allowed for the inclusion of future developments in avionics and associated ASW equipment. This foresight has meant that, through various upgrades, the aircraft has remained in service

as a cost-effective and highly capable machine. It also allowed Agusta to alter systems and specifications with the minimum of trouble, adding flexibility and matching the requirements of foreign air arms, to exploit a wide export market.

The Greek, Spanish and Turkish navies ordered the AB.212ASW and in South America, Peru and Venezuela bought the aircraft. Iranian machines, which were ordered in 1974, have been used against shipping in the Persian

Gulf, firing French-supplied AS.12 missiles. The delivery of 10 AB 212ASWs ordered by Iraq in 1983 was delayed and finally cancelled when Iraq invaded Kuwait.

Above: The AB.212 can also provide mid-course guidance corrections (via a Teseo TG-2 datalink under the nose) for OTO Melara TOMAT 2 anti-ship missiles used by the Italian navy.

Left: The Turkish navy bought 12 AB.212ASWs, which serve aboard 'Yavuz'-class frigates. These are fitted with British-built Sea Spray radar and Sea Skua air-to-surface missiles.

AB.212ASW

Type: ASW and ASV helicopter

Powerplant: one 1398-kW (1,875-hp.) Pratt & Whitney Canada PT6T-6 Turbo Twin-Pac

Maximum speed: 238 km/h (149 m.p.h.) at sea level

Endurance: 5 hours, or 4 hours 7 min on an ASV mission with two AS.12 missiles

Initial climb rate: 396 m/min (1,300 f.p.m.) at sea level

Service ceiling: 3200 m (10,500 ft.)

Weights: empty 3420 kg (7,524 lb.); maximum take-off 5070 kg (11,154 lb.)

Armament: two Mk 44, Mk 46 or MQ 44 torpedoes or two air-to-surface missiles

Dimensions:

main rotor diameter	14.63 m (48 ft.)
length	17.40 m (57 ft.)
height	4.53 m (14 ft. 10 in.)
main rotor disc area	168.10 m (1,809 sq. ft.)

AB.212ASW

'7-20' of the Italian navy wears the standard overall medium sea-grey camouflage scheme. Dayglo orange patches are also applied as an aid to visibility. This machine serves with 5° Gruppo Elicotteri.

Depending on the internal equipment fit and the type of mission to be flown, the cabin can hold up to two crew, in addition to the pilots, who operate the radar and dipping sonar. Alternatively, the cabin can hold seven passengers or four stretcher cases.

Unlike many naval helicopters, the AB.212ASW's main rotor cannot be folded to save valuable space on a ship's deck. The AB.212 retains Bell's distinctive twin-bladed rotor layout which was first used widely on the pioneering Model 47.

All but 12 of the Italian navy's AB.212ASWs are fitted with an APS-705 or -706 search radar. These have a range of 0.9 to 148 km (0.5 to 92 miles).

Power for the AB.212ASW is provided by a single Pratt & Whitney Canada Turbo Twin-Pac engine. It actually consists of paired PT6T turboshafts which are coupled together and drive via a common gearbox.

The simple, twin-bladed tail rotor is another typical Bell design feature. The tip of each blade is brightly painted in Italian national colours, making it easy for ground crew to see and avoid the spinning rotor.

MARINA 7-20

To cut down on drag, the floats are deflated. In an emergency, these inflate after a compressed air bottle is activated.

The AB.212ASW has an automated flight-control system which gives hands-off conversion under all weather conditions from the cruise state to hovering flight for dipping sonar.

ACTION DATA

MAXIMUM CRUISING SPEED

A somewhat aged design, the AB.212ASW is slower than the Advanced Sea King and the Panther. All three helicopters undertake ASW/ASV missions, where time on station is often more important than high speed. Despite its age, the AB.212ASW continues to offer cost-effective service.

AB.212ASW	185 km/h (115 m.p.h.)
AS 565 SA PANTHER	274 km/h (170 m.p.h.)
SEA KING Mk 42C	245 km/h (151 m.p.h.)

MAXIMUM TAKE-OFF WEIGHT

With its high maximum take-off weight the Sea King is able to carry more fuel and a heavier weapons load than the AB.212 or Panther. It is, however, more expensive and may not be suitable for air arms requiring lighter machines.

AB.212 ASW	AS 565 SA PANTHER	SEA KING Mk 42C
5070 kg (11,154 lb.)	4250 kg (9,350 lb.)	9752 kg (21,454 lb.)

MAXIMUM CLIMB RATE

Again as a result of its older design, the AB.212ASW offers a comparatively poor climb rate. In service, however, its performance has proved adequate, with many being flown from smaller ships that could not accommodate the larger, heavier Sea King.

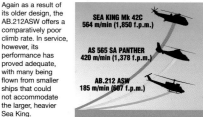

SEA KING Mk 42C	564 m/min (1,850 f.p.m.)
AS 565 SA PANTHER	420 m/min (1,378 f.p.m.)
AB.212 ASW	185 m/min (607 f.p.m.)

Agusta-Bell production

AB.47G: Agusta built many examples of Bell's first commercially successful helicopter and exported them widely.

AB.204: A specialised ASW/ASV variant of the 204 was developed by Agusta for the Italian navy. It was later replaced by the 212.

AB.205: Bell achieved phenomenal success with its UH-1D/H military helicopters and Agusta built several for both home and export customers.

AB.412: Agusta began building the 412 in 1981 and, in addition to the civilian version, has developed a specialised military variant.

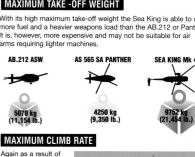

AGUSTA-SIKORSKY

AS-61

● Utility helicopter ● Anti-ship missiles ● Rescue missions

AGUSTA-SIKORSKY **AS-61**

▲ **Looking down**
A radome mounted on the lower fuselage
houses a sophisticated radar.

▲ **All-weather capability**
This Italian example has a nose-
mounted search radar to assist
during rescue operations.

▼ **Home grown**
The Italian company Augusta
obtained a license from Sikorsky
to build the Sea King.

▲ **Packing away**
To allow the helicopter to operate from
ships, the rotors fold down alongside the
fuselage for storage.

Civil operators ▶
Reliable and roomy, an enlarged version of the S-61
has found a welcome civil market. S-61s are often
used as air taxis for offshore oil platforms.

Agusta started to build Sikorsky's Model
61 – equivalent to the US Navy's SH-3D
Sea King – for the Italian navy in 1967. A
whole series of specialized military and civil
variants followed, and the HH-3F, operated by
the Italian air force as the S-61R Pelican, was
still in production 30 years later. Other S-61s
have been exported and license-built for military
and civil operators in Europe, the Middle East,
Asia and Latin America.

▲ *Despite its 1950s design, the Sea
King looks set to continue operating
with various navies across the world on
anti-submarine and rescue duties.*

FACTS AND FIGURES

➤ The S-61 designation applies to export
versions of the Anti-Submarines-Warfare
Sea King.

➤ The first flight of the helicopter was on
March 11, 1959.

➤ Mitsubishi also builds the S-61 under
license in Japan.

➤ For anti-ship operations, the Sea King can
carry two Exocet missiles, which have a
range of up to 145 km (90 miles).

➤ The helicopter is capable of landing on
water in an emergency.

➤ A British civil S-61N is used in the Falkland
Islands for transport duties.

PROFILE

Italian-built king of the sea

Below: The boat-like design of the S-61 is clear in this view, as are the two outer sponsons designed to keep the helicopter upright in the event of a crash at sea.

Aside from the Italian navy, operators of the original ASH-3D anti-submarine helicopter include the navies of Argentina, Brazil and Peru. The AS-61 VIP and logistic transport model was bought in small numbers by Egypt, Iran, Iraq, Saudi Arabia and Venezuela.

Another military variant is the AS-16R Pelican combat search-and-rescue helicopter, equivalent to the HH-3F, which is used by the Italian air force. Later versions have upgraded avionics

for night rescue missions.

In the course of its evolution, the AS-61 became a much more capable helicopter. Early S-61s had a weapon load of less than 400 kg (880 lb.), but the ASH-3D can carry much heavier loads, such as a pair of Exocet or Harpoon anti-ship missiles.

Agusta also built several civil variants. After producing 13 S-61L and 123 S-61N1 civil versions of the Sea King, Agusta produced the AS-61N1 Silver, which has a lightly shorter fuselage

Above: Often flown as a transport helicopter, the AS-61 is also capable of attacking enemy ships with missiles.

and seating for 28 passengers instead of the original 30. It has increased fuel capacity for longer range – it is capable of flying more than 966 km (600 miles) with 24 passengers.

AS-61 Sea King

Type: shipboard utility helicopter

Powerplant: two 1044 kW (1,400-hp.) General Electric T58-GE-10 turboshaft engines

Maximum speed: 267 km/h (166 m.p.h.); economical cruising speed 219 km/h (136 m.p.h.)

Initial climb rate: 670 m/min (2,200 f.p.m.)

Range: 1005 km (625 mi.)

Service ceiling: 4480 m (14,700 ft.)

Weights: Empty 5601 kg (12,322 lb.); max take-off 9525 kg (20,957 lb.)

Weapons: two anti-ship missiles/topedoes

Dimensions:
Rotor diameter	18.90 m (62 ft.)
Length (without rotor)	16.69 m (54 ft. 9 in.)
Height	5,13 m (15 ft. 6 in.)
Main rotor disc area	280,50 m² (3,013 sq. ft.)

AS-61 SEA KING

Developed in the late 1950s, the Sea King looks set to continue operations across the world, despite the development of more advanced designs.

The Sea King has a large five-blade rotor head. Naval variants have a specialised rotor head that allows the rotors to be folded back along the fuselage for easy storage on naval vessels.

The large fuselage allows the Sea King to undertake a wide variety of tasks. These have ranged from anti-submarine patrols and search and rescue to VIP transport and civilian commercial operations.

Two large sponsons protrude from either side of the fuselage. They have emergency flotation gear in the event of a crash at sea.

The unusual shape of the fuselage reflects the boat-like design of the helicopter. Though rarely practiced, the helicopter can land on water.

The folding tail rotor allows the helicopter to be stored below carrier decks and in the small hangars of frigates.

ACTION DATA

SPEED

The large AS-61R Pelican is a developed version of the Sea King. The Pelican offers a significant speed advantage over the French-built Super Frelon, but is a poor performer compared to the later-designed Cougar.

AS-61R PELICAN	261 km/h (165 m.p.h.)
AS 532C COUGAR	271 km/h (168 m.p.h.)
SA 321G SUPER FRELON	275 km/h (154 m.p.h.)

RANGE

Operating with the US Coast Guard, the Pelican is capable of an extremely long range, thanks to its auxiliary fuel tanks. Later variants had an inflight refueling probe. The Cougar has a poor range.

AS-61R PELICAN 1427 km (885 mi.)
AS 532C COUGAR 618 km (383 mi.)
SA 321G SUPER FRELON 1020 km (632 mi.)

CEILING

Restricted in ceiling due to its requirement to carry rescue equipment, the AS-61R is also used as a transport helicopter within various armed forces. Developed from the Aerospatiale Puma, the Cougar has exceptional performance.

AS-61R PELICAN 3385 m (11,100 ft.)
AS 532C COUGAR 4100 m (13,450 ft.)
SA 321G SUPER FRELON 3100 m (10,100 ft.)

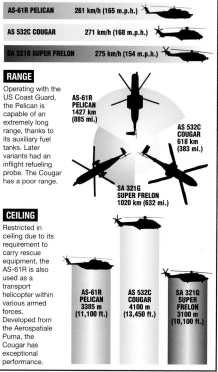

License-built Sea Kings

■ **BRAZIL:** A mixture of Agusta and Sikorsky-built SH-3Ds have been delivered to the Brazilian naval air arm. The helicopters perform a multitude of roles, including anti-submarine warfare.

■ **JAPAN:** This colourful helicopter is a Mitsubishi-built S-61AH of the Japanese Maritime Self-Defence Force. It is one of three procured for SAR duties.

■ **MALAYSIA:** Some 34 Sikorsky S-61A-4s remain in use for transport duties with the Royal Malaysian air force, though a more modern replacement is being sought.

ATLAS

ROOIVALK

● South African design ● Attack helicopter ● Battlefield support

▲ A fully armed Rooivalk carries V3C Darter air-to-air missiles, pods of 68-mm unguided rockets, enclosed four-round 80-mm anti-tank missile pods and a chin-mounted cannon.

Designed and produced in South Africa by Atlas Aviation, the Rooivalk or 'Red Kestrel', is an advanced armed attack helicopter. It can be deployed in support of highly mobile ground forces, in the anti-armour, deep penetration, close air support, reconnaissance and helicopter escort roles. A 20-mm high-speed cannon is carried in the nose turret and an assortment of missiles and other ordnance may be carried on the stub wings.

ATLAS ROOIVALK

Highly manoeuvrable ▶
A Rooivalk with ZT-3 anti-armour missiles and a 20-mm cannon shows that it can still be very agile in the battlefield area with up to 2000 kg (5 miles) of weapons aboard.

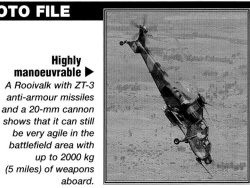

▲ Crash protection
The cockpits are similar, having head-up displays (HUDs) with night vision compatibility. Crash-worthy structure, protected systems and energy-absorbing seats give crew high crash survivability.

▼ Fast attack
With a top speed of over 300 km/h (185 m.p.h.) and a top climb rate of 670 m (2,200 f.p.m.) per minute, the Rooivalk can avoid detection during an attack thanks to its low radar and infra-red signature.

Tank-buster ▼
Up to 16 ZT-4 laser-guided or electro-optical fire-and-forget anti-tank missiles can be carried by the Rooivalk. These can be fired up to 8 km (5 miles) from the target.

▼ Adaptable
Operating away from its home base, the Rooivalk can be quickly changed between attack, support and escort roles.

FACTS AND FIGURES

➤ Development of South Africa's first attack helicopter began in 1981 with the XH-1 Alpha and XTP-2 Beta test aircraft.

➤ The Rooivalk uses some elements of the Aérospatiale Puma's rotor drive system.

➤ First flown on 11 February 1990, the Rooivalk entered service in late 1996.

➤ Special cockpit systems allow the crew to survive a crash, with sensors that cut off the electrics and fuel automatically.

➤ An automatic flight control system is fitted, with auto-hover and auto-land.

➤ The Rooivalk is designed to operate at low level (under 15 m/50 ft.) and at high speeds.

PROFILE

Red Kestrel – South Africa's attack helicopter

Designed and produced in South Africa, the Atlas CSH-2 Rooivalk or 'Red Kestrel' is a battlefield support and attack helicopter, capable of day/night and adverse weather operations. It was developed through the 1980s using the experience gained in producing the Puma helicopter for the South African Air Force and in building two experimental attack helicopters based on the older French Alouette design.

The Rooivalk's extra-strong fuselage is mostly metal but with some composites. It has stepped tandem cockpits, with the pilot in the rear and the co-pilot/gunner in the front. The cockpit canopies are formed from flat plate on single curvature sheets to minimise glint from the sun. The twin Topaz turboshaft engines are uprated versions of the Turboméca Turmo IV and the main rotor is similar to that fitted to the Aérospatiale Puma.

With a total of only 16 Rooivalks ordered for the South African Air Force, further production is uncertain. Foreign sales have yet to materialise.

Above: Rooivalk is able to fly a large number of sorties in the battlefield area, making a hot turnaround with full re-arming and refuelling in 15 minutes.

Left: Multi-role operations can be conducted with pairs of helicopters. One operates in the attack role. The other provides armed reconnaissance and escort or defends against enemy aircraft.

CSH-2 Rooivalk

Type: attack and battlefield support helicopter

Powerplant: two 1356-kW (1,818-hp.) Topaz turboshafts

Maximum speed: 315 km/h (195 m.p.h.)

Initial climb rate: 670 m/min (2,200 f.p.m.)

Range: 700 km (435 mi.) (without drop tanks)

Service ceiling: 6100 m (20,000 ft.)

Weights: empty 5910 kg (13,000 lb.); maximum take-off 8750 kg (19,250 lb.)

Armament: nose-mounted single-barrel 20-mm cannon or double-barrel 20-mm cannon, plus a variety of rockets and missiles on stub wings

Dimensions:
main rotor diameter	15.58 m (51 ft. 2 in.)
length overall	18.73 m (61 ft. 7 in.)
height	5.19 m (17 ft.)
rotor disc area	190.60 m² (2,051 sq. ft.)

CSH-2 ROOIVALK

The Atlas CSH-2 Rooivalk was based on engineering elements of the AS330 Puma and developed over a long period as an adaptable, multi-role, all-weather attack and battlefield support helicopter.

The four-bladed composite main rotor has a diameter of 15.58 m (51 ft. 2 in.) and is similar to that of the French Puma. It has a flapping hinge offset 3.8 degrees. An automatic flight control system provides automatic hovering and landing facilities.

The five-bladed composite tail rotor is located on the starboard side of the swept-back dorsal fin, with a horizontal stabiliser on the port side.

A nose-mounted, gyro-stabilised turret houses an automatic target detection and tracking system. Threat detection, warning and jamming self-protection systems are fitted.

The fuselage and engine cowlings have large access panels that, when lowered, can be used as platforms for maintenance workers. The engines have their own built-in automatic fault-detection systems.

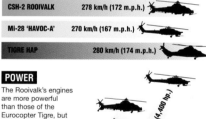

A typical weapons load consists of eight anti-armour and four air-to-air missiles as well as 400 rounds of 20-mm ammunition for the nose-mounted cannon.

The tricycle landing gear has two fixed high energy absorbing front main legs and a tailwheel at the base of the ventral tailfin.

COMBAT DATA

CRUISING SPEED

The Rooivalk has a cruising speed similar to that of these other modern attack helicopters, the Mil Mi-28 and Eurocopter Tigre HAP. Speeds vary according to the loads carried; during an attack mission a fully loaded helicopter will fly at an appreciably slower speed, limiting its manoeuvrability.

CSH-2 ROOIVALK	278 km/h (172 m.p.h.)
Mi-28 'HAVOC-A'	270 km/h (167 m.p.h.)
TIGRE HAP	280 km/h (174 m.p.h.)

POWER

The Rooivalk's engines are more powerful than those of the Eurocopter Tigre, but of a lower rating than the Russian Mi-28. Engine power has a major bearing on the speed and load-carrying abilities of these aircraft, more powerful attack helicopters being able to lift heavier loads.

CSH-2 ROOIVALK 2712 kW (3,636 hp.)

Mi-28 'HAVOC-A' 3280 kW (4,400 hp.)

TIGRE HAP 1916 kW (2,570 hp.)

ENDURANCE

An area in which the Rooivalk has a decided advantage over both the Tigre and Mi-28 is endurance. At 4 hr 55 min at 1525 m, the South African aircraft is able to spend twice as long as the Mi-28 on a mission and over an hour longer than the Tigre. This greatly increases the operational flexibility of the aircraft.

CSH-2 ROOIVALK 4 hours 55 min	Mi-28 'HAVOC-A' 2 hours	TIGRE HAP 3 hours 10 min

Modern attack helicopters

■ **EUROCOPTER TIGRE:** A Franco-German fast anti-tank and close air support helicopter to enter service in the late 1990s.

■ **KAMOV KA-50 WEREWOLF 'HOKUM':** A Russian single-seat attack helicopter with co-axial contra-rotating three-bladed rotors.

■ **MDH AH-64D LONGBOW APACHE:** US day/night and adverse weather attack helicopter developed from the AH-64A.

■ **MIL Mi-28 'HAVOC':** Russian battlefield attack helicopter planned to replace the successful Mi-24 'Hind' in the Russian army.

BELL

UH-1 IROQUOIS

● Troop carrier ● Helicopter gunship ● Medical evacuation

▲ The UH-1 was the workhorse of the US Army in Vietnam. By moving men quickly to the scene of action, the US Army could take on the highly mobile Viet Cong.

American soldiers in Vietnam won a prolonged, hand-to-hand battle with North Vietnamese infantry in the Ia Drang Valley in 1965, thanks to a new concept: air cavalry. The Bell UH-1 Iroquois helicopter, or 'Huey', enabled air cavalry soldiers to move from one firefight to another by air, leapfrogging the enemy and seizing the advantage. The 'Huey' revolutionised warfare, adding a new dimension to air mobility.

BELL UH-1 IROQUOIS

▼ Purple haze
Landing on a purple smoke signal from the ground troops, a 'Huey' lands at an artillery firebase to offload shells carried in a cargo net.

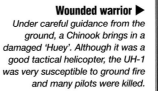

▲ Machine-gun
Fitted with twin 7.62-mm Browning machine-guns, the UH-1 was a devastating gunship.

Wounded warrior ▶
Under careful guidance from the ground, a Chinook brings in a damaged 'Huey'. Although it was a good tactical helicopter, the UH-1 was very susceptible to ground fire and many pilots were killed.

▼ Resupply mission
The 'Huey' allowed ground units to refuel anywhere. This UH-1D is carrying a cargo of fuel cans.

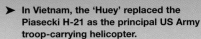

◀ Straight into action
Troops would often jump into a landing zone, especially if the pilots suspected that the area was mined.

FACTS AND FIGURES

➤ The 'Huey' helicopter was the first turbine-powered aircraft to serve with the US Army when it was adopted in 1959.

➤ The first prototype in the series made its first flight on 22 October 1956.

➤ Thousands of UH-1s were shot down in Vietnam, mainly by small-arms fire.

➤ In Vietnam, the 'Huey' replaced the Piasecki H-21 as the principal US Army troop-carrying helicopter.

➤ The UH-1D had a lengthened fuselage and was first flown on 16 August 1963.

➤ The total number of aircraft in the 'Huey' family exceeds 11,000.

PROFILE

Flying truck of the US Army

At the start of the Vietnam War, it had already been proven that helicopters could be useful to infantrymen. But when the Bell UH-1 'Huey' joined the massive US build-up in 1965, ground commanders were able to use it to lift battalion-sized units from one battlefield to another. This was the birth of the 'air cavalry' concept, made famous by the 1st Cavalry Division (Airmobile).

The 'Huey' was a straightforward, single-engined design with a crew of two pilots and a crew chief/door gunner. In combat, UH-1s flew three distinct missions as 'slicks' (troop transports), 'gunships' (armed battlefield helicopters) and 'dust-offs' (medical evacuation aircraft).

The Huey was armed with a door-mounted, flexible 7.62-mm M60 machine-gun, and gunship versions carried rocket pods,

grenade-launchers or four side-mounted guns. On the battlefield, a soldier might be put into action at the LZ (landing zone) by one 'Huey', given covering fire by another and taken to the field hospital by a third UH-1.

Left: 'Hueys' had to fly in extremely dangerous conditions. UH-1 crew casualties in Vietnam were exceeded only by the Marines and Army ground troops.

Right: Flying the 'Huey' in Vietnam required good handling skills. Carrying a full load of troops in 'hot-and-high' conditions, often landing in small jungle clearings while under intense ground-fire, the pilots soon learned tactical flying skills.

UH-1B Iroquois

Type: general-purpose helicopter

Powerplant: one 1044-kW (1,400-hp.) Avco Lycoming T5313B turboshaft

Maximum speed: 204 km/h (126 m.p.h.)

Range: 383 km (237 mi.) at sea level

Service ceiling: 5790 m (19,000 ft.)

Hover ceiling: 4635 m (15,200 ft.)

Weights: empty 2177 kg (4,789 lb.); maximum take-off 3856 kg (8,483 lb.)

Armament: up to 3800 kg (8,300 lb.) of guns, rockets, missiles and grenades, including 40-mm grenade-launcher, 70-mm air-to-ground rocket projectiles and 7.62-mm (.30 cal.) machine-guns

Dimensions:

rotor diameter	14.63 m (48 ft.)
length	12.31 m (40 ft. 5 in.)
height	3.77 m (12 ft. 5 in.)
rotor disc area	168.10 m² (1,809 sq. ft.)

UH-1D IROQUOIS

The standard US Army helicopter in Vietnam, the UH-1 was first introduced in 1959 and continues in service (in modified form) to this day. This aircraft is a 'slick' troop-carrier version, without external armament.

Pilots always checked the glass-fibre rotor blades before a flight to ensure that the surface was not delaminating. They also inspected the so-called 'Jesus nut' which held the main rotor blades securely.

The large, twin-bladed main rotor had a thick metal leading-edge spar, which allowed pilots to chop through vegetation in confined landing zones.

The secret of the UH-1's success compared to earlier machines was its powerful T531 gas turbine engine.

The main cabin door slid backwards to allow the troops to dismount or the gunner to fire. Gunships carried their armament on side-mounted sponsons.

The tail-rotor driveshaft ran along the top of the tailboom. An intermediate gearbox was located at the bend.

The main compartment could carry up to 10 troops in combat gear or six stretchers. The crew chief supervised loading of cargo, and a gunner operated the M-60 machine-gun.

A small elevator was fitted halfway along the tailboom to offload the main rotor in forward flight.

The twin-bladed tail rotor was protected by a small bumper, which very often struck the ground when pilots flared hard during combat landings.

UNITED STATES ARMY

Helicopter support in Vietnam

■ **BELL UH-1 IROQUOIS:** 'Huey' gunships escorted the troop-carrying 'slicks' into battle, blasting landing zones with rockets, machine-guns and SS-11 missiles.

■ **BOEING-VERTOL CH-47 CHINOOK:** The big muscle of the US helicopter force, the Chinook could recover shot-down 'Hueys' and was also used for transporting guns to firebases.

■ **PIASECKI H-21 SHAWNEE:** This twin-rotor machine was the first US Army helicopter deployed in Vietnam in support of the ARVN. It was soon replaced by 'Hueys' and Chinooks.

■ **SIKORSKY H-34 CHOCTAW:** Used mainly by the US Marine Corps, the H-34 was first used for undercover missions with the Special Forces in Laos. Westland based its Wessex on the H-34.

COMBAT DATA

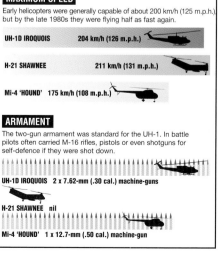

TROOP LOAD

The 'Huey' was smaller than the H-21 and Mi-4 but carried a respectable load. In Vietnam, they were often difficult to take off fully loaded.

UH-1D IROQUOIS 10 passengers

H-21 SHAWNEE 14 passengers

Mi-4 'HOUND' 12 passengers

MAXIMUM SPEED

Early helicopters were generally capable of about 200 km/h (125 m.p.h.) but by the late 1980s they were flying half as fast again.

UH-1D IROQUOIS 204 km/h (126 m.p.h.)

H-21 SHAWNEE 211 km/h (131 m.p.h.)

Mi-4 'HOUND' 175 km/h (108 m.p.h.)

ARMAMENT

The two-gun armament was standard for the UH-1. In battle pilots often carried M-16 rifles, pistols or even shotguns for self-defence if they were shot down.

UH-1D IROQUOIS 2 x 7.62-mm (.30 cal.) machine-guns

H-21 SHAWNEE nil

Mi-4 'HOUND' 1 x 12.7-mm (.50 cal.) machine-gun

BELL
UH-1B/C IROQUOIS

● Airborne jeep ● Multi-role helicopter ● NATO workhorse

PHOTO FILE
BELL UH-1B/C IROQUOIS

▲ **Navy rescue**
This TH-1L uses its sling hoist during a demonstration at Ellyson Field, Pensacola, Florida.

▲ **High speed bird**
Several test configurations were used on the 'Huey', increasing the speed to 402 km/h (250 m.p.h.).

▼ **Overseas success**
Built under licence by Agusta in Italy as the AB 204, this 'Huey' serves in the anti-submarine role. Early versions of the UH-1 remain in service throughout Europe.

▲ **Weapons platform**
An Italian example demonstrates the offensive capabilities of the UH-1 by lifting off with two pylon-mounted machine-guns and 21 rockets.

Anti-tank missiles▶
The 'Huey' was employed in the development of the first air-to-ground missile for the US Army, which was used in Vietnam.

Bell's Model 204 formed the basis for one of the most successful series of helicopters ever built. Flown for the first time in October 1956, it was designated XH-40, then HU-1 by the US Army (who called it the 'Huey'), before a designation change to HU-1A Iroquois. The HU-1B introduced a more powerful engine and the HU-1C had a new rotor system. Later still the HU- designation was changed to UH-. Variants were built by Agusta in Italy.

▲ A door-gunner rides 'shotgun' with his M60 as a pair of 'Hueys' fly over the Delta region in Vietnam. To many people, the war in Southeast Asia was symbolised by images of the UH-1.

FACTS AND FIGURES

➤ Four prototype YUH-1Bs were ordered in June 1959, with the first flight taking place in the following April.

➤ A total of 1,010 UH-1Bs were produced in Italy, Japan and the United States.

➤ The YUH-1B set an unofficial world speed record of 357 km/h (222 m.p.h.) in May 1964.

➤ Differences between the B and C models included a modified rotor system, wider rotor blades and a larger fin.

➤ The 'Huey' was the first helicopter to see widespread use as a gunship.

➤ The Royal Australian Air Force was the first non-US customer for 8 UH-1Bs.

PROFILE

Bell's ubiquitous 'Huey'

The turbine engine was one of the keys to the Model 204's success. Mounted on the cabin roof just behind the gearbox, it left the cabin unencumbered and provided the performance required by the US Army.

Early UH-1Bs retained the UH-1A's 716-kW (960 hp.) T53 engine, but an 820-kW (1100 hp.) powerplant soon became the standard. The new model was delivered from March 1961 and could be armed with rocket pods and machine-guns carried on the sides of the cabin.

UH-1Bs were also built by Fuji in Japan and Agusta in Italy. Agusta models included the AB 204AS anti-submarine variant for the Italian and Spanish navies, plus civil AB 204Bs with Lycoming T53, General Electric T58 or Rolls-Royce Gnome engines.

The UH-1C, which flew in September 1965, used a new rotor system with 'door hinges' and wider blades. This provided more lift, enabling the fuel load to be increased and improving the machine's manoeuvrability and speed. Variants of the UH-1C,

Above: This is one of six test YH-40s seen during a proving flight. There were few differences between these and the first production 'Hueys'.

Below: The glossy overall olive drab, with a yellow tail band and white lettering, soon gave way to dull green when the 'Huey' entered combat.

with new designations, were used by the US Air Force, Navy and Marine Corps in the training, rescue and assault roles.

TH-1L

Pictured in red and white training colours, this TH-1L, the navy designation for the 'Huey', is used for pilot training. This involves flying from aircraft carriers and over-water navigation.

UH-1C

Type: single-engined multi-role utility helicopter

Powerplant: one 820-kW (1,100-hp.) Lycoming T53-L-11 turboshaft engine

Maximum speed: 238 km/h (148 m.p.h.) at sea level

Initial climb rate: 427 m (1,401 ft.) per minute

Range: 615 km (382 mi.) with auxiliary fuel

Service ceiling: 3505 m (11,500 ft)

Weights: empty 2300 kg (5,070 lb.); maximum take-off 4309 kg (9,500 lb.)

Dimensions:
rotor diameter	13.41 m (44 ft.)
length	12.98 m (42 ft. 6 in.)
height	3.84 m (12 ft. 6 in.)
rotor disc area	141.26 m² (144 sq. ft.)

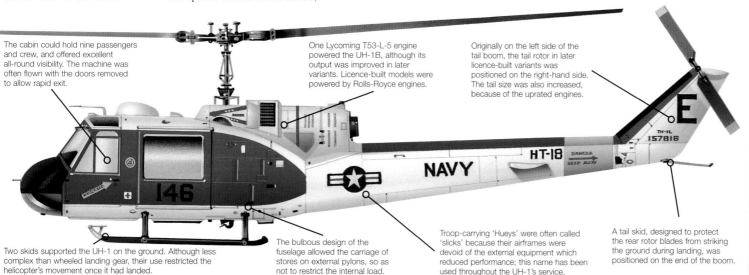

The cabin could hold nine passengers and crew, and offered excellent all-round visibility. The machine was often flown with the doors removed to allow rapid exit.

One Lycoming T53-L-5 engine powered the UH-1B, although its output was improved in later variants. Licence-built models were powered by Rolls-Royce engines.

Originally on the left side of the tail boom, the tail rotor in later licence-built variants was positioned on the right-hand side. The tail size was also increased, because of the uprated engines.

Two skids supported the UH-1 on the ground. Although less complex than wheeled landing gear, their use restricted the helicopter's movement once it had landed.

The bulbous design of the fuselage allowed the carriage of stores on external pylons, so as not to restrict the internal load.

Troop-carrying 'Hueys' were often called 'slicks' because their airframes were devoid of the external equipment which reduced performance; this name has been used throughout the UH-1's service.

A tail skid, designed to protect the rear rotor blades from striking the ground during landing, was positioned on the end of the boom.

COMBAT DATA

POWER

Although the Huey was the first practical transport helicopter to see widespread military use, the power of the early models was found to be lacking in the roles with which the helicopter was tasked. Later variants were fitted with improved engines.

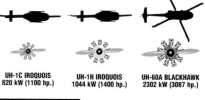

UH-1C IROQUOIS 820 kW (1100 hp.)	UH-1H IROQUOIS 1044 kW (1400 hp.)	UH-60A BLACKHAWK 2302 kW (3087 hp.)

MAXIMUM PAYLOAD

The early variants of the UH-1, although capable of lifting an acceptable load, required improvement. The advent of more powerful engines in later variants allowed an increased payload, although this was still restricted by the cabin size. The knowledge gained during the development of the 'Huey' was incorporated into the purpose-built Blackhawk.

UH-1C IROQUOIS 1361 kg (3,000 lb.)

UH-1H IROQUOIS 1759 kg (3,878 lb.)

UH-60A BLACKHAWK 3629 kg (8,000 lb.)

MAXIMUM SPEED

Because of its relatively light load the performance of the UH-1B was superior to that of later models which became much heavier, because of operational and design changes. The twin-engined Blackhawk offered improved performance in a streamlined fuselage while retaining the capability to carry large loads.

UH-1C IROQUOIS	238 km/h (148 m.p.h.)
UH-1H IROQUOIS	204 km/h (127 m.p.h.)
UH-60A BLACKHAWK	296 km/h (184 m.p.h.)

Improving the breed

■ **UH-1H:** An improvement of the UH-1B design, advances included increased lifting capability and an enlarged cabin area. This variant serves with the Taiwan air force.

■ **MODEL 212:** Offering the reliability of an improved twin engine and a weather radar located in the nose, this Singaporean example serves with the local VIP flight.

■ **MODEL 214ST:** Possessing little commonality with earlier designs, this Venezuelan 'Huey' features a stretched cabin, improved performance and composite rotor blades.

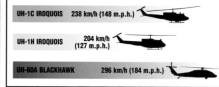

BELL
UH-1D/H IROQUOIS

● Classic design ● Thousands in service ● Vietnam veteran

On 16 August 1961, Bell test-flew a 'second-generation' 'Huey' helicopter, marking the start of a long career for the D and H models of the UH-1 Iroquois. This second-phase 'Huey' offered greater lifting capability, had a longer fuselage (by about one metre/yard) and a larger loading door than earlier helicopters in the series. The UH-1D/H helicopter began to arrive in Vietnam in 1965.

▲ Developed with the hindsight of initial combat experience in Vietnam, the UH-1D/H has become one of the great utility aircraft, and possibly the greatest military helicopter of all time.

BELL UH-1D/H IROQUOIS

▲ Spanish 'Huey'
Several UH-1H helicopters serve with the Spanish army and a handful fly as trainers with the country's air force. They are known as HU.10Bs.

▲ Antipodean Iroquois
Ten UH-1Hs and five UH-1Ds were delivered to the Royal New Zealand Air Force. They are flown by crews from the army and air force and are often used by overseas detachments.

▲ Into the 21st century
Having initiated a comprehensive upgrade programme to its UH-1 fleet in the late 1980s, the US Army is looking to further upgrade the aircraft with new engines and avionics. Bell's submission, the UH-1HP 'Huey II', first flew in August 1992.

▲ Built in Germany
Dornier built 352 UH-1Ds under licence. Manufacture has also taken place in Italy, Japan and Korea. Interestingly, few sales have been made to the civilian market.

South American SAR ▶
Brazil operates both the UH-1D and the slightly more powerful UH-1H. This aircraft is configured for search and rescue duties. Other South American operators include Argentina, Chile and Panama.

FACTS AND FIGURES

➤ Textron-Lycoming's T53-L-13 engine became standard on the UH-1H; Bell produced 5,435 of this model.

➤ New Zealand was the first overseas purchaser of UH-1H 'Hueys'.

➤ Between 1958 and 1980 the US Army purchased 9,440 'Hueys' of all versions.

➤ The UH-1H flew for the first time on 4 April 1966 at the same that the UH-1D was entering service.

➤ Other early UH-1H customers included Canada and the USAF.

➤ Many second-generation 'Hueys' flew medical evacuation missions.

Bell's immortal 'Huey'

Second-generation 'Huey' helicopters were bigger and had more power than earlier versions and were designed for rapid, simultaneous entry from both sides of the larger-volume cabin. This helped to minimise the exposure of aircraft and soldiers to enemy fire in a landing zone. Increased in size by about 12 per cent, the UH-1D and UH-1H were improvements on a design that was already proving itself in combat.

With the arrival of this second generation, the 'Huey'

became the most versatile and best-known combat helicopter of all time.

'Huey' pilots sat behind a Plexiglass windscreen that gave excellent visibility, but also made them vulnerable to ground fire during an assault landing to drop off troops. A crew chief was always carried and often doubled as a door gunner, shooting back at Viet Cong troops with a flexibly-mounted 7.62-mm M60 machine-gun.

Large numbers of 'Hueys' are still serving around the world,

and several are finding their way onto the second-hand civilian market, even though Bell found little commercial interest in new examples. Many operators look to the aircraft's proven reliability and global distribution to make flying their ex-military helicopters as economical as possible.

Bell's 'Huey' is set to be an important helicopter well into the next century.

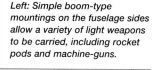

Left: Simple boom-type mountings on the fuselage sides allow a variety of light weapons to be carried, including rocket pods and machine-guns.

Right: UH-1s, often in UN colours, have been involved in military and humanitarian operations all over the world.

UH-1H Iroquois

Type: single-engined general-purpose military helicopter

Powerplant: one 1044-kW (1,400-hp.) Avco Lycoming T53-L-13 turboshaft engine

Maximum speed: 204 km/h (127 m.p.h.) (also maximum cruising speed)

Range: 511 km (317 mi.) at sea level

Service ceiling: 3840 m (12,600 ft.)

Weights: empty 2363 kg (5210 lb.); maximum take-off 4309 kg (9,500 lb.)

Accommodation: two pilots, crew chief, 12 to 14 fully-armed combat troops, or six stretchers plus three seats for medical evacuation work, or 1759 kg (3,878 lb.) freight

Dimensions:
main rotor diameter	14.63 m (48 ft.)
fuselage length	12.77 m (41 ft. 11 in.)
height 4.41 m	(14 ft. 5 in.)
rotor disc area	168.11 m² (1,809 sq. ft.)

UH-1H Iroquois

This UH-1 wears the typical drab green colours of the US Army and was one of many UH-1H helicopters to have served in Germany. 'Hueys' have been operated by US military forces in almost every theatre.

In November 1981 the US Army requested the development of new composite rotor blades for its UH-1H fleet. A contract for 6,000 blades was shared equally between Bell and Boeing. However, the blades may be changed yet again in a new series of upgrades.

The UH-1 features a two-bladed main rotor, with a stabilising bar at 90° to the rotor attachments.

Most 'Hueys' carry a distinctive VHF (very high frequency) antenna above the cockpit. The US Army flies a number of electronic countermeasures and electronic intelligence-gathering variants.

Mounting the engine above the fuselage and surrounding it with access panels made maintenance far easier than with previous US Army types.

None of the proposed upgrades has suggested replacing the all-metal tail rotor. One possibility is to move the rotor to the opposite side of the tail fin, where it would act as a tractor rather than pusher unit, to improve handling.

Although these glazed panels in the lower cockpit gave the crew good downward visibility, they also made the crew vulnerable to small arms fire. Many crews in Vietnam placed armoured plates behind the glazing.

The large sliding doors on either side of the fuselage made loading and unloading troops in the combat zone much faster. The doors could be removed to give straight-through access.

The UH-1's fuselage is of semi-monocoque all-metal construction. A skid at the rear protects the tail rotor in the event of a tail-down landing.

'Hueys' at work worldwide

POPULAR AROUND THE WORLD: After serving in Vietnam, the 'Huey' has become a popular utility helicopter in the West's air forces. Although it is beginning to be replaced, large numbers remain in service.

VIETNAM TROOP-CARRIER: The 'Huey', especially the UH-1D and H models, became synonymous with the war in Southeast Asia. Thousands were built for the general utility role.

SUPPORT ON ICE: The RNZAF has annually committed a UH-1 to the southern continent in support of New Zealand's scientific research operations in the Antarctic. With its Dayglo orange colour scheme, the aircraft has been nicknamed 'Orange Roughy' after a local species of fish.

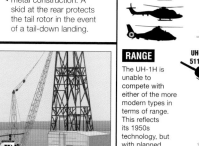

CIVIL OPERATIONS: Civil use of UH-1D/H (Bell Model 205) models has been minor compared to military service. Roles have included fire-fighting, logging, agricultural work and inshore oil exploration support.

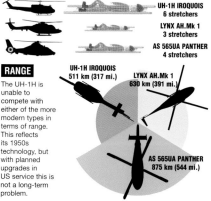

COMBAT DATA

MAXIMUM PAYLOAD

With its lengthened cabin, the UH-1H can carry a large payload. This makes refurbished or upgraded 'Hueys' an attractive proposition for air arms that might otherwise buy the Lynx or Panther.

UH-1H IROQUOIS	1759 kg (3,878 lb.)
LYNX AH.Mk 1	1361 kg (3,000 lb.)
AS 565UA PANTHER	1600 kg (3,527 lb.)

STRETCHERS

In common with many battlefield utility helicopters, the UH-1H is often used for medical evacuation missions. In this role it is far more effective than the Panther or the Lynx.

UH-1H IROQUOIS	6 stretchers
LYNX AH.Mk 1	3 stretchers
AS 565UA PANTHER	4 stretchers

RANGE

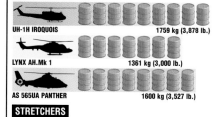

The UH-1H is unable to compete with either of the more modern types in terms of range. This reflects its 1950s technology, but with planned upgrades in US service this is not a long-term problem.

UH-1H IROQUOIS 511 km (317 mi.)
LYNX AH.Mk 1 630 km (391 mi.)
AS 565UA PANTHER 875 km (544 mi.)

BELL

AH-1 HUEYCOBRA (SINGLE)

● Gunship ● Tank killer ● Escort helicopter

Early Bell AH-1 HueyCobras opened a new era in warfare. From the dawn of rotary-wing aviation it was apparent that the helicopter could become a revolutionary weapon of war if it was armed. The HueyCobra was the first helicopter designed for armed battlefield duties. Although it had a number of features in common with the famous UH-1 'Huey', the AH-1 was the first of the real anti-tank helicopter gunships.

▲ *The AH-1 HueyCobra received its baptism of fire in the jungles of Southeast Asia with the US Army. The AH-1 took over the role of premier tank-busting and specialised assault helicopter from the UH-1D.*

BELL AH-1 HUEYCOBRA (SINGLE)

◄ Rocket strike
For the destruction of 'soft' targets the AH-1 carries up to four 70-mm LAU-68 pods, each containing seven unguided rockets.

Tank-busting missile ▶
The BGM-71A TOW used in Vietnam was a wire-guided anti-tank missile with a 3-km (1.8-mile) range.

Gun armament ▶
The AH-1's undernose turret contains a General Electric M197 three-barrelled 20-mm cannon which is aimed by the gunner in the front seat.

▲ US Army Cobra
The Cobra first saw service in 1968 after the Army ordered 38 examples. The current helicopters are much improved.

Slim lines ▶
The AH-1 (centre) was designed to present as small a target as possible to enemy ground fire.

FACTS AND FIGURES

➤ The AH-1 was designed with the rotor system, transmission and tailboom of the proven UH-1D 'Huey'.

➤ The AH-1 Cobra was first flown in prototype form on 7 September 1965.

➤ HueyCobras are equipped to carry TOW missiles.

➤ The US Army Aviation Association voted the AH-1 one of four 'most valuable weapons' of the Vietnam War.

➤ Bell produced more than 1,600 first-generation, single-engine Cobras.

➤ AH-1s were often armed with two 'thumper' 40-mm grenade-launchers.

The world's first attack helicopter

In 1965 the US Army finalised its requirement for the world's first armed battlefield helicopter, the Bell AH-1 Cobra, often called the HueyCobra.

The idea had arisen before Vietnam, but the Cobra arrived on the scene just when it was needed in the Southeast Asia conflict. The AH-1 featured a streamlined, narrow-width fuselage that accommodated a two-man crew in tandem seats with the pilot above and behind the co-pilot/gunner.

The US Army progressively improved this fine helicopter. The engine power, performance and armament had all been enhanced by 1972 when the AH-1 proved especially valuable during the North Vietnamese offensive. Already successful using guns and rockets for direct support of ground troops, the Cobras were pitched against Communist PT-76 light tanks.

The early design was so effective that improved versions of the AH-1 Cobra were ordered for the Army and the US Marine Corps. Beginning in the 1970s, twin-engined versions replaced 'first generation' HueyCobras. These newer combat helicopters still remain with some units.

The HueyCobra unleashes a deadly BGM-71 TOW (Tube-launched Optically-tracked Wire-guided) missile towards an unsuspecting tank. It is guided to the target by a trailing wire.

AH-1G/S HueyCobra

Type: attack/close-support helicopter

Powerplant: one 944-kW (1,266-hp.) Lycoming T53-L-13 or 1210-kW (1623 hp.)T53-L-703 turboshaft engine

Maximum speed: 277 km/h (172 m.p.h.)

Range: 574 km (357 mi.)

Service ceiling: 3530 m (11,600 ft.)

Weights: empty 2754 kg (6071 lb.); maximum take-off 4309 kg (9,500 lb.)

Armament: one M197 20-mm cannon in nose turret and 998 kg (2,200 lb.) of weapons (XM-18 Minigun pods and XM-157 70-mm rocket pods) on four racks

Dimensions:
main rotor diameter	13.41 m (44 ft.)
length, rotors turning	16.26 m (53 ft. 4 in.)
height	4.17 m (13 ft. 8 in.)
rotor disc area	141.26 m² (1,520 sq. ft.)

The cockpit has bulletproof panels, but the forward fuselage is narrow and only lightly armoured.

Both inboard pylons carry the classic armament of seven-round 70-mm LAU-68 unguided rocket packs for the destruction of light targets and unarmoured vehicles.

Outboard a heavier load of 19-round LAU-69 rocket pods is carried. In total the AH-1G can deploy 52 unguided 70-mm rockets.

AH-1G HUEYCOBRA

This HueyCobra is a US Army model in the three-colour camouflage used in the jungles of North Vietnam during the fighting of the early 1970s.

The AH-1 retained the UH-1's characteristically noisy two-bladed main rotor system and linkage.

The now common tandem seating of the gunner and pilot was first introduced into combat on a helicopter by the AH-1. In early Vietnam models, before the cannon was fitted, a single 40-mm grenade-launcher or twin 7.62-mm six-barrel Miniguns were carried.

Early Cobra's had a single Textron Lycoming T53 Turboshaft rated at 994 kW (1332 hp.). Later models have two.

The tail and fuselage are very slender. This enables the helicopter to fly tight and low at tree-top level to help mask its presence.

The twin-bladed tail rotor is identical to that of the UH-1.

16369

UNITED STATES ARMY

The HueyCobra has simple but very tough landing skids rather than a complex retractable undercarriage.

The AH-1 was designed and developed in such a short period of time that, wherever possible, systems were kept either the same as those in the UH-1 or were made simple like this primitive tail bumper.

COMBAT DATA

MAXIMUM CRUISING SPEED

Helicopters flying anti-armour missions often rely on stealth to ambush enemy columns. However, operating in enemy territory is very dangerous and these helicopters are amongst the fastest flying, using their speed to escape from threatening positions.

AH-1G HUEYCOBRA	**277 km/h (172 m.p.h.)**
LYNX AH.Mk 1	**259 km/h (161 m.p.h.)**
Mi-24 'HIND-A'	**270 km/h (168 m.p.h.)**

POWER

The 'Hind' is a far bigger helicopter as it is also designed as a troop carrier and is powered by two large engines. The AH-1G is at the other end of the spectrum, powered by a single, relatively small engine and relying on a streamlined shape and light construction for its performance.

AH-1G HUEYCOBRA 944 kW (1265 hp.)	LYNX AH.Mk 1 1342 kW (1800 hp.)	Mi-24 'HIND-A' 2238 kW (3001 hp.)

ARMAMENT

The main weapon used by all three helicopters is the anti-tank missile. The bigger 'Hind' can carry twice the number of missiles, but in reality would be more likely to carry a mixture of missiles and rockets. The cannon on the AH-1G and the gun on the Mi-24 are remote-controlled integrated systems; the gun on the Lynx can be fitted as required.

AH-1G HUEYCOBRA 8 anti-tank missiles 1 x 20-mm cannon

LYNX AH.Mk 1 8 anti-tank missiles 1 x 7.62-mm machine-gun

Mi-24 'HIND-A' 16 anti-tank missiles 1 x 12.7-mm machine-gun

Siege at An Loc

In 1972 North Vietnamese forces equipped with Russian-built tanks flooded into South Vietnam, invading both Saigon and the town of An Loc in an unprecedented large-scale conventional invasion.

AN LOC

SAIGON

AMERICAN RESISTANCE: American resistance was provided by AC-130 Spectre gunships and large numbers of nimble AH-1 attack helicopters.

URBAN WARFARE: The Cobra proved well-suited to fighting in an urban theatre. In one of its first operations, the BGM-71A TOW missile was used against the Viet Cong's T-54 heavy tanks. Several kills were made using the system.

BELL

206 JETRANGER

● Light turboshaft helicopter ● Multi-role civil and military variants

▲ The JetRanger is one of the most successful helicopters ever built. Combining simplicity and low operating costs, it has almost completely dominated the small helicopter market.

The Bell 206 JetRanger is one of the world's most popular helicopters. Manufactured by Bell in Canada and Agusta in Italy, this civil servant began as a military observation craft but has become a real champion of air commerce. For law enforcement, executive travel, crop spraying and countless other duties, it is one of the best aircraft in its class – a versatile and economical helicopter which is simple to operate and enjoyable to fly.

BELL 206 JETRANGER

▲ **Agile but simple to fly**
The JetRanger is agile enough to be used by display teams at air shows. The ease with which it can be flown means that it also makes a good helicopter trainer, both on land and at sea.

▲ **Kiowa warrior**
Known to the US Army as the OH-58 Kiowa, the latest armed versions of the Model 206 have four-bladed rotors and an anti-glare cockpit, and can carry Hellfire missiles and a mast-mounted sight.

▲ **All-rounder**
The 206 has performed most light helicopter tasks, but it is often used as an air taxi, typically flying businessmen to and from airports.

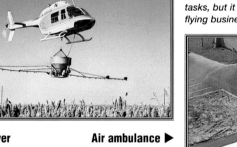

▲ **Crop sprayer**
With a tank and spray bar slung from a cargo hook, the JetRanger can fly crop-spraying missions with notable precision.

Air ambulance ▶
JetRangers have found a ready market as ambulance aircraft, being able to get casualties to hospital in minutes.

FACTS AND FIGURES

➤ The 1,394 JetRangers and 599 LongRangers on register make up 15 per cent of the US civil helicopter fleet.

➤ Full certification of the Model 206A occurred on 20 October 1966.

➤ The current 206B JetRanger III is built at Bell's facility in Mirabel, Canada.

➤ The normal interior of the JetRanger provides comfortable accommodation for five passengers.

➤ According to Bell figures, the 206 is the world's safest helicopter.

➤ US military trainer versions are the Navy TH-57 and Army TH-67.

PROFILE

Ranging the world with the Bell 206

The Bell 206 series – comprising the JetRanger and its longer, more powerful brother, the 206L LongRanger – virtually created the modern light helicopter market in North America, and have become familiar sights around the world. Bell 206s are seen everywhere, doing everything from ferrying VIPs to swanky race meetings to mounting fire-watching patrols over remote forests.

The 206 originated in Bell's unsuccessful 1964 bid for a US Army light observation helicopter contract. Although the majority of the 7,000 helicopters delivered by Bell have been for military use, well over 2,300 have been sold to civil operators, along with many of the 1,000 aircraft built by Agusta.

Commercial owners like the JetRanger's flexibility and low operating costs. Pilots speak well of its roominess, ease of handling and excellent visibility.

One image which represents what the Bell 206 is all about is that of a US Park Service LongRanger crew rescuing victims from Washington's icy Potomac River in the aftermath of the crash of Air Florida Flight 90 in January 1982.

Left: JetRangers can be used for air ambulance and rescue work. This US Park Police example was first on the scene at the Potomac River air crash of January 1982, which took place in the heart of Washington.

Above: JetRangers are often used by American TV stations to transport reporters to incidents quickly.

Model 206B-3 JetRanger III

Type: light general-purpose helicopter

Powerplant: one 313-kW (420-hp.) Allison 250-C20J turboshaft, flat-rated to 236 kW (316 hp.)

Maximum cruise speed: 216 km/h at 1525 m (134 m.p.h. at 5,000 ft.)

Range: 730 km (450 mi.) with maximum fuel

Service ceiling: 4115 m (13,500 ft.)

Weights: empty 737 kg (1,620 lb.); loaded 1520 kg (3,345 lb.) with external load

Accommodation: one or two pilots, three passengers; provision for medical attendant, litter, and up to 600 kg (1,320 lb.) of ambulance equipment; interior cabin of 2.35 m³ (83 cu. ft.)

Dimensions:
main rotor diameter	10.16 m (33 ft. 4 in.)
length (rotor turning)	11.82 m (38 ft. 9 in.)
height	2.91 m (9 ft. 6 in.)
rotor area	81.10 m² (873 sq. ft.)

ACTION DATA

MAXIMUM CRUISING SPEED

Light helicopters are not particularly fast by aviation standards, but for short journeys, typically from a city centre heliport to an airport about 50 km (30 miles) distant, they are the fastest means of travel. A journey which takes 10 minutes by JetRanger in those circumstances might take half an hour by train and, depending on the traffic, anything over an hour by limousine or bus.

MODEL 206B-3 JETRANGER III	216 km/h (134 m.p.h.)
BO 105	240 km/h (149 m.p.h.)
ECUREUIL	230 km/h (143 m.p.h.)

RANGE

Helicopters are not the most efficient of aircraft. They tend to use fuel much faster than a conventional aeroplane of similar size, and their range is generally shorter. But although fixed-wing aircraft might be more economical, they cannot put down in a city street to pick up a casualty, or make a rescue from a boat at sea, or land in a forest clearing to check for a possible fire.

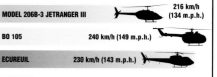

BO 105 600 km (370 mi.)

MODEL 206B-3 JETRANGER III 730 km (450 mi.)

ECUREUIL 730 km (450 mi.)

SERVICE CEILING

Since helicopters are most often used for short hops, they rarely need to climb very high. They can reach greatest altitudes in forward flight; in hovering flight their ceiling is much lower. The JetRanger is notable for the fact that its hovering ceiling, using the upwards wash of air known as ground effect, is only 200 m (660 ft.) less than its service ceiling.

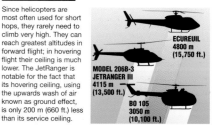

ECUREUIL 4800 m (15,750 ft.)

MODEL 206B-3 JETRANGER III 4115 m (13,500 ft.)

BO 105 3050 m (10,100 ft.)

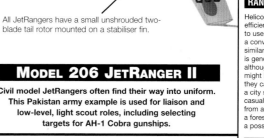

A spiky wirecutter is fitted to civil and military JetRangers routinely engaged in low-flying activity. It can make all the difference in surviving a wirestrike accident.

Transparent nose panels give the pilot an excellent view of the ground ahead.

The Allison 250-C20 engine is replaced by the more powerful 250-C30P variant in the modernised JetRanger III, or twin engines in the TwinRanger.

The two-blade main rotor has an alloy leading-edge spar with a glassfibre coating. The distinctive sound of the JetRanger comes from the two-blade configuration.

All JetRangers have a small unshrouded two-blade tail rotor mounted on a stabiliser fin.

The 'Noda-Matic' system is the company's patented anti-vibration equipment, designed to reduce discomfort for the passengers and crew.

MODEL 206 JETRANGER II

Civil model JetRangers often find their way into uniform. This Pakistan army example is used for liaison and low-level, light scout roles, including selecting targets for AH-1 Cobra gunships.

Evolution of the JetRanger

- **MODEL 206A:** Built as a losing submission for a 1962 US Army observation helicopter contest, the original civil JetRanger flew in 1966 and was an immediate success.

- **OH-58 KIOWA:** In 1967, the US Army ordered a modified Bell 206 to replace the Hughes OH-6, which won the original competition but proved costly and slow to produce.

- **LONGRANGER:** Deliveries of the stretched LongRanger began in 1975. Currently built in Canada and Italy, it shares the more powerful engine of the latest JetRanger III.

- **TWINRANGER:** The latest version of the Model 206 has twin engines. The greater power is expected to give improved payload and range, as well as increased safety.

- **MODEL 406:** Developed for the US Army as the OH-58D, the Model 406 has a more powerful engine and a four-bladed main rotor, and can carry advanced avionics and missiles.

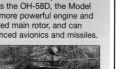

BELL 206

JETRANGER POLICE

● Airborne crime fighter ● Highway patrol ● Police chase

▲ Criminals no longer have anywhere to hide thanks to the heliborne camera. Here, a JetRanger lifts off to answer a request for assistance from a police patrol on the ground.

Orbiting high over every major American city are the 'eyes in the sky' of the police. The Bell 206 JetRangers, equipped with high-powered cameras, are a vital tool in the fight against crime. Recognising the success of the JetRanger in this role, numerous European police forces have adopted the helicopter for a wide range of duties. They include traffic control, rescue work and searches – all in the service of the public.

BELL 206 JETRANGER POLICE

▼ **Beach observer**
Keeping a watchful eye on bathing holiday-makers is a JetRanger operated by the New York Police Department. A number of American forces use Bell's JetRanger helicopter.

▲ **Eye in the sky**
Equipped with a powerful camera, the JetRanger can record activities for the police or TV stations.

◄ **European police**
Proudly displaying police titles on its fuselage, this Swedish JetRanger starts another patrol.

▼ **Highway patrol**
The California Highway Patrol is tasked with patrolling the extensive freeways of the state.

◄ **Proven design**
Operating over city skylines, the Bell JetRanger has proved to be an extremely reliable tool in the fight against crime.

FACTS AND FIGURES

➤ The prototype JetRanger first flew in December 1962. It was originally designed for a military role.

➤ Despite not winning the military contract, many civilian orders were received.

➤ Known as the Model 206, the JetRanger proved an instant sales success.

➤ American law enforcement agencies use the type for observation, traffic control and border patrols.

➤ More than 4,400 examples of the Model 206B were constructed.

➤ JetRangers are also built under licence by Agusta in Italy.

The 'bear in the air'

A police chase ends in a darkened alley; the culprit has escaped the pursuing police officers, and has concealed himself in the nearby woods. A few years ago similar situations often resulted in failure for the police, but now, having surrounded the immediate area, they can ask for airborne assistance.

Within minutes a police helicopter is circling overhead; using a sophisticated infra-red camera, it can detect the suspect through his own body heat. The pilot directs officers to the location, concluding in an arrest.

Despite failing to win the military contract for which it was designed, the JetRanger has gone on to become one of the most successful civilian helicopters of all time. Gradual upgrades of equipment have allowed police operations to take place at any time of day, in all weathers, leaving criminals little choice but to surrender to the police when they are tracked down.

In a more peaceful guise, airborne patrols are made along America's super-highways as police forces keep an eye on traffic problems.

Despite having been in service for nearly 20 years, the JetRanger will remain the US airborne police officer for years to come.

Below: Orbiting high over a city, the Bell JetRanger allows the police to extend their reach in the fight against crime.

Above: A police helicopter prepares to search for suspects. It is equipped with a powerful searchlight for night-time missions.

206B Jet Ranger III

Type: general-purpose light utility helicopter

Powerplant: one 313-kW (420-hp.) Allison 250-C20B turboshaft engine

Max speed: 225 km/h (140 m.p.h.) at sea level

Cruising speed: 214 km/h (133 m.p.h.)

Range: 579 km (359 mi.) with maximum load

Hover ceiling: 3870 m (12,700 ft.)

Weights: empty 660 kg (1,452 lb.); maximum take-off 1451 kg (3,192 lb.)

Accommodation: one pilot; three passengers

Dimensions:
span	1.88 m (6 ft. 2 in.)
length	9.50 m (31 ft. 2 in.)
height	2.91 m (9 ft. 6 in.)
main rotor disc area	81.10 m² (873 sq. ft.)

One of the key attributes of the JetRanger for police service was the excellent visibility afforded to the crew.

Many police helicopters have been fitted with the powerful Nitesun searchlight, which can produce a beam of over 1 million candlepower.

Most police pilots are ex-patrol officers who have requested training for airborne duty. Missions are often flown with an observer who controls the operation and radios.

A single Allison turboshaft engine powers the JetRanger. Police versions are equipped with an improved engine to allow for the additional weight of equipment associated with their mission.

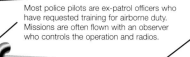

POLICE

N203FC

Most police helicopters are fitted with a skid undercarriage. If required, the JetRanger can be modified to carry large floats to undertake operations from water.

206A JetRanger

Having proved to be an extremely capable tool in the fight against crime, the JetRanger is operated across America by a host of police forces. This example flies with the Virginian state police.

POLICE PATROL

EUROPEAN POLICE: Developed by the European company Aérospatiale, the Ecureuil (pictured below) has been adopted by both military and police organisations. Proving to be a highly capable law enforcement helicopter, it has been successfully used on anti-drug operations throughout Europe.

BRITISH OPERATIONS: Despite the initial cost of acquiring a sophisticated helicopter, the British police have adopted a procedure in which several forces use one machine. An example of this is the MBB 105 (pictured below), which is used by the Devon and Cornwall police force but can also be operated by neighbouring constabularies.

Airborne officers

TRAFFIC COP: In the event of car crash, police helicopters are used to monitor the subsequent traffic congestion and send reports to the ground units.

NIGHT PATROL: Criminals no longer have the cover of night to hide their activities, because of the adoption of helicopters with a large searchlight on the nose.

ICE RESCUE: In January 1982 a Boeing 737 crashed into the frozen Potomac River. In a desperate bid to rescue the shocked survivors, a police JetRanger actually submerged its skids in the water.

BELL 206

JETRANGER TAXI

● Top-selling helicopter ● Comfort and refinement ● Thousands sold

▲ With its comfortable seating, excellent baggage capacity and enviable safety record, the JetRanger continues to be an international sales success.

One of the world's most popular helicopters, the Bell 206 started life as a loser. Designed to meet a US Army requirement for a utility helicopter in the early 1960s, it was beaten by the Hughes OH-6. When fitted with a bigger, more streamlined fuselage to become the JetRanger, however, the 206 was an immediate success in the civil market. Still in production after 30 years and with more than 4,000 in service, it is one of the mainstays of the air taxi business.

BELL 206 JETRANGER TAXI

JetRanger II in Canada ▶
Three major variants of the 206B have been produced. These Canadian-registered machines are examples of the JetRanger II.

▼ European air taxi
This JetRanger is painted in one of the smart colour schemes often worn by charter company aircraft. The machine carries a German registration.

▼ Bell in the city
Demonstrating the helicopter's unique ability to operate over cities from the smallest of helipads, this JetRanger flies past London's Big Ben. The helicopter is ideal for transporting personnel to inner-city areas and avoids the problems associated with the road.

▲ Luxury interior
Customers may specify individual requirements. This JetRanger is a luxury version.

Versatile taxi ▶
With its skid undercarriage the JetRanger has the versatility to operate from a variety of surfaces. Ground handling can be difficult however, and some aircraft are fitted with auxiliary wheels.

FACTS AND FIGURES

➤ Although it lost to the Hughes OH-6 in the US Army competition, Bell later sold 2,200 JetRangers to the service.

➤ Bell delivered the first Model 206B JetRanger in 1966.

➤ All JetRangers are now built in Canada by Bell Helicopter Textron Canada.

➤ Between 5 August 1982 and 22 July 1983 Dick Smith piloted a JetRanger III around the world, flying 56,742 km (35,180 miles) in 320 hours.

➤ Bell introduced the JetRanger II in 1971 and the JetRanger III in 1977.

➤ Over 7,000 JetRangers have been built.

PROFILE

Bell's flying taxi cab

Left: Passenger-friendly features of the JetRanger include wide cabin access doors and steps fitted to the skid undercarriage struts.

Below: As one of the world's most significant helicopter operators, Bristow uses the JetRanger as an air taxi, trainer and utility aircraft.

As an air taxi the JetRanger has many attractions. When it first became available perhaps the most important were its comparatively low levels of noise and vibration. The engine and other mechanical components are fitted on top of the fuselage, keeping the main sources of noise away from the passenger cabin.

The 206 is also safe. One reason for this is that the energy stored in the two heavy rotor blades makes autorotation easy in the event of engine failure. Statistically, JetRangers have suffered fewer accidents than any other single-engined aircraft, either fixed- or rotary-winged.

For the air taxi pilot, no two days are the same. A typical day might include ferrying businessmen to meetings or celebrities to parties, delivering urgent packages or providing the platform for aerial photography. One factor that these tasks have in common is that they all benefit from the unique versatility of the helicopter, as exemplified by the JetRanger.

Although usually made from airports, flights could be from a hospital roof or the grounds of a country hotel. Wherever it is, the chances are that if a helicopter can land there, then a JetRanger has.

206B JetRanger III

Type: general-purpose light helicopter

Powerplant: one 313-kW (420-hp.) Allison 250-C20B flat-rated at 236 kW (316 hp.)

Maximum cruising speed: 214 km/h (133 m.p.h.) at sea level

Climb rate: 384 m/min (1,260 f.p.m.) at sea level

Range: 676 km (443 m.p.h.)

Hover ceiling: 2680 m (8,790 ft.) at maximum take-off weight out of ground effect

Weights: empty 742 kg (1,632 lb.); maximum take-off weight 1451 kg (3,192 lb.)

Accommodation: pilot and five passengers

Dimensions:
rotor diameter	10.16 m (33 ft. 4 in.)
length	9.50 m (31 ft. 2 in.)
height	2.91m (9 ft. 6 in.)
main rotor disc area	81.10 m² (873 sq. ft.)

Bell used its tried and tested twin-bladed rotor layout for the JetRanger, keeping rotorhead complexity to a minimum. The main rotor blades are constructed entirely of aluminium.

A 313-kW (420-hp.) Allison 250-C20B powers the JetRanger III. The engine is flat-rated to 236 kW (316 hp.) to maximise engine life.

206B JetRanger III

This JetRanger is seen in the colours of Cabair, based in the UK. Painted in this colourful blue and white scheme, it flies air taxi services and general charters.

In normal operations the aircraft is flown by the pilot from the right seat. Dual controls may be fitted as an option, and with a co-pilot in the left-hand seat this reduces passenger capacity to four.

A distinctive shaped and angled tailplane is mounted on either side of the tailboom. It is positioned to ensure that the helicopter assumes the correct nose-up or nose-down attitude during climb and descent.

G-BPIE

CABAIR

Up to 113 kg (250 lb.) of baggage may be stowed behind the rear bench seat. This door provides access to the baggage compartment, while passengers enter the main cabin by large doors on either side of the fuselage.

Flight control is by hydraulically-actuated, powered collective and cyclic controls. The tail rotor is controlled by the pilot's foot. Optional equipment includes an autostabiliser, autopilot and instrument flying equipment.

ACTION DATA

ACCOMMODATION

Able to carry a maximum of five passengers, the JetRanger cannot match the MD500E or AS 350B in terms of accommodation. Air taxi work often involves smaller payloads of only two or three passengers, however, and makes the 206B an economical choice.

206B JETRANGER III	5
AS 350B ECUREUIL	6
MD500E	7

MAXIMUM CRUISING SPEED

Compared to some of its rivals the JetRanger is lacking in maximum cruising speed at sea level. Over the short sectors typical of air taxi operations this is not a problem, however, and the JetRanger's proven record ensures its continued popularity.

206B JETRANGER III 214 km/h (133 m.p.h.)

AS 350B ECUREUIL 232 km/h (144 m.p.h.)

MD500E 248 km/h (154 m.p.h.)

RANGE

The JetRanger III has a good range at sea level. Of the types compared here, the AS 350B has marginally better range. It is a larger helicopter, however, and cannot offer such an economical package on low-density taxi services.

206B JETRANGER III 676 km (419 mi.)

AS 350B ECUREUIL 700 km (434 mi.)

MD500E 431 km (267 mi.)

JetRanger civilian operations

OFFSHORE SUPPORT: Unusually for a single-engined helicopter, some JetRangers are used for rig support flying. The aircraft in the foreground is a 206L LongRanger, a seven-seat development which has a longer cabin.

CROP SPRAYING: The versatility and load-carrying capabilities of the JetRanger are shown to advantage by its use in the crop-spraying role. Its reliability, economical operating costs and comparative lack of complexity make it ideal for the job.

FIRE-FIGHTING: Many helicopters have been adapted to the fire-bombing role. While the JetRanger's lifting capacity may be marginal for such duties, it is a useful secondary capability for aircraft serving with police or para-military forces.

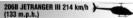

BELL

206 JETRANGER RECORD BREAKER

● Solo flights ● Around the world ● Epic journey

▲ Record-breaking pilots stand in front of a Bell JetRanger. This highly successful helicopter has been used for a number of record-breaking flights around the world.

Seven men have flown a total of five helicopters in round-the-world record-breaking flights. The first three flights were made in Bell Model 206s – two JetRangers and a 206L LongRanger – and each set a new record. Perhaps the most remarkable was that of Dick Smith, whose 56,740-km (35,257-mile) flight was a solo effort. Ross Perot Jr, who set the first record, had a C-130 for navigation, communications and logistic support, while Ron Bower had GPS navigation to help him beat Perot's record.

206 JETRANGER RECORD BREAKER

▼ **Colourful example**
Having flown around the world in 1994, this Bell 206B-3 is now used by a helicopter training school, to teach the fine art of helicopter flying to new pilots.

▲ **Reliable design**
Bell has continued to improve the JetRanger, and a number of pilots have achieved fame after accomplishing long-distance flights in the type.

Spirit of Texas ▶
Owned and operated by Ross Perot Jr and Jay Coburn, the   was used to accomplish the record in 1982, after which it was donated to a museum.

▼ **Best seller**
The qualities that the JetRanger family showed in their record breaking flights were reflected in the high sales figures the type gained.

▲ **Setting off**
Crowds cheer and wave as Dick Smith takes off on his record attempt from Fort Worth on 5 August 1982. Ahead lay long solo flights across the world's oceans and deserts that would test both pilot and helicopter to the limit.

➤ Like the Boeing 747, the Bell Model 206B JetRanger is one of the most recognised aircraft in the world.

➤ Ron Bower began his flight on 28 June 1984 from Fort Worth, Texas.

➤ Ross Perot Jr is the youngest son of the Texas oil billionaire.

➤ At the end of a round-the-world flight, a total of at least 37,966 km (23,540 miles) must have been flown.

➤ Pilots maintain that the record can be accomplished in 200 flying hours.

➤ Pilots usually aim to complete the flight in just 28 days.

PROFILE

Around the world in a helicopter

In August 1982, Australian Dick Smith flew solo in a JetRanger III. He was followed by Texans Ross Perot Jr and Jay Coburn in a LongRanger II.

Perot and Coburn completed their flight in 29 days, three hours and eight minutes, to set the first record with an average speed of around 57 km/h (35 m.p.h.). Dick Smith postponed the second half of his journey until the following year, though his total time of 10 months was still a record because his was the first solo flight.

Perot's record stood for 12 years until Ron Bower took up the challenge. Setting off from Bell's factory near Houston, Texas in a brand new 206B-3 JetRanger, he completed the planned 38000-km trip in 24 days, four hours and 36 minutes at an average speed of nearly 65.5 km/h (41 m.p.h.). The total flight time was 229.22 hours, giving an average flying speed of nearly 166 km/h (103 m.p.h.) for the official distance, although Bower actually covered more than 40000 km (24,800 miles).

In 1996 Bower broke his own record in a Model 430, with Bell test pilot John Williams.

In 1997 Mike Smith and Steve Good took the record from Bower flying around the world in their McDD Model 500D in a mere 13 days.

Above: Dick Smith comes in to land in front of cheering and waving crowds, having completed his round-the-world flight on 22 July 1983.

Below: During his record-breaking flight Ross Perot Jr had to obtain his fuel in some extremely isolated and desolate locations.

260B JETRANGER

Inspired by the aviators of a bygone era, Dick Smith embarked on long solo flights across the world's oceans and deserts. Equipped with the latest advances in aviation, he still faced many dangers.

206B JetRanger III

Type: general-purpose light helicopter

Powerplant: one 313-kW (420-hp.) Allison 250-C20B turboshaft

Max speed: 225 km/h (140 m.p.h.) at sea level

Cruising speed: 214 km/h (133 m.p.h.)

Initial climb rate: 487 m/min (1,600 f.p.m.)

Range: 579 km (359 mi.) with max fuel load

Hover ceiling: 3870 m (12,700 f.p.m.)

Weights: empty 660 kg (1,452 lb.); maximum take-off 1451 kg (3,192 lb.)

Accommodation: 3 passengers and 2 pilots

Dimensions:
span	1.92 m (33 ft. 4 in.)
length	9.50 m (31 ft. 2 in.)
height	2.91 m (9 ft. 6 in.)
rotor disc area	81.10 m² (873 sq. ft.)

AVIATION PIONEERS

THE FIRST SOLO FLIGHT from England to Australia was the achievement of Sqn Ldr 'Bert' Hinkler in his Avro 581 Avian light aircraft prototype G-EBOV, as seen below. Flying from Croydon to Darwin, he covered the 17711 km (11,000 miles) via such destinations as Karachi and Singapore. After this flight, the aircraft was placed on display in the Brisbane Museum.

Amy Johnson in her de Havilland 60 named *Jason*, similar to that pictured below, set out for the same destination as 'Bert' Hinkler in an effort to equal his record.

Following this flight was Capt. P. G. Taylor in his Lockheed Altair, called *Lady Southern Cross* (the aircraft pictured below). He was the first to fly between Australia and the United States, in October 1934, leaving from Brisbane and landing in California. He completed the trip on 4 November, after staging through Fiji and Hawaii.

Before take-off, Dick Smith was presented with numerous letters and gifts to carry with him on his trip. Of these, the most treasured was a large white Texan hat which he vowed to wear upon his return.

Sponsorship for the flight was provided by the Australian airline Qantas and the Australian division of Mobil Oil. Their only request was that the names of the respective companies be displayed on the fuselage of the helicopter in an eye-catching colour scheme.

Standard skids were fitted to the helicopter, as this would offer the best solution for landing on the various types of terrain that would be encountered, including ice-floes.

Very few modifications were made to the JetRanger, most being concerned with the addition of survival equipment in the cockpit in the event of a mishap. Additional radio equipment was fitted to allow communication with the various air-traffic control networks that would be encountered.

Ron Bower's World Tour

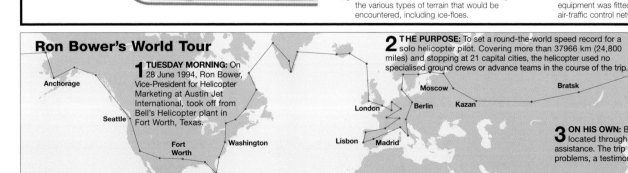

1 TUESDAY MORNING: On 28 June 1994, Ron Bower, Vice-President for Helicopter Marketing at Austin Jet International, took off from Bell's Helicopter plant in Fort Worth, Texas.

2 THE PURPOSE: To set a round-the-world speed record for a solo helicopter pilot. Covering more than 37966 km (24,800 miles) and stopping at 21 capital cities, the helicopter used no specialised ground crews or advance teams in the course of the trip.

3 ON HIS OWN: Bell's Customer Service Facilities located throughout the world provided the only assistance. The trip was completed without any major problems, a testimony to the capabilities of the JetRanger.

BELL

MODEL 212/214/412

● Commercial transport ● Twin and single engines ● Military use

▲ Developed as a civil version of the UH-1N, the twin-turboshaft Model 212 has found military operators, too, and has been successfully followed by the more powerful single-engined Model 214.

The product of a contract between Bell Helicopters and the Canadian government, the successful 212/214/412 series began when the first twin-turbine development of the Model 205 took to the air. The USAF took 79 examples (as the UH-1N), and to date the series has been adopted by more than 40 different military services and numerous other civil operators. Licence production around the world continues.

BELL MODEL 212/214/412

◄ **Airborne crane**
A Bell Model 214B of the Sultan of Oman's Air Force demonstrates the type's load capacity, lifting a disabled Skyvan. The 214B was a derivative of the 214A Isfahan developed for the Iranian armed forces in the early 1970s.

Commercial ►
derivative
The Bell 212 Twin Two-Twelve was based upon the UH-1N, itself an improved version of the UH-1 Huey.

▲ **Fire fighter**
For the fire-bombing role, the Model 212 may be fitted with high ground-clearance skids to accommodate an under fuselage water tank.

Alternative ►
undercarriage
A version of the Model 412SP with wheeled landing gear is offered by Bell Textron, for operations from places where ground manoeuvrability is important.

▲ **Model 214's single turbine**
The 214A is one of Bell's largest helicopters. It boasts a 2185-kW (2930-hp.) turbine engine producing more power than the twin engines of the 212.

FACTS AND FIGURES

➤ The Model 212 was the first helicopter to be certified by the FAA for single-pilot instrument-flying fixed-float operations.

➤ Initial deliveries of the military 212 or UH-1N were made to the USAF in 1970.

➤ The Norwegian armed forces operate the 412SP from portable landing pads.

➤ The US Marine Corps flies the VH-1N as a dedicated VIP transport; the US Navy's UH-1Ns of VXE-6 are for Antarctic flights.

➤ Iran's Bell 214s were operational in the war with Iraq, flying alongside CH-47Cs.

➤ Indonesia constructs the Model 412 under licence, as the NBell-412.

PROFILE

Powerful cousins of the Iroquois

As part of one the world's most successful series of helicopters, the first development of the basic Huey was the Model 212. As well as joint US-Canadian production, the original 212 was licence-built in Italy by Augusta, where it was also further developed.

Military variants of the 212 are operated by Canada (as the CH-135 Twin Huey) and Sri Lanka (with infra-red reflecting paint and fuselage cannon), and by 38 other nations.

Following the 212 came the Model 214, a privately-funded dedicated civil version of the civilian Huey. Iran received 287 of the type, known as the

Isfahan. These examples saw action against Iraqi Model 214ST gunships during the 1980s.

Civil variations on the Model 214 theme include the 214C for search and rescue and the 214B BigLifter.

The ultimate Huey is without doubt the Model 412, with a new four-bladed main rotor and improved systems. First flying in 1979, the 412 is available as the higher gross weight and fuel capacity 412SP and the 412HP with improved transmission.

One of the latest Model 412 customers is the UK's Defence Helicopter Flying School at Shawbury which flies civilian-operated Griffon HT.Mk 1s.

Above: Differing from the military 212 in cabin furnishing and avionics, the 14-seat commercial version is also known as the Twin Two-Twelve.

Below: The Canadian Armed Forces know the Model 412HP as the CH-146 Griffon and use the aircraft as an assault transport, equipped with wire-cutting blades and night-vision goggles for the pilots. The Griffon flies alongside the CH-135 Twin Huey (Model 212).

Model 412SP

Type: light utility helicopter

Powerplant: one 1342-kW (1,800-hp.) Pratt & Whitney Canada PT6T-3B-1 Turbo Twin Pac turboshaft flat-rated at 1044 kW (1400-hp.)

Maximum speed: 259 km/h (161 m.p.h.)

Initial climb rate: 411 m/min (1,350 f.p.m.)

Range: 695 km (432 mi.) with max payload

Service ceiling: 4970 m (16,306 ft)

Hover ceiling: 2805 m (9,203 ft)in ground effect

Weights: empty 2935 kg (6470 lb.); maximum take-off 5397 kg (11,900 lb.)

Dimensions:
main rotor diameter	14.02 m (46 ft.)
fuselage length	12.92 m (42 ft. 4 in.)
height	4.32 m (14 ft. 4 in.)
rotor disc area	154.4 m² (1,662 sq. ft.)

For flying in a war theatre, the AB.412 may be equipped with optional infra-red emission-reduction devices on the exhaust pipes. An internal hoist is fitted if required.

The conventional tail boom and twin-bladed tail rotor unit confirm the Model 412's relationship to the earlier UH-1 Iroquois/Model 204 series.

Each of the four folding rotors has elastomeric hub bearings and composite construction, a glassfibre spar, titanium abrasion strip and Nomex honeycomb filler. The four-bladed rotor is an identifying feature of the 412; the 212 has a two-bladed main rotor.

Though described as a single engine unit, the Pratt & Whitney Canada Turbo Twin Pac engine actually consists of two turbines.

The AB.412 cabin has energy-absorbing armour-protected seats for up to 14 passengers or troops. Cabin floor fittings allow conversion into medevac aircraft.

AB.412

The AB prefix of this Lesotho Police Mobile Unit Air Wing aircraft, denotes an example built by Agusta in Italy. Lesotho Police fly a pair of AB.412s. Agusta call their military version of the 412 the Grifone.

LP◉F24

Short heavy-duty tubular landing skids allow for speedy knee-high movement to and from the cabin. One or two side-mounted cannon may be fitted, as well as cable-cutters for battlefield operations.

ACTION DATA

CRUISING SPEED

The Model 212, whose heritage lies in the veteran UH-1 design, is not as quick as more sophisticated, aerodynamically refined aircraft such as the S-76, or the Dauphin. However, for military use in typical medevac and communications roles, it is quite fast enough.

MODEL 212	230 km/h (143 m.p.h.)	
SA 365C DAUPHIN 2	255 km/h (158 m.p.h.)	
S-76 SPIRIT	269 km/h (167 m.p.h.)	

POWER

The key to the success and load-carrying ability of the 212 series is its turbine powerplant, a great improvement over that of the Model 204. Though a smaller design, the power of the Model 212 compares well with its competitors.

MODEL 212 962 kW (XX hp.)	SA 365C DAUPHIN 2 970 kW (XX hp.)	S-76 SPIRIT 969 kW (XX hp.)

MAXIMUM WEIGHT

The Model 212 has a higher gross weight than the larger, if somewhat under-powered SA 365C Dauphin 2. Its loaded weight is also close to that of the Sikorsky S-76, but the Model 212 is a much more flexible design, capable of being adapted for a large number of military roles.

212 5080 kg (11,200 lb.)	SA 365C DAUPHIN 2 3400 kg (7,496 lb.)	S-76 SPIRIT 5171 kg (11,400 lb.)

Model 212/214/412 military operators

■ SINGAPORE: No. 120 Squadron operates the Model 212 for search and rescue. Based at Sembawang, this aircraft carries a nose-mounted weather radar to provide an all-weather capability.

■ IRAN: Before the 1979 revolution, Iran's army took delivery of 287 Bell Model 214As, known locally as Isfahans. As many as 180 were believed to remain in service in the late 1990s.

■ VENEZUELA: The Venezuelan air force flies two Model 412s on utility missions. For shipboard and land-based anti-submarine warfare, the navy flies the Agusta AB.212.

BELL

OH-58 KIOWA/TH-57 SEARANGER

● JetRanger military variants ● USAF and Navy service ● Exports

▲ The versatility of the civil JetRanger has been exploited in the military variants. These are used by all three US service branches in a variety of training and offensive roles.

JetRangers have been big sellers on civil markets throughout the Western world. The Model 206 has also found numerous military buyers, both in the U.S. and abroad. With the U.S. Army, as the OH-58 Kiowa battlefield observation helicopter, it saw service in Vietnam and has recently been reordered as the TH-67 Creek, for primary rotary-wing training. The Navy employs the same craft for helicopter flight training as the TH-57 SeaRanger.

BELL OH-58 KIOWA/TH-57 SEARANGER

▼ SeaRangers in training
All TH-57As have been replaced by newer TH-57Bs and TH-57Cs equipped as instrument trainers.

▲ Dual-control TH-57A trainer
Selected in January 1968, 40 Bell 206A JetRangers filled the Navy's rotary-wing trainer needs.

▲ First blood
The Kiowa was deployed to Vietnam from late summer 1969 and was used throughout the war. Though intended as an observation platform, it was in demand as a transport due to its size and agility.

▲ Off-the-shelf service
Numerous air forces operate civil off-the-shelf JetRangers for training purposes, including Brunei.

◄ Down under Kiowas
Commonwealth Aircraft Corporation assembled 44 Model 206B-1 Kiowas (adding to 12 from Bell) for the Australian army and navy in the 1970s.

FACTS AND FIGURES

➤ According to Bell, the OH-58 surpasses all others, even the UH-1 'Huey,' as the Army's safest helicopter.

➤ Canadian Armed Forces Kiowas are designated CH-136; trainers are CH-139s.

➤ The Royal Australian Navy nicknamed its Kiowas 'Battle Budgies.'

➤ This helicopter traces its origins to a military prototype, the OH-4A, which first flew in December 1962.

➤ Bell claims that military Model 206s have flown over 17 million flight hours.

➤ Army OH-58As, Cs and Ds were widely used during the 1991 Gulf War.

PROFILE

JetRangers in uniform

Though not offered a production contract for a new observation and artillery spotting helicopter, Bell improved its OH-4 design, developing the civil Model 206 JetRanger. When, in 1968, the Army reopened the competition, this design was to be selected by the Army as the OH-58 Kiowa to augment the Hughes OH-6 Cayuse that had won the original competition.

Early examples of the 2,200 Kiowas built were sent immediately to the Vietnam War, where they distinguished

themselves as agile transports able to go places the OH-6 could not.

The Navy soon adopted the 206, but in a different role, as the TH-57 SeaRanger pilot trainer. Almost 20 years later, with the JetRanger still in civil production, the Army has ordered still more, this time as TH-67 Creek trainers.

Exports to foreign air forces have been numerous, though many of these have been civil

machines. Training and liaison are common unarmed roles, though Sweden and Chile use armed Model 206s for anti-submarine work.

Below: Sweden's navy operates seven Italian-built Agusta-Bell AB 206A JetRangers as Hkp 6As. These can carry a torpedo or depth charges.

Above: The U.S. Army has adopted the JetRanger as its New Training Helicopter (NTH) or TH-67 Creek.

TH-57C SeaRanger

Type: Dual-control advanced training and transport helicopter

Powerplant: One 313-kW (420-hp.) Allison 250-C20J turboshaft engine flat-rated to 236-kW (316 hp.)

Cruising speed: 214 km/h (133 m.p.h.)

Rate of climb: 467 m/min (1,538 f.p.m.) at sea level

Range: 845 km at 3048 m (525 mi. at 10,000 ft.)

Service ceiling: Over 6096 m (20,000 ft.)

Weights: Empty 838 kg (1,848 lb.); max takeoff 1518 kg (3,348 lb.)

Dimensions:
Rotor diameter	10.16 m (33 ft. 4 in.)
Fuselage length	9.5 m (31 ft. 2 in.)
Height	2.9 m (9 ft. 6 in.)
Rotor disc area	81.9 m² (882 sq. ft.)

OH-58A KIOWA

Beginning in May 1969, the U.S. Army took delivery of 2,200 OH-58As. Several hundred OH-58As and Cs have since been retired, 332 in 1995 alone. By 2000 as few as 300 are expected to remain in service.

Between 75 and 84 OH-58As have been upgraded with forward-looking infrared (FLIR) and communications links for civilian law enforcement agencies and are assigned to Army National Guard units in 27 states.

A total of 435 OH-58As have been converted to OH-58C standard with a flat glass canopy to reduce glint, an upgraded T63 engine, infrared (IR) suppressed exhausts and internal improvements. Wire cutters are often fitted above and below the forward fuselage.

While the OH-58A used a 236-kW (316-hp.) Allison T63-A-700 turboshaft (a military derivative of the 250-C found in the JetRanger), the OH-58C introduced the improved 313-kW (420-hp.) T63-A-700 variant. A common feature of the Kiowa is an exposed tail rotor drive shaft on the tail boom, covered on this example.

Many OH-58Cs are now able to be fitted with Stinger air-to-air missiles on mountings on each side of the fuselage behind the main cabin door. These provide protection from other helicopters, but are seldom fitted.

A number of OH-58s were converted to OH-58D standard, radically changing the look of the aircraft and optimizing it as a support helicopter to work with the AH-64 Apache anti-tank helicopter. OH-58Ds have since been armed as Kiowa Warriors.

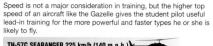

ACTION DATA

SPEED

Speed is not a major consideration in training, but the higher top speed of an aircraft like the Gazelle gives the student pilot useful lead-in training for the more powerful and faster types he or she is likely to fly.

TH-57C SEARANGER	225 km/h (140 m.p.h.)
GAZELLE HT.Mk 3	309 km/h (192 m.p.h.)
Mi-2T 'HOPLITE'	209 km/h (130 m.p.h.)

CLIMB RATE

With a 30 per cent more powerful engine fitted into an airframe only 11 per cent heavier, the Gazelle demonstrates a better climb rate than the SeaRanger. The Mi-2 is a much older design with a significantly inferior power-to-weight ratio compared to newer designs due to its smaller engine and heavier airframe.

Mi-2T 'HOPLITE' 270 m/min (886 f.p.m.)
TH-57C SEARANGER 469 m/min (1,538 f.p.m.)
GAZELLE HT.Mk 3 540 m/min (1,771 f.p.m.)

RANGE

In the training role, good range means longer endurance. This allows longer training flights further away from the training base. The Gazelle's higher top speed and better climb rate are partly due to its proportionally smaller airframe. Smaller aircraft tend to have a smaller fuel load and thus shorter range.

TH-57C SEARANGER 845 km (525 mi.)
GAZELLE HT. Mk 3 668 km (415 mi.)
MI-2T 'HOPLITE' 795 km (494 mi.)

U.S. Army observation helicopters

■ **BELL OH-13 SIOUX:** Famous for its exploits during the Korean War, Bell's Model 47 entered service in 1946, the first of many Bell types.

■ **HILLER OH-23 RAVEN:** The first Ravens were air ambulances delivered to the Army in 1950, the last OH-23s arrived in 1967.

■ **HILLER YOH-5:** This turbine-engine LOH prototype was not put into production, but served as the basis for the civil FH-1100.

■ **HUGHES OH-6 CAYUSE:** Later to become a big seller as the civil Model 500, the OH-6 'Loach' was awarded the first LOH contract.

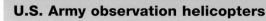

BELL

AH-1 HUEYCOBRA (TWIN)

● The first 'gunship' ● Close support ● Precision anti-armour

▲ In the front cockpit sits the HueyCobra gunner. At his disposal is a fearsome array of guns and missiles which he can bring to bear with frightening rapidity.

Bell's AH-1 HueyCobra was the first true attack helicopter. Twenty-five years after bringing purpose-built gunships to Vietnam, upgraded versions are still deadly weapons, reaching out with guns and missiles to halt the enemy in its tracks. Today the twin-engined HueyCobra is flown by Marine pilots, elite warriors who use the AH-1's speed and power to fight and win, no matter what the odds.

BELL AH-1 HUEYCOBRA (TWIN)

▲ **Minigun**
Early HueyCobras carried the Minigun, a six-barrelled machine-gun which fired at rates of up to 100 rounds per second. Today the slower but harder-hitting M197 20-mm cannon is fitted.

▲ **In the weeds**
Like its serpentine namesake, the HueyCobra is designed to fight down among the trees and bushes, where it can lurk undetected until it is time to rear up and strike.

◀ **Riding 'shotgun'**
As well as taking out enemy tanks, the HueyCobra is charged with the vital task of escorting assault helicopters. These US Army helos are seen on exercise in Egypt during 1982.

▼ **Rapid turnaround**
When it is out of missiles, the HueyCobra can be re-armed in minutes by a well-drilled ground team. The TOW missiles are pre-packed in their launch tubes and are strapped straight on to the helicopter.

▲ **SuperCobra**
Derived from a project to supply the Shah of Iran with an upgraded version of the AH-1T, the SuperCobra prototype with its twin T-700 engines served as the basis for the development of the current Marine Corps AH-1W.

FACTS AND FIGURES

➤ The AH-1 first flew on 7 September 1965; new HueyCobras are produced today.

➤ Building a HueyCobra requires 38,500 hours of factory-worker time.

➤ In Operation Desert Storm, four Marine squadrons flew 1,000 missions, including one which destroyed 60 tanks.

➤ The HueyCobra's stub wing provides some of the lift which keeps it in the air.

➤ HueyCobra pilots use night vision goggles and electronic sensors to fight in darkness and bad weather.

➤ The AH-1W 'Whiskey Cobra's' cannon fires a depleted uranium shell.

PROFILE

Strike like a snake

The AH-1 HueyCobra evolved from the famous Bell UH-1 Huey. When the AH-1G model arrived in Vietnam it became the first rotorcraft designed specifically to carry arms to enter combat. With the helicopter's miraculous ability to leap in and out of tight places, and with a deadly powerhouse of weapons hanging under its stub wings, the HueyCobra is the infantryman's best friend.

New, hard-hitting Cobras are at work today. The US Army introduced TOW missiles to fight tanks. The Marines went a step further with the laser-guided Hellfire missile, fired from many kilometres away to kill a tank with pinpoint accuracy.

Today, Marines use the AH-1W 'Whiskey Cobra', a warrior for the hi-tech battlefield: as formidable in many situations

as the Army's newer Apache, which came along years later. The 'Whiskey Cobra' excels at amphibious warfare, flying from ship decks or from land. Pilots of this thin, graceful ship praise its nimble flying qualities and its flexibility and fighting prowess.

AH-1W SuperCobra

Spearheading the Marine assault is the AH-1W, sweeping ahead of the ground troops to root out enemy armour and artillery before they can do any damage.

Helicopter killer – the HueyCobra can carry the Sidewinder missile on its stub pylons to shoot down other helicopters.

For use against 'soft' targets such as troops and trucks, the Cobra carries seven-round rocket pods on the stub pylons.

The stub pylons provide not only the means to carry a large weapon load but also act as miniature wings, providing valuable extra lift when the Cobra is in forward flight.

AH-1W SuperCobra

Type: two-seat attack helicopter

Powerplant: two General Electric T-700 turboshafts, each rated at 1212-kW (1,625-hp.)

Maximum speed: 352 km/h (219 m.p.h.)

Range: 590 km (367 mi.)

Hover ceiling: 4495 m (14,747 ft.)

Weights: empty 4627 kg (10,200 lb.); loaded 6690 kg (14,749 lb.)

Armament: one M197 20-mm cannon in undernose turret and four underwing hardpoints for guided anti-armour or air-to-air missiles, Minigun pods, or unguided high explosive rockets

Dimensions:
rotor diameter	14.63 m (48 ft.)
fuselage length	13.87 m (45 ft. 6 in.)
height	4.11 m (13 ft. 6 in.)
rotor disc area	168.11 m² (1,809 sq. ft.)

The Cobra's tail rotors are made from an aluminium honeycomb with a stainless steel skin and leading edge.

The two-man crew works as a team. The pilot is in the rear cockpit, sitting high up so he can get a good all-round view over the head of the gunner in the front seat. The gunner has a commanding view of the battlefield, and has night vision sights to help him fire the weapons.

Above and below the pilot's cockpit are special blades which cut cables. Such obstructions are a very real danger at the altitudes at which Cobras normally work.

Cobras have been powered by a variety of engines over the years. Marine aircraft generally have two engines, as an added safety factor for long over-water operations.

Bell designed the Cobra before the days of modern composite materials. Its structure is conventional, with a semi-monocoque aluminium skin.

Under the AH-1W's chin is a General Electric turret which houses the deadly 20-mm M197 cannon. This weapon has three barrels, and can fire at a rate of 675 rounds per minute, although each burst is limited to just 16 rounds. The turret can swing through 110° either side of the nose.

Marine Cobras fly in a bewildering variety of colour schemes, usually applied according to the type of terrain to be encountered. This strange sand-and-grey scheme was applied for the Gulf War.

COMBAT DATA

COMBAT RADIUS

Because of their unique abilities, helicopters do not need vulnerable fixed bases. Operating from hides very close to the battle area, they can get into action very quickly, and their lack of range when carrying a full load of fuel, troops and weapons is no handicap.

AH-1W SUPERCOBRA 250 km (155 mi.)

AH.Mk 7 LYNX 270 km (168 mi.)

Mi-24F 'HIND' 160 km (99 mi.)

Firing the TOW

TOW stands for Tube-launched, Optically-sighted, Wire-guided, and is an admirably succinct explanation of how the missile is operated.

TARGET IN SIGHT

WIRE GUIDANCE: When it is fired, the TOW trails wires behind it which remain attached to the helicopter. These transmit guidance commands from the gunner, who literally 'flies' the missile to its target.

TRACKING: On the back of the missile are small flares which allow the gunner to follow its progress. He keeps the sight centred on target, and the missile is automatically guided to the point of aim.

WIRE GUIDANCE

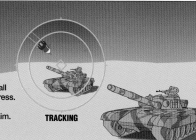

TRACKING

BELL

UH-1N IROQUOIS

● Civil/military utility helicopter ● Twin-engine reliability

The most widely produced helicopter in the Western world, the single-engine Bell 'Huey' won eternal fame in the Vietnam War. An extensive development programme produced the more powerful UH-1H, from which came the 'November' model with extended range and greater safety of twin engines. Its load carrying capacity was also increased and, like its predecessors, the UH-1N was bought by US and foreign armed forces.

▲ *The original
single-engine versions of the Huey
became famous as rugged troop carriers in
Vietnam. Troop transport continues to be a
major role of the UH-1N for many operators.*

BELL UH-1N IROQUOIS

▲ VIP transport
*One of several USAF staff
transport UH-1Ns over
Washington D.C.*

▲ Oil exploration support
*With flotation gear fitted to the
fuselage and weather radar in the
nose, this 212 is used in support
of oil rig operations.*

Twin-engine security ▶
*For the Marine Corps, which
routinely operates its UH-1Ns
from amphibious assault vessels,
the extra safety of two engines is
a major asset.*

▼ Inconspicuous Hueys
*Operators paint their UH-1Ns according to their
role; camouflage implies use near a battlefield.*

Twin Huey to the rescue ▶
*Search and rescue is often an important role for
any helicopter, the UH-1N being no exception.*

FACTS AND FIGURES

➤ In 1972, a UH-1N dropped a parachutist over McMurdo Sound, Antarctica for a record jump of 6247 m (20,497 ft.).

➤ The 'Huey' nickname comes from the original U.S. Army HU-1 designation.

➤ The US Navy unit VXE-6 operates about six bright-red UH-1Ns in the Antarctic.

➤ The USAF's crack 1st Special Operations Wing in Florida is one of the main users of the UH-1N.

➤ UH-1Ns are often fitted with door-mounted machine guns for protection.

➤ The original Huey, a Bell 204, flew for the first time in 1956.

PROFILE

Twin-engine Huey

Beginning life as the Bell Model 212, the UH-1N benefitted from an agreement between the US manufacturer and United Aircraft of Canada to supply license-built Pratt & Whitney engines for a more powerful model of the UH-1H transport helicopter. Twin engines for greater reliability gave the 212/UH-1N wider customer appeal, Bell aiming to attract both military and civil orders.

Fitted with the PT6T-3 'Turbo Twin-Pac' (T400), the first production Model 212 made its maiden flight in April 1969 and the first machine for the Canadian Armed Forces was handed over in May 1971. As the CUH-1N (later CH-135 Twin Huey) the new type was operated on liaison, utility and rescue sorties, the typical variety of duties for which the 'Huey' became internationally famous.

UH-1Ns were subsequently ordered by the US Army, Air Force, Navy and Marines, all of which appreciated the additional capability available from the Bell twin. The Navy and Marines particularly liked

Above: Most USMC UH-1Ns fulfil a light attack/forward air control role with AH-1 Sea Cobra and Super Cobra attack helicopters.

the extra safety afforded by two engines, especially important over long open stretches of water.

Italian company Agusta, which license-built the earlier Hueys, also produced 212s and developed an anti-submarine and anti-shipping version for the Italian navy and for export.

Below: Many of the UH-1Ns in USAF service, like this one, are employed on staff transport tasks. The first of 73 ordered was delivered on 2 October, 1970.

UH-1N Iroquois

Type: Twin-engine, multirole (civilian/military) utility helicopter

Powerplant: Two 962-kW (1,290-hp.) Pratt & Whitney Canada T400-CP-400 (PT6T-3B) twin turboshaft engines

Max speed: 257 km/h (160 m.p.h.)

Service ceiling: 4328 m (14,200 ft.)

Range: 418 km (260 mi.)

Weights: Empty 2899 kg (6,392 lb.); loaded 5069 kg (11,176 lb.)

Dimensions:
Span (main rotor)	14.6 m	(48 ft.)
Length	17.37 m	(57 ft.)
Height	4.57 m	(15 ft.)
Rotor disc area	167.8 m²	(1,807 sq.ft.)

ACTION DATA

SPEED

With its twin-engines, the more powerful UH-1N out performs its forerunner the UH-1C. The increased speed of the UH-1N is useful when flying troops into a combat zone helping to reduce the time in the danger area. The Puma can carry a bigger load but is slower and larger than the UH-1 making it more vulnerable.

UH-1N IROQUOIS	257 km (160 m.p.h.)
UH-1C IROQUOIS	238 km (148 m.p.h.)
SA 330C PUMA	202 km (126 m.p.h.)

In recent years the flight deck crew of two aboard HH-1Ns have benefitted from updated communications and avionics and Doppler navigation equipment.

The twin PT6T (T400) engines power a combining gearbox so that in the event of one engine failing, the other will still provide power to drive the rotor blades.

Some US Navy HH-1Ns have been fitted with composite main rotor blades, which are interchangeable and non-folding.

High-visibility 'day glo' paint is used on the tail and nose of the HH-1N to aid conspicuity.

158284

GUAM

NAVY
NAS AGANA

RESCUE

Perspex windows in the lower nose and above their seats provide the crew with good all-round visibility.

An optional external cargo hook has an underslung load capacity of 1814 kg (4,000 lb.).

When fitted, optional flotation gear is attached to the landing skids of the UH-1N and inflates automatically if the aircraft ditches.

RATE OF CLIMB

As the UH-1N is basically a twin-engine version of the earlier single-engine Huey utilising a similarly sized airframe, the extra power means a much improved climb rate as well as improved agility. While the Puma is more powerful, it is considerably larger and heavier and therefore has a lower power-to-weight ratio.

UH-1N IROQUOIS 704 m/min (2,309 ft./min)

SA 330C PUMA 552 m/min (1,811 ft./min)

UH-1C IROQUOIS 427 m/min (1,400 ft./min)

HH-1N

One of a batch of UH-1Ns purchased by the US Navy and converted to HH-1N standard, this example is a rescue machine based at Naval Air Station Agana, Guam. The HH-1N is the standard Navy local base rescue helicopter.

TROOP LOAD

Once again, the size of the Puma allows it to hold a larger complement of troops. The UH-1C was the military version of the original Bell 204, which had a smaller fuselage than the later 205 (UH-1D and H), on which the 212 was based. It therefore has a smaller load capacity.

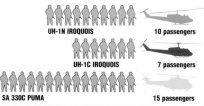

UH-1N IROQUOIS — 10 passengers

UH-1C IROQUOIS — 7 passengers

SA 330C PUMA — 15 passengers

Bell 212/UH-1N variants

■ **AGUSTA-BELL AB 212ASW:** Equipped with a large search radar above the cabin, sonar, anti-shipping missiles and homing torpedoes, this Italian-built 212 is one of 60 purchased by the Italian navy. Other operators include Greece, Spain and Turkey.

■ **VH-1N:** Purchased originally as a UH-1N and later converted by the US Marine Corps, this aircraft was outfitted as a luxurious VIP transport with extra communications equipment. One other was similarly converted and six purchased new as VH-1Ns.

■ **TWIN TWO-TWELVE:** Several air forces use the civil 212 in the transport role, an example being that of Peru. The civil version first received FAA certification in October 1970. Other South American users include Argentina, Chile and Ecuador.

BELL

222 POLICE PATROL

● Police patroller ● Major event surveillance ● Quick-reaction transport

Based at Lippitts Hill in Essex, the Metropolitan Police Air Support Unit found the Bell 222 to be an ideal crime-busting helicopter. Powerful twin engines and stable flight characteristics, as well as good speed, are vital when tracking criminals. The pilots who fly the regular patrols over London's streets are actually employed by Bristow Helicopters and have extensive experience. Whether flying by day or night, the Bell 222 proved to be an invaluable asset in the fight against crime.

▲ The crews of the Metropolitan Police enjoy some of the most varied flying available today. Operating over a large city calls for quick-thinking, good teamwork and accurate flying.

BELL 222 POLICE PATROL

◀ **Low level over London**
Although London's police helicopters sometimes fly very low, for example during a chase, they normally operate at around 300 metres (1,000 ft.) to avoid noise nuisance and for safety reasons. Accurate navigation and meticulous attention to air traffic control procedures are vital as the local area contains approach lanes for Heathrow airport.

▲ **Speed trapper** ▶
Using timing marks painted on the motorways, a Bell crew can instantly work out the precise speed of a car and arrange a roadblock.

▲ **Round the clock surveillance**
The heli-tele system enclosed in the ball on the starboard side provides a close-in view of an incident. The infra-red camera on the port side allows the capability to be maintained at night.

◀ **Police pilot**
Police helicopter pilots are actually employed by the Bristow company. Usually ex-military, they are trained in firearms and the use of the heli-tele and thermal-imaging systems. Conversion to the Bell 222 was undertaken in the USA.

FACTS AND FIGURES

➤ The first Scotland Yard aerial unit used an airship to observe the crowds at the 1923 Derby.

➤ Just before the war, the Metropolitan Police were using Cierva autogyros.

➤ In the 1970s police helicopters only carried an observer and a radio.

➤ The Air Support Unit started flying the Bell 222 in 1980.

➤ The helicopters carry Nitesun searchlights, stabilised heli-tele TV cameras and infra-red cameras.

➤ The 'Met' always has one helicopter airborne over London in daylight hours.

PROFILE

London police force's eye in the sky

London's famous Metropolitan Police have been using aircraft for observation since 1923. In those days they used an airship, but modern equipment has included the more sophisticated Twin Squirrel and Bell 222 helicopters equipped with advanced sensors and communications systems.

The pilot of the police helicopter works in conjunction with two specialised observers. 'Obs 1' sits beside the pilot and interprets the incoming police messages before guiding him to the location. 'Obs 2', who is positioned behind the pilot in the passenger cabin, locates and follows the target and is responsible for co-ordinating the operation with ground units. Through a large window he observes the scene below using an array of equipment. This includes gyrostabalised binoculars as well as infra-red thermal-imaging and conventional camera systems. During night operations he is also responsible for operating the powerful Nitesun searchlight. This combination of personnel and equipment makes the Bell 222 a highly effective crime-fighting machine.

The Bell 222 is an excellent choice for a police helicopter, having twin-engined clearance for work over crowded cities, and enough capacity to carry dog teams or special firearms officers if needed.

Assignments are numerous and range from searching for missing persons with the infra-red system to covering convoys transporting important criminals to court. Most of this work involves diverting from routine patrols.

Bell 222A

Type: police patrol helicopter

Powerplant: two 462-kW (620-hp.) Lycoming LTS101-750C-1 turboshafts

Maximum speed: 250 km/h (155 m.p.h.)

Range: 523 km (325 mi.) or 2 hours 30 minutes' endurance at economical cruising speed

Service ceiling: 6100 m (20,000 ft.)

Weights: empty 2204 kg (4,850 lb.); loaded 3560 kg (7,832 lb.)

Accommodation: two pilots, two observers or up to six passengers. Observers are equipped with searchlight, stabilised TV camera, infra-red, thermal imaging and video cameras

Dimensions: rotor diameter 12.12 m (40 ft.)
fuselage length 10.98 m (36 ft.)
height 3.51 m (12 ft.)
rotor disc area 115.29 m² (1,240 sq. ft.)

The 222 rotor consists of a stainless-steel 'D' spar, with a honeycomb core behind it, covered in a glass-fibre skin.

Bell helicopters have traditionally been equipped with twin-bladed rotors.

Police Bell 222s are powered by a pair of Lycoming LTS101-750C-1 turboshafts.

The Bell 222 retains its passenger-carrying capacity, and is sometimes used to ferry special firearms teams to major incidents.

The cockpit of the 222 is fully equipped for instrument flying, although most of the work is carried out under Visual Flight Rules conditions.

The nose fairing hinges to one side for access to the weather radar.

The rear fuselage area contains baggage space and a fuel tank.

A steerable Nitesun searchlight is fitted to the rear fuselage. This can be focused to cover a wide or narrow area.

The tailplane is a fixed unit with a built-in slot, with fixed endplates.

BELL 222A 'G-METC'

The Metropolitan Police Air Support Unit operated a pair of Bell 222s, with the serials G-METB and G-METC, and a leased Eurocopter Ecureuil. The unit is based at Lippitts Hill, near Loughton, on London's eastern edge.

ACTION DATA

MAXIMUM SPEED

Although helicopters are not as fast as fixed-wing aircraft, they are still considerably quicker than any land-based transport available in a city. A Bell 222 on patrol over central London can reach an incident anywhere in the the metropolis in minutes.

MODEL 222	250 km/h (155 m.p.h.)	
AS 350 ECUREUIL	230 km/h (143 m.p.h.)	
BO 105	240 km/h (149 m.p.h.)	

ENDURANCE

Excellent though the Bell 222 is for most patrol duties, it is a larger and heavier helicopter than other types in use by police forces around the world. Because of this, it uses more fuel and needs to land for replenishment more often than otherwise less-capable machines.

MODEL 222 2 hours 30 minutes	AS 350 ECUREUIL 4 hours	BO 105 3 hours 30 minutes

CAPACITY

Although the Bell 222's main task is to patrol, it can be pressed into duty as a transport. The helicopters are especially useful for special duty units, such as heavily-armed anti-terrorist teams, who can reach any major incidents with the minimum of delay.

MODEL 222
1 pilot and 7 passengers

AS 350 ECUREUIL
1 pilot and 4 passengers

BO 105
1 pilot and 4 passengers

The long arm of the law

■ **SUSPICIOUS BEHAVIOUR:** Two youths have been seen breaking into cars. A report to the police brings the Bell 222 to the scene, which quickly locates a pair of suspects.

■ **GROUND UNITS CALLED:** As the suspects take a shortcut through an industrial estate, the helicopter directs ground-based police units to cut them off.

■ **POLICE MOVE IN:** The youths are approached and questioned by officers, while the helicopter remains in a surveillance position in case the suspects flee.

■ **AN ARREST IS MADE:** The suspects are found to be carrying goods which may have been stolen. There are now sufficient grounds for holding them, and they are arrested.

BELL

222/230

● Twin-engined light helicopter ● Fifteen years of service ● Exports

 ▲ Bell 222s have been produced for customers worldwide and the later 230 and 430 have continued this success. In 1992 production of the 230 and 430 models was switched to a new factory at Mirabel, Quebec.

Bringing real elegance to the everyday job of carrying people and cargo, the Bell 222 and 230 are considered by many to be the best-looking helicopters on the market. The Bell 222 was launched in 1974, first flew in 1976 as a private venture, and was enthusiastically by helicopter operators around the world. Since it was first delivered in 1980, the 222 has proved popular in roles from executive transport to ambulance.

PHOTO FILE

BELL 222/230

▼ Model 430
Bell's 430 is a nine-seat version of the 230 with two 605-kW (810-hp.) Allison engines.

▲ Helikopter Service 222B
This Norwegian-registered 222 flew with Helikopter Service AS of Oslo. The 222B and 222B Executive variants were the original models with a hydraulically retracted wheeled undercarriage.

▼ Fenestron trials
This 222 was fitted with a shrouded tail rotor, or fenestron, as used on a number of European designs.

▲ Chilean SAR helicopter
In 1993 this modified 230 was leased to the Chilean navy. Modifications for the search-and-rescue role included a nose-mounted Honeywell radar, Nitesun searchlight, thermal imager and hoist. GPS navigation was also installed, as were extra fuel tanks.

FACTS AND FIGURES

➤ For offshore operations, the 222 can carry a water-activated emergency flotation system and auxiliary fuel tanks.

➤ The first prototype Bell 222 made its maiden flight on 13 August 1976.

➤ A 222 delivered in January 1981 was the 25,000th helicopter built by Bell.

➤ In January 1980 the offshore oil-drilling company Petroleum Helicopters became the first user of the Bell 222.

➤ As of January 1997 Bell 222s were operating in at least 11 countries.

➤ The 430, a stretched version of the 230 with a four-bladed rotor, flew in 1994.

PROFILE

America's first light twin helicopter

The 222 was the first commercial light twin-engined helicopter built in the USA. Its successor, the 230, was manufactured in Canada, which is now the centre for Bell's civil production.

When the 222 first appeared Bell was one of the most experienced helicopter manufacturers in the world, and the new helicopter profited from this experience. The result was a clean, sleek aircraft with retractable landing gear and provision for a number of passenger and cargo configurations.

A single pilot can fly the 222 even under IFR (instrument flight rules) conditions, although on difficult or long-range missions most companies prefer to use two pilots.

So far, the bulk of sales has been to the civil market, but the 222 and 230 have demonstrated great potential for military use. A naval patrol version, with light armament, has been proposed

and a variant for the search-and-rescue role has been employed by the Chilean navy. Civil duties remain the most common, however, and include executive transport and aeromedical and police operations. Succeeded by the 430, Model 230 production ended in 1995, after 38 had been built.

Left: The 230 is distinguished from the 222 by its revised engine air intakes and repositioned exhausts.

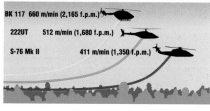

Above: The 222B Executive, fitted with retractable wheeled landing gear, has become a favourite with companies as a luxury transport.

230 Utility

Type: light commercial helicopter

Powerplant: two 522-kW (700-hp.) Allison 250-C30G2 or 510-kW (685-hp.) Textron Lycoming LTS 101-750C-1 turboshaft engines

Maximum cruising speed: 254 km/h (157 m.p.h.) at sea level

Range: 702 km (435 mi.)

Service ceiling: 4815 m (15,800 ft.)

Weights: empty 2245 kg (4,940 lb.); maximum take-off 3810 kg (8,380 lb.)

Accommodation: pilot and seven passengers

Dimensions:
main rotor diameter	12.80 m (42 ft.)
fuselage length	12.97 m (42 ft. 6 in.)
height	3.66 m (12 ft.)
rotor disc area	128.71 m² (1,385 sq. ft.)

222UT

The skid-equipped 222UT (Utility Twin) is widely used in the air ambulance role. N77UT carries the livery of the University of Tennessee Research Center and Hospital, Knoxville, Tennessee.

While more modern and updated designs (like the 430) have four-bladed main rotors, the 1970s-designed 222 and 230 are fitted with a two-bladed rotor. This has a stainless steel spar and leading edge with a Nomex body and fibre-glass skin.

Both the 222 and 230 have a two-bladed tail rotor. The 230 and skid-equipped 222s have a curved bar at the rear of the tail boom to protect the tail rotor from ground strikes.

The standard accommodation available in the 222UT is one pilot and six to eight passengers. An optional high-density layout in the 222B allows for up to nine passengers. There is room in both models for 1.05 m³ (37 cu. ft.) of baggage aft of the cabin.

While the 222 was fitted with two AVCO Lycoming (later Textron Lycoming) LTS 101 engines, the 230 is offered with the option of Allison 250-C turboshafts. The latter has been one of the most successful turboshafts and is fitted to many other types, including the Bell 206 JetRanger and Hughes (later McDonnell Douglas) 500.

Those aircraft fitted with wheeled landing gear have hydraulic forward-retracting units. The rear wheels are stowed in sponsons on the outside rear of the cabin. Skid-equipped versions can be fitted with ground handling wheels and retain sponsons, as these contain fuel tanks.

ACTION DATA

MAXIMUM SPEED

A top speed of around 270 km/h (167 m.p.h.) is typical of turbine-powered, light commercial helicopters. The popularity of these machines with executive users and air ambulance operators is due to their speed performance and the adaptability of their airframes.

222UT	270 km/h (167 m.p.h.)
BK 117	270 km/h (167 m.p.h.)
S-76 Mk II	278 km/h (172 m.p.h.)

RATE OF CLIMB

The Eurocopter-Kawasaki BK 117 has a superior rate of climb to the similarly sized Bell 222. The S-76 Mk II is a much heavier machine, but has more powerful engines and, consequently, a greater lifting capacity.

BK 117	660 m/min (2,165 f.p.m.)
222UT	512 m/min (1,680 f.p.m.)
S-76 Mk II	411 m/min (1,350 f.p.m.)

PASSENGER LOAD

The larger S-76 Mk II carries a greater passenger load, although the Bell 222 can be configured for up to nine passengers in a high-density layout. All three types have been used in the air ambulance role, equipped to carry stretchers and medical equipment.

222UT	7
BK 117	7
S-76 Mk II	10

Bell's civil helicopter line-up

■ **206B-3 JETRANGER III:** First flown in 1966, the top-selling JetRanger is still in production. NTH is the US Army's trainer version.

■ **206L-4 LONGRANGER:** Agusta in Italy continues to produce this 'stretched' seven-seat version of the JetRanger.

■ **407:** A development of the 206, the 407 is a single-engined helicopter intended to replace the JetRanger. It first flew in 1994.

■ **412:** Announced in 1978, this development of the 212 has a four-bladed main rotor. The 412 is also built in Indonesia and Italy.

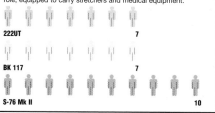

BELL

214ST

● Oil rig support ● Military transport ● Gulf War gunship

Originally intended as a military transport for Iran, the Bell 214ST contract was put in jeopardy with the advent of the Islamic revolution in 1979. Only 100 of these helicopters were built. Although the majority found military customers in utility and support roles, a few ended up in oil rig support. Since then, the 14ST has been replaced by more modern Bell designs and the type is now a rare sight.

▲ Often working
alongside other Bell designs, a handful of Bell 214STs were used by British Caledonian helicopters in the North Sea, transporting oil rig workers.

PHOTO FILE

BELL 214ST

'Huey' heritage ▶
Despite the extensive modifications from the standard Bell 214, the 214ST still has a large twin-blade rotor and twin-blade tail rotor.

▲ Desert colours
Eventually, the 214ST arrived in the Middle East as a gunship, albeit in the hands of Iran's enemy, Iraq.

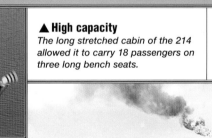

▲ High capacity
The long stretched cabin of the 214 allowed it to carry 18 passengers on three long bench seats.

▲ Thai navy
Thailand's navy operates five 214STs, and the air force and army operate two each.

Civil colours▶
Painted a distinctive colour, this experimental Bell 214ST carried out testing flights to oil rigs.

FACTS AND FIGURES

➤ Originally, ST stood for Stretched Twin, but was subsequently changed to mean Super Transport.

➤ Oman, Peru und Venezuela all operate three Bell 214STs.

➤ Between 1987 and 1988, Iraq bought 45 Bell 214STs and used them in combat.

➤ The original requirement for Iran was improved hot-and-high performance over the older Bell 214.

➤ The composite rotor blades of the 214ST are wider than the standard Bell 214.

➤ The last of the 100 214STs was prodiced in 1990; the first was built in 1980.

PROFILE

Biggest of the Bell twins

In the 1970s, the Imperial Iranian armed forces were shopping for new equipment, with a great deal of money. Impressed by the United States Air Cavalry's performance in Vietnam, the air force ordered an upgraded Bell 214.

Bell proposed a substantially improved machine, the 214ST, with increased capacity and power, twin engines and vastly improved hot-and-high performance. The project, worth $575 million to Bell, was suddenly cancelled when the nation's Islamic revolution occurred in 1979. Bell continued development, and began production in November of that year, hoping for sales to civilian operators as well as other military users.

Luckily for Bell, the 214ST was a success, and despite a modest production run, it was popular with users. Ironically, the largest single user was Iran's mortal enemy in the 1980s, Iraq, which took 45 aircraft in 1987 and recconfigured them as gunships and operated them alongside Soviet-built Mi-24s.

A few were sold to civil operators, especially for oil rig support where the type's single-engine flight capability was paramount. In 1982 the FAA approved an upgrade capacity to 18 passengers to enhance the appeal of the 214ST to civil users; it has had limited sales.

Left: The North Sea is home to a wide variety of helicopters, including Chinooks, Bell 212s, Pumas and Super Pumas, MBB 105s, Sikorsky S-61s and a few 214STs.

Below: Examples of the 214ST with wheeled undercarriage are extremely rare, but some were sold to China.

214ST

The Fuerza Aérea Venezolana operated three Bell 214STs in the communications role, serving with 42 Escuadrón. Venezuela also operates the Bell 212 and Bell 412 in the VIP transport role.

214ST

Type: medium utility helicopter

Powerplant: two General Electric CT7-2 turboshafts rated at 1212 kW (1,625 hp.) each

Max cruise speed: 259 km/h (161 m.p.h.)

Hover ceiling: 1950 m (6,400 ft.)

Initial climb rate: 543 m/min (1,780 f.p.m.)

Combat radius: 858 km (530 mi.) with standard fuel

Ferry range: 1019 km (630 mi.)

Weight: empty 4284 kg (9,425 lb.); loaded 7938 kg (17,465 lb.)

Dimensions:
Rotor diameter	15.85 m (52 ft.)
Length	18.95 m (62 ft. 2 in.)
Height	4.84 m (15 ft. 10 in.)
Wing area	197.29 m² (2,123 sq. ft.)

Bell used a new rotor suspension system known as Noda-Matic nodal suspension for the rotors. The nodal beam reqires no lubrication. The avanced rotor blades have a glass-fibre spar as well as the more useful glass-fibre coating.

Pilot and co-pilot have full controls. Both crew doors are jettisonable. Avionics can include radar, VLF navigation system, ADF, DME and nav coupling

The main transmission has a one-hour run-dry capability, so the aircraft can still operate safely in the event of loss of lubricant. The twin turboshaft engines are coupled through a combiner gearbox. Single-engine operation is also possible.

Emergency flotation gear can be fitted to the undercarriage. Pop-out life rafts can be installed in the fairing under the rotor mast.

Additional baggage can be stored behind the passenger compartment. The seats can be removed to provide additional cargo space. A special roll-over protection ring is installed in the fuselage structure.

The tail rotor is a conventional design with steel leading edge, honeycomb core and glass-fibre trailing edge. The electronically controlled elevator minimizes trim changes with alternations of power or centre of gravity, and improves stability.

FUERZA AEREA VENEZOLANA

FAV 214

ACTION DATA

TAKE-OFF WEIGHT

The demand for a larger helicopter was not lost on Bell and development of the proven 212 was undertaken. The resulting Bell 214 ST differed little in comparison to the earlier models, but offered a take-off weigt that was significantly greater.

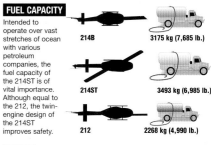

214B
7257 kg
(17,465 lb.)

214ST
7938 kg
(15,965 lb.)

212
5080 kg
(11,176 lb.)

FUEL CAPACITY

Intended to operate over vast stretches of ocean with various petroleum companies, the fuel capacity of the 214ST is of vital importance. Although equal to the 212, the twin-engine design of the 214ST improves safety.

214B — 3175 kg (7,685 lb.)

214ST — 3493 kg (6,985 lb.)

212 — 2268 kg (4,990 lb.)

SPEED

Despite the increase in weight due to the larger cabin area and additional engine, the cruising speed is equal to the earlier and lighter Bell 212. Developments in the helicopter series have enabled Bell to meet the increasing demands of the civilian helicopter market.

214B	259 km/h (161 m.p.h.)
214ST	259 km/h (161 m.p.h.)
212	230 km/h (143 m.p.h.)

Bell rotorcraft

■ **BELL 206 JETRANGER:** The standard by which light civil turbine helicopters are judged, the 216 is still an extremely popular helicopter.

■ **BELL 212:** Based on the 'Huey', the 212 is a twin-engine design. It has proven popular with civil and military users.

■ **BELL 222:** Competing against the Agusta 109 and S-76 Spirit, the Bell 222 was itself further developed into the Bell 230.

■ **BELL/BOEING V-22:** Due to enter service with the US Marine Corps, the V-22 was developed from Bell's XV-15 prototype.

BELL

OH-58D KIOWA

● Two-seat armed scout helicopter ● Special mast-mounted sight

Bell's OH-58D Kiowa Warrior combines a proven design, increased power and hi-tech equipment in its important role as the US Army's main battlefield scout. The Kiowa Warrior goes into combat in careful co-ordination with ground commanders and heavier helicopters like the Apache. The OH-58D's main duty is to reconnoitre the enemy and pinpoint his forces, although it can also carry guns, rockets and guided missiles.

▲ The OH-58D was originally an unarmed helicopter. In 1987, however, when Iran began to threaten ships in the Persian Gulf, armed Kiowas were used to protect oil tankers against gunboat attacks.

PHOTO FILE

BELL OH-58D KIOWA

▲ **Mast-mounted sight**
The MMS is mounted on a non-vibrational bearing. It can swivel through 360° and tilt up or down 30°.

▲ **Dual-role scout**
The OH-58D Kiowa Warrior has two main roles: as a scout helicopter for the army's land and airborne forces and, when required, as an armed attacker in its own right.

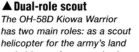

◀ **Modern 'glass' cockpit**
The OH-58D has a state-of-the-art cockpit with large multi-function displays (MFDs) for aircraft systems, navigation and targeting data. The MFDs are designed to be used at night when the crew wear night-vision goggles. These were not used in the Gulf War because of smoke from burning oil wells.

▼ **Naval support**
The 4th Squadron, 17th Cavalry, US Army, is trained to operate from US Navy vessels if necessary. OH-58D operations were mounted at sea during the 1991 Gulf War.

▲ **Hellfire anti-tank missile launch**
The MMS also contains a laser rangefinder and designator. The latter can be used to guide the OH-58D's own missiles or those of larger attack helicopters, like the AH-64 Apache.

FACTS AND FIGURES

➤ The US Army's 1/17th Cavalry flies a stealth version with a laser-proof windscreen and more pointed nose.

➤ Saudi Arabia's 15 Bell 406 Combat Scouts have a roof-mounted sight.

➤ The main rotor turns at 395 rpm and the tail rotor at 2,381 rpm.

➤ The OH-58D is named after the native American Kiowa tribe. Other US Army helicopters are also named in this way.

➤ The stealth version of the Kiowa Warrior first flew on 6 August 1990.

➤ The first production unarmed OH-58D was delivered in March 1986.

PROFILE

The Cavalry's armed scout

The army uses the OH-58D to cope with the speed and complexity of modern warfare. Ground commanders need flexibility to stay on top of an enemy's manoeuvres, and the Kiowa Warrior uses a mast-mounted sight – a 'ball' above its whirling rotors – to spot the enemy, aim its own weapons and guide those of others.

In combat, the OH-58D hides beneath the horizon, using the contours of the ground to shield it, rising only to use its mast sight – known as 'nap of the earth', or NOE, flying. At the right moment, the OH-58D attacks on its own, or directs weapons from artillery batteries, larger attack helicopters or close air support fighter-bombers.

The Kiowa Warrior combines the aerodynamic shape of the earlier OH-58A/C spotter with a four-bladed rotor, a more powerful engine and a respectable weapons capacity.

Bell also builds an export version of the OH-58D known as the 406 Combat Scout. In 1988 Saudi Arabia ordered 15 of these.

Above: On 26 January 1991, during the Gulf War, two OH-58Ds flying from a US Navy frigate liberated an Iraqi-held island in the Gulf and took 29 prisoners.

A Hydra-70 seven-tube 70-mm rocket pod is fitted on the port side weapons pylon.

As well as the infra-red countermeasures turret on the tailboom, the Kiowa Warrior also uses two types of radar-warning receiver and a laser detection set for self-protection.

Two AGM-114C Hellfire anti-armour missiles are carried by this helicopter.

OH-58D Kiowa Warrior

Type: two-seat single-engined armed scout helicopter

Powerplant: one 485-kW (650-hp.) Allison T703-AD-700 turboshaft

Maximum speed: 237 km/h (147 m.p.h.) 'clean' at 1220 m

Maximum climb rate: 469 m/min (1,539 f.p.m.) at sea level

Range: 463 km (288 mi.)

Weights: empty 1381 kg (3045 lb.); maximum take-off 2041 kg (4500 lb.)

Armament: 12.7-mm machine-guns, seven-tube 70-mm rocket pods, plus provision for Stinger air-to-air missiles and Hellfire anti-armour missiles

Dimensions: main rotor diameter 10.67 m (35 ft.)
main rotor disc area 89.37 m² (962 sq. ft.)
length 12.85 m (42 ft. 2 in.)
height 3.93 m (12 ft. 10 in.)

OH-58D KIOWA WARRIOR

Assigned to the 4th Squadron, 17th Cavalry, US Army, this OH-58D carries the unit's nickname ('Thugs').

The OH-58D's key sensors are located in the mast-mounted sight. Behind the two windows are a TV sensor and an imaging infra-red, which provide targeting and navigational information in all light and weather conditions.

High-tension wires can cause a helicopter to crash if its rotors become entangled. Wire-cutters are fitted above and below the cockpit to deal with these hazards.

The ALQ-144 IRCM turret provides protection against heat-seeking missiles.

The exhaust is located in the upper panel of the engine fairing. Hot gases are ejected straight into the downwash, where they are rapidly diffused to reduce infra-red signature.

10553

UNITED STATES ARMY

THUGS

Under the cabin, inboard of each main skid, a caving ladder is carried. This is dropped down for the rapid rescue of personnel.

Some Kiowa Warriors are intended to be air transportable, with collapsible skids, folding stabiliser and fin, removable wire-cutters and a support frame for the mast-mounted sight.

COMBAT DATA

MAXIMUM SPEED

Of these scout helicopters, the single-engined Kiowa Warrior is by far the best equipped. It is therefore heavier and slightly slower than the Gazelle and Bo 105.

OH-58D KIOWA WARRIOR	237 km/h (147 m.p.h.)
SA 341B GAZELLE	264 km/h (164 m.p.h.)
Bo 105M	242 km/h (150 m.p.h.)

RANGE

With the space in its fuselage taken up by avionics, the OH-58D does not have as much room available for fuel tanks as the other two less well-equipped helicopters. It therefore lacks their range.

OH-58D KIOWA WARRIOR 463 km (288 mi.)

SA 341B GAZELLE 670 km (416 mi.)

Bo 105M 658 km (409 mi.)

HOVER CEILING

The ability to operate in most conditions is vital for a scout helicopter, especially the Kiowa Warrior. Rotor blade and engine design are important factors when flying in 'hot and high' conditions. Most OH-58 operations are flown below 1000 m (3,250 ft).

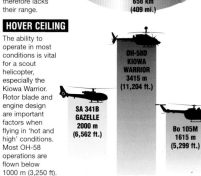

OH-58D KIOWA WARRIOR 3415 m (11,204 ft.)

SA 341B GAZELLE 2000 m (6,562 ft.)

Bo 105M 1615 m (5,299 ft.)

OH-58D scout mission

A major part of the Kiowa Warrior's job is to act as a scout working with gunship/anti-armour helicopters like the AH-64 Apache. In this role the OH-58D uses natural and manmade features as cover while scouting for targets.

HI-TECH SIGHT: The mast-mounted sight (MMS) contains a TV sensor, an infra-red imaging system and a laser designator/rangefinder.

INTO THE TRAP: Hiding behind a building, this OH-58D is using the extra height of its MMS to track the tanks beyond, without exposing itself to enemy fire.

APACHE SUPPORT: With the target in sight the scout can then radio for an anti-armour gunship helicopter to engage with rockets, missiles or gunfire.

DESTRUCTION: Using its laser designator, the scout can guide Hellfire anti-tank missiles from the gunship, without the latter being able to see the target.

BENSEN

AUTOGYROS

● Do-it-yourself flying ● Evaluated by the USAF ● Low cost

▲ In the 1950s Bensen Aircraft of Raleigh, North Carolina developed the concept of a low-cost, home-built gyrocopter which did not require a pilot's licence to be flown.

Doctor Igor Bensen, former chief of research at Kaman Aircraft, saw the potential for marketing a series of light autogyros and rotary-winged gliders. First flying in the mid-1950s, these strange craft proved very successful, remaining in production for nearly 30 years. Two key factors to their incredible success were a very competitive price and the fact that under US regulations any member of the general public could build and fly one.

BENSEN AUTOGYROS

Gyro-Boat ▶
One of Bensen's most innovative designs was the Gyro-Boat. This craft could only 'fly' while being towed by a normal boat.

◀ Flying Scooter
The 'Sky Skooter' was one of many Benson aircraft. Little is known about this ingenious but apparently unsuccessful design.

Wright tribute ▶
This particular gyrocopter was named Spirit of Kitty Hawk in tribute to the brothers Orville and Wilbur Wright, who made their first ever flight there.

▼ Star Autogyro
Gyrocopters were used for a variety of different roles. This heavily modified example appears to have been used for filming purposes.

▲ VTOL 'shopping trolley'
The strange twin-rotored 'Prop-Copter' resembled something from the supermarket.

FACTS AND FIGURES

➤ When its flight testing was completed *Spirit of Kitty Hawk* was donated to the Smithsonian Museum in Washington, DC.

➤ The original Bensen Autogyro, first seen in 1959, was known as the B-7M.

➤ Neither machine evaluated by the USAF was adopted by the service.

➤ From his experience at Kaman Aircraft Bensen built a one-off true helicopter which featured twin co-axial rotors.

➤ A single gyrocopter flew non-stop from California to the Catalina Islands.

➤ In 1987 Bensen Aircraft said it was ceasing the production of autogyros.

Flight for the masses

Both unusual and outstanding, the Bensen series of autogyros and gliders represented the first serious attempt to put flying within reach of the average person in the street.

The first craft to be built was the B-8 Gyro-Glider, a simple unpowered device that was towed behind a motorised form of transport such as a car or boat. From this, Bensen developed its series of motorised versions, known as Gyro-copters, of which the most famous was the B-8M. This aircraft proved highly successful, generating half of the total production orders for the company. Among the most interesting variants was a single autogyro acquired by the USAF for parachute experiments.

In 1986, Bensen unveiled its last and possibly best Gyro-copter, known as the Powergyro, at an air show at Lakeland, Florida. Within a year, however, the firm announced that it was ceasing production of all aircraft.

Above: Recreation was a popular advertising theme in 1950s America and signified a new age of optimism. Bensen Aircraft was quick to appreciate the trend.

Right: Hovering in the only true Bensen helicopter, which incorporated co-axial rotors, company founder Igor Bensen demonstrates the relay winch.

Bensen B-8M

Type: single-seat lightweight autogyro

Powerplant: one 54-kW (72-hp.) McCulloch 4318E air-cooled flat-four engine

Maximum speed: 137 km/h (85 m.p.h.)

Endurance: 1.5 hours

Initial climb rate: 610 m/min (2,000 f.p.m.)

Range: 160 km (100 mi.)

Service ceiling: 5030 m (16,500 ft.)

Weights: empty 112 kg (247 lb.); loaded 227 kg (500 lb.)

Take-off run: 15.25 m (50 ft.)

Dimensions:
rotor diameter	6.10 m	(20 ft.)
length	3.45 m	(11 ft. 4 in.)
height	1.90 m	(6 ft. 3 in.)

THE BENSEN BIRD EXPERIMENTS

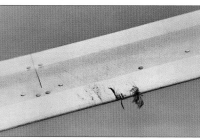

Bird strike tests: What happens when a bird flies into the rotor of a B-8M Gyro-copter? The bird comes out second best! Although this picture may appear rather brutal, tests conducted by Bensen Aircraft showed that, on average, three out of four birds would survive such an incident unscathed. Bensen made it clear that no live birds were used during the experiments. The primary objective was to test the strength of the rotor blades.

The end result: This was the outcome of a collision. Bird strikes were, and still are, a serious hazard during normal aircraft operations. If large aircraft could suffer severe damage after such a collision, then a small autogyro would fare even worse. Bensen took the matter seriously and the tests were exhaustive. As can be seen from the photo, the damage actually done to the blades was minimal. Happily, such accidents did not occur frequently.

X-25A

Two Bensen aircraft, a B-8M Gyro-copter and an unpowered B-8 Gyro-glider, were acquired by the USAF in 1968. Known as X-25s, they were used for research into the use of controlled parachutes.

Wooden rotor blades were standard fitments for Bensen B-8Ms, though fabric-covered steel ones could be specified. Quickly detachable blade supports permitted storage in small spaces and enabled the craft to be transported on public roads.

Powering the B-8M was a 1600-cc McCulloch horizontally opposed four-cylinder engine originally designed for unmanned drone targets. This very light engine was powerful for its size and gave the autogyro surprising performance.

Flight instruments on the B-8M were rudimentary, consisting of a propeller-driven air-speed indicator, altimeter and compass, with an extremely crude artificial horizon mounted above the instrument panel.

Basic flight controls consisted of a large centre-mounted stick with the throttle located to the right of the centre spar. On the original design, the main control column was attached to the rotor head bearing and hung down. Some examples had the stick relocated to a more conventional position and the flight controls reversed for easier handling in the air.

For directional stability one vertical and twin horizontal stabilisers were fitted. The latter were fixed, but the vertical surface featured a large rudder to aid control in flight.

Igor Bensen's amazing B-8

■ **FLYING AUTOMOBILE:** An interesting feature of the Gyro-Copter was its ability to run on normal automotive fuel. When out on the road, just pull into the nearest filling station for some petrol and groceries!

■ **CIVILISED IN TRAFFIC:** Despite being designed primarily as an airborne vehicle, the B-8 was surprisingly capable on the road.

■ **RUSH HOUR IN THE BENSEN:** Negotiating a busy junction, especially in a craft as small as the B-8 Gyro-copter, was no easy task.

■ **SUPER BUG:** Two main variants of the powered B-8 Gyro-Copter were available, the B-8M and B-8V. The 'V' designation referred to the fitment of a more or less standard 1600cc air-cooled flat-four Volkswagen engine.

BOEING HELICOPTERS

CH-47 CHINOOK

● Tactical airlift ● Twin-rotor helicopter ● Heavy lifter

▲ The Chinook is an extremely capable helicopter. If a new variant is produced to replace the CH-47D, the Chinook will still be around 50 years after its introduction in 1962.

From Vietnam to the Gulf War, the Boeing Chinook has been the most successful Western tactical medium-/heavylift helicopter. Fast, massively powerful and with a large rear loading ramp and long interior, the Chinook takes loads that other helicopters cannot: it can transport heavy guns, light vehicles and even other helicopters. Now uprated with better engines and new avionics as the CH-47D, the Chinook remains in production over 30 years after it first flew, and remains unbeatable.

PHOTO FILE

BOEING HELICOPTERS CH-47 CHINOOK

◀ **Battle wagon** ▼
Transporting troops and their gear to the front is the Chinook's main role. The twin-rotor layout has the advantage of not needing a vulnerable tail rotor and allows a long cabin section.

◀ **Ladder climb**
The large rear door is very useful for special forces insertion techniques, using ropes or ladders to land troops.

▼ **Trucking flight**
The first Chinook (CH-47A) had only a single cargo hook, but the modern versions have three, allowing safer carriage of heavy loads like this five-tonne truck.

▼ **Oil rig support**
With its large capacity and range, civil versions of the Chinook were very useful heli-liners in offshore locations like the North Sea. One Chinook was lost in a ditching incident in 1984 after the gearbox failed in flight.

▲ **Huey rescue**
In Vietnam the Chinook was one of the few machines capable of lifting downed aircraft. The wrecked Huey's rotor blades have been tied to stop them rotating in the wind.

FACTS AND FIGURES

➤ In the Falklands War in 1982, a British Chinook carried 82 paratroopers in a single lift and survived a minor crash.

➤ The MH-47E is a special operations version, with night-flying capability.

➤ A Chinook pilot was killed in the First Gulf War after flying into a tower.

➤ The new CH-47D has triple hooks, night goggle-compatible cockpit, advanced rotors and improved crash protection.

➤ The lower fuselage is completely sealed to allow emergency ditching in water.

➤ RAF Chinooks inserted teams of SAS commandos into Iraq in the First Gulf War.

Boeing's twin-rotor heavy helicopter

Designed to meet a US Army requirement for a heavylift helicopter, the CH-47 Chinook first flew in 1962. It remains one of the few helicopters to successfully use the 'twin-rotor' layout. Each engine can drive both rotors if one fails, and a synchronisation unit keeps the intermeshing rotors clear of each other.

Vietnam proved that the Chinook was a superb performer. It could lift artillery pieces, trucks, fuel bladders and even shot-down UH-1 Hueys, as well as performing routine troop lifts and medevac missions.

Good though it was, the war showed that it could be improved, and many foreign buyers specified new equipment, including pressure refuelling and improved crash resistance. The US Army ordered an upgrade of its fleet in the 1980s to CH-47D standard, and also ordered the highly sophisticated MH-47E for special forces operations. These are equipped with Stinger missiles, laser and missile warning kit, inertial navigation systems and an air-to-air refuelling probe.

Chinooks were widely exported, and are operated by several nations including Argentina (which lost some in the Falklands War), Australia Egypt, Iran, Italy, Japan, Libya and Taiwan.

Below: Chinooks can carry armament like these rocket pods, but the best defence is speed and low-level flight.

Above: Helikopter Service is one of many North Sea operators who value the Chinook for its range and capacity, although its large size prevents it using small heli-decks.

CH-47D Chinook

Type: medium-/heavylift battlefield helicopter

Powerplant: two 3264-kW (4377-hp.) Textron Lycoming T55-L-712 SSB turboshafts

Max speed: 298 km/h (185 m.p.h.) at sea level

Combat radius: 190 km (118 mi.) with maximum internal load; 60 km (37 mi.) with maximum external load

Service ceiling: 6735 m (22,069 ft.)

Weights: empty 10151 kg (22,379 lb.); max take-off 22679 kg (50,000 lb.)

Payload: internal 6300 kg (13,890 lb.); external 10340 kg (22,800 lb.)

Dimensions:
rotor diameter	30.14 m (99 ft. 11 in.)
fuselage length	15.54 m (51 ft.)
height	5.77 m (18 ft. 11 in.)
rotor disc area	525.34 m² (5,655 sq. ft.)

The CH-47D has glass-fibre rotors in place of the original metal ones. The projected future Chinook will have even more advanced 'swept-tip' blades, possibly of carbon-fibre composite construction.

A flexibly mounted machine-gun can be fitted to the small starboard door for the loadmaster to give covering fire when operating in hostile landing zones.

The CH-47's maximum payload of more than 10 tonnes can be slung from one, two or three cargo hooks beneath the fuselage.

The rear pylon carries both engines and the gearbox synchronisation unit. Chaff and flare dispensers and infra-red jammers can be mounted on the pylon.

The Lycoming T-55 turboprop is powerful and reliable. It is likely to be replaced by an engine in the 3500-kW (4690 hp.) class if an advanced future Chinook is built.

Fifty-five equipped troops or 24 litters can be accommodated in the main cabin. Small vehicles can also be carried inside the main fuselage.

The crew consists of a pilot and co-pilot with full dual controls, and a loadmaster in the rear compartment.

CH-47C CHINOOK

The Royal Moroccan air force received 12 CH-47Cs built by Meridionali in Italy. The Chinook is also operated in North Africa by Libya and Egypt.

Fuel is carried in the long bulged fairings along the fuselage sides.

COMBAT DATA

CARGO CAPACITY

The Chinook is only beaten in the West by the even larger CH-53E, which has three engines. The Chinook can carry the same number of troops, thanks to its cabin shape. The Russian Mil Mi-17VM, a modified version of the Mi-8, is much smaller than these two helicopters, although other Russian helicopters dwarf the Chinook; the Mi-26, for example, can carry a C-130 Hercules.

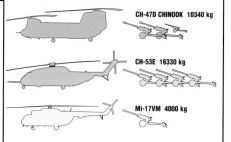

CH-47 CHINOOK 10340 kg

CH-53E 16330 kg

Mi-17VM 4000 kg

Twin-rotor helicopters

■ **BOEING VERTOL:** Piasecki became Vertol, which was taken over by Boeing. The highly successful CH-46 Sea Knight is still in service with the US Navy and US Marine Corps.

■ **BRISTOL:** The slender Bristol Belvedere was developed from the Bristol 173, Britain's first multi-engine helicopter, and served in the UK, the Middle East and the Far East.

■ **FOCKE-ACHGELIS:** The first practical twin-rotor helicopter was the Focke-Achgelis Fa 223 Drache, which was used operationally in the last years of World War II.

■ **PIASECKI:** Twin rotors were a trademark of the Piasecki company, and their naval HUP Retriever and military H-21 'Flying Banana' saw service in the 1950s and 1960s.

■ **YAKOVLEV:** The only major Soviet helicopter of this type was the Yakovlev Yak-24 'Horse', which first flew in 1955 and served with Aeroflot and the Soviet military.

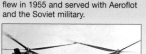

BOEING HELICOPTERS

234 CHINOOK

● Civil CH-47 variant ● Oil exploration support ● Limited production

Representing the muscle among the Western world's helicopter designs, the Chinook was seen as an ideal aircraft for companies specialising in construction, logging and petroleum exploration. Although the Chinook was designed for military use and is well-known for its US Army duty in Vietnam, this big, durable, rotary-wing craft can handle heavy cargoes and travel respectable distances making it ideal for commercial applications.

▲ *The Model 234*
Commercial Chinook was a civil version of the popular heavy-lift CH-47 Chinook military transport helicopter. It was built only in small numbers, however.

BOEING HELICOPTERS 234 CHINOOK

◀ **Dual-role heavy lifter**
Boeing Helicopters marketed the Commercial Chinook as an aircraft combining heavy-lift capabilities (nine tonnes internally or 12.7 tonnes externally) with a useful 44-seat passenger load.

◀ **Prototype**
The first military CH-47 Chinook took to the air in 1961. It was not until 19 August 1980 that this, the 234LR prototype, was first flown.

◀ **Forestry work**
Columbia Helicopters of Portland, Oregon use their five ex-British Airways Helicopters 234s for logging and fire-fighting duties.

▼ **Cold weather versatility**
Alaska's oldest and largest helicopter operator, ERA Helicopters, took delivery of a 234ER in 1985 to support oil exploration rigs in the Bering Sea.

▲ **Arriving in the US**
After British International Helicopters (formerly British Airways Helicopters) withdrew their 234s, they were sold and airlifted across the Atlantic with the engines and rotor blades removed.

FACTS AND FIGURES

➤ In all-passenger versions of the 234, a galley and toilet are fitted. A passenger attendant can also be carried.

➤ The first Commercial Chinook made its maiden flight on 19 August 1980.

➤ British Airways Helicopters accepted the first of its six 234s in December 1980.

➤ Columbia Helicopters reported the 234 'an excellent success' in logging operations in mountainous areas.

➤ Model 234s carry external cargoes slung from as many as four separate hooks.

➤ Boeing engineers claim that the Chinook fuselage will hold 180,000 golf balls.

PROFILE

Oil rig logistics and 'flying crane' duties

Below: For a demonstration tour of the People's Republic of China in 1987, this 234 was painted in the colours of the Chinese national airline, CAAC.

In 1978, Boeing Helicopter began development of the Model 234, a civil version of the famous CH-47 Chinook helicopter. The Commercial Chinook was offered in all-passenger, combined passenger-freight and all-cargo models, the first examples entering airline service in Britain in 1981. These machines carried people and cargo from Scotland to offshore oil platforms in the North Sea.

Model 234s were available in four versions, each configured for differing roles from

passenger transport to 'flying crane' duties. Principal differences centred on interior fittings and fuel capacity. Production aircraft were of the 234LR 'Long Range' and 234ER 'Extended Range' variants, the latter having extra fuel tanks which boosted range by more than 1500 km (930 miles).

Only a small number were built, including six aircraft for British Airways Helicopters and three for Helikopter Service SA of Norway. From the mid-1980s, five survivors of the ex-BAH

Above: British Airways Helicopters was the first and largest Model 234 operator, taking delivery of six 234LRs during 1981 and 1982. They were finished in the standard BA colour scheme of the day.

fleet were engaged in logging operations with Columbia Helicopters in Oregon, USA and other examples were in use in Alaska. Trading as USAir Shuttle, Shuttle Incorporated operated two 234s between New York and Atlantic City from 1989.

In all-passenger guise, the Commercial Chinook's interior held up to 44 seats, with fuel tanks fitted in the fuselage fairings. For extended-range flights, fuel tanks could also be installed in the cabin, reducing passenger accommodation. As a freighter, 9072 kg (20,000 lb.) could be carried internally, while in a 'flying crane' role, up to 12701 kg (28,000 lb.) could be slung under the aircraft.

Model 234LR

Type: commercial transport helicopter

Powerplant: two 3039-kW (4.075-hp.) (take-off rating) Textron Lycoming AL 5512 turboshaft engines

Max speed: 278 km/h (172 m.p.h.) at sea level

Cruising speed: 269 km/h (167 m.p.h.) at 610 m (2,000 ft.) at 29411 kg (64,700 lb.) all-up weight

Range: 1149 km (950 mi.) with 17 passengers and reserves (average load)

Weights: empty 12020 kg (26,444 lb.); maximum take-off 23133 kg (50,893 lb.)

Accommodation: two pilots, maximum of 44 passengers, or up to 9072 kg (20,000 lb.) of freight internally or up to 12701 kg (28,000 lb.) externally

Dimensions:
rotor diameter	18.29 m (60 ft.)
fuselage length	15.87 m (52 ft.)
height	5.77 m (18 ft. 11 in.)
rotor disc area (total)	525.34 m² (5,653 sq. ft.)

Among the optional equipment offered by Boeing for the Model 234 were a 272-kg (600-lb.) capacity rescue hoist, glass fibre wheel-skis, an ice detector probe and ditching equipment (including two life rafts with overload capacity for 36 persons).

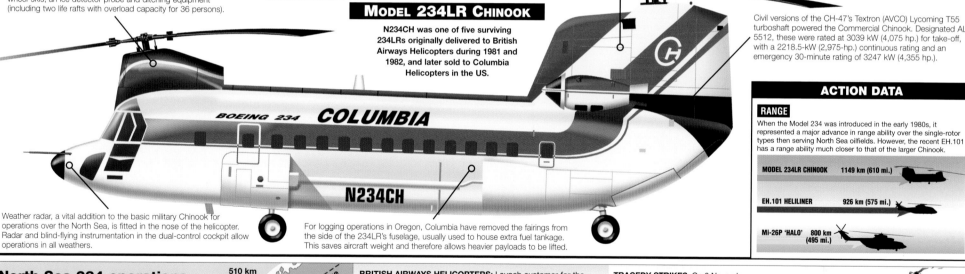

MODEL 234LR CHINOOK

N234CH was one of five surviving 234LRs originally delivered to British Airways Helicopters during 1981 and 1982, and later sold to Columbia Helicopters in the US.

Civil versions of the CH-47's Textron (AVCO) Lycoming T55 turboshaft powered the Commercial Chinook. Designated AL 5512, these were rated at 3039 kW (4,075 hp.) for take-off, with a 2218.5-kW (2,975-hp.) continuous rating and an emergency 30-minute rating of 3247 kW (4,355 hp.).

BOEING 234 COLUMBIA

N234CH

Weather radar, a vital addition to the basic military Chinook for operations over the North Sea, is fitted in the nose of the helicopter. Radar and blind-flying instrumentation in the dual-control cockpit allow operations in all weathers.

For logging operations in Oregon, Columbia have removed the fairings from the side of the 234LR's fuselage, usually used to house extra fuel tankage. This saves aircraft weight and therefore allows heavier payloads to be lifted.

ACTION DATA

RANGE

When the Model 234 was introduced in the early 1980s, it represented a major advance in range ability over the single-rotor types then serving North Sea oilfields. However, the recent EH.101 has a range ability much closer to that of the larger Chinook.

MODEL 234LR CHINOOK	1149 km (610 mi.)
EH.101 HELILINER	926 km (575 mi.)
Mi-26P 'HALO'	800 km (495 mi.)

North Sea 234 operations

LONG-RANGE ABILITY: The Commercial Chinook's range made it an obvious choice for North Sea oil rig operations. Most were well within the Model 234's range from their Aberdeen base.

510 km (315 mi.)

1149 km (950-mi.) range

Rig support air bases
● North Sea oil rigs
--- Model 234 range
— Chinook routes
--- Fixed-wing routes
— Other helicopter routes

BRITISH AIRWAYS HELICOPTERS: Launch customer for the Model 234LR was British Airways Helicopters, which ordered six examples for delivery in 1981-82. This operation was eventually taken over by British International Helicopters, although the aircraft were operated in BAH colours.

TRAGEDY STRIKES: On 6 November 1986, one of BIH's 234LR fleet, G-BWFC, was returning to the Shetland Islands from the Brent oilfield. About 7 km (4 mi.) from land, a loud bang was heard by crew and passengers aboard G-BWFC. The tail of the aircraft dropped violently and, out of control, it plummeted into the sea. Of 45 passengers and crew aboard, only two survived. Subsequent investigations into the cause of the mechanical failure were concluded in court, 234s being withdrawn from North Sea service.

BOEING HELICOPTERS

MH-47E CHINOOK

● Special operations ● In-flight refuelling ● Amphibious

W ith the Boeing MH-47E, the US Army enhanced its ability to carry out secret missions deep in enemy territory at night and in foul weather. The dark, dangerous-looking MH-47E is today's special operations version of the much-admired Chinook of the Vietnam era. With high-tech terrain-following radar and an infra-red sensor, the MH-47E is the trump card of the US Army's famous 'Night Stalkers'.

▲ Designed to operate behind enemy lines, the MH-47 is packed with fire power in the form of two window-mounted machine-guns, and Stinger air-to-air missiles.

BOEING HELICOPTERS MH-47E CHINOOK

▼ All weather
The MH-47 cockpit is fully compatible with night vision goggle (NVG) systems.

▲ Weekend warriors
Smaller saddle tanks identify this as an early MH-47D operating with an Oklahoma unit of the Army National Guard.

Missile attack ▶
The avoidance of enemy missiles relies on low flying and a series of chaff dispensers situated on each side of the fuselage.

▼ Night vision
Situated in the nose is an AAQ-16 forward-looking infra-red (FLIR) turret, which is essential for low-level night operations.

▲ Special Ops kit
The MH-47E features numerous additions to the standard model CH-47, including radar, an in-flight refuelling probe, a complete set of defensive modifications and additional fuel tanks.

FACTS AND FIGURES

➤ Fifty-one MH-47Es are in production; all will be operated by the Special Operations Aviation Regiment.

➤ Operational equipment includes terrain-following and mapping radar.

➤ The contract for development of the MH-47E was awarded to Boeing in 1987.

➤ Missions include global clandestine, long-range airlift infiltration/exfiltration into hostile territory.

➤ A platoon of Rangers can be airlifted in one mission.

➤ The Chinook can be completely refuelled in less than 4 minutes.

PROFILE

Special Forces hauler

Below: This MH-47E is seen during maintenance. The type has proved to be very reliable and looks set to equip special operations units into the next century.

The special operations MH-47E can quickly be distinguished from other Chinooks by the air-refuelling probe extending from its nose. Other vital changes in the MH-47E lie beneath the skin – the latest avionics allow this clandestine warrior to fly behind enemy lines at night and in almost any adverse weather conditions.

According to US Army experts, the primary objective of the MH-47E is to give a 90 per cent probability of successfully completing a five-hour, deep-penetration, clandestine mission over a 560-km (348-mile) radius. Special Operations Forces (SOF), including the Army's elite 160th 'Night Stalkers', routinely train for agent drops, counter-terrorist work, combat rescue, and sabotage. The capabilities of the MH-47E make these difficult jobs much easier.

Operating with specialised Hercules refuelling aircraft, the transfer of fuel – although difficult – can be accomplished in under four minutes in all weathers, thereby extending the striking reach of the SOF raiders.

Although in service with the Army, Chinooks often support Navy SEAL special forces. The MH-47E is the only remaining American military helicopter that is capable of landing on water to launch or

Above: The main transport assets of the SOF are seen here: a Chinook taking off on an exercise with an accompanying CH-53E.

recover SEAL teams.

Establishment of forward arming areas and refuelling points is another role assigned to the MH-47, for which three 3028-litre fuel tanks are carried internally; these are known as 'fat cow' operations.

MH-47E Chinook

Type: Special Forces support helicopter

Powerplant: two Textron Lycoming T55-I-714 turboshaft engines

Max speed: 285 km/h (177 m.p.h.) at sea level

Max cruising speed: 259 km/h (161 mi.) at sea level

Endurance: 5 hr 30 min

Combat radius: 560 km (348 mi.)

Range: ferrying 2224 km (1,382 mi.); typical 1136 km (706 mi.)

Weights: empty 12210 kg (26,918 lb.); maximum take-off 24,494 kg (54,000 lb.)

Armament: two 12.7-mm machine-guns; Stinger air-to-air missiles

Dimensions:
rotor diameter	18.28 m (60 ft.)
length	15.87 m (52 ft.)
height	5.59 m (18 ft. 4 in.)
rotor area	282.6 m² (3,042 sq. ft.)

MH-47E CHINOOK

Developed in response to a request from the Special Operations Forces, the MH-47E was derived from the standard CH-47D, but is fitted with extremely sophisticated avionics.

Operational requirements specified an up-rated version of the Lycoming engine to improve handling at low level and when hovering.

To undertake long-range operations, the Chinook was the first helicopter to be fitted with an in-flight refuelling probe, allowing refuelling from a C-130 Hercules. With a length of 11 m (36 ft.), it is the longest probe attached to any aircraft.

Located in the nose is an APQ-174 terrain-following all-weather radar, and mounted under the chin is an AAQ-16 FLIR turret; this avionics suite means that operations can be carried out below 30 m (98 ft.).

Additional fuel tanks can be bolted on to the sides of the fuselage, although this requires moving the nosewheels forward to accommodate the extra volume.

The rear cargo ramp is often left open during operations to allow rapid exit of troops. Occasionally, a rearward-firing machine-gun is fitted, increasing the armament further.

COMBAT DATA

MAXIMUM SPEED

The twin-rotor design of the CH-47 means it will never have the performance to match others in its class, although this is more than compensated for by the operational equipment.

MH-47E CHINOOK	285 km/h (177 m.p.h.)
CH-47D CHINOOK	298 km/h (185 m.p.h.)
MH-53J PAVE LOW III ENHANCED	315 km/h (196 m.p.h.)

HOVERING CEILING

The extra equipment needed by the Special Operations Forces has meant that the MH-47E's performance is reduced when compared to cargo versions. The larger MH-53J is used where longer range is required, as the internal fit is similar.

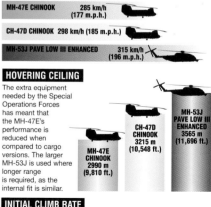

- MH-47E CHINOOK 2990 m (9,810 ft.)
- CH-47D CHINOOK 3215 m (10,548 ft.)
- MH-53J PAVE LOW III ENHANCED 3565 m (11,696 ft.)

INITIAL CLIMB RATE

Operational requirements have left the Special Forces helicopters with reduced climb performance also, but the ability to operate anywhere in adverse conditions outweighs any disadvantage.

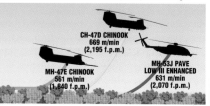

- CH-47D CHINOOK 669 m/min (2,195 f.p.m.)
- MH-47E CHINOOK 561 m/min (1,840 f.p.m.)
- MH-53J PAVE LOW III ENHANCED 631 m/min (2,070 f.p.m.)

Special Forces operations

EXTENDED RANGE: To operate behind enemy lines, the MH-47 is fitted with a telescopic in-flight refuelling probe which extends forward. This enables contact with a Hercules tanker aircraft which trails a drogue behind its fuselage.

NIGHT-HAWK: A comprehensive fit of terrain-following radar and FLIR turret lets the MH-47 fly at extremely levels in all weathers, allowing the rapid deployment of Special Forces.

DEPLOYMENT: Once in the area of deployment, troops can leave the MH-47 by abseiling from the rear cargo ramp. During this stage, defensive firepower is provided by the two machine-guns.

BOEING-VERTOL

CH-46 SEA KNIGHT

● Assault transport ● Medium-lift helicopter ● US Marine Corps

▲ Twin-rotor lifting power gives the old CH-46 impressive performance, and the aircraft will be more than 35 years old when it retires. The Sea Knight has notched up a good combat record.

With its familiar tandem-rotor configuration, the CH-46 Sea Knight is easily recognised as the US Navy's and Marine Corps' version of the civil Model 107. This practical, versatile workhorse has operated since the 1960s and saw action in Vietnam and the Persian Gulf. The Navy relies upon the Sea Knight to supply its warships at sea, while the Marine Corps uses it as an assault helicopter. Despite its age, the CH-46 is still in service.

◀ **Resupply at sea**
Transporting stores at sea is the UH-46's main task, ferrying loads from replenishment ships to warships. HH-46s serve in a similar role, but have a winch for search-and-rescue duties.

▼ **Frozen North**
In support of US Marine Corps detachments CH-46s are deployed to Norway. This is especially challenging as crews have to fly over the mountainous terrain in extreme weather.

▼ **Shot down**
This CH-46 was shot down during the American intervention in Grenada. One of the weaknesses of the Sea Knight is that it has little armour and is vulnerable to small arms fire.

▼ **Jeep carrier**
The CH-46 can even carry a light vehicle in its hold, thanks to its integral rear loading ramp. This can be opened in flight to allow paratroop drops, or while the Sea Knight is on the water for rescue duties.

Storm service ▶
The biggest deployment for the CH-46 in recent years was Operation Desert Storm. Sixty were used for such varied tasks as casualty evacuation, resupply and vertical replenishment.

FACTS AND FIGURES

➤ The prototype flew on 22 April 1958, with the first production CH-46 following on 16 October 1962.

➤ The US Army tested a version of the CH-46 but decided not to operate it.

➤ In 1965 the Sea Knight replaced the Sikorsky H-34 with Marine units in Vietnam.

➤ Some 669 Sea Knights were built; US Navy and Marine Corps models served in Operation Desert Storm.

➤ Other military versions of this helicopter are employed in Canada, Japan and Sweden.

➤ The V-22 tilt rotor has begun replacing the CH-46.

PROFILE

The Marine Corps' 'flying bullfrog'

When the twin-turbine CH-46 Sea Knight was introduced it provided a new standard of performance to the Navy and Marine Corps. Both needed a strong, roomy, versatile helicopter for combat support. To the Navy, this meant 'vertical replenishment' – using helicopters to haul cargoes to ships at sea. The Marine Corps used the CH-46 to carry combat troops directly into battle, and many who served in Vietnam are alive today because the

The CH-46 has earned a good reputation with the US Marine Corps despite its tendency to turn upside down when ditched at sea.

Sea Knight snatched them to safety from the battlefield.

After more than three decades of service many Sea Knights are now approaching their limit of 10,000 flying hours. A number of improvements have been made to these valiant warriors, but the fleet is now ready to be replaced. The US Navy is evaluating the Kaman K-Max

helicopter to take over the CH-46's supply mission, while the Marine Corps is planning to buy 425 Bell-Boeing V-22 Ospreys to replace its 238 remaining Sea Knights.

CH-46E Sea Knight

Type: troop-carrying military helicopter

Powerplant: two 1394-kW (1869-hp.) General Electric T58-GE-16 turboshaft engines

Maximum speed: 256 km/h (159 m.p.h.)

Cruising speed: 225 km/h (140 m.p.h.) at sea level

Range: 996 km (206 mi.)

Weights: empty equipped 5100 kg (11,243 lb.); maximum take-off 9707 kg (21,400 lb.)

Accommodation: two pilots, up to 25 troops or up to 1415 kg (3,119 lb.) of cargo internally, plus up to 1000 kg (2,204 lb.) in an external sling

Dimensions:
rotor diameter	15.24 m (50 ft.)
length, rotors turning	25.4 m (83 ft. 4 in.)
height	5.09 m (16 ft. 9 in.)
rotor disc area	182.41 m² (1,963 sq. ft.)

Painted in a high-visibility orange paint scheme, this Sea Knight is an HH-46 variant; 38 of these aircraft were modified to this standard. Many are based at Point Mugu, California, for search-and-rescue duties.

Another improvement retrofitted to the CH-46E is the use of glassfibre rotor blades. All CH-46s have a powered blade folding system.

CH-46E SEA KNIGHT

The CH-46 is still in service with 15 front-line units and two training squadrons in the US Marine Corps.

The cockpit seats two pilots and a loadmaster. Improved avionics were fitted to the CH-46F.

Provision exists for fitting 12.7-mm machine-guns in the side doors. Troops usually exit through the rear door, with the side doors only used for crew exit and in emergencies.

The three-bladed main rotors rotate in different directions. The use of high-mounted engines allows the cabin area to be very roomy, but makes the Sea Knight top heavy and very vulnerable to turning over when the aircraft has ditched in a rough sea.

All CH-46s remaining in service contain the T58-GE-16 engine, which was adopted together with glass-fibre rotor blades as part of a modification programme.

Up to 25 fully equipped combat troops can be carried in the fuselage. The floor of the cabin is fitted with rollers to facilitate cargo loading, and there is a cargo hook for underslung loads under the fuselage.

The undercarriage is non-retractable, but is strengthened to withstand the high rates of vertical sink common to assault helicopters operating from aircraft-carriers.

The undercarriage sponsons contain large self-sealing fuel tanks. The CH-46E has greatly enlarged sponsons.

16 MARINES

156423

COMBAT DATA

MAXIMUM SPEED

Most assault helicopters are not very fast, having fairly bulky airframes designed for carrying capacity rather than speed. They generally avoid flying in areas of extreme danger.

CH-46E SEA KNIGHT	256 km/h (159 m.p.h.)
Ka-29TB 'HELIX'	265 km/h (164 m.p.h.)
COMMANDO	226 km/h (140 m.p.h.)

PAYLOAD

By using a twin-rotor configuration, the CH-46 can carry a large number of troops in its cargo bay. The Kamov 'Helix' is a more compact aircraft, designed to operate from small ships like frigates.

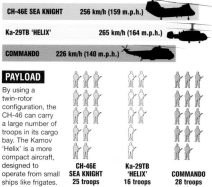

CH-46E SEA KNIGHT	Ka-29TB 'HELIX'	COMMANDO
25 troops	16 troops	28 troops

Rescue under fire in Grenada

COBRA DOWNED: During the American assault on Grenada, a Cobra gunship was shot down at the Tanteen sports field near St Georges. The pilot, Captain Jeb Seagle, dragged his wounded co-pilot Tim Howard to safety and called for help on the emergency radio.

SEA KNIGHT RESCUE: A Marine Corps CH-46 from USS *Guam* landed and picked up Howard. The crew then waited on the ground for Captain Seagle despite the incoming gunfire. However, unknown to his rescuers, Seagle had been shot and killed.

ESCAPE TO SAFETY: Under the cover of suppressive fire from a Cobra, the Sea Knight returned to base, having suffered damage to its stabilising equipment. Tim Howard survived but lost his forearm in the incident.

BRANTLY

B-2

● Two-seat light helicopter ● US design ● Hundreds built

▲ Thanks to their small size and affordability, B-2s sold well worldwide. They were easily transported and could be handled with ease on the ground because of their light weight. The B-2 was a comfortable two-seater.

I n 1946 the first of Brantly's helicopter designs, the over-complex B-1, flew for the first time. Undaunted by the unpopularity of his initial design, Brantly went on to produce the best-selling B-2. Through at least three changes of company ownership, the B-2 remained in constant production, a testimony to the soundness of the basic design. Constant improvements allowed the type to remain in production from 1958 until 1994.

BRANTLY B-2

▲ Model 305
Basically an enlarged B-2, the 305 was potentially a more versatile design, but did not sell well.

▲ Attractive presentation
Finished in a bright colour scheme, the Brantly B-2 is an attractive and sleek-looking helicopter. Several examples remain in regular service.

Unchanging design ▶
This early B-2A demonstrates the original lines of the type and how little they were to change during three decades of production.

▼ In the business
This immaculate B-2B is seen under the ownership of Helicopter International Magazine.

▲ Army evaluation
Five B-2s were tested by the US Army under the designation YHO-3-BR. No production order resulted from this evaluation and the B-2 also failed to win orders from the British Army.

FACTS AND FIGURES

➤ When Brantly was taken over by Hynes, the B-2 became the Brantly-Hynes B-2. It continued in production until 1994.

➤ Brantly also developed the 305, a larger, five-seat helicopter based on the B-2.

➤ Float, skid or wheeled landing gear was an option on all B-2s.

➤ James T. Kimura was the third owner of the B-2 type certificate, and delivered his first B-2B on 25 August 1990.

➤ British Executive Air Services acquired a production licence for the B-2.

➤ In 1992, a B-2B cost US$120,000 to US$135,000 depending on equipment fit.

Lightweight success story

Abandoning the co-axial rotor system of his B-1, Brantly turned to the more conventional layout of main rotor and anti-torque tail rotor for the B-2. A simple two-seat design, the prototype flew for the first time on 21 February 1953, before entering production in 1958.

From 1963 the improved B-2A introduced a reprofiled cabin roof, which was bulged upwards to give an improved all-round view. The other modifications included a cabin redesign and improved installation for the engine.

In excess of 200 B-2s had been delivered when production switched to the B-2A. Although the latter type failed in a bid to gain British Army orders, it continued to sell well until it was replaced by the B-2B and subsequently the B-2E which introduced fuel injection and allowed a higher maximum take-off weight.

Michael K. Hynes had purchased the type certificate for the B-2 on 1 January 1975, and initially provided support for helicopters already in service, before establishing a new production line. A new owner was reported in 1989, using the old Brantly facilities, but by 1994 the company had failed.

Above: British Executive Air Services acted as UK agent for Brantly helicopters and found a ready market.

Below: A choice of undercarriage gave the B-2 added flexibility. These floats seem overly large for such a small machine, however, and must have reduced performance dramatically.

B-2B

Type: two-seat light helicopter

Powerplant: one 134-kW (180-hp.) Textron Lycoming IVO-360-A1A flat-four piston engine

Max speed: 161 km/h (100 m.p.h.) at sea level

Max cruising speed: 145 km/h (90 m.p.h.) at 75 per cent power

Initial climb rate: 580 m/min (1,900 f.p.m.) at sea level

Range: 400 km (250 mi.) with maximum fuel and reserves

Service ceiling: 3290 m (11,000 ft.)

Weights: empty 463 kg (1,020 lb.) (with skids); maximum take-off 757 kg (1,665 lb.)

Dimensions:
main rotor diameter	7.24 m (23 ft. 9 in.)
fuselage length	6.62 m (21 ft. 9 in.)
height	2.06 m (6 ft. 9 in.)
main rotor disc area	41.16 m² (443 sq. ft.)

Each main rotor blade is in two sections, the outboard half detaching for easy stowage in confined spaces. A stainless steel leading-edge strip is fitted to the non-removable section.

With the introduction of bulged glazing, the B-2A and B provided a much better all-round view from the cabin. Blind flying equipment was available as an option.

A compartment in the forward part of the tailcone provides space for a maximum of 22.7 kg (50 lb.) of baggage. This makes the B-2 a useful touring machine.

B-2B

This colourful helicopter is jointly operated by two private owners in the UK. Most B-2s belong to private owners or companies since the B-2 failed to break into the military market.

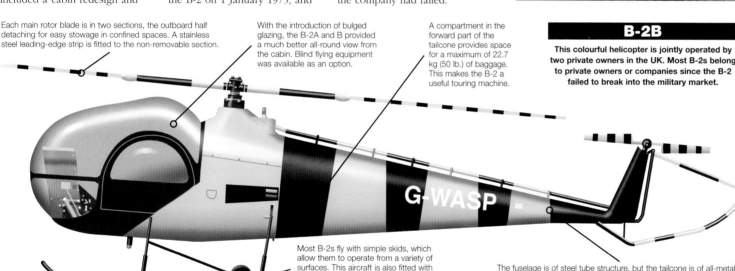

G-WASP

Most B-2s fly with simple skids, which allow them to operate from a variety of surfaces. This aircraft is also fitted with ground-handling wheels. Other landing gear options are floats or skis.

The fuselage is of steel tube structure, but the tailcone is of all-metal stressed skin construction. The looped tailskid also provides protection for the tail rotor when the aircraft is flown into tight spaces.

ACTION DATA

MAXIMUM SPEED

Most owners of the B-2A were interested in its use either as a cross-country transport or for pure fun. In either case, good speed performance was important and the aircraft comfortably outperformed the less streamlined Hughes 269.

Brantly B-2A   161 km/h (100 m.p.h.)

Enstrom F-28   185 km/h (115 m.p.h.)

Hughes 269A 138 km/h (86 m.p.h.)

INITIAL CLIMB RATE

With its light weight and streamlined fuselage, the B-2A outclimbed the Model 269A and the F-28, both of which used a similar 134-kW engine. Brantly flew his B-2 before Hughes had produced its Model 269, but chose a radically different approach.

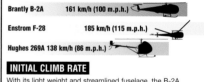

F-28
407 m/min
(1,335 f.p.m.)

269A
442 m/min
(1,450 f.p.m.)

B-2A
482 m/min
(1,580 f.p.m.)

MAXIMUM TAKE-OFF WEIGHT

Substantially heavier than the other types shown, the F-28 offered accommodation for a third person, even though the prototype was flown as a two-seater. Brantly achieved an outstanding blend of light weight and good performance with the B-2.

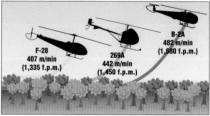

B-2A
726 kg (1,600 lb.)

F-28
885 kg (1,950 lb.)

269A
703 kg (1,550 lb.)

1960s light helicopters

AGUSTA A 104 HELICAR: First flown in December 1960, the Helicar was designed for easy assembly and dismantling by one person. It failed to steal orders from the American types.

BELL 47: One of the earliest production helicopters, having been produced from 1946, the Model 47 was still in production during the 1960s. Many hundreds were built.

ENSTROM F-28: Having entered production during the autumn of 1963, the F-28 was intended to offer exceptional value for a three-seat lightweight helicopter.

HUGHES 269: Hughes found a very successful formula with its rather ungainly-looking Model 269. Hundreds of aircraft were built in the US and under licence.

BRISTOL
SYCAMORE

● Army co-operation ● Ambulance/search and rescue ● Trainer

▲ Although the Sycamore was of limited capability due to the lack of power from its radial piston engine, it provided operators with an insight into just how useful helicopters could be.

Conceived at the end of World War II, the Sycamore was designed by Raoul Hafner and was the first British helicopter to gain a civil certificate of airworthiness. It was used for search-and-rescue duties and as an air ambulance by the Royal Air Force, and was also tested by the British Army. The Sycamore was even used by the Federal German army and navy, and British examples saw combat service in Borneo, Cyprus and Malaya.

BRISTOL SYCAMORE

Picking up survivors ▶
Sycamores pioneered helicopter search-and-rescue flights around the United Kingdom. Most units used the HR.Mk 14 version in this role.

▲ Transport Command
Used by the RAF's Transport Command, this Sycamore had a bulged port observer's window.

▲ Australian delivery
The aircraft-carrier HMAS Vengeance took delivery of the Royal Australian Navy's first three Sycamore HC.Mk 51s.

▲ Evaluation flight
The first Sycamore for Fighter Command, WV781, was flown to St Mawgan by two RAF pilots who had just been trained by Bristol company crews.

Company colours ▶
This Sycamore is flying over the Severn Estuary not far from the Bristol factory at Filton. The company gave up helicopter production after the Belvedere.

FACTS AND FIGURES

➤ The rotor blades were constructed of spruce and ply ribs with a plywood covering and a Hydrulignum spar.

➤ Originally known as the Type 171, the Sycamore was Bristol's first helicopter.

➤ The Sycamore had a simple auto-throttle which the pilot could override.

➤ The last Sycamore version was the HR.Mk 14, which served with Fighter Command's No. 275 Squadron.

➤ In early Sycamores the pilot sat to port, but this was later changed to starboard.

➤ The main production version was the Type 177 Mk 4, which had taller landing gear.

PROFILE

Multi-purpose piston helicopter

By the end of World War II the helicopter had been born, with great strides being made in America, Germany and the Soviet Union. Britain was developing its own designs, and Raoul Hafner of the Bristol company produced the Sycamore using the pre-war experience of his A.R. III Gyroplane.

The Sycamore was a typical late-1940s helicopter with wooden rotor blades, a conventional light alloy fuselage containing four or five seats and an Alvis Leonides radial piston

engine. The aircraft first flew in 1949, and its rotor blades disintegrated on the second flight.

Sycamores went on to achieve great success, however, serving with a variety of customers, including British European Airways, the Belgian air force (which used the machine in action in the Congo), the Royal Australian Navy and the German army and navy (as the Mk 52). The Royal Air Force used no less than 80 Sycamores for search-and-rescue duties, and the type also saw action in the

light-assault role in Malaya. The Sycamore HC.Mk 11 was evaluated as an air ambulance and communications aircraft by the Army Air Corps.

Below: Federal Germany bought 50 Sycamores. Two served as VIP transports and the others performed a range of military duties.

Above: Unfortunately for the Sycamore, it never survived into the turbine era. If it had it been re-engined with a gas turbine it may have been in service for far longer.

Sycamore HR.Mk 14

Type: five-seat multi-role piston-engined military helicopter

Powerplant: one 410-kW (550-hp.) Alvis Leonides 73 radial piston engine

Maximum speed: 204 km/h (127 m.p.h.)

Initial climb rate: 280 m/min (918 f.p.m.)

Range: 430 km (265 mi.)

Service ceiling: 4724 m (15,500 ft.)

Weights: empty 1877 kg (4,129 lb.); maximum 2452 kg (5,394 lb.)

Accommodation: five, including pilot

Dimensions:
diameter	14.8 m (48 ft. 6 in.)
length	18.63 m (61 ft. 2 in.)
height	3.71 m (12 ft. 2 in.)
tail rotor diameter	2.93 m (9 ft. 7 in.)

SYCAMORE Mk 52

The Sycamore Mk 52 was first delivered to the Federal German government in 1955, and was successfully used by the army and navy.

The Sycamore had conventional controls. The collective lever had a simple 'twist-grip' throttle and an auto-throttle.

Medical evacuation Sycamores had large Perspex blisters fitted to allow stretchers to be accommodated sideways across the cabin.

Like many early helicopters, the Sycamore had wooden rotors with a metal leading edge. Metal tabs were fitted on each root and rotor tip to correct aerodynamic balance. The blades were fully articulated in both flapping and dragging planes.

The three-blade anti-torque rotor was equipped with a free-wheel so it could continue turning during auto-rotation.

The nose section was of metal monocoque with a Perspex and metal fairing.

If a hinge pin was removed the rotor blades could be folded away for parking. The rotors were built to Bristol's own design.

AS ✠ 322

ACHTUNG →

A side exhaust was fitted to avoid scorching the deck when landing on ships. The nine-cylinder radial engine drew air in through an intake above the fuselage, and was cooled by an engine-driven fan.

A long tail bumper protected the tail rotor, which was susceptible to damage if the pilot flared in a nose-high attitude on landing.

Flying helicopters

COLLECTIVE: The pilot takes off by raising the collective pitch lever and increasing the power using the throttle.

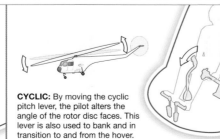

PITCH AND POWER: This alters the pitch on the blades, via control rods to the swash plate, giving greater lift to the rotors.

CYCLIC: By moving the cyclic pitch lever, the pilot alters the angle of the rotor disc faces. This lever is also used to bank and in transition to and from the hover.

PEDALS: The pedals affect the anti-torque rotor tail, allowing the pilot to yaw the aircraft left and right.

ACTION DATA

MAXIMUM SPEED

The early single-engined helicopters had limited speed due to their poor power-to-weight ratio, especially when carrying a useful load and fuel. However, speed was not a primary requirement of these utility machines.

SYCAMORE HR.Mk 14	204 km/h (127 m.p.h.)
Mi-1	170 km/h (105 m.p.h.)
Ka-18	160 km/h (99 m.p.h.)

RANGE

Early helicopters had short range due to engine limitations. The figures given are for unladen aircraft; range dropped dramatically when the aircraft carried full fuel and loads. However, these helicopters were still a big improvement on machines like the Ka-10 and Sikorsky R.4 which could barely carry their own weight.

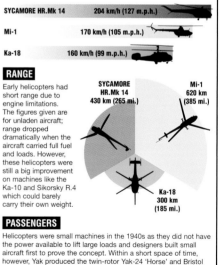

SYCAMORE HR.Mk 14 430 km (265 mi.)

Mi-1 620 km (385 mi.)

Ka-18 300 km (185 mi.)

PASSENGERS

Helicopters were small machines in the 1940s as they did not have the power available to lift large loads and designers built small aircraft first to prove the concept. Within a short space of time, however, Yak produced the twin-rotor Yak-24 'Horse' and Bristol built the Belvedere, which were both capable of carrying large numbers of troops or even light artillery pieces.

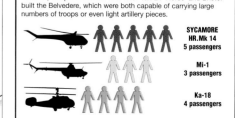

SYCAMORE HR.Mk 14 5 passengers

Mi-1 3 passengers

Ka-18 4 passengers

BRISTOL
BELVEDERE

● First RAF twin-rotor ● Heavy-lifter ● Search and rescue

▲ The Belvedere underwent many changes in configuration before the definitive Model 192 entered production. Here a Model 191 airframe undergoes engine tests on a test rig in 1957.

Bristol's excellent Belvedere gave new muscle to the Royal Air Force in the 1950s at a time when helicopters were becoming bigger and more versatile. With twin engines and tandem rotors, the slender, cigar-like Belvedere lifted and carried more than any previous RAF helicopter. Never successful in its original purpose as a naval craft, the Belvedere performed well hauling troops, supplies and weapons from land bases.

PHOTO FILE

BRISTOL BELVEDERE

▲ **Malayan mission**
With emergency floats fitted to the side, Belvederes flew search and rescue missions and heavy lift sorties in the jungles of Malaya.

▲ **Heavy-lifter**
Part of the RAF's requirement for the Belvedere was an ability to lift bulky loads on an external sling. A loadmaster kept a watchful eye on the load, like this Bloodhound missile, from the large upward-opening fuselage door.

▲ **Flying crane**
Due to the lack of roads and the dense tropical jungle, the Belvedere was used for transporting heavy items in the Far East.

▼ **Back to the drawing board**
The Type 173 was the initial prototype. On its first flight the test pilot found it would only fly backwards.

▲ **Naval trials**
The Belvedere was initially developed to meet a Fleet Air Arm requirement for a ship-based transport and anti-submarine helicopter, but it was never ordered.

FACTS AND FIGURES

➤ The first Belvedere suffered noise and stability problems – rectified by redesigning the rotor hubs and tailplane.

➤ On 24 August 1952 the prototype for the Belvedere series made its maiden flight.

➤ The prototype was demonstrated at the Farnborough air show in September 1952.

➤ British European Airways leased a Belvedere briefly but never used it in commercial service.

➤ The first production aircraft with Gazelle engines made its initial flight in July 1958.

➤ The Belvedere had a long career, ending its RAF service in March 1969.

Bristol's biggest chopper

Below: Due to some handling and stability problems the designers settled on anhedral tailplanes originally fitted with large endplates.

In the 1950s and early-1960s, when brushfire wars raged in Aden and Borneo, the Belvedere was the right aircraft at the right time. Britain needed a rotary-wing aircraft that could carry a payload over more than 100 km (70 miles) to support troops in the field and to help maintain combat forces in regions that had little to offer in the way of roads, railways or even paved runways.

Bristol developed the Belvedere in 1952 based on its experience with the single-engine Sycamore, an earlier helicopter that had been a great success. The original version of the Belvedere looked promising for both naval and civil use, but there were many problems during the development of this helicopter and only the Royal Air Force used it operationally. In final form, the Belvedere had four-bladed metal rotors and proven Gazelle engines.

Pilots who flew the Belvedere recall it with fond memories. From the cold of Scotland to the tropical heat of Malaya it

Above: British European Airways evaluated the Alvis Leonides-powered Type 173. The dihedral tailplanes were a feature of the early prototypes.

performed with distinction. Though never easy to fly and always a challenge to maintain, the Belvedere did a fine job in the infancy of large helicopters.

66 SQUADRON
ROYAL AIR FORCE
"The Flying Longhouses"

Left: Based at RAF Seletar in Singapore, No. 66 Squadron Belvederes became known as 'The Flying Longhouses'.

Belvedere HC.Mk 1

Type: short-range tactical transport

Powerplant: two 1092-kW (1,465-hp.) Napier Gazelle N.Ga.2 turboshaft engines

Max speed: 231 km/h (145 m.p.h.)

Max cruising speed: 222 km/h (138 m.p.h.)

Rate of climb: 305 m/min (1,000 f.p.m.)

Range: 121 km (75 mi.)

Ferry range: 740 km (460 mi.)

Service ceiling: 5275 m (17,302 ft.)

Weights: empty 5277 kg (11,609 lb.); maximum overload take-off 9072 kg (19,958 lb.)

Dimensions: rotor diameter, each 14.91 m (49 ft.)
length rotors turning 27.36 m (90 ft.)
height 5.26 m (17 ft.)
rotor disc area, both 349.30 m² (3,758 sq. ft.)

The original Type 173 had three-bladed wooden rotors. The production version for the RAF had much more efficient four-bladed metal rotors.

Prototypes used Leonides Major engines, which did not produce adequate power. When the excellent Napier Gazelle turboshafts were fitted the Belvedere began to fulfil its potential.

BELVEDERE HC.MK 1

This Belvedere of No. 26 Squadron wears the original transport command colour scheme. The squadron's Belvederes saw active service in the Far East where they adopted jungle camouflage.

A winch on the port side of the fuselage could lift weights of up to 270 kg (600 lb.).

The heated cockpit was fully equipped for day and night instrument flying. It had dual-controls and provision for an automatic pilot.

Although fairly frail in appearance, the undercarriage was an excellent design allowing operation from rough surfaces. The castoring front wheels gave good manoeuvrability on the ground.

The production Belvedere for the RAF had steep, anhedral tailplanes which provided good stability and extra lift.

XG474

COMBAT DATA

MAXIMUM SPEED

Thanks to its excellent Gazelle turboshaft engines the Belvedere had good performance and set a number of point-to-point records in the early-1960s. The Yak-24 was slower but could carry bigger loads.

BELVEDERE HC.MK 1 222 km/h (138 m.p.h.)

YAK-24 'HORSE' 175 km/h (109 m.p.h.)

H-21 211 km/h (131 m.p.h.)

TROOP LOAD

As well as being able to carry 20 fully armed troops the Belvedere could also carry up to 12 stretcher cases together with medical attendants. The larger Yak-24 could carry up to 30 troops, which was a very impressive achievement for the late-1950s. The H-21 could also carry stretchers for casualty evacuation duties.

BELVEDERE HC.MK 1 20 troops

YAK-24 'HORSE' 30 troops

H-21 20 troops

MAXIMUM LOAD

Lifting capability was a primary consideration in the design and all three helicopters could carry a useful payload. They also had provision for carrying underslung loads.

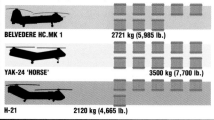

BELVEDERE HC.MK 1 2721 kg (5,985 lb.)

YAK-24 'HORSE' 3500 kg (7,700 lb.)

H-21 2120 kg (4,665 lb.)

Lifting in the jungle

LANDING SITE: With the supplies carried on a sling the Belvedere did not need to land to supply troops on the ground. A small clearing in the jungle is all that was needed.

LOW LEVEL: The RAF crews practised flying their supply missions at very low level to prevent detection by enemy fighters or ground forces. This task required great care and skill.

ESSENTIAL SUPPLIES: In addition to artillery, the Belvedere also supplied the troops with extra ammunition, food and other essential supplies which would otherwise take days to arrive by road.

CIERVA

AUTOGYROS

● Rotary-winged aircraft ● Spanish inventor ● British manufacture

Juan de la Cierva was born in September 1895. He designed and built a glider when he was 15, and his first three-engined aeroplane in 1918. His true aim was to design an aircraft that would be able to maintain lift, and land safely after an engine failure. Practical helicopters were impossible with the engines and materials then available, so he turned to the concept of an aircraft using an unpowered rotor for lift and a conventional propeller for propulsion.

▲ Cierva's autogyros were among the first practical rotorcraft. However, it was not until the mid-1930s that vertical take-off in an autogyro was possible. By the end of World War II, the helicopter had demonstrated unbeatable versatility.

CIERVA AUTOGYROS

Vertically rising C.40 ▶
The C.40 of 1938 was able to make a direct vertical take-off. This was accomplished by spinning the main rotor at a high speed with the blades at zero incidence, then selecting positive pitch to create lift.

◀ First successes
With subsidies from the Spanish government, Cierva built the C.6 series, using Avro 504K fuselages. Such was its success that Cierva established a company in the UK.

Commercial successes ▶
The most commercially successful early design was the C.19, the first purpose-built autogyro. Twenty-nine were built.

Air Ministry craft ▶
British Air Ministry interest in Cierva's designs began in the 1920s with the C.6. Avro was among several British companies eventually licensed to build autogyros. The RAF evaluated several prototypes, including C.6s, a C.8L and C.19s. In 1934/35, 12 C.30As were delivered.

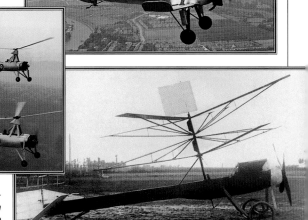

Cierva's first autogyro ▶
Using the fuselage of a French Deperdussin monoplane, Cierva built the C.1, an aircraft that refused to fly!

FACTS AND FIGURES

➤ Twelve C.30As (designated Rota Mk I) were delivered to the RAF in the 1930s, followed by 13 civil examples after 1939.

➤ Among preserved Autogyros is a Rota Mk I (C.30A) at the RAF Museum, London.

➤ British-built C.19s were sold in countries like New Zealand, Japan and Australia.

➤ During World War II, a Jeep was fitted with a rotor and towed behind an aircraft, using the autogyro principle.

➤ Juan de la Cierva became the first autogyro passenger in a C.6D on 30 July 1927.

➤ In the late 1920s, Cierva learned to fly his own autogyros.

PROFILE

Spanish rotary-wing pioneer

Cierva patented the autogyro (or autogiro) design for his aircraft. Their key feature – and a vital contribution to helicopter development – was the articulated rotor hub. Its drag and flapping hinges allowed the individual rotor blades to rise and fall and thus 'evened out' the lift. The first workable craft, the C.4, flew in January 1923 and covered 4 km (3 miles). By September 1928, Cierva's C.8L Mk II design, powered by a 149-kW (200 hp.) Lynx engine and based on an Avro 504 fuselage, made a 40-km (25-mile) flight across the English Channel and on to Paris.

Cierva died in an airliner crash at Croydon in December 1936, by which time his ideas had been accepted and he had formed his own company in England. The C.40 had a newly developed tilting rotor, allowing it to take off vertically.

Above: de Havilland's distinctive lines were evident in the C.24, designed and built by the company in 1931.

Below: Early autogyro flights were plagued by accidents. The first three designs failed to become airborne; it was the C.4 that finally flew in 1923.

Cierva C.30A

Type: utility autogyro

Powerplant: one 104-kW (140-hp.) Armstrong Siddeley Genet Major IA radial engine

Maximum speed: 177 km/h (110 m.p.h.)

Cruising speed: 153 km/h (95 m.p.h.)

Range: 459 km (285 mi.)

Service ceiling: 5800 m (19,000 ft.)

Weights: empty 553 kg (1,217 lb.); maximum take-off 816 kg (1,795 lb.)

Accommodation: pilot and observer

Dimensions:
main rotor diameter	11.28 m (37 ft.)
fuselage length	6.01 m (19 ft. 9 in.)
height	3.38 m (11 ft. 1 in.)
rotor disc area	99.89 m² (1,075 sq. ft.)

ROTA MK IA

One of three Cierva C.30s impressed into RAF service in World War II, this aircraft was previously G-ACWH. No. 529 Squadron employed a number of Rotas for radar calibration duties during 1943-44.

To start the main rotor spinning before take-off, the C.19 and later designs introduced a drive transmission system from the main engine. This was controlled by a rotor clutch and brake operated from the cockpit.

The C.30 was a two-seater, the pilot occupying the rear cockpit. The pilot was able to unlock and tilt (laterally, as well as fore and aft) the main rotor using the control column attached to the rotor head.

For yaw stability, the C.30's vertical surfaces were of a sizeable area. A large fixed fin had a small trimmer at the extreme rear. A small ventral fin was also fitted. The horizontal fins had upturned ends for extra stability.

A seven-cylinder Armstrong Siddeley Genet Major IA radial rated at 104 kW (140 hp.) was installed in the C.30A. To the RAF, the engine was known as the Civet I.

Although the initial Cierva designs used existing aircraft fuselages, the C.19 and subsequent models were purpose-built. Sixty-six were licence-built by A.V. Roe and Co. Ltd, all at Manchester. In France, Lioré-et-Olivier built 25 designated LeO C301, while Focke-Wulf built 40 examples.

The C.30's fuselage structure was of Duralumin tubing with a fabric skin covering. The later C.40 used wooden skinning over a metal internal frame.

Among the new features of the C.30A were folding rotor blades to allow easier hangarage, and a reverse aerofoil section on the port tailplane to counteract rotor torque.

ACTION DATA

MAXIMUM SPEED

Rota Mk Is (C.30As) had a top speed comparable to the fixed-wing Fieseler Storch. Although RAF Rotas were attached to the School of Army Co-operation, they were soon assigned a coastal radar calibration role. The Storch was a widely-used German STOL liaison aircraft.

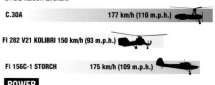

C.30A	177 km/h (110 m.p.h.)
FI 282 V21 KOLIBRI	150 km/h (93 m.p.h.)
Fi 156C-1 STORCH	175 km/h (109 m.p.h.)

POWER

With an engine of little more power, the FI 282 search-and-rescue and spotting helicopter was able to accomplish vertical flight using two intermeshed rotors. The Storch STOL aircraft had a larger engine but none of the versatility of the rotary-winged types, relying on an airstrip from which to operate.

C.30A	FI 282 V21 KOLIBRI	Fi 156C-1 STORCH
104 kW (140 hp.)	119 kW (160 hp.)	179 kW (240 hp.)

RANGE

Cierva C.30As had a good range performance, comparable to that of the Storch. Lack of range was a shortcoming of early helicopter designs. The Kolibri was a small two-seater with little internal fuel capacity, whereas the Cierva used a larger fuselage, similar to a fixed-wing aircraft, with more tankage.

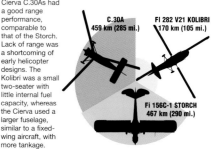

C.30A	459 km (285 mi.)
FI 282 V21 KOLIBRI	170 km (105 mi.)
Fi 156C-1 STORCH	467 km (290 mi.)

Getting airborne in an autogyro

CIERVA'S AUTOGYRO: The term 'autogyro' was coined by Juan de la Cierva to describe his aircraft, in which the freewheeling main rotor provided lift for vertical flight.

FORWARD MOTION: With the rotor locked, the engine was started and pulled the aircraft forward. On early designs the rotor was unlocked and air flow made the rotor rotate.

TILTING ROTOR: The C.30 used a driveshaft from the engine to initiate rotor rotation. Once the rotor had reached the required number of revolutions per minute, it was tilted backwards.

LIFT FROM THE ROTOR: Combined with the aircraft's forward motion, the spinning rotor disc provided lift, much like a helicopter. This allowed the autogyro to make very short take-offs.

EH INDUSTRIES

EH.101 MERLIN

● Anti-submarine warfare ● Assault transport ● Heli-liner

The EH.101 Merlin is the West's most promising large naval anti-submarine and rescue helicopter. It is a big, attractive craft with a five-bladed rotor and a long fuselage, with the capacity for diverse military missions. Britain and Italy are equipping surface warships with EH.101s, and pilots praise its stability, handling and performance. Land-based military and civilian models will soon follow the successful maritime version.

▲ A large maritime helicopter can perform many other useful roles at sea besides anti-submarine warfare. The EH.101 will undoubtedly follow in the footsteps of the S-61 in carrying out oilrig support missions.

EH INDUSTRIES EH.101 MERLIN

Heli-liner ▶
Another former Sea King job that the EH.101 is sure to take up is the heli-liner role. It will carry passengers faster and much more safely, thanks to its third engine.

▼ Avionics testbed
Number PP4 was the naval avionics test aircraft, engaged in testing the systems for anti-submarine warfare. The aircraft was destroyed in an accident early in 1995, but the crew escaped safely.

▲ Leaning fin
The tailfin of the EH.101 has a pronounced lean to port, to counteract the effects of the main rotor.

▲Trials family
The EH.101 systems were first tested in the Sea King furthest from the camera. It is flying with the civilian trials EH.101 and the Royal Navy's PP5.

◀ Advanced head
The five-bladed rotor head is designed to be resistant to cannon fire, and can continue operating even after a gearbox oil leak.

FACTS AND FIGURES

➤ The EH.101 prototype, with few of the features of the final aircraft, flew on 9 October 1987.

➤ The Merlin makes extensive use of hi-tech composite materials.

➤ The EH.101 will have a special 'harpoon' system for landing on frigate decks.

➤ An Italian Merlin was lost in an accident on 21 January 1993, causing a brief delay in flight testing.

➤ British Merlins will fly from the decks of Type 23 frigates like HMS *Iron Duke*.

➤ Merlin production began at the rate of one new helicopter every seven weeks.

New king of the seas

The attractive EH.101 Merlin was conceived as a replacement for the busy but antiquated Sikorsky/Westland Sea King. It was designed as a co-operative venture by Westland and Agusta, who established a company called European Helicopter, later EH Industries, to build this advanced, multi-purpose machine.

The Merlin is a large and costly helicopter and may prove too costly for some navies. In its state-of-the-art anti-submarine form it may nevertheless become a common sight on the world's oceans, especially on the flight decks of larger frigates and destroyers.

The Merlin offers sturdiness, range and endurance. It is a complex aircraft, however, and this, combined with its cost, has seen Canada cancel its order. Britain and Italy have ordered more than 80 copies between them though, to operate on both land- and carrier-based duties.

With a rear fuselage ramp added, the Merlin is ideal for

The utility version of the EH.101 has better prospects for export than the naval version, but it faces stiff competition from another European design, the NH.90.

other uses, including army operations, civil oil industry work and executive transport. As a utility transport, Merlin can haul 30 infantry soldiers, 5445 kg (11,980 lb.) of cargo, or 17 passengers in comfortable seats.

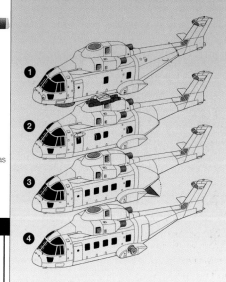

Side-facing air intakes are one of the many anti-icing features fitted to the EH.101. Another feature is thermal de-icing mats fitted to the rotor leading edges.

EH.101 has advanced swept-tip rotor blades, derived from the British Experimental Rotor Project Lynx that broke the helicopter world speed record.

The undercarriage is a hydraulically retractable tricycle unit with a steerable nosewheel. EH.101 prototypes have survived simulated hard landings at vertical speeds of more than 10 metres (33 ft.) per second.

Merlin HAS.Mk 1

Type: four-/six-seat maritime helicopter

Powerplant: three 1724-kW (2,310-hp.) Rolls-Royce/Turboméca RTM322-01 turboshafts (Italian helicopters have three 1279-kW (1,714-hp.) General Electric T700-GE-GE-T6A turboshafts)

Maximum speed: 309 km/h (192 m.p.h.)

Endurance: 5 hours

Weights: empty 7121 kg (15,666 lb.); loaded 13530 kg (29,766 lb.)

Armament: four Marconi Sting Ray torpedoes; two sonobuoy dispensers; options for Exocet, Harpoon, Sea Eagle and Marte Mk 2 missiles

Dimensions:
main rotor diameter	18.59 m (61 ft.)
length	22.81 m (75 ft.)
height	6.65 m (22 ft.)
rotor disc area	271.70 m² (2,924 sq. ft.)

EH.101 MERLIN 'PP5'

PP5 is the Royal Navy's EH.101 trials aircraft. First flown in October 1989, the helicopter was the first with a complete set of mission systems, including the Blue Kestrel radar and computerised avionics.

The EH.101 is powered by three engines. Italian aircraft will have the General Electric T700 turboshaft, but British ones will use the more powerful Rolls-Royce/Turboméca RTM322.

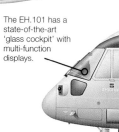

The EH.101 has a state-of-the-art 'glass cockpit' with multi-function displays.

The Blue Kestrel radar can be used for sea search, navigation and over-the-horizon targeting.

The rear cabin contains the dipping sonar and its winch, sonobuoy racks and dispensers, a sonar operator and a tactical systems officer.

Orange Reaper electronic support measures antennas are fitted to the front and rear of the helicopter. This system warns the crew of the presence of enemy radar transmissions.

EH.101 variants

1 MERLIN: Built for the Royal Navy, the primary anti-submarine variant of the EH.101 has a fully computerised avionics suite and a 360° scanning Blue Kestrel radar.

2 CH-148 PETREL: Canada intended to use the EH.101 as its primary shipborne ASW helicopter. But rising costs and a new government saw its cancellation in 1993.

3 MILITARY UTILITY: On order for the Royal Air Force, the military utility variant has a rear loading ramp and can carry six tonnes of cargo or 30 fully-equipped troops.

4 HELI-LINER: The main commercial variant will fly up to 30 passengers in an airline-style cabin at a range of 1000 km (620 miles). Key markets include city-centre routes and oil rig supply.

COMBAT DATA

MAXIMUM SPEED

The Merlin's three powerful engines, well-shaped fuselage and rotor blades of extremely advanced aerodynamic shape make it one of the fastest helicopters in the world, even when carrying a full load of weapons or personnel. It will use that speed to patrol large areas of the ocean.

EH.101 MERLIN	309 km/h (192 m.p.h.)
SH-60 SEAHAWK	234 km/h (145 m.p.h.)
Ka-29 'HELIX'	250 km/h (155 m.p.h.)

ENDURANCE

Successful anti-submarine warfare is a long and involved process, which calls for considerable endurance on the part of the hunter. A helicopter can never match a fixed-wing ASW aircraft when it comes to staying aloft, but modern machines like the EH.101 are far more capable than their predecessors.

EH.101 MERLIN	5 hours with full weapons load
SH-60 SEAHAWK	4 hours
Ka-29 'HELIX'	4 hours 30 minutes

ARMAMENT

The Merlin's size is a considerable advantage when it comes to carrying weapons. Four torpedoes instead of two is only part of the story, however; the EH.101 is also capable of operating with full-size long-range anti-ship missiles such as Harpoon or Exocet.

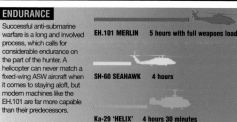

EH.101 MERLIN four torpedoes; Exocet, Harpoon, Sea Eagle or Marte air-to-surface missiles

SH-60 SEAHAWK two torpedoes or Penguin air-to-surface missiles

Ka-29 'HELIX' two lightweight wire-guided torpedoes or depth charges

ENSTROM

SHARK

● Observation helicopter ● Passenger transport ● Trainer

▲ Demonstrating the F-28's ability to remain stable in the hover, a brave employee is hauled into the air in front of the cameras as a marketing sales gimmick.

First flown in its original form in 1962, the Enstrom 280 has been one of the most successful light piston helicopter designs ever. Whether teaching students to master the basics of helicopter flight, spraying crops, transporting businesspeople across cities or patrolling pipelines, the Shark has proved popular with pilots and customers alike. Remarkably, the successful design has not changed much as the Shark remains an excellent utility helicopter.

PHOTO FILE

ENSTROM SHARK

▼ Blended body
The streamlined fuselage of the Shark – the result of a careful design study – is displayed for the camera.

▲ Light transport
Later versions of the helicopter were capable of carrying three passengers seated abreast. Although cramped, visibility from the cockpit was excellent.

Military service ▶
Operated by the Peruvian army, the helicopter is used for light observation and training duties, replacing the early Bell 47.

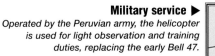

◀ High performance
Due to its lightweight design, the manoeuvrability of the Shark is exceptional, as demonstrated by this flying display at an air show.

Later Versions ▶
This late-model Enstrom development is test flown. A gradual upgrading of the design has taken place in an attempt to bring the helicopter wider service.

FACTS AND FIGURES

➤ First flight of the Enstrom Shark was on 26 May, 1962. it was the first of two three-seat pre-production models.

➤ The helicopter features a light alloy and glass-fibre cabin section.

➤ The US Army has shown an interest in the design, as a training helicopter.

➤ Military versions of the Shark serve with the Chilean and Peruvian armies as observation helicopters.

➤ A four-seat version was developed and flew in 1978; it was called the Hawk.

➤ The most recent development of the Shark is the five-seat Eagle.

Enstrom's Shark of the air

Enstrom was formed in 1959 specifically to build a light helicopter. The F-28, designed by Rudy J Enstrom, first flew in 1962. By the time the improved F-28A was built in 1968, Enstrom had been purchased by a bigger corporation. A turbocharged F-28B was built, along with a T-28 turbine-powered variant. By 1975, production of the F-28C had begun; this variant was phased out in 1981, when the current F-28F and 280 appeared.

These models became very popular and by 1993, over 900 of these helicopters had been built. With a redesigned main gearbox, main rotor shaft, and an optional exhaust silencer, the F28 can be configured for crop-spraying with easily removeable hoppers, and is also available as a police variant (F28F Sentinel) with a searchlight. The 280FX is a substantially upgraded version, with new seats, tail fins, faired landing gear and a covered tail rotor shaft. More than 170 F-28F and 280FXs were in service in 1993.

The 280 achieved some success as a military trainer,

Below: A US Army request for a new training helicopter saw a developed model of the Shark enter the competition. Though test flown by service pilots on occasion, the helicopter has not received an order and remains under development.

Above: Operating with the Chilean army, the Shark has proven to be an excellent utility helicopter.

with Chile, Colombia and Peru operating the type. The military-optimised TH-28, which lost out to the Bell TH-67 for the new US Army training helicopter requirement, is a similar aircraft.

F28F Shark

- **Type:** Light trainer/transport helicopter
- **Powerplant:** one Textron Lycoming HIO-360F1 rated at 168 kW (225 hp.)
- **Maximum speed:** 180 km/h (112 m.p.h.)
- **Cruising speed:** 165 km/h (102 m.p.h.)
- **Range:** 423 km (262 mi.)
- **Endurance:** 3.5 hours
- **Climb rate:** 442 m/min (1,150 f.p.m.) from sea level
- **Hover ceiling:** 2345 m (7,700 ft.) out of ground effect
- **Dimensions:**

Rotor diameter:	9.75 m (32 ft.)
Length:	8.92 m (29 ft. 3 in.)
Height:	2.79 m (9 ft. 2 in.)
Rotor disc area:	74,66 m² (804 sq. ft.)

ACTION DATA

SPEED

Due to the small dimensions of the F-28F, its speed is limited by its engine size. The streamlined design allows respectable performance compared to larger types such as the twin-engine German-designed BO 105CB.

F28F SHARK	180 km/h (112 m.p.h.)
R22 BETA	180 km/h (112 m.p.h.)
BO 105 CB	242 km/h (150 m.p.h.)

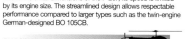

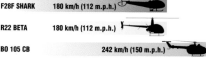

POWER

Although progressively updated during the course of development, the F-28F offers better performance in all flight areas than the Robinson R22. Although not as powerful as the Bo 105CB, the F-28F does not require as large of a load-carrying capacity.

F28F SHARK	R22 BETA	BO 105 CB
168 kW (225 hp.)	119 kW (160 hp.)	626 kW (420 hp.)

ROTOR DISC AREA

A large three-blade rotor disc offers excellent handling qualities for the F28F in the hover – a key selling point for the helicopter. Compared to the larger BO 105CB, the disc area seems too large for the small helicopter.

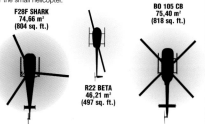

F28F SHARK	BO 105 CB
74,66 m² (804 sq. ft.)	75,40 m² (818 sq. ft.)

R22 BETA 46,21 m² (497 sq. ft.)

Although cramped for travellers on long flights, the cabin can accomodate three passengers in comfort for short trips. The pilot is positioned on the port side and has excellent visibility in all directions.

The helicopter is powered by an Avco Lycoming engine that has been progressively improved and updated to incorporate design changes to the airframe. Later versions are powered by Allison turboshafts.

A single rotor tail is positioned at the end of the boom. In later, larger variants it was moved to the port side to improve their handling qualities. The main rotor diameter has changed little during the course of development.

N2019H

Constructed from a light alloy and glass fibre, the fuselage offers exceptional strength at no penalty in weight. The tail boom is of an all-metal semi-monocoque construction. The resulting weight of the helicopter is surprisingly little.

280FX SHARK

Bringing helicopter travel to the masses has always been a driving principle for manufacturers. The Enstrom company has gone a long way to resolve this with its designs.

Light utility helicopters

■ **ROBINSON R22 MARINER:** Developed in the US, the R22 has been exported worldwide to serve as a utility and training helicopter. The design has proved very successful.

■ **EUROCOPTER ECUREUIL 2:** The AS 350 is larger than the Shark, but both are used in the same roles. The Enstrom achieves this at a lower operational cost thanks to a less fuel-thirsty engine.

■ **EUROPCOPTER GAZELLE:** The streamlined design looks very similar to the Enstrom Shark but the Gazelle has proved to be far more adaptable, serving widely in both civil and military roles.

EUROCOPTER

AS 350/550 ECUREUIL

● Anti-tank helicopter ● Air taxi ● Advanced rotor design

▲ *Despite the standard layout of Aérospatiale's Ecureuil, the helicopter has gone on to achieve notable sales success in both the civilian and military markets.*

Known as the Ecureuil, the Squirrel or, in North America, the AStar, the AS 350 was developed to replace the Aérospatiale Alouette. First flown in June 1974, it has been produced in military and civil versions. Military models include the AS 550U2 utility, A2 armed and C2 anti-tank versions. The AStar is fitted with a single Textron Lycoming LTS 101, whereas the civilian 355 Twin Squirrel, or TwinStar, and military 555 Fennec have two engines.

EUROCOPTER AS 350/550 ECUREUIL

▲ **Citywide travel**
Several companies have purchased the Ecureuil and use it as a safe and reliable method to overcome city congestion.

▼ **American flyer**
Operated in the United States as the AStar, the AS 350 is used as an executive transport.

▲ **Personal transport**
Although it has not replaced the family car as first stated by the helicopter manufacturers, it is very useful for those who have the money.

Shipboard down under ▼
Operated by the Australian navy, the AS 350B has a lightweight Doppler navigation system for overwater flights.

▼ **Rocket attack**
Seen launching unguided rockets during a test flight, the Ecureuil has been purchased by a number of armed forces.

FACTS AND FIGURES

➤ The first flight of the AS 350 occurred on 24 June, 1974, followed by a second example on 14 February, 1975.

➤ A fully-armed version of the Ecureuil is capable of launching anti-tank missiles.

➤ The helicopter has been assembled under licence in Brazil.

➤ The Ecureuil is marketed as the AStar in the US, where it has achieved considerable sales success.

➤ A gunship version of the Ecureuil has a 20-mm cannon and twin gun pods.

➤ Emergency flotation gear can be fitted to the skids for operations over water.

Europe's utility helicopter

Continued development has kept the AS 350 and its many derivatives on the market for more than 20 years. Operators use them for a variety of tasks, from passenger transport to police work, aerial filming to construction work. They have captured 60 per cent of the civil and public service market for single-engine, six- to eight-seat helicopters.

The first twin-engine model flew in September 1979. Most examples have Allison 250 engines, but the French air force's 44 AS 555ANs use the 340-kW (456-hp.) Turboméca Arrius. AS 550s and 555s have been produced in both armed and unarmed configurations for several military customers, and there are naval variants as well. Helibras of Brazil has assembled versions of both the single- and twin-engine Fennec, known as Esquilos. Armament options include guns, rocket pods, anti-tank missiles and torpedoes.

The latest AS 350B3, flown for the first time in March 1997, has more powerful Arriel 2 engines for improved performance in hot weather and at extreme altitudes. The maximum load has been increased to 1397 kg (3,080 lb.), while new avionics, displays and controls make it safer and easier to operate.

Below: Versatility is a major selling point for the AS 350, as demonstrated by the Alaskan-operated example, which is using the rear of a ship as a helipad.

Above: Displaying a more war-like role, this French army example has rocket pods.

AS 550 Fennec

Type: General-purpose 6-seat helicopter

Powerplant: one 546-kW (732-hp.) Turboméca Arriel 1D1 engine

Maximum speed: 287 km/h (178 m.p.h.)

Initial climb rate: 534 m/min (1,750 f.p.m.) from sea level

Range: 666 km (413 mi.)

Service ceiling: 4800 m (15,750 ft.)

Weight: empty 1220 kg (2,684 lb.); max take-off 2250 kg (4,950 lb.)

Weapons: one 20-mm M621 cannon and twin 7.62-mm (.30-cal.) gun pods when installed

Dimensions:
Main rotor diameter:	10,69 m (35 ft. 1 in.)
Length:	10,93 m (42 ft. 5 in.)
Height:	3,14 m (10 ft. 11 in.)
Rotor disc area:	89,75 m² (966 sq. ft.)

AS 550 FENNEC

Operated by Singapore, the Fennec has seen use as both a utility and attack helicopter. Intended as a replacement for the Alouette, the AS 550 is proving to be a worthy successor.

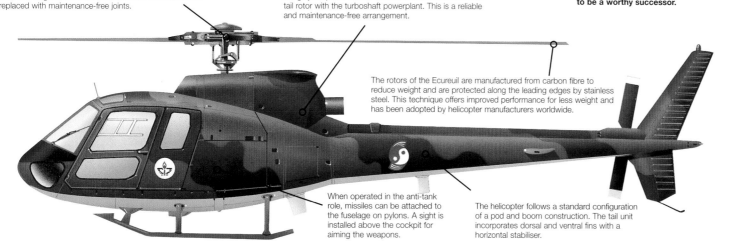

Building on experience gained from earlier designs, the Ecureuil features a three-blade main rotor with a glass-fibre hub. The hinges have been removed from the blades and replaced with maintenance-free joints.

A highly simplified transmission unites the main rotor and tail rotor with the turboshaft powerplant. This is a reliable and maintenance-free arrangement.

The rotors of the Ecureuil are manufactured from carbon fibre to reduce weight and are protected along the leading edges by stainless steel. This technique offers improved performance for less weight and has been adopted by helicopter manufacturers worldwide.

When operated in the anti-tank role, missiles can be attached to the fuselage on pylons. A sight is installed above the cockpit for aiming the weapons.

The helicopter follows a standard configuration of a pod and boom construction. The tail unit incorporates dorsal and ventral fins with a horizontal stabiliser.

ACTION DATA

TAKE-OFF WEIGHT

The high take-off weight of the AS 550 allows it to be used for a wide range of duties, from attck to air ambulance. Compared to the later Mi-34, its performance is excellent.

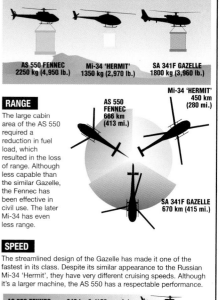

AS 550 FENNEC 2250 kg (4,950 lb.) — Mi-34 'HERMIT' 1350 kg (2,970 lb.) — SA 341F GAZELLE 1800 kg (3,960 lb.)

RANGE

The large cabin area of the AS 550 required a reduction in fuel load, which resulted in the loss of range. Although less capable than the similar Gazelle, the Fennec has been effective in civil use. The later Mi-34 has even less range.

AS 550 FENNEC 666 km (413 mi.) — Mi-34 'HERMIT' 450 km (280 mi.) — SA 341F GAZELLE 670 km (415 mi.)

SPEED

The streamlined design of the Gazelle has made it one of the fastest in its class. Despite its similar appearance to the Russian Mi-34 'Hermit', they have very different cruising speeds. Although it's a larger machine, the AS 550 has a respectable performance.

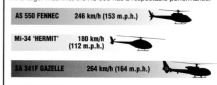

AS 550 FENNEC	246 km/h (153 m.p.h.)
Mi-34 'HERMIT'	180 km/h (112 m.p.h.)
SA 341F GAZELLE	264 km/h (164 m.p.h.)

Eurocopter's diverse designs

AS 330 SUPER PUMA: Capable of long range while carrying a large payload, the Puma is the ultimate in civilian helicopter travel. Continually improved, the design is in widespread service.

SA 341 GAZELLE: A compact design capable of a high cruising speed, the Gazelle is only hindered by its small cabin for carrying passengers.

AS 365 DAUPHIN: A development of the Dauphin 1, the improved twin-engine design has a greater range and improved lifting capacity. it has been sold around the world.

EUROCOPTER

AS 332 SUPER PUMA

● Oilrig support ● Search and rescue ● Tactical transport

▲ The Super Puma has been a great success in North Sea operations. It has proved very reliable, and can operate in marginal weather conditions that would severely inhibit less capable helicopters.

Eurocopter's family of heavylift helicopters – Puma, Cougar and Super Puma – perform many duties around the world, but none more challenging as those in the petroleum industry. This is high adventure only a helicopter can provide – heading out over raging seas to bring supplies to oilrigs on the ocean. Fortunately, helicopters like the Super Puma handle extremely well when the going is rough.

EUROCOPTER AS 332 SUPER PUMA

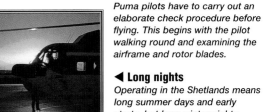

▲ Bristow Puma
The British operator Bristow Helicopters works its Pumas very hard. There is an average of 55 sorties a day leaving Dyce heliport near Aberdeen, heading out to the oilrigs and support vessels and back.

▲ Pre-flight checks
Puma pilots have to carry out an elaborate check procedure before flying. This begins with the pilot walking round and examining the airframe and rotor blades.

◄ Long nights
Operating in the Shetlands means long summer days and early starts, but long winter nights allow few daylight flying hours.

▲ Ready to go
With a close eye on the vicious and changeable weather and fuel states carefully calculated, the crew taxis out. The number of passengers is variable, depending on the fuel load needed.

▲ Night maintenance
Where possible work is carried out at night, as the Super Pumas have a very busy day schedule.

◄ Norwegian Puma
AS Lufttransport operates in the Norwegian sector, often flying in Arctic conditions.

FACTS AND FIGURES

➤ The prototype Puma first flew on 15 April 1965.

➤ The Super Puma took to the air for its maiden flight on 13 September 1978.

➤ About 420 Super Puma/Cougar helicopters have been built, about half of them used by civil operators.

➤ Petroleum Helicopters, the world's largest user of helicopters, uses Pumas and Super Pumas.

➤ The military Puma variant, the AS 532 Cougar, is used by 32 countries.

➤ The Super Puma Mk II introduced new main and tail rotors and transmission.

PROFILE

Flying for oil in the North Sea

Aérospatiale (now Eurocopter) has built a superb helicopter family with the AS 330 Puma, AS 332 Super Puma and AS 332L2 Super Puma II. With twin-engine reliability and an interior of 11.40 m³ (403 cu. ft.), the Super Puma offers brute hauling power. A survey of petroleum companies recognised the Super Puma as the most cost-effective helicopter in its class.

The Super Puma retains the original Puma's retractable undercarriage and adds glass-fibre rotor technology. The Super Puma is identified by its ventral fin and nose radome for weather radar.

For oilrig support, pilots praise its qualities, which also appeal to military users. Just as the rotors are deemed strong enough for 40 flying hours after hits by 12.7-mm (.50 cal.) small-arms fire, the fuselage and main rotors of the Super Puma can endure salt-water corrosion, high winds and the other challenges of petroleum industry flying.

The Super Puma supplements the older and larger Sikorsky S-61 Sea King (below) to service the oil industry. It has been a great success for the manufacturers, now called Eurocopter. The British operating company Bristow ordered 31 of a special variant known as the Tiger for offshore support work, and others are serving as far afield as the South Pacific and Abu Dhabi.

AS 332 Super Puma

Type: medium-size transport helicopter

Powerplant: two 1184-kW (1,590-hp.) Turboméca Makila 1A1 turboshafts

Maximum cruising speed: 266 km/h (165 m.p.h.)

Weights: empty 4460 kg (9,812 lb.); loaded 8600 kg (18,920 lb.)

Accommodation: crew of 2; 24 passengers in high-density configuration, or nine stretchers and three seated casualties, or 4500 kg (9,900 lb.) of cargo slung externally; some models have twin freight doors to accommodate bulky cargoes such as oil-drilling equipment

Dimensions:
main rotor diameter	15 m (49 ft. 2 in.)
length	18.15 m (59 ft. 6 in.)
height	5.14 m (16 ft. 10 in.)
rotor disc area	177.00 m² (1,905 sq. ft.)

A protective grille is fitted to the engine intakes to prevent ingestion of ice or debris. The engines drive at over 23,000 rpm, reduced by the gearbox to 265 rpm at the main rotor.

The Super Puma can be flown by a single pilot in visual flight conditions, but instrument flying in poor weather requires two pilots.

The more powerful Makila turboshaft replaces the original Turboméca Turmo of the original Puma.

The four-bladed main rotor is made of glass-reinforced plastic with a carbon fibre stiffening and moltoprene filler.

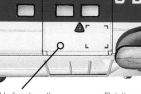

Offshore Pumas usually have a nose-mounted weather radar.

As in all helicopters, the passenger cabin of the Super Puma is quite noisy.

Flotation gear is essential when operating in bad weather over the dangerous North Sea.

The Puma airframe is of conventional aluminium with titanium skinning in critical areas.

In 1994 lightning struck the tail rotor of a Bristow Super Puma, causing it to ditch into the North Sea, miraculously without injury to any passengers.

G·BFEU **BRISTOW**

AS 332 SUPER PUMA

The Super Puma serves in large numbers in the North Sea. Known as the Tiger to Bristow Helicopters, it serves with other operators including Helikopter Servis and Bond Helicopters.

ACTION DATA

CRUISING SPEED

The Super Puma is a thoroughly modern design, and is capable of maintaining a high-speed cruise through bad weather conditions. This is important, since in its unceasing search for new supplies the oil industry operates in some of the most hostile environments on Earth, from the violent winter storms of the North Atlantic to the Polar wastes of Siberia and Alaska.

MODEL 214	256 km/h (159 m.p.h.)
AS 332 SUPER PUMA	266 km/h (165 m.p.h.)
Mi-8	225 km/h (140 m.p.h.)

RANGE

North Sea helicopters need plenty of range, since the oil and gas production platforms they service are exploiting reserves in deeper and deeper water, at ever increasing distances from the nearest shore bases. The ability to fly those distances in severe weather conditions is also essential.

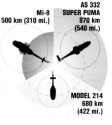
Mi-8 500 km (310 mi.) — AS 332 SUPER PUMA 870 km (540 mi.) — MODEL 214 680 km (422 mi.)

PASSENGER CAPACITY

Modern marine drilling platforms, especially those geared for deep-water operations in bad weather areas such as the North Sea, are massive structures housing hundreds of people. There is constant movement of men and equipment over wide areas, so large-capacity helicopters become essential to the smooth running of the oilfields.

AS 332 SUPER PUMA 24 passengers
Mi-8 28 passengers
MODEL 214 18 passengers

The Puma family

■ **SA 330 PUMA:** Developed initially as a military transport, the Puma could carry between 16 and 20 passengers. It was one of the first helicopters cleared for all-weather operation.

■ **AS 332 SUPER PUMA:** Based on the highly successful SA 330, the Super Puma has more powerful engines, better avionics, and a tougher airframe and landing gear.

■ **SUPER PUMA II:** The latest version of the Puma, first certified in 1992, is the Super Puma II. It is the longest in the series, with a stretched fuselage seating up to 29 passengers.

EUROCOPTER
AS 355/555 TWIN STAR

● Versatile lightweight ● Air taxi ● Police, ambulance, fire service

▲ The Twin Squirrel is popular with everybody from air taxi services to TV stations, who appreciate the perfect view it gives when breaking stories.

Known in the United States as the Eurocopter Twin Star, the bouncy little Aérospatiale Twin Squirrel is one of the world's most versatile flying machines. It is small, modest and relatively inexpensive, but it is an amazingly practical helicopter with dozens of everyday uses. From air taxi services to police and rescue work, the Twin Star gives solid performance at reasonable cost.

EUROCOPTER AS 355/555 TWIN STAR

▼ **Police support**
The Twin Squirrel is used by several police forces around the world, including Britain's Metropolitan police, who use it alongside the larger Bell 222.

▲ **Safety tests**
Modern helicopters undergo strict testing, such as stability analysis, before entering service.

Power-line surveillance ▶
Several UK electricity companies operate the AS 355. Its primary task is to locate damaged power cables allowing swift repair.

Neat interior ▶
The Twin Star has found its real niche as a comfortable air taxi. Its compact cabin can accommodate four passengers.

◀ **Fennec**
The military version of the Twin Star is known as the AS 555 Fennec. It is used for light utility work such as liaison and scouting, and can be armed with a Giat 20-mm cannon pod and pylon-mounted rockets.

▲ **Light rescue**
Equipped with a winch above the port door and a cargo hook, the Twin Squirrel can be used for search and rescue and light transport duties. The large mirrors under the starboard nose window allow the pilot to see the load carried by the aircraft's central cargo hook, essential for safety.

FACTS AND FIGURES

➤ A naval variant, the AS 555MN, is equipped with a chin-mounted radar, but is unarmed.

➤ The first Twin Squirrel made its maiden flight on 28 September 1979.

➤ The Twin Star has the best safety record of any helicopter in its class.

➤ Brazilian company Helibras builds Twin Squirrels with the designation CH-55 and VH-55 for the Brazilian air force.

➤ The Twin Squirrel's FADEC control system allows automatic engine starting.

➤ About 750 Ecureuils and Astars have been delivered to operators in 19 nations.

PROFILE

Eurocopter's versatile baby

The Eurocopter Twin Star is one of the world's best-selling light helicopters. Combining the twin-engined safety (essential for operating above dense urban areas) with the versatility and low costs of the AS 350 Squirrel, the AS 355 has been a great success. It has sold very well in North America, despite the dominance of the light helicopter market by the Bell 206 and Hughes 500.

The Twin Squirrel is derived from the single-engined AS 350 Ecureuil, driven by a single Turboméca Arriel turboshaft.

This aircraft featured a new rotor system and 'Starflex' rotor hub.

Like many helicopters in general use, the Twin Star can be equipped with a variety of flight instruments, avionics, radios and equipment options.

In use with civil operators, oil firms and police departments, the Twin Squirrel makes a superb air taxi. It is also ideal for primary training of fledgling rotary-wing pilots. The military AS 555 Fennec comes in naval and scout versions, and a missile-carrying version is under development,

armed with anti-armour TOW rockets.

The naval AS 355M2 has a chin-mounted 360° radar and can be armed with a pair of lightweight homing torpedoes. This version is in use with the Brazilian navy, which operates 11 UH-12Bs.

The AS 355 has a combined gearbox, with a shaft from each engine delivering power to the rotors.

The Starflex rotor system replaces the three conventional rotor hinges with a maintenance-free steel and rubber balljoint.

The main rotor blades are of glassfibre construction with a steel leading-edge sheath, combining strength, flexibility and light weight.

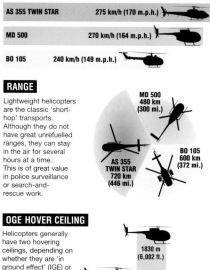

AS 355 Twin Star

Type: five-/six-seat general-purpose helicopter

Powerplant: two 340-kW (455-hp.) Turboméca Arrius turboshaft engines driving a three-bladed main rotor

Maximum speed: 275 km/h (170 m.p.h.)

Range: 720 km (446 mi.)

Service ceiling: 4000 m (13,120 ft.)

Weights: empty 1382 kg (3,040 lb.); loaded 2540 kg (5,580 lb.)

Accommodation: one or two pilots; six seats or up to 1134 kg (2,495 lb.) as an underslung load; various military loads can be carried including HOT or TOW anti-armour missiles, 20-mm Giat cannon pod or two homing torpedoes

Dimensions:
main rotor diameter	10.69 m (35 ft.)
length	13 m (43 ft.)
height	3.08 m (10 ft.)
rotor disc area	89.75 m² (966 sq. ft.)

COMBAT DATA

MAXIMUM SPEED

Helicopters are not the fastest of aircraft, but modern machines like the Twin Star can cruise quite comfortably at more than 200 km/h (125 m.p.h.). Coupled with their ability to operate from city centre heliports, they are often the fastest way of travelling from city to city.

AS 355 TWIN STAR	275 km/h (170 m.p.h.)
MD 500	270 km/h (164 m.p.h.)
BO 105	240 km/h (149 m.p.h.)

RANGE

Lightweight helicopters are the classic 'short-hop' transports. Although they do not have great unrefuelled ranges, they can stay in the air for several hours at a time. This is of great value in police surveillance or search-and-rescue work.

MD 500 480 km (300 mi.)
BO 105 600 km (372 mi.)
AS 355 TWIN STAR 720 km (446 mi.)

The Twin Squirrel has a simple two-bladed tail rotor, unlike the 'fenestron' or 'fan in fin' of its predecessor, the Aérospatiale Gazelle.

The latest AS 355 is powered by two Allison 250-C20F turboshafts. The original Ecureuil had a single Textron Lycoming or Arriel turboshaft. The twin-engined version first flew in 1979.

G-BOSK

POLICE

AS 355 TWIN SQUIRREL

The AS 355, known as the Twin Star for the American market, is known to most users as the Twin Squirrel. The Metropolitan Police was the first force in Britain to buy its own AS 355.

All AS 355s have a skid-type undercarriage for simplicity and low cost. This is slightly lengthened in military models.

Police Twin Squirrels often have a spot-light mounted under the belly, trained from the cockpit.

OGE HOVER CEILING

Helicopters generally have two hovering ceilings, depending on whether they are 'in ground effect' (IGE) or 'out of ground effect' (OGE). Using ground effect involves riding on the air generated by the rotor wash, which under certain conditions bounces back off the ground and acts as a cushion beneath the helicopter.

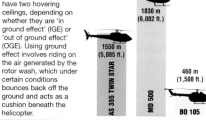

1830 m (6,002 ft.)
1550 m (5,085 ft.) AS 355 TWIN STAR
MD 500
460 m (1,508 ft.) BO 105

Aérospatiale's lightweights

■ **ALOUETTE II:** One of the most important helicopters in history, the Alouette II was the first turbine-powered rotary-winged craft to enter large-scale service.

■ **ALOUETTE III:** Taking the original Alouette concept a stage further, the Alouette III has a bigger cabin, a more efficient rotor system and more powerful engines.

■ **LAMA:** For operations in extreme conditions, Aérospatiale (now Eurocopter) introduced the high-altitude Lama, which is an Alouette II airframe with an Alouette III powerplant.

EUROCOPTER

AS 565 DAUPHIN/PANTHER

● Tactical transport ● Search and rescue ● Civil heli-liner

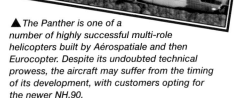

▲ The Panther is one of a number of highly successful multi-role helicopters built by Aérospatiale and then Eurocopter. Despite its undoubted technical prowess, the aircraft may suffer from the timing of its development, with customers opting for the newer NH.90.

Flown around the globe by both commercial and military operators, the twin-engined Dauphin is built in three continents. Its ability to carry up to 13 passengers or a load of more than 3000 kg (6,600 lb.) internally or on an external sling makes it the ideal vehicle for a wide range of tasks. It has been particularly successful as a flying ambulance, and its dedicated military descendant, the Panther, is used by both naval and land forces.

EUROCOPTER AS 565 DAUPHIN/PANTHER

▲ Heli-liner
The AS 365N2 is used by many city helicopter airlines, including Hankyu Airlines of Japan with its distinctive 'Footwork' logo.

▲ Gunship
Armed with rocket pods, or the clip-on gun pods seen here, the Panther is used as a gunship.

▲ Multi-role machine
The Panther has been bought by many users for such varied missions as anti-tank attack and search and rescue.

Fenestron tail ▶
Like the Gazelle, the Dauphin and Panther have a shrouded tail rotor for improved crosswind performance.

▲ Dauphin family
The Dauphins were progressively upgraded with greater use of composite construction, a retractable undercarriage and an 11-bladed fenestron. The first Dauphins used the Astazou engine which also powered the Gazelle.

FACTS AND FIGURES

➤ The Maryland State Police operates AS 365s with radar, forward-looking infra-red, searchlights and hoists.

➤ The French navy uses the AS 565 MA for plane-guard duty aboard its carriers.

➤ A Dauphin AS 365X set a speed record in March 1991 flying a 3-km (2-mi.) course.

➤ The Panther was designed around the AS 365 but with radar, infra-red and significantly reduced noise signatures.

➤ Chile operates four AS 565 MAs fitted with radar warning and Exocet missiles.

➤ Saudi Arabia uses AS 565s equipped with the AS.15TT short-range anti-ship missile.

PROFILE

Multi-mission, rotary wing helicopter

Flown in 1972, the first Dauphin was an updated Alouette III with a more powerful engine. In 1973 it set a new speed record for its class of 303 km/h (188 m.p.h.).

Aérospatiale then built the twin-engined AS 365C, and started a long line of versatile utility helicopters. The US Coast Guard chose the 366G version as its standard short-range rescue helicopter, and Israel bought 20 to operate from naval patrol boats. Harbin in China builds the 365N as the Z-9. A multi-role military version, the AS 365M, was first flown in February 1984 and carried 12 soldiers and HOT anti-tank missiles or SNEB rockets. The more powerful AS 565 Panther serves aboard French navy frigates and is built by Brazil for its army. Naval Panthers are equipped with the 'Harpoon' deck landing system.

The Panther has been sold widely to Angola, China, Ireland (fishery protection), Saudi Arabia, Taiwan and to Thailand's naval air arm. Fitted with T800 engines, the type was even offered to the US Army as a UH-1 'Huey' replacement.

Civil Dauphins are used around the world by fire and police departments and ambulance services. Commercial operators use them to support offshore oil operations and for executive transport. One is used the French air force for VIP transport, with the GLAM flight based at Villacoublay.

Above: Most armed Panthers are naval aircraft, but army versions can carry GIAT 20-mm cannon pods, MATRA Mistral missiles or unguided Thomson-Brandt 68-mm rockets.

AS 565UA Panther

Type: twin-engined multi-role medium-utility and naval helicopter

Powerplant: two 584-kW (780-hp.) Turboméca Arriel 1A1 turboshaft engines

Maximum speed: 296 km/h (183 m.p.h.)

Initial climb rate: 420 m/min (1,375 f.p.m.)

Maximum range: 875 km (540 mi.) with standard fuel

Service ceiling: 2600 m (8,500 ft.)

Weights: empty 2193 kg (4,825 lb.); loaded 4250 kg (9,350 lb.)

Armament: AS.15 or Exocet anti-ship missiles, gun and rocket pods

Dimensions: rotor disc width 11.94 m (39 ft. 2 in.)
length 13.68 m (44 ft. 10 in.)
height 3.52 m (11 ft. 6 in.)
rotor disc area 111.97 m² (1,205 sq. ft.)

Z-9

China builds the AS 365N Dauphin as the Harbin Z-9. The current Z-9A-100 army helicopter carries Red Arrow wire-guided anti-tank missiles.

The main rotor is a four-bladed Starflex structure with quick-disconnect pins for manual folding. They rotate at 350 rpm.

The Z-9 is powered by two licence-built IC 2 Arriel turboshafts. The Panther is powered by the Arriel 1A1, and has been trial fitted with the LHTEC T800.

The anti-torque rotor is shrouded within the fin, which is designed to reduce noise, increase efficiency and help avoid possible damage to the blades.

The dual flying controls are hydraulically powered. The pilot has a full instrument flying panel and an autopilot and optional radar.

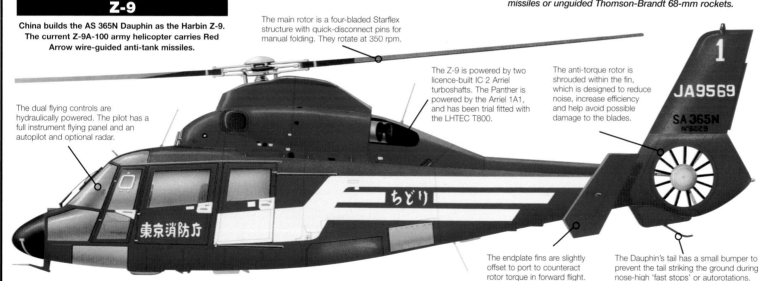

JA9569
SA365N
ちどり
東京消防庁

The endplate fins are slightly offset to port to counteract rotor torque in forward flight.

The Dauphin's tail has a small bumper to prevent the tail striking the ground during nose-high 'fast stops' or autorotations.

COMBAT DATA

PASSENGERS

These small tactical helicopters must be able to carry a squad of troops, but the airframe also needs to be small enough to fit on a ship's deck.

AS 565UA PANTHER	12 passengers
LYNX AH.Mk 9	10 passengers
UH-60 BLACKHAWK	11 passengers

MAXIMUM CRUISING SPEED

With twin engines and a sleek airframe, the Panther, Blackhawk and Lynx can all fly troops into battle very quickly to avoid hostile ground fire.

AS 565UA PANTHER	278 km/h (172 m.p.h.)
LYNX AH.Mk 9	259 km/h (161 m.p.h.)
UH-60 BLACKHAWK	278 km/h (172 m.p.h.)

COMBAT RADIUS

The Panther has an excellent combat radius and appears to outperform the other two types. However, the figure for the AS 565 is for an unladened aircraft, whereas the others are fully loaded values.

AS 565UA PANTHER 875 km (540 mi.)
UH-60 BLACKHAWK 592 km (365 mi.)
LYNX AH.Mk 9 685 km (425 mi.)

Dauphin and Panther operators

■ **GLAM:** A single SA 365 is operated by the Group de Liaison Aériennes Ministerielles, the French air force ministerial transport flight.

■ **CATIC FIRST:** This SA 365N2 is one of two sent to CATIC of China to allow the company to set up its own Dauphin production line.

■ **BOND HELICOPTERS:** Bond operates the Dauphin on oilrig support duties, alongside Sikorsky S-61s and Super Pumas.

■ **BRAZILIAN ARMY:** Known as the HM-1 in Brazilian service, 10 of the 36 Panthers were built under licence by Helibras in Brazil.

EUROCOPTER

TIGER

● Multi-role attack helicopter ● Fighting by day and by night

H overing menacingly among the trees, the helicopter lies in wait for its prey like a huge jungle cat. But no cat ever had such a sharp set of senses, nor such lethal claws. The helicopter needs those senses and claws; after all, natural predators have never had to deal with prey as tough as a 60-tonne Main Battle Tank, which is what the Eurocopter Tiger is designed to fight.

▲ The design of the Tiger was started at a time when the armoured hordes of the Warsaw Pact seemed poised to overrun western Europe, and Soviet tanks were to be its prime target.

EUROCOPTER TIGER

◀ **Tank-buster**
In German service as the PAH-2, the Tiger is equipped with a full day/night sensor fit designed to control long- and medium-range anti-tank missiles.

▼ **Gunship**
The pilot is seated in the front cockpit with the weapons operator positioned above and behind. This staggered arrangement allows good all-round visibilty.

◀ **Predecessor**
The Tiger will have twice the fighting power of the MBB 105, Germany's current anti-tank helicopter.

Tigre ▶
In French service, the helicopter is known as the HAC (Hélicoptère Anti-Char) Tigre. It has a similar weapons and sensor fit to the Tiger, differing only in the air-to-air missiles that it carries.

▼ **Tiger's teeth**
Helicopters are vulnerable to air attack, so the Tiger is equipped with Mistrale, seen here, or Stinger air-to-air missiles. Its main weapons, however, are the Trigat pods (below right), containing four heavy anti-armour missiles.

FACTS AND FIGURES

➤ The Tiger development programme is reported to have cost, to date, more than £1 billion (US$1.4 billion).

➤ Initial planning calls for the Bundeswehr to acquire over 200 PAH-2 Tigres.

➤ France was to order 75 HAP Gerfauts and 140 HAC Tigres, but may reduce that total.

➤ Tiger is 80 per cent manufactured from composite materials.

➤ The plastic, carbon-fibre and Kevlar fuselage is protected from lightning by an embedded copper-bronze grid.

➤ Tiger will be able to destroy any tank likely to appear in the next decade.

PROFILE

Europe's airborne tank-destroyer

In an age when missiles rule the battlefield, the main anti-tank helicopters in both Germany and France were converted light utility machines, and were horribly vulnerable.

In 1984 the two countries decided to produce a new, potent battlefield helicopter. Named the Tiger, it was to be a state-of-the-art gunship.

Equipped with infra-red, television and laser sensors, the Tiger can fly and fight in all weathers and at all times. It is armed with the latest anti-tank missiles, potent against even the latest super tanks.

But the Tiger is more than just a tank-killer. It forms the basis for the French army's Gerfaut, or Gyrfalcon. The Gerfaut is an escort and fire support aircraft armed with air-to-ground rockets and a powerful cannon, and is designed to work closely with supporting troops on the ground. Air-to-air missiles also mean that it can hunt down opposing helicopters.

First deliveries of the Tiger took place in 1998, and it will be on the front line until well into the 21st century.

Although designed for the Cold War in Europe, the Tiger will prove equally effective as a weapon for the rapid deployment and peacekeeping roles which are likely to be its lot for many years to come.

Tiger

Type: two-seat anti-tank and ground-attack helicopter

Powerplant: two MTU/Rolls-Royce/Turbornéca MTR 390 turboshafts, each delivering 1160 kW (1,171 hp.) of emergency power

Maximum speed: 280 km/h (175 m.p.h.)

Initial rate of climb: more than 600 m/min (1,900 f.p.m.)

Battlefield endurance: 2 hours 50 min

Weights: empty 3300 kg (7,275 lb.); loaded 6000 kg (13,225 lb.)

Armament: four wing stations for up to eight HOT or Trigat anti-armour missiles, and four air-to-air missiles; Escort version has a 30-mm cannon turret and can carry four air-to-ground rocket pods

Dimensions:
rotor diameter	13 m (42 ft. 7 in.)
length	14 m (46 ft.)
height	4.32 m (14 ft. 1 in.)

TIGER (HAC)

Tiger was originally to be produced in three slightly differing variants, this aircraft being the prototype Hélicoptère Anti-Char (HAC) for use with the anti-tank helicopter units of the French army.

Tiger's mast-mounted gunner's sight enables the helicopter to operate from behind cover with minimum vulnerability. The sight can feed display units in both cockpits, and contains a TV camera, a thermal imager and a laser rangefinder.

Made from a flexible fibre-plastic, the rotor blades are of advanced design. They are designed to withstand combat damage and birdstrike.

Tiger's nose-mounted sight is part of the pilot's night vision system. It incorporates a thermal imager, allowing the pilot to see in complete darkness. It can be linked to the pilot's helmet-mounted sight, so that wherever he looks the sight follows instantly.

Twin turboshaft engines are mounted side by side above the fuselage. They are armoured against both incoming fire and shock.

F-ZWWW

The fuselage of the Tiger is mostly made from an immensely strong sandwich carbon-fibre plastic and Kevlar, and is intended to be proof against 23-mm cannon fire.

COMBAT DATA

ARMAMENT

HÉLICOPTÈRE ANTI-CHAR TIGRE:
The HAC can carry eight HOT or Trigat missiles, or as shown here a combination of both, together with Mistral air-to-air missiles for self-defence.

PANZER ABWEHR HUBSCHRAUBER-2 TIGER:
The PAH-2 is of similar configuration, here carrying eight HOT missiles. For self-defence, however, it is equipped with the American-designed Stinger.

HÉLICOPTÈRE D'APPUI ET DE PROTÉCTION GERFAUT:
The HAP version can also carry four air-to-air missiles but its main armament is a 30-mm cannon in a nose turret and unguided air-to-ground rockets.

Tiger anti-armour attack

1 The Tiger can use its cannon against lightly armoured, low-threat targets like personnel carriers and trucks, or buildings.

2 To engage high-value, high-threat targets at long range, Tiger uses the Trigat missile system. Priority targets are enemy anti-aircraft systems such as ZSU-30 mobile guns and SA-8 missile launchers. Trigat has sufficiently long range to engage armoured vehicles outside the range of shoulder-launched air defence systems like the SA-14.

AIR-TO-AIR COMBAT: The Tiger is lethal. It is more agile than older helicopters like the Mi-24 and can engage them from high 'off-boresight' angles.

TIGER

Main anti-helicopter weapons are the nose-mounted 20-mm cannon, or the Mistral heat-seeking air-to-air missile.

Mi-24 'HIND'

EUROCOPTER
AS 532 COUGAR

● Multi-role ● First Gulf War veteran ● Operated worldwide

▲ Over the horizon
After a period of troubled development and budget cut-backs, a single AS 532 with Orchidée radar flew 24 missions during the Gulf War. An improved AS 532UL/Horizon combination is now entering service with the French army.

▲ Naval attack
For the anti-submarine warfare (ASW) and anti-surface vessel (ASV) roles, Eurocopter offers the AS 532SC Cougar. In the ASV role, the aircraft carries two AM39 Exocet missiles with a reported range of 48–64 km (30–40 miles).

◄ Keep on truckin'
With its underfloor cargo hook, the Cougar is able to carry external loads to a maximum of 4490 kg (9,900 lb.).

▼ Submarine killer
Thomson-CSF Varan located in the nose radome combines with an Alcatel/Thomson Sintra HS 312 dipping sonar in the rear fuselage to make the AS 532SC a formidable ASW helicopter.

▲ Rapid-reaction Cougar
Equipped with infrared-suppressing exhaust shrouds, this Cougar flies as part of the French army's rapid-reaction force. It was delivered by Aérospatiale as an SA 332M1 Super Puma and is now regarded as an AS 532UL Cougar.

In January 1990, Aérospatiale changed the name of its military Super Puma variants to Cougar. Now built by Eurocopter, this range of big, powerful machines includes tactical transports, Exocet-armed naval helicopters and a specialized combat search and rescue aircraft. Armed versions of the land-based models can carry guns and rocket pods, while the prototype of a specialised battlefield surveillance model proved highly successful during the First Gulf War.

▲ Both the Super Puma and Cougar serve in some numbers worldwide. The family has proven successful in the face of fierce competition and flies a range of missions from basic utility transport to battlefield surveillance and control.

FACTS AND FIGURES

➤ By 1 January, 1995, 42 countries had ordered Super Pumas/Cougars, two-thirds of them military.

➤ Five of Abu Dhabi's VIP aircraft have been given Exocet capability.

➤ Turkey ordered 20 AS 532U2 Cougars at a cost of US$253 million.

➤ Aérospatiale based the Super Puma on the highly successful SA 330 Puma, incorporating much new technology.

➤ The AS 532's gearbox will operate for one hour after all oil has been lost.

➤ In South Africa, Atlas used many AS 532 components in its Oryx helicopter.

PROFILE

Super Puma sharpens its claws

Two layouts form the basis of the Cougar family, the 15.5-m (50-ft. 11-in.) short fuselage variant and the 16.3-m (53-ft. 5-in.) long fuselage aircraft. The AS 532UC and AC are respectively the unarmed and armed versions of the former variant, while the AS 532UL and AL are the longer machines, each carrying an extra four troops in the utility version. The naval version uses the longer fuselage and is designated AS 532SC.

These versatile helicopters are widely used, most significantly by Argentina, France and Turkey. The AS 532SC also serves with the navies of Chile, Kuwait and Saudi Arabia.

Six of the AS 532UL Horizon battlefield surveillance version are being supplied to the French army. Special equipment enables the helicopter to act as a real-time reconnaissance aircraft, co-ordinating friendly airborne and surface forces and monitoring enemy movements.

In April 1987, the first AS 532U2, or Cougar Mk 2, was

Above: The AS 332M incorporated a .76-m (30-in.) fuselage stretch, allowing it to carry four additional passengers.

flown. Equipped with a 'glass' cockpit, highly automated systems and more powerful engines, the aircraft has been adopted by the French army for use in the combat search and rescue role.

Below: The Spanish air force operates a number of Cougars in a variety of roles. This AS 332B is seen prior to delivery to 803 Escuadrón of Ala 48 based at Cuatro Vientos near Madrid. Their primary role is search and rescue, plus secondary VIP duties.

AS 532 UC

Type: Military utility helicopter.

Powerplant: Two 1398-kW. (1,875-hp.) Turboméca Makila 1A1 turboshafts.

Maximum speed: 261 km/h (162 m.p.h.) at sea level.

Climb rate: 420 m/min (1,378 f.p.m.) at sea level.

Range: 616 km (383 mi.) with standard fuel capacity.

Weights: Empty 4321 kg (9,526 lb.); max take-off (8981 kg) 19,800 lb. with an internal load; 9330 kg (20,570 lb.) with an external load.

Weapons: 2 crewmembers plus 21 commandoes or 4490 kg (9,900 lb.) external load.

Dimensions: Rotor diameter 15.6 m (51 ft. 2 in.)
Length 15.5 m (50 ft. 11 in.)
Height 4.9 m (16 ft. 2 in.)
Rotor disc area 239 m² (2,570 sq. ft.)

ACTION DATA

SPEED
Sikorsky's Blackhawk is perhaps the Cougars closest rival on the international market. The UH-60A is slightly faster than the Cougar and is based on a more recent design.

AS 532UC COUGAR	261 km/h (162 m.p.h.)
UH-60A BLACKHAWK	267 km/h (166 m.p.h.)
Mi-17U 'HIP-H'	230 km/h (143 m.p.h.)

PAYLOAD
Cougar is a reasonably large helicopter and as such has a considerable payload capacity. In this respect, it outperforms both the Blackhawk and Mil Mi-17U 'Hip-H'.

AS 532UC COUGAR	4490 kg (9,900 lb.)
UH-60A BLACKHAWK	3622 kg (7,985 lb.)
Mi-17U 'HIP-H'	3991 kg (8,800 lb.)

RANGE
Eurocopter's product also has the edge on range, although the Blackhawk is able to carry up to four external fuel tanks when fitted with the external stores support system pylons. The Mi-17U is the current production version of this popular Russian helicopter, which is not noted for its range abilities.

AS 532UC COUGAR 616 km (383 mi.)
UH-60A BLACKHAWK 590 km (367 mi.)
Mi-17U 'HIP-H' 494 km (307 mi.)

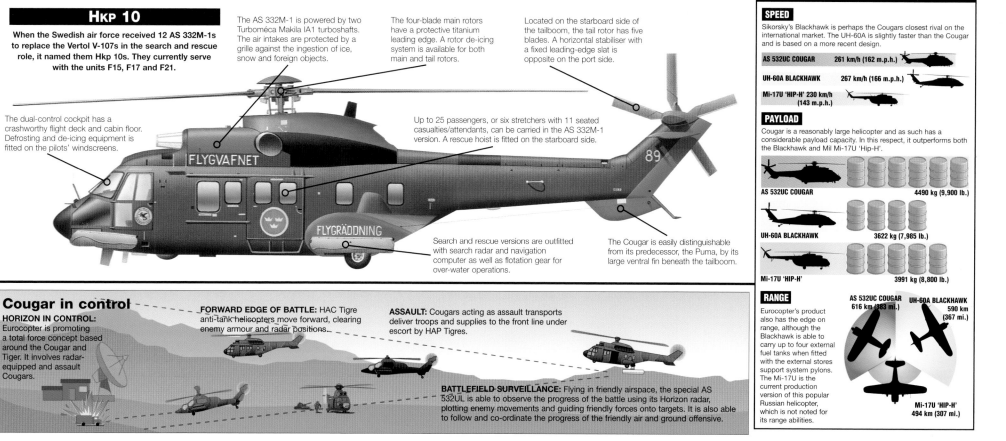

Hkp 10

When the Swedish air force received 12 AS 332M-1s to replace the Vertol V-107s in the search and rescue role, it named them Hkp 10s. They currently serve with the units F15, F17 and F21.

The AS 332M-1 is powered by two Turboméca Makila IA1 turboshafts. The air intakes are protected by a grille against the ingestion of ice, snow and foreign objects.

The four-blade main rotors have a protective titanium leading edge. A rotor de-icing system is available for both main and tail rotors.

Located on the starboard side of the tailboom, the tail rotor has five blades. A horizontal stabiliser with a fixed leading-edge slat is opposite on the port side.

The dual-control cockpit has a crashworthy flight deck and cabin floor. Defrosting and de-icing equipment is fitted on the pilots' windscreens.

Up to 25 passengers, or six stretchers with 11 seated casualties/attendants, can be carried in the AS 332M-1 version. A rescue hoist is fitted on the starboard side.

Search and rescue versions are outfitted with search radar and navigation computer as well as flotation gear for over-water operations.

The Cougar is easily distinguishable from its predecessor, the Puma, by its large ventral fin beneath the tailboom.

FLYGVAFNET
FLYGRÄDDNING
89

Cougar in control

HORIZON IN CONTROL: Eurocopter is promoting a total force concept based around the Cougar and Tiger. It involves radar-equipped and assault Cougars.

FORWARD EDGE OF BATTLE: HAC Tigre anti-tank helicopters move forward, clearing enemy armour and radar positions.

ASSAULT: Cougars acting as assault transports deliver troops and supplies to the front line under escort by HAP Tigres.

BATTLEFIELD SURVEILLANCE: Flying in friendly airspace, the special AS 532UL is able to observe the progress of the battle using its Horizon radar, plotting enemy movements and guiding friendly forces onto targets. It is also able to follow and co-ordinate the progress of the friendly air and ground offensive.

EUROCOPTER
EC 120/135

● European design ● Latest technologies ● Quiet operations

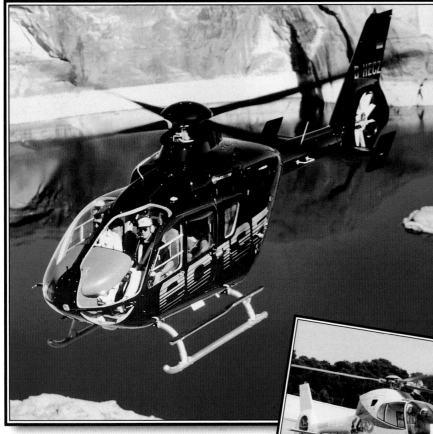

▲ Both the EC 120 and EC 135 represent the cutting edge of helicopter technology for the next century. The Eurocopter company was formed in 1992 by the merger of the Aérospatiale and MBB helicopter divisions.

I n order to match helicopter requirements in the next century, Eurocopter has produced its advanced EC 135 and EC 120 Colibri helicopters. Developed from the BO 108 technology demonstrator, the EC 135 is a high-tech successor to the MBB/Eurocopter BO 105, while the EC 120 is generally in the same class as Eurocopter's own Ecureuil and Gazelle. It meets the Bell JetRanger and MD 500 series head on, and is likely to sell well.

EUROCOPTER EC 120/135

Prototype ▶ formation
D-HECY, seen in the middle of this view of all three EC 135 prototypes, is the sole EC 135D-1 powered by the Pratt & Whitney PW206B engine.

▲ Before the EC 135
Messerschmitt-Bolkow-Blöhm (MBB) flew the first example of its Allison-powered BO 108 on 15 October 1988. The design subsequently evolved into the EC 135.

First flight ▼
Eurocopter considers all EC 135 prototypes to be pre-production prototypes. D-HECX was the first example and is seen on its maiden flight.

▼ French assembly
F-WWPA, the first EC 120 prototype, was assembled at Eurocopter's Marignane facility in France. The EC 135 was developed mostly in Germany.

Colibri programme ▶
By April 1997 two prototypes of the EC 120 were operational and had completed 250 hours of flight testing in preparation for certification.

FACTS AND FIGURES

➤ Having aimed to build 30 EC 135s in 1997, Eurocopter expects to increase production to 60 per annum thereafter.

➤ Eurocopter foresees a requirement for 700 EC 135s up to 2007.

➤ An Emergency Medical Service (EMS) layout is being developed for the EC 120.

➤ A number of EC 135s were flying with police forces in Germany and Spain by early 1997.

➤ The McDonnell Douglas MD 900 Explorer is a serious EC 135 competitor.

➤ Operating costs of the EC 135 are 25 per cent below those of the BO 105.

PROFILE

European helicopter challenge

With an upturn in the world economy causing a boom in the international helicopter market, Eurocopter was optimistic about the future of its EC 120 and EC 135 helicopters at the HeliExpo '97 trade show.

After certification during the summer of 1996, EC 135 deliveries totalled 10 by the year's end. Having first predicted orders for 20 EC 135s per year, Eurocopter has been forced to increase production to 30 in 1997 to meet demand.

Announced in February 1990,

the EC 120 Colibri is a joint venture between Eurocopter, CATIC/HAMC in China and Singapore Technologies Aerospace. The aircraft was officially launched at HeliExpo '97 and gained certification during the same year after, extensive flight testing. The Colibri is to be offered in a range of executive, police, training and utility layouts. A market of 1,600 to 2,000 examples is expected.

Both helicopters make extensive use of composites, the EC 120 being almost

entirely constructed from composite materials, and both employ a distinctive fenestron anti-torque system. This offers benefits in ease of maintenance and noise reduction, the latter being especially important in the policing and EMS roles.

Above: Eurocopter added an advanced fenestron anti-torque system to the MBB BO 108.

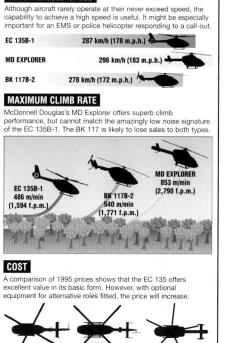

Above: Wearing its smart dark green colour scheme, D-HECZ introduced the EC 135 to America at HeliExpo '95 in Las Vegas. Strong competition for the type comes from the McDonnell Douglas MD 900 Explorer.

EC 135B-1

Type: five/seven-seat light helicopter

Powerplant: two 417-kW (560-hp.) (continuous rating) Turboméca Arrius 2B turboshafts

Maximum cruising speed: 261 km/h (162 m.p.h.) at sea level

Endurance: 4 hours at sea level

Maximum climb rate: 486 m/min (1,594 f.p.m.) at sea level

Range: 715 km (443 mi.) at sea level with standard fuel

Weights: empty 1370 kg (3,014 lb.), maximum take-off 2500 kg (5,500 lb.)

Accommodation: maximum of six passengers

Dimensions:
main rotor diameter	10.20 m (33 ft. 6 in.)
fuselage length	10.16 m (33 ft. 4 in.)
height	3.62 m (11 ft. 11 in.)
main rotor disc area	81.71 m² (879 sq. ft.)

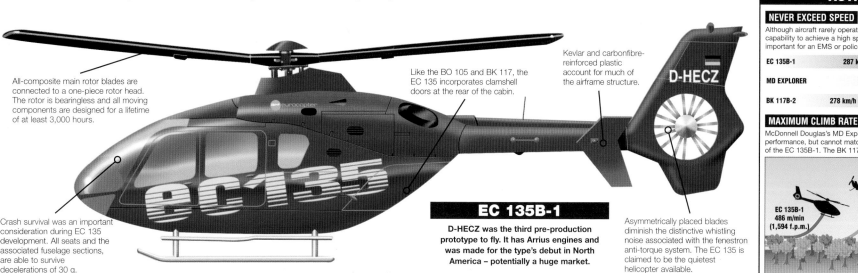

All-composite main rotor blades are connected to a one-piece rotor head. The rotor is bearingless and all moving components are designed for a lifetime of at least 3,000 hours.

Like the BO 105 and BK 117, the EC 135 incorporates clamshell doors at the rear of the cabin.

Kevlar and carbonfibre-reinforced plastic account for much of the airframe structure.

Crash survival was an important consideration during EC 135 development. All seats and the associated fuselage sections, are able to survive decelerations of 30 g.

EC 135B-1

D-HECZ was the third pre-production prototype to fly. It has Arrius engines and was made for the type's debut in North America – potentially a huge market.

Asymmetrically placed blades diminish the distinctive whistling noise associated with the fenestron anti-torque system. The EC 135 is claimed to be the quietest helicopter available.

ACTION DATA

NEVER EXCEED SPEED
Although aircraft rarely operate at their never exceed speed, the capability to achieve a high speed is useful. It might be especially important for an EMS or police helicopter responding to a call-out.

EC 135B-1	287 km/h (178 m.p.h.)
MD EXPLORER	296 km/h (183 m.p.h.)
BK 117B-2	278 km/h (172 m.p.h.)

MAXIMUM CLIMB RATE
McDonnell Douglas's MD Explorer offers superb climb performance, but cannot match the amazingly low noise signature of the EC 135B-1. The BK 117 is likely to lose sales to both types.

EC 135B-1 486 m/min (1,594 f.p.m.)
BK 117B-2 540 m/min (1,771 f.p.m.)
MD EXPLORER 853 m/min (2,798 f.p.m.)

COST
A comparison of 1995 prices shows that the EC 135 offers excellent value in its basic form. However, with optional equipment for alternative roles fitted, the price will increase.

EC 135B-1 US$1.98 million
BK 117B-2 US$3.50 million
MD EXPLORER US$3.33 million

Eurocopter product line-up

AS 355 ECUREUIL 2: Still strong sellers, the AS 355 and single-engined AS 350 are especially popular with police forces, as well as private and corporate operators.

AS 332 SUPER PUMA: Also available as the military AS 532 Cougar, the Super Puma has been updated since Eurocopter inherited the design from Aérospatiale.

AS 365N2 DAUPHIN 2: Developed from Aérospatiale's initially unsuccessful single-engined SA 360, the Dauphin 2 offers customers high equipment and performance levels.

BK 117: Designed and built jointly with Kawasaki in Japan, the BK 117 was originally designed in co-operation with MBB. The aircraft is a competitor of the EC 135.

105

EUROCOPTER

HH-65A DOLPHIN COAST GUARD

● Search and rescue ● Coastal patrol ● Utility helicopter

Speeding to the rescue with the US Coast Guard, the HH-65 Dolphin has saved hundreds of lives since its was introduced in 1987. Serving in coastal locations across America, this short-range recovery version of the Eurocopter Dauphin multi-role helicopter has demonstrated impressive versatility. Fitted with advanced avionics and search equipment, the Dolphin is first to the rescue whatever the weather.

▲ *A stretcher can be attached to the Dolphin's winch cable, which is particularly useful when picking up a casualty from a ship. The HH-65A is the US Coast Guard's most numerous asset, with nearly 100 examples currently in service.*

EUROCOPTER HH-65A DOLPHIN COAST GUARD

▼ **High-visibility paint scheme**
The US Coast Guard has replaced its Dolphin's original white and red colour scheme (shown left) with an all-over high-visibility red, reflecting the helicopter's dedicated civil rescue role.

▲ **Short-range rescue**
The HH-65A is the short-range component of the modernised Coast Guard fleet, operating alongside the longer ranged HH-60J Jayhawk and fixed-wing HU-25 Guardian, a version of the French Dassault Falcon 20.

Advanced cockpit ▶
The Dolphin's modern cockpit is designed for minimum effort all-weather operations and includes comprehensive radio systems and datalink. The flight deck normally houses two, but it can be flown by a single pilot.

▼ **Safety record**
The HH-65A has a reputation as a very safe helicopter, thanks to its automatic flight control system, airspeed regulator, flotation bags, Rockwell-Collins navigation and Northrop SeeHawk FLIR.

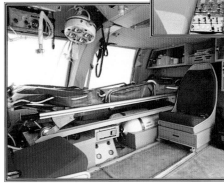

◀ **Rescue equipment**
In addition to a winch and searchlight, the cabin contains first-aid gear, a removable stretcher and a sliding seat for the engineer.

FACTS AND FIGURES

➤ Israel purchased two HH-65s, and in trials operated them from the navy's fleet of fast patrol craft.

➤ Two HH-65s are used by the US Navy test centre at Patuxent River, Maryland.

➤ Flotation bags allow waterborne ditchings in bad weather – up to sea state five.

➤ The Dolphin was criticised for lacking power in hot and high conditions, but a re-engining programme was cancelled.

➤ The crew can be supplemented by a rescue diver for special missions.

➤ Dolphins were purchased to replace the elderly Sikorsky HH-52.

PROFILE

Coast Guard rescue helicopter

Around the coast of America, the United States Coast Guard waits patiently for calls for help. Teams of swimmers and boat crews are used for inshore rescues, and fixed-wing and larger rotary-wing aircraft, such as the Sikorsky HH-60J 'Jayhawk' and special versions of the C-130 Hercules transport, carry out the long-range work. The responsibility of the HH-65A Dolphin, a modernised version of the Eurocopter SA 366 Dauphin purchased in 1987 to replace the elderly single-engined Sikorsky HH-52, is to undertake rescues at ranges up to 760 km (472 miles). Although built in France, the new HH-65A incorporates 70 per cent American components.

A total of 96 Dolphins serve around the United States from Astoria to San Diego. Fitted with advanced infra-red search systems, a winch, all-weather avionics and a searchlight, the HH-65A is ideal for short-range rescue work.

Although the Dolphin has been a success, there was controversy over complaints voiced by the US Coast Guard that the aircraft lacked power, especially in the hot conditions around the coastlines of California and Florida in the summer. Re-engining the helicopter was considered, but rejected on the grounds of cost.

The HH-65A is seen here with its stablemate, the improved Eurocopter Panther 800. A more powerful and upgraded development, the Panther seems unlikely to serve with the USCG, which was not entirely satisfied with the Dolphin.

HH-65A Dolphin

Type: short-range coast guard search-and-rescue helicopter

Powerplant: two 507-kW (680-hp.) Textron Lycoming LTS101-750 turboshaft engines

Maximum speed: 324 km/h (200 m.p.h.)

Operational radius: 760 km (470 mi.) with maximum fuel and 400 km (250 mi.) with maximum passenger payload; no external fuel carried

Endurance: 4 hours

Weights: empty 2718 kg (5,980 lb.); loaded 4050 kg (8,910 lb.)

Dimensions:
span	11.94 m (38 ft. 4 in.)
length	13.88 m (45 ft. 6 in.)
height	3.98 m (13 ft. 5 in.)
rotor disc area	119.90 m² (1,290 sq. ft.)

HH-65A DOLPHIN

The Eurocopter SA 366G Dolphin has been employed by the US Coast Guard since 1982, replacing the larger amphibious Sikorsky HH-52A in most units.

The HH-65's twin engines drive four-bladed rotors measuring 11.68 m (38 ft. 4 in.). Like the Gazelle and Panther, the tail rotor is the fenestron 'fan-in-fin' type.

Typically, the HH-65's crew will consist of a pilot, co-pilot and flight engineer/winch operator. The helicopter has a 1200-kg (2,640-lb.) stressed winch mounted above the starboard door.

The Coast Guard refit their French Dolphins with more powerful American-built Textron Lycoming LTS101 turboshafts, making the aircraft capable of a maximum speed of 324 km/h (200 m.p.h.).

The Dolphin carries a sophisticated Planar array weather and search radar, plus equipment to allow joint missions with Coast Guard HU-25s, HH-60Hs, RG-8s and C-130s.

If the HH-65 is unfortunate enough to suffer a double engine failure over the sea, a successful ditching will be aided by the helicopter's pop-out inflatable floats.

The Dolphin's tailboom is sealed for enhanced buoyancy and contains an increased size all-composite Fenestron tail rotor. The aircraft's mainly composite structure leads to its nickname of 'plastic puppy'.

ACTION DATA

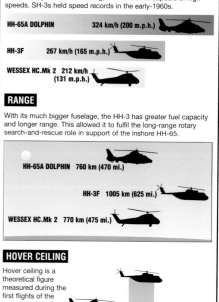

MAXIMUM SPEED

A generation ahead of the HH-3 or the Wessex and with considerably more streamlining, the HH-65A is capable of high speeds. SH-3s held speed records in the early-1960s.

HH-65A DOLPHIN	324 km/h (200 m.p.h.)
HH-3F	267 km/h (165 m.p.h.)
WESSEX HC.Mk 2	212 km/h (131 m.p.h.)

RANGE

With its much bigger fuselage, the HH-3 has greater fuel capacity and longer range. This allowed it to fulfil the long-range rotary search-and-rescue role in support of the inshore HH-65.

HH-65A DOLPHIN	760 km (470 mi.)
HH-3F	1005 km (625 mi.)
WESSEX HC.Mk 2	770 km (475 mi.)

HOVER CEILING

Hover ceiling is a theoretical figure measured during the first flights of the prototype. It can be affected very significantly by high temperature (this figure is calculated at a standard temperature of 15°C/59°F). The HH-65 often flies in hot weather at sea level.

HH-65A DOLPHIN	HH-3F	WESSEX HC.Mk 2
1627 m (1,000 ft.)	2500 m (1,550 ft.)	1220 m (760 ft.)

On patrol with the US Coast Guard

HC-130H: With a large APS-137 radar on the fuselage sides, the HC-130H can search large areas of ocean with great accuracy.

HH-52 SEAGUARD: The single-engined predecessor to the HH-65, the old HH-52 could land on the water, unlike the HH-65.

HU-25 GUARDIAN: Derived from the Dassault Falcon 20, the HU-25 can fly counter-smuggling or long-range rescue missions.

SCHWEIZER RV-8: For covert spying against smugglers, the low-light TV-equipped RV-8 wears a low-visibility paint scheme.

EUROCOPTER/KAWASAKI

BK 117

● European/Japanese co-operation ● Ambulance, rescue and utility

▲ With its large clamshell rear doors and twin-engined reliability, the BK 117 is a popular aircraft with civilian rescue and ambulance operators. It has also been licence produced by IPTN in Indonesia.

On 25 February 1977 Messerschmitt-Bölkow-Blohm and Kawasaki signed an agreement for the joint production of a new utility helicopter. Although the aircraft itself has been reasonably successful, it was the programme as a whole that demonstrated what can be achieved by a harmonious international project. BK 117s have found their most lucrative market in the rescue/emergency service role and continue to give life-saving service.

PHOTO FILE

EUROCOPTER/KAWASAKI BK 117

Armed and dangerous ▶
MBB displayed a multi-role military BK 117A-3M version at the 1985 Paris air show. The helicopter could carry the HOT anti-tank missile.

◀ Mountain rescue
Equipped with a cabin-mounted rescue winch and a searchlight, the BK 117 is a useful light search-and-rescue helicopter.

Off-shore support ▶
With its twin engines and 11-seat capacity, the BK 117 has considerable potential for maritime operations.

▼ Executive transport
Most BK 117s have been bought by civilian customers, and some are operated as corporate transports.

Fighting fires in Scotland ▶
Emergency services around the world appreciate the value of the helicopter for a variety of tasks. Many companies, such as McAlpine in the UK, lease aircraft to agencies such as the Strathclyde fire brigade.

FACTS AND FIGURES

➤ MBB abandoned its armed military BK 117A-3M, but 'civilian' machines have been sold to military customers.

➤ Kawasaki flew the first production BK 117 on 24 December 1981.

➤ Several features of the BO 105 were retained or modified in the BK 117.

➤ MBB abandoned its BO 107 design and Kawasaki its KH-7 project in favour of joint BK 117 production.

➤ The first aircraft from the MBB production line flew on 23 April 1982.

➤ Germany's ministry of defence used one BK 117 as a composites testing aircraft.

International multi-role project

Few international programmes have operated with as little controversy as that of the BK 117. Development costs were split equally between MBB (the German arm of Eurocopter) and Kawasaki and final assembly takes place in Donauwörth (Germany) and Gifu (Japan). Each company supplies the components it is responsible for, for example all fuselages are produced by Kawasaki and all rotor systems by MBB.

The majority of the BK 117's structure and production techniques was based on the BO 105, but, unlike its illustrious predecessor, the BK 117 failed to find any real military customers and this has limited the number of orders.

On the civilian market the BK 117 has proved ideal for emergency and rescue work, but this niche market has not allowed this helicopter to achieve the market success it truly deserves.

Above: MBB's BK 117A-3M demonstrator is armed with HOT missiles. Although more than 20 military customers exist, none uses the BK 117 offensively.

Right: Kobe City Fire Department's BK 117 is equipped with powerful spotlights for fire-spotting and other emergency duties.

BK 117B-2

Type: twin-turboshaft multi-purpose helicopter

Powerplant: two Textron Lycoming LTS 101-750B-1 turboshafts, each with 528-kW (708-hp.) take-off rating and 516-kW (692-hp.) continuous rating

Maximum speed: 278 km/h (172 m.p.h.)

Initial climb rate: 660 m/min (2,165 f.p.m.)

Range: 541 km (335 mi.) at sea level

Weights: empty 1727 kg (3,800 lb.) ; maximum take-off 3350 kg (7,370 lb.)

Accommodation: one pilot and a maximum of 10 passengers

Dimensions:
main rotor diameter	11 m (36 ft. 1 in.)
length	13 m (42 ft. 8 in.)
height	3.85 m (55 ft. 3 in.)
main rotor disc area	95.03 m² (1,023 sq. ft.)

BK 117

This BK 117 serves with the air proving wing of the Japanese Air Self-Defence Force.

The four-bladed rotor head is almost identical to that of the MBB BO 105. It is made of titanium. As an option, two of the blades can be made to fold.

A two bladed, semi-rigid tail rotor was specially designed to produce minimum noise. The tail rotor operates at 2,169 revolutions per minute.

Glass fibre-reinforced plastic (GFRP) is used for the main rotor blades, with a stainless-steel anti-erosion leading-edge strip. The blades are similar to, but larger than, those of MBB's previous design, the BO 105.

A pilot and up to six passengers can be accommodated when the BK 117 is used as an executive transport, but nine passengers are standard in Eurocopter-supplied machines. Ten passengers may be carried in a high-density layout.

Single pilot VFR (Visual Flight Rules) operations are possible with the BK 117's standard equipment fit. Kawasaki aircraft are equipped to a slightly higher level.

MBB is responsible for such components as the rotor system and tail section. Kawasaki manufactures the fuselage, fuel systems, transmission and other items.

Wheels may be attached to the skids to aid ground handling. Emergency flotation equipment and snow skids are optional.

ACTION DATA

MAXIMUM SPEED

Although it can carry only two more passengers than the BK 117, the Dauphin 2 is far more powerful and hence faster. The comparatively low-powered Explorer does not use a tail rotor, which decreases drag.

BK 117B-2	278 km/h (172 m.p.h.)
AS 365N2 DAUPHIN 2	296 km/h (184 m.p.h.)
MD EXPLORER	296 km/h (184 m.p.h.)

MAXIMUM CLIMB RATE

Both of the lighter helicopters offer good climb performance. The much newer technology used in the Explorer is reflected in its superior performance.

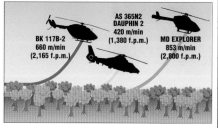

BK 117B-2 660 m/min (2,165 f.p.m.)

AS 365N2 DAUPHIN 2 420 m/min (1,380 f.p.m.)

MD EXPLORER 853 m/min (2,800 f.p.m.)

RANGE

Larger airframes have greater fuel capacity and therefore the Eurocopter AS 365N2 Dauphin 2 has the longest range. The BK 117, although incorporating older technology, offers a range almost as great as that of the Explorer. The BK 117 can be fitted with two internal and two external auxiliary tanks to increase its range.

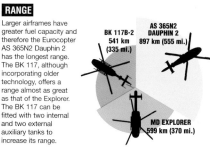

BK 117B-2 541 km (335 mi.)

AS 365N2 DAUPHIN 2 897 km (555 mi.)

MD EXPLORER 599 km (370 mi.)

Kawasaki aerospace projects

■ **KH-4:** Licensed manufacture of the Bell 47G-3B, as the KH-4, began in 1962. This aircraft was exported to the Thai police force.

■ **KV-107:** Kawasaki built the Boeing-Vertol Model 107 under licence, but production ceased in the early-1990s.

■ **OH-6:** Beginning in March 1969, Kawasaki manufactured the Hughes OH-6 under a licence agreement.

■ **369:** Civilian variants of the OH-6, designated the 369, have also been built in Japan, mostly for Japanese customers.

FLETTNER

FL 282 KOLIBRI

● Operational helicopter ● Highly manoeuvrable ● All weather

▲ Kolibris quickly proved their worth flying a variety of missions with the German navy. The aircraft were very stable and performed well.

Flettner, together with Sikorsky, pioneered the design and production of the military helicopter. The Fl 282 Kolibri was the result of Flettner's experience with rotorcraft and was fitted with intermeshing rotors mounted side-by-side. The aircraft was operated successfully as a reconnaissance platform for the German navy, from both shore bases and ships. The Luftwaffe also used the Kolibri for rescue and resupply missions in the later stages of the war.

FLETTNER FL 282 KOLIBRI

▼ Post-war testing
Three aircraft were claimed by the Allies. Two, including the V15 prototype shown here, went to the US, and one went to the USSR.

▲ Kolibri prototypes
To speed up development, 30 prototypes were ordered in 1940. Here V23 is seen in the US.

◄ Enclosed single-seater
Only the first three prototypes were completed with enclosed cockpits, as seen on V3. These were the only single-seat Fl 282s.

◄ Into service
With 20 aircraft completed by 1943, some, including V6, were assigned to convoy protection in the Aegean and Mediterranean.

Shipborne ▶ operations
V5 paved the way for naval operations in harsh conditions by flying from a platform above a gun turret on the cruiser Köln in the Baltic. Here V6 is recovered by a ship in the Aegean.

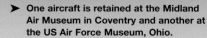

FACTS AND FIGURES

➤ Only 24 of the 30 prototypes and 15 pre-production aircraft were completed before the end of the war.

➤ One Fl 282 accumulated 95 flying hours without any repairs.

➤ Pulling back violently on the controls could cause the rotors to strike the fin.

➤ One aircraft is retained at the Midland Air Museum in Coventry and another at the US Air Force Museum, Ohio.

➤ Using his Fl 282 experience, Flettner began designing the 20-passenger Fl 339.

➤ Hans E. Fuisting performed most of the Fl 282 test-flying.

PROFILE

Hummingbird goes to war

Anton Flettner had tried several schemes for helicopters before hitting on the 'egg-beater' system. The two twin-bladed rotors cancelled out each other's torque, so there was no need for additional rotors. In 1938 Flettner's Fl 265 won a small order from the German navy.

In addition to flying trials from surface ships and submarines, one of the six Fl 265s was tested in simulated combat against Bf 109 and Fw 190 fighters. It was able to evade their gunsights for a full 20 minutes and led to

increased military confidence in the improved Fl 282.

The Kolibri had an additional seat for an observer behind the engine. Two dozen were delivered for service trials with the Luftwaffe and navy. Operating from escort ships in the Aegean, they were used to hunt for hostile submarines.

The Kolibri's success led to an order for 1,000 aircraft. These were to be built by BMW at Munich and Fisenach, but Allied bombing raids in 1944/45 disrupted production, and none had been completed by the end of the war.

Once the Kolibri had landed and been secured to the deck, its rotor blades were carefully tied down to prevent damage.

The two rotor blades were mounted so that they were parallel at the 45° position.

Each rotor blade was made of wooden ribs on tubular steel spars, with a fabric-over-plywood covering.

FL 282 V21 KOLIBRI

Shown while flying evaluation tests in 1943, this aircraft was the 21st of 24 prototypes built. Most Kolibris were destroyed to avoid their capture just before the German capitulation.

Although of considerable size, the horizontal stabiliser was fitted only for trimming purposes. The inter-meshing rotor system allows designers to dispense with a tail rotor.

An experienced pilot could fly the Kolibri from a ship in almost any weather. Conditions for the pilot must have been severe, however, especially during trials in the Baltic, since the forward cockpit was completely open.

An observer's cockpit was provided in the rear fuselage. It was open and provided excellent visibility. An observer was carried at the expense of fuel, and range was therefore limited.

For maximum ground manoeuvrability, the nosewheel could be steered via the rudder pedals. A crude instrument panel was mounted forwards of the controls.

Mounting the engine in this central position gave both crewmembers an excellent view. Air was drawn into the engine from below the fuselage by a wooden fan.

An abnormally large rudder was fitted to the vertical fin. The shape of the rear fuselage was not ideal and caused a great deal of turbulence, which meant that much of the rudder area was ineffective.

Rotorcraft in World War II

■ **FLETTNER Fl 265:** Having proved Flettner's ideas for a practical military helicopter, only six examples of the Fl 265 were built before it gave way to the more promising Fl 282.

■ **FOCKE ACHGELIS Fa 223 DRACHE:** Designed to satisfy a Lufthansa requirement, only a few military Fa 223s were completed due to continuous Allied bombing.

■ **SIKORSKY R-4:** An R-4 achieved the first helicopter landing aboard a ship in May 1943 and later went on to perform a number of combat rescue missions.

■ **SIKORSKY R-5:** A completely new design, the R-5 first flew on 18 August 1943. The all-metal aircraft was later built in large numbers in the US and the UK.

Fl 282B Kolibri

Type: single- or two-seat reconnaissance and transport helicopter

Powerplant: one 119-kW (160-hp.) Bramo Sh 14 seven-cylinder radial piston engine

Maximum speed: 150 km/h (93 m.p.h.) at sea level

Vertical climb rate: 91.5 m/min (300 f.p.m.) at loaded weight

Range: 300 km (185 mi.) with pilot only

Service ceiling: 3292 m (10,800 ft.)

Weights: empty 760 kg (1,672 lb.); maximum take-off 1000 kg (2,200 lb.)

Dimensions:
main rotor diameter	11.96 m (39 ft. 3 in.)
fuselage length	6.56 m (21 ft. 6 in.)
height	2.20 m (7 ft. 3 in.)
total rotor disc area	224.69 m² (2,148 sq. ft.)

ACTION DATA

MAXIMUM SPEED

The Fl 282 was not only a practical helicopter design, it also offered good performance. Sikorsky's YR-4B had similar capabilities and looked more advanced, but it could not match the Kolibri's speed.

Fl 282 V21 KOLIBRI	150 km/h (93 m.p.h.)
YR-4B HOVERFLY	121 km/h (75 m.p.h.)
R-5B DRAGONFLY	171 km/h (106 m.p.h.)

MAXIMUM TAKE-OFF WEIGHT

Early helicopters had limited payloads, with an empty Fl 282 weighing only 240 kg (528 lb.) less than its maximum take-off weight. Sikorsky, unhindered by the enemy bombing which troubled Flettner, was able to develop the larger R-5B.

Fl 282 V21 KOLIBRI	YR-4B HOVERFLY	R-5B DRAGONFLY
1000 kg (2,200 lb.)	1150 kg (2,530 lb.)	2189 kg (4,816 lb.)

RANGE

In full operational configuration with pilot and observer, the Fl 282 V21 had less range than the American machines. The majority of its operational missions were flown around a convoy, however, and refuelling was not a problem.

Fl 282 V21 KOLIBRI 170 km (105 mi.)

YR-4B HOVERFLY 209 km (130 mi.)

R-5B DRAGONFLY 579 km (359 mi.)

FOCKE-ACHGELIS

FA 223 DRACHE

● Transport helicopter ● Twin-rotor layout ● Post-war service

In the years immediately preceding World War II Germany had become one of the world's leading helicopter nations. In 1932 Prof. Heinrich Karl Focke began a series of experiments commencing with licence-built autogyros and culminating in the Fa 266 Hornisse. This outrigger-mounted twin-rotor design was the world's first genuine transport helicopter, and when war arrived it was developed for military use as the Focke-Achgelis Fa 223 Drache.

▲ Using experience gained with the smaller Fa 266 Hornisse, Focke-Achgelis sought to develop a larger aircraft capable of undertaking transport and rescue missions.

FOCKE-ACHGELIS FA 223 DRACHE

◄ Mountain operations
The Drache proved suitable for use in a variety of environments and was often employed by high-ranking German military officers to attend important meetings at Hitler's secluded mountain-top command post in Bavaria.

Rotor position ►
To provide a stable lifting platform the rotors were positioned on outriggers on either side of the fuselage. This allowed larger blades to be used.

Indoor flight ►
Prior to the outbreak of World War II the helicopter was seen as a tool for propaganda use, with flight demonstrations even taking place at indoor conferences.

▲ Post-war service
After World War II, two Fa 223s were constructed in Czechoslovakia from German-manufactured aircraft components. They saw limited service.

Early birds ►
Numerous configurations were tested before a practical design was adopted for operational use with the Luftwaffe during the war.

FACTS AND FIGURES

➤ The first flight of the Fa 223 Drache occurred in August 1940. The project was under military control.

➤ After the first successful flight, 39 pre-production examples were ordered.

➤ The roles envisaged for the Drache were rescue and anti-submarine patrols.

➤ One variant was to be fitted with machine guns and two 250-kg (550-lb.) bombs for armed reconnaissance missions.

➤ An Fa 223 became the first helicopter to cross the English Channel.

➤ After the war both France and Czechoslovakia developed the design.

PROFILE

Pioneering transport helicopter

Designed for the German national airline Lufthansa, the Fa 266 was developed from the earlier twin-rotor Fa 61. When war broke out, the military potential of the aircraft was realised and 39 pre-production examples of the newly designated Fa 223 were ordered. Intended roles were to include anti-submarine patrol, reconnaissance, rescue, transport and training.

When production commenced at Bremen, problems were immediately encountered because the factory was bombed. Production was switched to Laupheim, near Stuttgart, and, by early 1942, 17 Fa 223s had been completed and operational trials had commenced.

Despite more delays caused by bombing the trials were generally successful and 100 production examples were ordered. Allied bombing again hampered production and, although strenuous efforts were made, only 10 aircraft had flown

by 1944. The Fa 223 did, however, demonstrate many of the roles that the helicopter has made its own in the postwar years. Successful rescue missions using a winch were carried out and deployments of troops to confined areas were also achieved by Luft-Transportstaffel 40. Only three machines were serviceable by the end of the war and one of these became the first helicopter to cross the English Channel.

Left: Unconventional in layout, the Fa 223 Drache proved itself a highly capable helicopter during the war.

Above: The prototype Drache was initially flown tethered to the ground to allow the pilot to explore its handling safely.

Fa 223 Drache

Type: transport/rescue/reconnaissance helicopter

Powerplant: one 746-kW (1,000-hp.) BMW 301 R nine-cylinder radial engine

Maximum speed: 175 km/h (109 m.p.h.)

Cruising speed: 120 km/h (74 m.p.h.)

Range: 700 km (434 mi.), with auxiliary fuel tank

Service ceiling: 2010 m (6,600 ft.)

Weights: empty 3175 kg (6,985 lb.); maximum take-off 4310 kg (9,480 lb.)

Armament: one 7.92-mm MG 15 machine-gun and two 250-kg (550-lb.) bombs

Dimensions:
span	24.5 m (80 ft. 4 in.)
length	12.25 m (40 ft. 2 in.)
height	4.35 m (14 ft. 3 in.)
rotor disc area	226.19 m² (2,434 sq. ft.)

A heavily glazed cockpit afforded the pilot excellent visibility, particularly when coming in to land when a downward view was required. Pilots found the Drache relatively easy to master and this was demonstrated by two German pilots flying one across the Channel to Britain for evaluation at the conclusion of World War II.

Positioned on outriggers the twin rotors were powered by a single nine-cylinder radial engine. Providing enough power for the helicopter was a particular problem that the makers had to overcome in order to achieve military backing.

After numerous trials the tail configuration that offered the best handling qualities during the hovering phase was a high-set design. This allowed the Drache to make precise landings at mountain heli-pads even when fully loaded with troops.

DM+SP

Roles envisaged for the Drache were battlefield transport, observation and rescue work. For the last of these an extra fuel tank and rescue winch were provided.

Substantial tyres were fitted to the Fa 223 Drache to allow the helicopter to land on unprepared airfields. These were adapted from other German transport aircraft. Steering on the ground was accomplished through the large nose wheel.

FA 223 DRACHE

Revolutionary for its time, the Focke-Achgelis Fa 223 Drache achieved only limited service because of Allied bombing of the production line. Despite this, those that saw service use were a complete success.

ACTION DATA

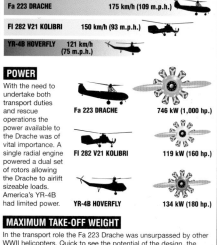

MAXIMUM SPEED

Despite its relatively large size, the Fa 223 had good performance and was faster than the American Sikorsky Hoverfly and the light-weight observation Fl 282 Kolibri. Such fine performance also meant that the Fa 223 could operate in many difficult locations.

Fa 223 DRACHE	175 km/h (109 m.p.h.)
FI 282 V21 KOLIBRI	150 km/h (93 m.p.h.)
YR-4B HOVERFLY	121 km/h (75 m.p.h.)

POWER

With the need to undertake both transport duties and rescue operations the power available to the Drache was of vital importance. A single radial engine powered a dual set of rotors allowing the Drache to airlift sizeable loads. America's YR-4B had limited power.

Fa 223 DRACHE	746 kW (1,000 hp.)
FI 282 V21 KOLIBRI	119 kW (160 hp.)
YR-4B HOVERFLY	134 kW (180 hp.)

MAXIMUM TAKE-OFF WEIGHT

In the transport role the Fa 223 Drache was unsurpassed by other WWII helicopters. Quick to see the potential of the design, the Luftwaffe hoped to operate the helicopter as a battlefield transport but Allied bombing of the factories halted its wider use.

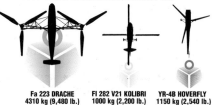

Fa 223 DRACHE	FI 282 V21 KOLIBRI	YR-4B HOVERFLY
4310 kg (9,480 lb.)	1000 kg (2,200 lb.)	1150 kg (2,540 lb.)

Pioneering rotors

■ **FLETTNER FI 282 KOLIBRI:** Used as an observation helicopter, the Fl 282 was operated by the German navy allowing ship captains to view Allied shipping over the horizon.

■ **HAFNER R-11:** Utilising a standard army Willys jeep, the English company Hafner adapted the vehicle to be used as a battlefield air observation platform. The project met with limited success and was soon cancelled.

■ **SIKORSKY R-4:** The most successful helicopter of World War II, the R-4 was used in the rescue and scout roles and saw extensive service in the Pacific theatre.

HILLER

UH-12 RAVEN

● Lightweight 1950s design ● US Army's H-23 ● War veteran

F lagship for an exceedingly successful helicopter family which included the Model 360 and the military H-23 Raven, the UH-12 was created in 1948 by helicopter genius Stanley Hiller. As a test bed for his innovative 'Rotor-Matic' control system, it went on to be built in large numbers. At least 2,300 examples have provided excellent service to civil and military users, and many are still on duty, from Britain to New Zealand.

▲ Popular with civil and military operators alike, the Hiller was produced throughout the 1950s and until the late-1960s. After Hiller was taken over by Fairchild, production was restarted in 1973.

PHOTO FILE

HILLER UH-12 RAVEN

▼ Army H-23 Raven
The US Army operated the UH-12 as the H-23 Raven from 1950. This H-23B carries the wing of an L-20 Beaver.

▲ Powerful light helicopter
Hiller billed the UH-12E as the most powerful US-built light helicopter.

Piston-engined ▶
The earliest Hiller UH-12s were powered by Franklin engines, while later models used more powerful Lycoming flat-six powerplants. The final UH-12E-4s had an Allison 250 turboshaft as fitted to machines like the Bell 206 JetRanger.

▲ Over San Francisco Bay
Hiller marketed the civil Hiller 12C for land- or ship-based port work, such as personnel transport and the off-loading of light priority cargoes.

Large US Army orders ▶
US Army Ravens were delivered for 17 years from 1950. The most common variant was the OH-23G; 793 were built.

FACTS AND FIGURES

➤ An early UH-12 was the first commercial helicopter to log a transcontinental flight across the United States.

➤ Over 1,600 UH-12s went to the US Army and were used in Korea and Vietnam.

➤ As a flying ambulance, the UH-12 can carry two stretcher cases.

➤ UH-12s were exported to at least 18 countries, many via the Mutual Defense Aid Program.

➤ The Hiller UH-12 was the US Army's primary trainer until 1965.

➤ UH-12s were manufactured by Hiller in Palo Alto, near San Francisco, California.

PROFILE

Light helicopters from Palo Alto

In 1971 the US Army held a celebration to mark 100,000 accident-free miles flown by one of its veteran Hiller H-23 Ravens (the military designation for the UH-12). This kind of satisfaction by those who rely on the UH-12 is far from unusual. For decades the versatile Hiller UH-12 has enjoyed a reputation for safety and reliability in roles like police work and agricultural spraying, as well as military operations.

The UH-12 is of simple construction, incorporating two-blade main and tail rotors with a sturdy, upswept tailboom. Built in highly successful two-, three- and four-seat configurations, the type was fitted with a variety of Franklin and Lycoming piston engines. Aircraft built in the 1970s had almost twice the installed horsepower of the earliest models; there was even a turboshaft-powered version.

Production of what was at first known as the Model 360 began in the late-1940s and continued as the Fairchild-Hiller UH-12 and Model 12 until 1965. At least 300 Hillers were exported to overseas customers, both military and civil.

Stanley Hiller's son, Jeffrey, took over the business in 1994. The compnay continues to develop the UH-12 in piston- and turbine-engined versions and as a new five-seater – a testimony to the soundness of the 1940s design.

Left: Numerous civil UH-12s have been used for agricultural tasks such as crop spraying. In New Zealand most UH-12s have undergone conversion and been fitted with Allison 250 turboshaft engines.

Below: A number of UH-12s in the US are employed in a major insect control campaign in the Atlantic coast states. Over 1,000 UH-12s are still flying worldwide.

H-23D Raven

Type: three-seat light observation and training helicopter

Powerplant: one 186-kW (250-hp.) Lycoming VO-450-23B flat-six air-cooled piston engine

Max speed: 153 km/h (95 m.p.h.) at sea level

Cruising speed: 132 km/h (82 m.p.h.)

Initial climb rate: 320 m/min (1,246 f.p.m.)

Range: 317 km (200 mi.)

Weights: empty 824 kg (1,812 lb.); loaded 1225 kg (2,695 lb.)

Armament: normally none, although small-arms were often carried by crew in active service

Dimensions:
main rotor diameter	7.44 m (24 ft. 5 in.)
length	8.47 m (27 ft. 9 in.)
height	2.98 m (9 ft. 9 in.)
rotor disc area	91.51 m² (985 sq. ft.)

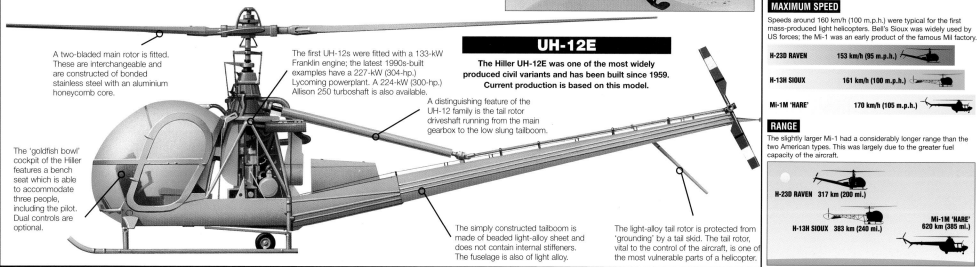

A two-bladed main rotor is fitted. These are interchangeable and are constructed of bonded stainless steel with an aluminium honeycomb core.

The first UH-12s were fitted with a 133-kW Franklin engine; the latest 1990s-built examples have a 227-kW (304-hp.) Lycoming powerplant. A 224-kW (300-hp.) Allison 250 turboshaft is also available.

UH-12E

The Hiller UH-12E was one of the most widely produced civil variants and has been built since 1959. Current production is based on this model.

A distinguishing feature of the UH-12 family is the tail rotor driveshaft running from the main gearbox to the low slung tailboom.

The 'goldfish bowl' cockpit of the Hiller features a bench seat which is able to accommodate three people, including the pilot. Dual controls are optional.

The simply constructed tailboom is made of beaded light-alloy sheet and does not contain internal stiffeners. The fuselage is also of light alloy.

The light-alloy tail rotor is protected from 'grounding' by a tail skid. The tail rotor, vital to the control of the aircraft, is one of the most vulnerable parts of a helicopter.

Hiller vertical risers

■ **UH-5:** Hiller's first helicopter with a main rotor/tail rotor configuration, the UH-5 also saw the first use of its 'Rotor-Matic' control system.

■ **HJ-1 HORNET:** Twelve of these two-seat ramjet-powered helicopters were built, plus a further 12 for the US Army as the YH-32.

■ **FH-1100:** Hiller's attempt to build a machine to rival the Bell JetRanger and Hughes 500 was derived from the unsuccessful military OH-5.

■ **X-18:** This unusual machine was flown in 1959 to test the practicality of tilt-wing aircraft. It was short-lived and the results were inconclusive.

ACTION DATA

MAXIMUM SPEED

Speeds around 160 km/h (100 m.p.h.) were typical for the first mass-produced light helicopters. Bell's Sioux was widely used by US forces; the Mi-1 was an early product of the famous Mil factory.

H-23D RAVEN	153 km/h (95 m.p.h.)
H-13H SIOUX	161 km/h (100 m.p.h.)
Mi-1M 'HARE'	170 km/h (105 m.p.h.)

RANGE

The slightly larger Mi-1 had a considerably longer range than the two American types. This was largely due to the greater fuel capacity of the aircraft.

H-23D RAVEN 317 km (200 mi.)
H-13H SIOUX 383 km (240 mi.)
Mi-1M 'HARE' 620 km (385 mi.)

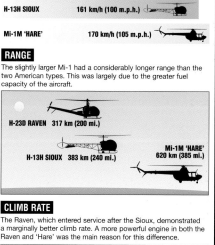

CLIMB RATE

The Raven, which entered service after the Sioux, demonstrated a marginally better climb rate. A more powerful engine in both the Raven and 'Hare' was the main reason for this difference.

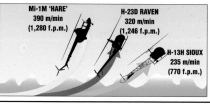

Mi-1M 'HARE' 390 m/min (1,280 f.p.m.)
H-23D RAVEN 320 m/min (1,246 f.p.m.)
H-13H SIOUX 235 m/min (770 f.p.m.)

HUGHES

OH-6 CAYUSE

● Vietnam veteran ● Hundreds in service ● Top-secret missions

Hughes overcame competition from Bell and Hiller to win a contract for the US Army's new LOH (light observation helicopter). The OH-6 went on to become the US Army's primary observation helicopter in Vietnam. Although some problems were encountered during the OH-6's production, new variants based on the civil Model 500 found success. Recently, the aircraft has been tasked with a new role, flying special forces missions with the US Army.

▲ Well-armed, small and agile, the OH-6A performed well in Vietnam. Many Cayuses have been exported and the Model 500 has breathed new life into the series.

HUGHES OH-6 CAYUSE

▼ Post-war service
OH-6As which survived the Vietnam War were passed on to National Guard and Reserve units. Some were modified for special duties.

▲ 'People planks' and Special Forces
This MH-6H serves with the US Army's 160th Special Operations Air Regiment (SOAR). It is able to carry personnel on the 'people planks'.

▼ Testing time in the navy
Four ex-US Army OH-6As are on loan to the US Navy Test Pilots' School at Patuxent River. They are used to give students light helicopter experience.

▲ Armed for support
AH-6Gs are not used as traditional gunships. They are most likely to lend fire support to a covert mission if it is compromised and attacked.

No tail rotor (NOTAR) ▶
McDonnell Douglas' NOTAR concept allows operations from tight spots, but with the cost of diminished speed and increased fuel consumption.

FACTS AND FIGURES

➤ For observation duties the US Army received 1,434 Cayuses from an originally planned 4,000.

➤ The first service OH-6s were delivered to the US Army in September 1965.

➤ Soldiers nicknamed the OH-6 'Loach' because of its LOH role designation.

➤ Cayuse and Model 500 variants serve in Japan, where some are dubbed 'chisai baggu' (little bug).

➤ In Vietnam damaged Cayuses numbered 420; many were returned to flying status.

➤ McDonnell Douglas still produces civil helicopters inspired by the OH-6 design.

PROFILE

Cayuse for the aerial cavalry

Seeking a replacement for its first-generation Bell and Hiller types, the US Army issued a requirement for a high-performance, easily maintained and cost-effective observation helicopter. After announcing the OH-6A Cayuse as the winner, the Army received its first in September 1965 and the helicopter soon went into combat in Vietnam.

Hughes struggled to meet the pressures of wartime production and, with Bell offering its improved OH-58A Kiowa in a renewed competition, manufacture of the OH-6A was prematurely terminated after 1,434 had been completed.

Hughes also developed a civilian variant of the OH-6A, the Model 500. This machine went on to spawn a range of new military helicopters, including a family of special operations variants. These

black-painted MH- and AH-6s were first used in the 1983 US invasion of Grenada and later in the Gulf. Their operations are kept highly secret.

Left: With its small-diameter, four-bladed main rotor, the OH-6A was ideal for riverine support operations in the jungles of Vietnam.

Right: A tight formation of four Cayuses flies before a setting sun. The aircraft is far from being in the twilight of its career.

OH-6A Cayuse

Type: light observation helicopter

Powerplant: one 237-kW (318-hp.) Allison T63-A-5A turboshaft engine derated to 160 kW (214 hp.) for continuous running and 188 kW (252 hp.) for take-off

Maximum speed: 241 km/h (150 m.p.h.)

Economic cruising speed: 216 km/h (134 m.p.h.) at sea level

Range: 611 km (380 mi.) at 1525 m (5000 ft.)

Weights: empty equipped 557 kg (1,228 lb.); maximum take-off 1225 kg (2,700 lb.)

Armament: one XM27 7.62-mm machine-gun or XM-75 40-mm grenade-launcher; provision for two M60 7.62-mm machine-guns

Accommodation: one pilot and one observer plus up to four passengers, or one pilot and one medic and up to two stretchers

Dimensions:
main rotor diameter	8.03 m (26 ft. 4 in.)
fuselage length	7.01 m (23 ft.)
height	2.48 m (8 ft. 2 in.)
main rotor disc area	50.60 m² (555 sq. ft.)

OH-6A CAYUSE

'Loaches' served in huge numbers in Vietnam, where 658 were lost in combat and a further 297 in accidents. Non-standard markings were a feature of operations in Southeast Asia.

With its four-bladed main rotor, the OH-6A has excellent control response and little vibration at high speeds. The rotor is also of small diameter – a feature useful among the tree-tops of Vietnam.

Each of the rotor blades is attached to the one opposite by 15 flexible stainless steel straps. Up to six can fail before a blade is lost.

The Cayuse has excellent all-round vision, with only a small blindspot to the rear.

In the event of a crash the tailboom and engine separate from the crew compartment, improving the survival chances of the crew.

Mounted in the rear fuselage at an angle of 45°, the T63 turboshaft engine drives the main rotor and tail rotors from a single shaft. A bevel gear splits the drive from this and transfers it to the respective rotor shafts.

In its YOH-6A prototype form the Cayuse did not have a vertical tailfin. Production aircraft feature a fin above and below the tail boom, with the upper fin braced to the angled side fin.

A maximum of five people can be carried by the OH-6A. In combat the aircraft seldom carried such a load, however, and was usually flown with a crew of two or three.

UNITED STATES ARMY 16208

COMBAT DATA

MAXIMUM SPEED

The OH-6A is faster than its close contemporary the Aérospatiale SA 318C Alouette II. Although the more recent Gazelle AH.Mk 1 has greater speed still, it is vulnerable in combat.

OH-6A CAYUSE 241 km/h (150 m.p.h.)
GAZELLE AH.Mk 1 310 km/h (193 m.p.h.)
SA 318C ALOUETTE II 205 km/h (127 m.p.h.)

CLIMB RATE

The OH-6A and Alouette II are closely matched in terms of climb rate. The Gazelle can climb faster, but over the battlefield agility and survivability are more important.

SA 318C ALOUETTE II 396 m/min (1300 f.p.m.)
GAZELLE AH.Mk 1 540 m/min (1772 f.p.m.)
OH-6A CAYUSE 381 m/min (1,250 f.p.m.)

RANGE

Comparatively short range is perhaps the one weak point of the OH-6A. In Vietnam the aircraft frequently flew from forward bases, so range was less of a problem. And in operations since then, the Army has operated them from US Navy ships and covert bases.

OH-6A CAYUSE 611 km (380 mi.)
GAZELLE AH.Mk 1 670 km (416 mi.)
SA 318C ALOUETTE II 720 km (447 mi.)

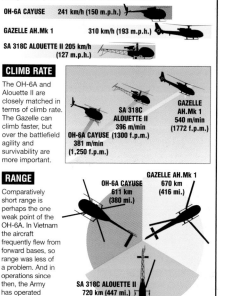

Suppression and insertion

From Vietnam to the Gulf, the 'Loach' and its descendants have proved highly capable combat helicopters.

VIETNAM OPS: Operations in Vietnam typically involved engagements with Viet Cong troops at less than tree-top height.

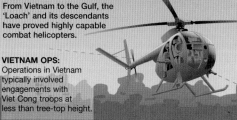

FIRE SUPPORT: Rocket and gun-armed AH-6Gs of the US Army's 160th SOAR fly in support of insertion/exfiltration missions by the same unit's MH-6Hs. The AH-6Gs also provides support for pre-placed special forces teams.

INSERTION FROM THE PLANK: With a 'people plank' on either side of its fuselage, the MH-6H is able to drop or pick up two personnel extremely rapidly. Some sources claim that the 'plank' can also be used as a sniper platform.

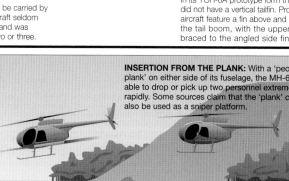

HUGHES/SCHWEIZER
300/TH-55 OSAGE

● Lightweight helicopter ● Police operations ● Military trainer

▲ The success of the Model 269/300 family paved the way for the Model 369/500 design, which placed Hughes among the world's leading producers of light helicopters.

I n 1948 the Hughes Aircraft Company began specialising in helicopters. Its second design, the Model 269/300, served as the basis for one of the most successful families of light helicopters. Having evaluated five examples as potential observation aircraft in 1958, the US Army adopted this simply constructed two-seater as its standard primary helicopter trainer in the 1960s. Hughes went on to build nearly 3,000 for both civil and military users.

HUGHES/SCHWEIZER 300/TH-55 OSAGE

▼ Traffic watching
Robust and fuel-efficient, the 300 is an ideal machine for monitoring traffic conditions.

▲ Police service
More than 17 US city police departments have operated the Model 300 as a relatively economical surveillance platform. The 300 has also proved its military potential in the training role.

◄ Over California
A lieutenant from Whittier, California, keeps in touch with a police department 300.

▼ In the US Army
The Osage provided experience for the first generation of US Army chopper pilots.

▲ Schweizer production
By the time Schweizer began building Hughes 300s in July 1983, more than 2,800 had been built.

FACTS AND FIGURES

➤ Schweizer Aircraft bought the entire Model 300 programme in 1986; its 500th 300C was delivered in 1994.

➤ In 1996 a Model 300C training helicopter was priced at $187,500.

➤ Iraq acquired 30 Model 300Cs for crop-dusting, but used them for pilot training.

➤ In 1996 12 nations operated military Model 269s, including Indonesia, North Korea, Pakistan, Paraguay and Honduras.

➤ Kawasaki assembled 38 TH-55As as TH-55Js for the JGSDF.

➤ Schweizer builds a turbine development of the Model 300 – the Model 330.

PROFILE

Hughes' first successful chopper

Designated TH-55A Osage, the Hughes Model 269A-1 was delivered to the US Army after being selected in 1964. The Osage was a refinement of the civil Model 200 Utility, which was derived from the original Model 269 that had first flown in October 1966.

The next major variant was the three-seater Model 300 (269B), which, with an uprated Lycoming engine, became the Model 300C in 1969. This was the most widely produced version, with more than 1,000 being built by Hughes. Licence production was also undertaken by BredaNardi in Italy, as the NH-300C.

Popular with civil operators, the Model 300 has being used for roles as diverse as crop-spraying and policing duties. For the latter, the Hughes 300C Sky Knight, with a public address system and an infra-red sensor, was introduced.

In military service, several countries have adopted the type, principally for pilot training. TH-55As were supplied to Algeria, Haiti, Nigeria, Spain (designated HE.20s) and Sweden (as Hkp 5Bs). Other nations have acquired Model 300s, including Colombia and Japan.

Having acquired the programme from Hughes' new owners, McDonnell Douglas, in 1986, Schweizer introduced a new TH-300C trainer variant. Turkey was an early customer.

Above: This Hughes 300, based at Lakewood, Los Angeles, is fitted with a searchlight, a siren and warning light. Police versions often carry armour.

Below: For agricultural operations, the Hughes 300 often carries a crop-spraying or dry powder dispersal kit. Stetcher kits, cargo racks and slings may also be fitted.

Model 300C

Type: three-seat light utility/training helicopter

Powerplant: one 168-kW (225-hp.) Textron Lycoming HIO-360-D1A piston engine derated to 142 kW (190 hp.)

Max cruising speed: 153 km/h (95 m.p.h.)

Endurance: 3 hours 24 min at sea level

Initial climb rate: 229 m/min (751 f.p.m.) at sea level

Range: 360 km (225 mi.) at 124 km/h (77 m.p.h.) at 1220 m (4,000 ft.)

Weights: empty 474 kg (1,043 lb.); maximum take-off 930 kg (2,046 lb.), with external load of 975 kg (2,145 lb.)

Dimensions:
rotor diameter	8.18 m (26 ft. 10 in.)
fuselage length	9.4 m (22 ft. 2 in.)
height	2.66 m (8 ft. 9 in.)
rotor disc area	52.50 m² (565 sq. ft.)

The Hughes 300 series tail rotor is of the teetering type, with just two blades freely pivoted as one unit. Each comprises a steel tube spar with glass-fibre skin. A spring-mounted bumper protects the blades.

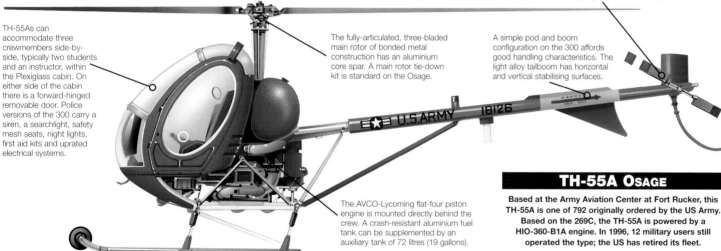

TH-55As can accommodate three crewmembers side-by-side, typically two students and an instructor, within the Plexiglass cabin. On either side of the cabin there is a forward-hinged removable door. Police versions of the 300 carry a siren, a searchlight, safety mesh seats, night lights, first aid kits and uprated electrical systems.

The fully-articulated, three-bladed main rotor of bonded metal construction has an aluminium core spar. A main rotor tie-down kit is standard on the Osage.

A simple pod and boom configuration on the 300 affords good handling characteristics. The light alloy tailboom has horizontal and vertical stabilising surfaces.

The AVCO-Lycoming flat-four piston engine is mounted directly behind the crew. A crash-resistant aluminium fuel tank can be supplemented by an auxiliary tank of 72 litres (19 gallons).

U.S.ARMY 18126

TH-55A OSAGE

Based at the Army Aviation Center at Fort Rucker, this TH-55A is one of 792 originally ordered by the US Army. Based on the 269C, the TH-55A is powered by a HIO-360-B1A engine. In 1996, 12 military users still operated the type; the US has retired its fleet.

ACTION DATA

NEVER-EXCEED SPEED

Never-exceed speed, or velocity (Vne), is greater than the true maximum safe speed of the aircraft. The older Series 300C is slower than its more recent, aerodynamically efficient and stronger counterparts, the Robinson R22 and Enstrom F-28F.

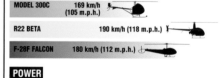

MODEL 300C	169 km/h (105 m.p.h.)
R22 BETA	190 km/h (118 m.p.h.)
F-28F FALCON	180 km/h (112 m.p.h.)

POWER

The Hughes 300 has more power than the smaller, but more recent, R22. Also flown by police forces, the Enstrom has the same powerplant as the Hughes, albeit turbocharged, and the 300C has its motor derated to 142 kW (190 hp.).

MODEL 300C	R22 BETA	F-28F FALCON
168 kW (225 hp.)	119 kW (160 hp.)	168 kW (225 hp.)

CLIMB RATE

The Hughes 300C lags behind in this category, but performed well against its 1960s contemporaries. For the military training role, as well as crop-dusting and observation, the practicality and economy of operation are more important factors.

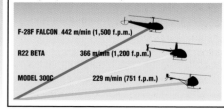

F-28F FALCON	442 m/min (1,500 f.p.m.)
R22 BETA	366 m/min (1,200 f.p.m.)
MODEL 300C	229 m/min (751 f.p.m.)

Piston-engined military training helicopters

■ **BELL MODEL 47:** Bell's Model 47 Sioux first flew in 1945, was used by at least 30 air arms. It stayed in production until 1974.

■ **HILLER UH-12:** A contemporary of the 300, more than 2,200 UH-12s were built. Military operators included the Royal Navy.

■ **ROBINSON R22:** Designed in the late 1970s, the R22 was bought by only one military customer, the Turkish army.

■ **SAUNDERS-ROE SKEETER:** Designed by Cierva, the two-seat Gipsy Major-powered Skeeter served with both Britain and Germany.

KAMAN

H-43 HUSKIE

● Intermeshing rotor ● Firefighter ● Rescue

D eveloped in the 1950s, the
box-shaped HH-43 Huskie provided
the US Air Force with a helicopter
that was able to put out fires and perform
rescues. In its role as a local airbase
firefighter, the Huskie was very effective.
Built with the twin-meshing rotors that are
the signature of inventor and entrepreneur
Charles Kaman, the Huskie ended its career
in the Vietnam War.

▲ Charles Kaman invented his
intermeshing rotor design using tools at home,
and the system remains unique. The concept
has most recently been rejuvenated in the
company's K-Max utility transport helicopter.

KAMAN H-43 HUSKIE

▼ Huskie rescue
When flying aircrew rescue sorties in Vietnam, the
Huskie was painted in camouflage. Due to the
H-43's limited range, it was generally used only
over South Vietnam, although its small size allowed
it to operate in small jungle clearings.

▲ Firefighter
With its underslung load of firefighting chemicals
contained in a special tank and fully-equipped
firefighters in the rear cabin, the Huskie was
effective in the airfield firefighting role.

◀ Delta delivery
Huskies were used over the
Mekong Delta area of South
Vietnam, operating in a support
role for the US Navy's inshore
PBR (Patrol Boat, River) force.

▼ Red fins
Huskies based in friendly territory
wore bright 'rescue' colours. The
rotors could be stored in the 'fore
and aft' position to save space.

▲ Box body
The advantage of the Kaman
rotor system is that the
helicopter does not require a
tail rotor, so it can be designed
with a capacious interior.

FACTS AND FIGURES

➤ Ex-US Huskies have served with the
air forces of Burma, Colombia, Morocco,
Pakistan and Thailand.

➤ The Huskie established seven world
records using its T53-1 engine.

➤ The first flight of the prototype in this
series took place on 13 December 1958.

➤ The USAF received 263 Huskies
(18 H-43As, 203 HH-43Bs and
42 HH-43Fs) between 1958 and 1968.

➤ The rescue hoist of the Huskie has a
capacity of 272 kg for lifting personnel.

➤ A few civilian Huskies remain in use
undertaking logging operations.

PROFILE

Two rotors are better than one

Best known for its service with the US Air Force, this fine helicopter began in the late-1950s as a US Navy training and observation craft. The Huskie was created to help the Air Force to deal with accidents and fires on its airfields.

Speed and range were not important. What mattered was the ability of this helicopter to spring quickly into action, to maintain a stable hover, and to carry firefighting and rescue equipment. The Huskie was also fitted with a pair of loudspeaker horns, which were used to transmit directions during a firefighting emergency.

The two pilots of the HH-43 had almost unprecedented visibility through the Plexiglass cockpit. And the Huskie gave the pilot a degree of responsiveness and stability not found on many helicopters.

Typically, the Huskie also carried two para-jumpers (known as PJs), who were trained in medical treatment and rescue work. As the US's role in Vietnam grew, the Huskie's job of local airbase rescue was expanded and a number flew missions behind enemy lines.

Left: The Huskie crew often had to operate under dangerous and terrifying conditions. This burning C-97 was part of a training session, but the H-43 tackled many other fires for real.

Right: One of the H-43's many unusual features was the exhaust boom that projected over the tail to keep the rear door area safe.

H-43B Huskie

Type: three-place rescue helicopter

Powerplant: one 615-kW (825-hp.) Avco Lycoming T53-L-1B turboshaft engine

Maximum speed: 165 km/h (102 m.p.h.)

Range: 560 km (350 mi.)

Service ceiling: 7740 m (25,400 ft.)

Weights: empty 2095 kg (4,609 lb.); loaded 4150 kg (9,130 lb.)

Accommodation: useful load of 2054 kg (4,520 lb.) including crew, passengers and rescue/ firefighting equipment; seating for eight passengers, 12 combat troops on folding seats, or four stretchers and a medical attendant

Dimensions:
main rotor diameter	14.55 m (47 ft. 9 in.)
length	7.8 m (25 ft. 7 in.)
height	3.88 m (12 ft. 9 in.)
rotor disc area	52.49 m² (565 sq. ft.)

Unusually, the Huskie had wooden main rotor blades. These were attached to the rotor head only by dragging hinges.

H-43 HUSKIE

Pakistan operated six Huskies, none of which remains in service. The H-43 was also exported to Burma (12), Columbia (six), Morocco (four) and Thailand (three).

The H-43 was powered by a T53 turboshaft engine. When one of the first Kaman K-225s (developed from the H-43) was fitted with a Boeing YT 50 engine, it became the world's first gas-turbine-powered helicopter.

The H-43 had twin rotors on different shafts, with the rotors turning in an intermeshing pattern.

Each rotor blade has a servo-flap which makes the cyclic pitch changes by twisting the blade.

Despite its unorthodox rotor system, the H-43 had conventional helicopter controls consisting of cyclic and collective pitch levers. Visibility from the cockpit was excellent.

Huskies had an unusual undercarriage system of four struts fitted with wheels and skis. The forward struts were longer than the rear ones, giving the H-43 a tail-down appearance on the ground.

Similar to the Kamov twin-rotor designs, the H-43 had large, wide fins at the rear for directional control.

Fire crews or cargo could be loaded through the wide twin clamshell doors. The main fuel supply of 755 litres (200 gallons) of kerosene was stored under the cabin floor.

PAKISTAN AIR FORCE HH-43F 62-4556B B 4556

COMBAT DATA

MAXIMUM SPEED

The Huskie has the least-impressive top speed of these three similarly sized aircraft. The Kamov Ka-25 is also a twin-rotor helicopter but uses two co-axial rotors. The SH-2G is the most modern of the three and, like the Ka-25, is turboshaft-powered.

H-43B HUSKIE	165 km/h (102 m.p.h.)
Ka-25 'HORMONE'	209 km/h (129 m.p.h.)
SH-2G SEASPRITE	256 km/h (159 m.p.h.)

PAYLOAD

The powerful H-43 has the most impressive load-carrying capacity. This is especially noteworthy given its modest power compared to the other types. Speed and range were never important considerations in the Huskie's design.

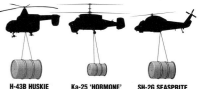

H-43B HUSKIE	Ka-25 'HORMONE'	SH-2G SEASPRITE
2054 kg (4,520 lb.)	1300 kg (2,860 lb.)	1814 kg (4,000 lb.)

RANGE

The Kamov Ka-25 is hampered by its lack of range, and the more recent Seasprite has twice the range of the Russian machine. The H-43 is similarly short on range, but in its given role this was not as important. Responsiveness, stability and its lifting ability were more important in the air rescue role.

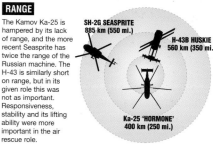

SH-2G SEASPRITE 885 km (550 mi.)
H-43B HUSKIE 560 km (350 mi.)
Ka-25 'HORMONE' 400 km (250 mi.)

Huskie missions

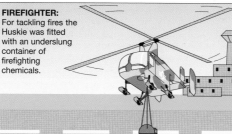

NAVAL SUPPORT: Huskies were used in support of the 'brown water navy', the force of patrol craft deployed in the Mekong Delta area of South Vietnam. The helicopter usually carried door guns for these missions, as Viet Cong snipers were a threat.

FIREFIGHTER: For tackling fires the Huskie was fitted with an underslung container of firefighting chemicals.

JUNGLE RESCUE: Confined to the southern half of the country, the H-43 carried out numerous rescues at the scene of crashed aircraft in Vietnam.

KAMAN

SH-2 SEASPRITE

● Anti-submarine ● Search and rescue ● Anti-patrol vessel

Kaman's SH-2F Seasprite and SH-2G Super Seasprite are the current models of a sturdy, versatile helicopter that has been a familiar sight on the world's oceans for four decades. Originally a Vietnam-era rescue helicopter hampered by limited range, this Kaman design has shown extraordinary growth potential. New engines and systems have kept the SH-2 up-to-date and make it a formidable anti-submarine weapon.

▲ Kaman's Seasprite is an unremarkable but enduring design that has given excellent service for nearly four decades. Fulfilling roles as varied as combat search and rescue and anti-submarine patrol, the Seasprite may still remain in service well past 2010.

KAMAN SH-2 SEASPRITE

▼ Watching the Soviets
The SH-2 was often used to shadow Soviet naval auxiliaries, like this research vessel of the Pacific fleet in the Sea of Japan. The SH-2 could detect ships with its own radar, or by homing in on their radar emissions.

LAMPS ▶
The original H-2 was upgraded to Light Airborne Multi-Purpose System standard in 1969/70 with major avionics improvements.

▲ Torpedo attack
The Seasprite's main anti-submarine weapon is the homing torpedo. Having located the target with sonar buoys or magnetic detection equipment, the weapon is released. The SH-2G will carry the new lightweight and more capable Mk 50 torpedo.

Modernised ▶
Current SH-2Gs are fitted with improved T700 turboshafts and composite rotor blades, and are painted grey.

▲ In the hangar
With rotors stowed away the SH-2 could fit in the hangar of frigates such as the 'Knox' class, originally designed to carry a drone helicopter.

FACTS AND FIGURES

➤ Early Seasprite models were rebuilt in Connecticut to become advanced SH-2Fs and SH-2Gs.

➤ The Seasprite helicopter known as HU2K-1 first flew on 2 July 1959.

➤ Egypt bought the SH-2F, and the SH-2G has been selected by the Australian navy.

➤ Kaman is flying an SH-2F with the company's Magic Lantern anti-ship mine detector housed in a pod.

➤ The first flight of the new SH-2G took place on 28 December 1989.

➤ Turkey received 14 surplus SH-2Fs under an agreement proposed in 1994.

PROFILE

Sub-chasing Seasprite

The Seasprite and SH-2G Super Seasprite are the only helicopters from Charles Kaman's Connecticut company that do not use the famous inventor's twin meshing rotors having instead a conventional single-rotor system.

The Seasprite first flew in 1959 and entered service in the 1960s as a ship-launched US Navy rescue and utility helicopter. An early Seasprite flew a dramatic mission on 19 June 1968, when Commander Clyde Lassen went deep into North Vietnam under heavy fire to rescue a downed Phantom crewman; he was one of only two US naval aviators to be awarded the Medal of Honor in that conflict.

In the 1970s and 1980s, the single-engine craft with three-bladed rotors evolved into a twin-engine helicopter with four-bladed rotors and considerable anti-submarine capability. Today's more powerful, better-equipped SH-2G Super Seasprite is perhaps not quite in the class of the newer Sikorsky SH-60B Sea Hawk, but it is a weapon that no submarine skipper can ignore. SH-2F and SH-2G helicopters serve with half-a-dozen air arms outside the United States.

Clearly visible on the starboard sponson of this SH-2G is the ASQ-81 magnetic anomaly detector 'bird'.

The Seasprite has emergency flotation devices for ditching in calm water.

SH-2 Seasprite

Powerplant: two 1285-kW (1,722-hp.) General Electric T700-GE-401/403C; SH-2F has two 1007-kW (1,343-hp.) T58-GE-8F turboshafts

Max speed: 265 km/h (164 m.p.h.) at sea level

Max cruising speed: 230 km/h (143 m.p.h.)

Range: 679 km (421 mi.)

Service ceiling: 5670 m (18,598 ft.)

Weights: empty 3193 kg (7,025 lb.); maximum take-off 6033 kg (13,273 lb.)

Armament: up to two Mk 46 or Mk 50 lightweight torpedoes; 7.62-mm machine-gun may be pintle-mounted in each doorway; the SH-2G can carry the AGM-65 Maverick air-to-ground missile

Dimensions:
rotor diameter	13.51 m (44 ft.)
length	16.08 m (53 ft.)
height	4.58 m (15 ft.)
rotor disc area	143.41 m² (1,543 sq. ft.)

SH-2F SEASPRITE

This SH-2F served with HSL-33 of the US Navy. The variant is rapidly being replaced by the modified SH-2G aboard US Navy frigates and destroyers.

The main improvement of the SH-2G is the replacement of the old T-58 turboshaft with more efficient T700 engines. These deliver about 10 per cent more power and use about 20 per cent less fuel.

The SH-2F used a conventional aluminium spar and fibreglass covered rotor blade, replaced by long-life composite blades in the SH-2G.

Originally painted dark blue with large national and unit markings, all SH-2s are now receiving a light sea-grey scheme and toned-down national markings.

The cockpit accommodates the pilot and co-pilot. The rear compartment houses a systems officer who operates a tactical navigation system and sensor suite.

A Litton LN 66 search radar for detecting surface ships and submarine periscopes and snort masts was fitted. Updated SH-2s have an undernose infra-red turret.

The undercarriage retracts into fairings in the side of the fuselage.

The Mk 46 homing torpedo is the standard NATO anti-submarine air-launched torpedo. Developments in Soviet submarine hull technology have meant that it is now almost obsolete. The SH-2G has recently been cleared to fire the AGM-65 Maverick missile for anti-ship operations.

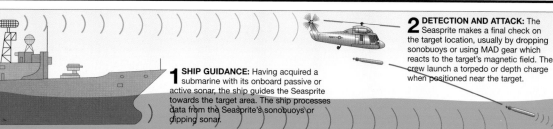

Attacking submarines from small ships

1 SHIP GUIDANCE: Having acquired a submarine with its onboard passive or active sonar, the ship guides the Seasprite towards the target area. The ship processes data from the Seasprite's sonobuoys or dipping sonar.

2 DETECTION AND ATTACK: The Seasprite makes a final check on the target location, usually by dropping sonobuoys or using MAD gear which reacts to the target's magnetic field. The crew launch a torpedo or depth charge when positioned near the target.

3 TARGET SUBMARINE: The Mk 46 torpedo makes a spiral search pattern to acquire the target, using active and passive homing.

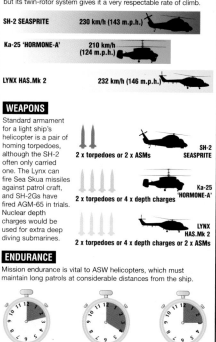

COMBAT DATA

MAXIMUM CRUISING SPEED

Anti-submarine helicopters do not need to travel at high speed. The Ka-25 is slower than the Seasprite due to its bulky shape, but its twin-rotor system gives it a very respectable rate of climb.

SH-2 SEASPRITE 230 km/h (143 m.p.h.)

Ka-25 'HORMONE-A' 210 km/h (124 m.p.h.)

LYNX HAS.Mk 2 232 km/h (146 m.p.h.)

WEAPONS

Standard armament for a light ship's helicopter is a pair of homing torpedoes, although the SH-2 often only carried one. The Lynx can fire Sea Skua missiles against patrol craft, and SH-2Gs have fired AGM-65 in trials. Nuclear depth charges would be used for extra deep diving submarines.

SH-2 SEASPRITE 2 x torpedoes or 2 x ASMs

Ka-25 'HORMONE-A' 2 x torpedoes or 4 x depth charges

LYNX HAS.Mk 2 2 x torpedoes or 4 x depth charges or 2 x ASMs

ENDURANCE

Mission endurance is vital to ASW helicopters, which must maintain long patrols at considerable distances from the ship.

SH-2 SEASPRITE	Ka-25 'HORMONE-A'	LYNX HAS.Mk 2
2½ hours	4 hours	3 hours

KAMAN

K-MAX

● Twin-engined 'flying crane' ● Single-seater ● Intermeshed rotors

▲ 'WARNING: APPROACH FROM FRONT' reads the legend below the aircraft's rotor. While on the ground, the intermeshed rotors pass much lower than those on conventional helicopters.

Charles Kaman launched his helicopter company in 1945 when he was 26 years old. The K-MAX is the latest product from this now elderly trailblazer. The last living aviation pioneer of the 20th century, Kaman's principal contribution was the intermeshing rotor arrangement that dispenses with the need for a tail rotor. This arrangement is used on the K-MAX, known as the 'aerial truck', a machine capable of lifting almost 3 tonnes.

PHOTO FILE

KAMAN K-MAX

Sales in Europe ▶
Helog of Switzerland became the first European K-MAX operator in May 1995, when this colourful example was delivered. Others have been delivered to France and Sweden.

◀ Versatility
Without a tail rotor, the K-MAX is able to manoeuvre into tight spots otherwise inaccessible to conventional helicopter designs.

▲ Slim profile
In this view of a Helog aircraft with an underslung load, the slim frontal profile of the design is seen. Angled cockpit windows give the pilot an excellent view.

▲ Connecticut factory
Pilots are trained using ex-military Kaman HH-43F Huskie helicopters. H-43s have a similar intermeshing rotor system.

◀ Prototype N3182T
In December 1991 the first K-MAX took to the air. This aircraft consisted of the basic airframe structure without a tailplane and fins.

FACTS AND FIGURES

➤ The K-MAX was originally known as MMIRA (pronounced 'Myra') for Multi-Mission Intermeshing Rotor Aircraft.

➤ The US Navy evaluated the type for use in resupplying warships at sea.

➤ In 1996 the price for one of these helicopters was $3.5 million.

➤ The K-MAX was the first helicopter structurally designed for repetitive external lift operations.

➤ Production rate at Kaman's Connecticut factory in 1996 was six per year.

➤ Kaman claims a 20-year life for K-MAX's airframe, at 1,000 hours per year.

PROFILE

Kaman's unique 'aerial truck'

Above: This view of the inside of the Kaman factory shows the light alloy construction of a partly completed K-MAX.

Above: Kaman's helicopter designs have been intended to fill market niches. The company's vast experience with intermeshing rotors benefited the K-MAX design.

When Charles Kaman revealed his company's K-MAX in March 1992, he signalled the introduction of a very special 'aerial truck' that has brought a revolution in the way helicopters handle cargo-hauling duties.

Kaman felt that the helicopter industry was focused on, and dominated by, 'people movers', the flying equivalent of the family car. Until the K-MAX, there were no helicopters designed specifically for operators wanting logging, fire-fighting, construction, and cargo-hauling capabilities in a purpose-built machine.

The K-MAX, described by its Connecticut manufacturer as 'an efficient lifting workhorse', was designed as a twin-engined, single-seat heavy hauler to provide unsurpassed visibility for its pilot and to set new low levels of maintenance and operating expenses. Kaman's intermeshing rotors mean that a conventional tail rotor is not required; this allows the aircraft to go into some otherwise dangerous or inaccessible locations.

First flown in late 1991, the K-MAX sold initially in the USA and Canada and has since found customers in Europe and Asia.

K-MAX

Type: single-seat external lift intermeshing-rotor helicopter

Powerplant: one 1118-kW (1,500-hp.) AlliedSignal T53-17A-1 turboshaft flat rated to 1007 kW (1,350 hp.)

Maximum speed: 185 km/h (115 m.p.h.) clean; 148 km/h (92 m.p.h.) with external load

Service ceiling: 7620 m (25,000 ft.) at 2722 kg (6,000 lb.) weight in standard atmospheric (ISA) conditions

Weights: operating empty 2132 kg (4,690 lb.); maximum take-off 2721 kg (6,000 lb.) without jettisonable load, 5216 kg (11,475 lb.) with external load

Dimensions:
rotor diameter (each)	14.73 m (48 ft. 4 in.)
length overall	15.85 m (52 ft.)
wheel track	3.56 m (11 ft. 8 in.)
wheelbase	4.11 m (13 ft. 6 in.)

AlliedSignal's (formerly Textron Lycoming's) T53-17A-1 turboshaft is a civil version of the military-specification T53 used in large numbers in aircraft like single-engined variants of the Bell UH-1 Iroquois.

Glass-fibre reinforced plastic (GFRP) and carbonfibre reinforced plastic (CFRP) are used in the construction of the rotor blades and tabs, for strength and lightness. Like the aircraft's engine (which is designed with a 10,000-hour life with a 1,500-hour time-between overhauls), these are designed to have a minimum maintenance requirement and therefore savings in operating costs.

K-MAX

First flown on 12 January 1994, N132KA was the first production K-MAX and the first of two leased to Oregon-based Erickson Air Crane on a $1,000 per hour, 1000 hours per year basis. Both aircraft were returned in 1995.

A narrow fuselage and cockpit means that the K-MAX is a single-seat aircraft. The pilot sits in an impact-absorbing seat with a five-point harness. The K-MAX was also designed for unmanned radio-controlled operation in hazardous conditions.

N132KA — ERICKSON AIR-CRANE

Constructed of light alloy, the K-MAX's airframe is both light and strong. The tail assembly weighs just 36.3 kg (80 lb.) and can be quickly removed by two people.

A wheeled tricycle undercarriage is a feature of the K-MAX and facilitates ground manoeuvring. Foot-operated brakes are standard. A 'bear paw' plate fits around each wheel for operations from soft ground.

ACTION DATA

MAXIMUM HOOK CAPACITY

The K-MAX is able to lift more than 2.7 tonnes on its single under-fuselage hook, thanks to its design which makes a higher proportion of the aircraft's engine power available for lifting. A minimal fuselage means that 'dead' weight is kept to a minimum.

K-MAX	W-3A SOKOL	TWIN TWO-TWELVE
2721 kg (6,000 lb.)	2100 kg (4,620 lb.)	2268 kg (5,000 lb.)

POWER

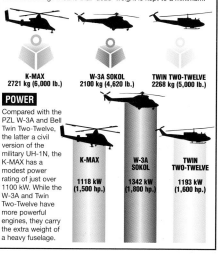

Compared with the PZL W-3A and Bell Twin Two-Twelve, the latter a civil version of the military UH-1N, the K-MAX has a modest power rating of just over 1100 kW. While the W-3A and Twin Two-Twelve have more powerful engines, they carry the extra weight of a heavy fuselage.

K-MAX	W-3A SOKOL	TWIN TWO-TWELVE
1118 kW (1,500 hp.)	1342 kW (1,800 hp.)	1193 kW (1,600 hp.)

Logging by K-MAX

OPERATION ROANOKE: As part of Kaman's type testing, two pilots from logging helicopter operators took part in a five-day test in Virginia.

MARCH 1994 TEST: Selectively cut trees over an area of 162000 m² (531,360 sq. ft.) of inaccessible hillside were lifted out in 40 hours of operations in sub-zero temperatures.

SUCCESS: Only 90 minutes of unscheduled maintenance was required after the test. Kaman claims that, at a rate of 30 return logging sorties per hour, the K-MAX will have an airframe life of 20,000 flight hours.

KAMOV

KA-25 'HORMONE'

● Twin-rotor submarine hunter ● Missile guidance platform

Bulky and square-shaped, the Ka-25 'Hormone' was developed by the Kamov design bureau in the late-1950s. Its Cold War task was to detect NATO submarines. This is one of the most challenging jobs of modern warfare, and although the chunky 'Hormone' is far from graceful it performs this duty with precision. Once a principal anti-submarine weapon in the Soviet Union, the 'Hormone' continues to serve Russia today.

▲ *Kamov's designs have not only been a success in operation, but have set world female-piloted payload and height records with instructors like Tatyana Zuyeva and Nadezhda Yeremina at the controls.*

KAMOV KA-25 'HORMONE'

From ship to shore ▶
With fewer Russian carriers in service now, many Ka-25s are confined to land bases. The pilots here are wearing special waterproof survival suits.

▲ Kamov's trademark
All Kamov helicopters have the twin-rotor layout. This needs no compensating tail rotor, and allows the design to be short and compact.

◀ Folded up
The large tapes holding down the rotor blades when the Ka-25 is stored on deck are essential to stop them flapping in the wind and hitting the airframe. They also allow tight storage on deck.

▼ More of the same from Kamov
The Ka-27 'Helix' is the successor to the Ka-25. Of similar dimensions and built along the same lines, it has twice the power and is a much more capable machine.

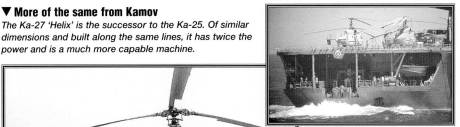

▲ Sub-chaser
The Ka-25 first went to sea aboard 'Moskva'-class helicopter-carrying cruisers. They operated from a large flight deck at the stern, beneath which was the ship's variable-depth sonar. This was used to locate enemy submarines at long ranges.

FACTS AND FIGURES

➤ About 400 aircraft, known in the West as 'Hormone-A', '-B' and '-C', were built.

➤ The Soviet Union constructed four 'Kiev'-class carriers which used 'Hormones' for anti-submarine warfare.

➤ This family of helicopters began with the Ka-20 'Harp', first flown in 1960.

➤ Not normally armed, the Ka-25 can carry bombs, depth charges or torpedoes.

➤ Only the 'Hormone-B' has retractable landing gear which can be lifted out of the scanning beam of the nose radar.

➤ The 'Hormone' is cluttered inside and does not give its crew room to stand.

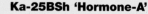

Kamov's pocket heavyweight

The Ka-25 family of shipborne helicopters have justified the faith placed by Nikolai Kamov's design bureau in contra-rotating helicopter rotors mounted on the same axis, a concept which eliminates the need for a tail rotor. The chunky Kamov design takes up far less space on deck than helicopters of more conventional configuration.

When used for anti-submarine warfare, the Ka-25 is readily identified by its chin-mounted radar, known in the West as 'Big Bulge'. It also carries a dipping sonar which is lowered into the sea from the hover, as well as electro-optical and magnetic-anomaly sensors. These have become the standard hi-tech tools used to seek and pinpoint an undersea vessel deep in its lair.

The Kamov Ka-25 was exported to India, Syria, Yugoslavia and Vietnam, and remains in use in these countries. When not used for anti-submarine work, the 'Hormone' can accommodate up to a dozen passengers, making it a useful utility transport and search-and-rescue machine.

The bulbous 'Big Bulge' radar is designed to pick out a submarine's periscope, or find ships for a missile attack.

The Ka-25 lowers its dipping sonar into the sea for an 'active' search. The 'Hormone' uses its passive sonobuoys for a first search, and then active sonar and magnetic anomaly detection in the closing stages of an attack.

Ka-25BSh 'Hormone-A'

Type: six-seat anti-submarine helicopter

Powerplant: two 671-kW (888-hp.) OMKB 'Mars' (Glushenkov) GTD-3F turboshafts in early helicopters; 738-kW (986 shp.) GTD-3BMs in later aircraft

Max speed: 210 km/h (130 m.p.h.) at sea level

Range: 650 km (250 mi.)

Weights: empty 4765 kg (10,500 lb.); loaded 7500 kg (15,875 lb.)

Armament: weapons are not normally carried; 'Hormones' detect submarines and provide guidance to ship-launched weapons

Dimensions:
rotor diameter	15.72 m (51 ft. 7 in.)
length	9.75 m (32 ft.)
height	5.37 m (17 ft. 7 in.)
rotor disc area	389.15 m² (4,190 sq. ft.)

KA-25 'HORMONE-C'

The Kamov Ka-25 'Hormone-C' is a dedicated search-and-rescue helicopter. The 'Hormone-C' remains in limited service, but is now being replaced by the Ka-27 'Helix'.

Ka-25s can fly on a single engine in an emergency.

The twin contra-rotating rotors on a single axis are characteristic of the Kamov design bureau. They offer significant advantages in a naval helicopter: most notably, since there is no need for a tail rotor, in overall compactness.

A rescue winch is mounted above the doors. It can lift a load of 300 kg 660 lb.), and is hydraulically driven.

The nose of the Ka-25 carries the 'Odd Rods' identification system, and some aircraft also have the 'Yagi' system for homing in on pilots' distress beacons.

The three tailfins help give stable hovering while the helicopter dips its sonar system.

The 'Hormone-C' has a large searchlight with an anti-glare shield to enable the crew to undertake night rescues.

All Kamov naval helicopters have wide, strong undercarriages – essential for shipborne operations.

The Ka-25's cabin is bigger than it looks, and can hold up to 12 people.

COMBAT DATA

CRUISING SPEED

Ka-25 'HORMONE'	190 km/h (130 m.p.h.)	
SH-2 SEASPRITE	220 km/h (136 m.p.h.)	
LYNX	230 km/h (143 m.p.h.)	

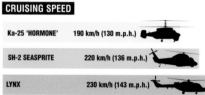

The 'Hormone' design dates basically from the late-1950s, and while it performs well enough it is not as fast as more recent and more powerful designs. The later Ka-27 is a much faster machine, with Lynx-like capability.

RANGE

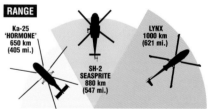

Ka-25 'HORMONE' 650 km (405 mi.)

LYNX 1000 km (621 mi.)

SH-2 SEASPRITE 880 km (547 mi.)

Helicopters do not have very great range, and naval machines are no exception. But they are fully capable of their main task, which is to extend the range of a warship's sensors and its anti-submarine and anti-ship weaponry out beyond the horizon, and stay on station to attack and hopefully kill the threat.

ARMAMENT

Unlike Western helicopters, the 'Hormone' was designed primarily as an unarmed sensor platform, leaving the mothership to engage the target. But it is capable of carrying a variety of lightweight torpedoes, missiles or depth charges.

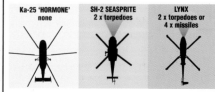

Ka-25 'HORMONE' none	SH-2 SEASPRITE 2 x torpedoes	LYNX 2 x torpedoes or 4 x missiles

Anti-submarine 'Hormones' in action

TARGET DETECTION: The 'Hormone' is equipped with a wide variety of detection systems. Among the most effective is the dipping sonar, a sensitive microphone on a long cable which can be lowered into the water to listen for hostile submarines.

ENGAGEMENT: 'Hormones' were not originally armed. However, they are able to carry a pair of lightweight homing torpedoes, with which they can mount attacks on submarines detected by their sensitive onboard systems.

KAMOV

KA-26 'HOODLUM'

● Co-axial rotor system ● Multi-role versatility ● Twin piston engines

First flown in 1965, the Ka-26 is widely used as an agricultural, ambulance, fire-fighting, survey and search and rescue helicopter. Its adaptability is largely a result of its unusual configuration. The piston engines are mounted on short wings and this allows a variety of payloads, including chemical spraying equipment, to be mounted aft of the enclosed cabin. It is a very compact design because the contra-rotating rotors mean that a tail rotor is not required.

▲ The layout of the Ka-26 'Hoodlum' has resulted in a practical helicopter which has sold well in at least 15 countries. It has a capacious fuselage and is easily adapted to different roles

PHOTO FILE

KAMOV KA-26 'HOODLUM'

▼ **Turboshaft conversion**
After developing the Ka-126, Kamov passed responsibility for the production to IAR in Romania. Some customers have had their older Ka-26s modified to Ka-126 standard.

▲ **Passenger pod**
This Ka-26, fitted with spraying equipment, is shown alongside the alternative passenger/ambulance pod and the flat cargo platform. Conversion between roles is very rapid.

▼ **Geological study**
When configured for geophysical prospecting, the Ka-26 carries a large ring which produces electro-magnetic pulses.

German Kamovs ▶
Ka-26s were in use in both East and West Germany before reunification. This example was operated by the East German airline Interflug for short-range passenger or cargo flights.

▲ **Compact people carrier**
Even when configured for the carriage of seven passengers, the Ka-26 is a remarkably small helicopter. Few Russian aircraft have been exported so successfully.

FACTS AND FIGURES

➤ Kamov announced the Ka-26 in 1964 and the aircraft entered large-scale agricultural use in the USSR in 1970.

➤ Search-and-rescue variants have a winch for towing rescue boats.

➤ Full instrumentation is provided for flying by day or night, and in all weathers.

➤ In 1962 Ka-26s joined other helicopters transporting demolition teams whose task was to keep Soviet rivers free of ice.

➤ A towed 'bird' receives reflections from the emitter of the prospecting version.

➤ All payloads are carried at the Ka-26's centre of gravity.

Kamov's agricultural export

The compact dimensions of the Ka-26 allow it to fly from small ships as well as from land bases. It has even been fitted with floats and flown as a spotter aircraft from fishing boats. Military versions, designated 'Hoodlum' by NATO, were delivered to Bulgaria and Hungary for border patrol and liaison, and others may also be in service with Benin and Russia.

In 1981 Kamov started work on a turbine-powered version of the Ka-26. The original scheme involved replacing the piston engines by two small turbines, but this was abandoned in favour of a single 537-kW TV-O-100 above the cabin.

One Ka-26 was used as a testbed for Kamov's jet thrust anti-torque system, which was similar to the NOTAR (no tail rotor) concept developed by McDonnell Douglas Helicopters. Kamov intended to use this system in the development of the Ka-118, which was planned as a five-seat business helicopter with just one main rotor.

By 1993 nearly 900 Ka-26s had been built and production was continuing at the Kumertaou Aviation Production Association. With its strength and versatility, the 'Hoodlum' is likely to remain in service for many years.

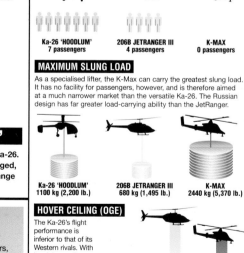

For crop-spraying the Ka-26 can carry 900 kg (200 lb.) of liquid, and when used as a duster capacity increases by 165 kg (360 lb.). Most Russian Ka-26s are used to treat orchards and vineyards.

Ka-26 'Hoodlum-A'

Type: general-purpose light helicopter

Powerplant: two 242.5-kW (325-hp.) Vedeneyev M-14V-26 nine-cylinder air-cooled radial piston engines

Maximum speed: 170 km/h (105 m.p.h.)

Range: 400 km (250 mi.) with seven passengers

Hover ceiling: 800 m (2,625 ft.) out of ground effect

Weights: empty in passenger configuration 2100 kg (4,620 lb.); maximum take-off 3250 kg (7,150 lb.)

Accommodation: pilot plus seven passengers, up to 1065 kg (2,340 lb.) of chemicals or cargo, or an 1100-kg (2,200-lb.) externally slung load

Dimensions:
rotor diameter	13 m (42 ft. 7 in.)
fuselage length	7.75 m (25 ft. 5. in.)
height	4.05 m (13 ft. 4 in.)
main rotor disc area	265.50 m² (871 sq. ft.)

The Ka-26 uses the co-axial contra-rotating rotor system which he had been used on the earlier Ka-25 'Hormone'.

Each of the air-cooled engines has a large fan fitted in the front of its nacelle. These ensure a sufficient supply of cooling air, even at slow airspeeds.

Kamov was one of the first helicopter manufacturers to use glass-reinforced plastic (GRP) rotor blades. They weigh only 25 kg (55 lb.) each and are de-iced by an alcohol-glycerine mixture.

Operations are normally flown by a single pilot but a second pilot or passenger can be seated in the cabin, which is lightly pressurised. Agricultural models have an air filter system which prevents chemicals from entering the cockpit.

Like the rotor blades, the tailbooms are manufactured largely from GRP. A tailplane is mounted at the rear of the booms and carries the twin endplate fins and rudders.

With its simple, but sturdy, four-leg undercarriage, the Ka-26 is able to carry a variety of payloads, attached directly to the fuselage between the rear legs. Only the rear wheels have brakes.

This detachable pod can accommodate six passengers. It has also been used to transport firemen and ice demolition teams.

Each of the fins is canted inwards at 15° and a large rudder is fitted to both. The external skin stiffening ribs on the tailplane are a characteristic feature of the Ka-26. They were previously used, but to a lesser extent, on the Ka-25.

KA-26 'HOODLUM-A'

Aeroflot has been a major user of the Ka-26. Very few military customers have emerged, but civilian operators appreciate the range of payload options available.

ACTION DATA

MAXIMUM PASSENGERS

Like the K-Max, the Ka-26 is used as a flying crane. The JetRanger III can also transport slung loads, but neither of the American helicopters can match the versatility of the Ka-26, which is able to carry seven passengers or fly as a crane.

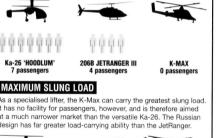

Ka-26 'HOODLUM' 7 passengers
206B JETRANGER III 4 passengers
K-MAX 0 passengers

MAXIMUM SLUNG LOAD

As a specialised lifter, the K-Max can carry the greatest slung load. It has no facility for passengers, however, and is therefore aimed at a much narrower market than the versatile Ka-26. The Russian design has far greater load-carrying ability than the JetRanger.

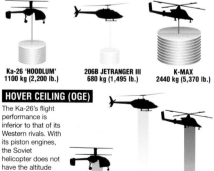

Ka-26 'HOODLUM' 1100 kg (2,200 lb.)
206B JETRANGER III 680 kg (1,495 lb.)
K-MAX 2440 kg (5,370 lb.)

HOVER CEILING (OGE)

The Ka-26's flight performance is inferior to that of its Western rivals. With its piston engines, the Soviet helicopter does not have the altitude capabilities of the turbine-engined machines. This poor performance led to development of the Ka-126.

Ka-26 'HOODLUM' 800 m (2,625 ft.)
206B JETRANGER III 2680 m (8,790 ft.)
K-MAX 2440 m (8,000 ft.)

Piston-powered crop-sprayers

■ BRANTLY-HYNES B-2: Typical of the older generation of helicopters which have found use as sprayers, the B-2 is a lightweight two-seater.

■ HILLER UH-12: Used for agricultural spraying and power line inspection, the UH-12 is a common sight around the world.

■ HUGHES 300: In 1983 Schweizer acquired all rights for the 300. It has since developed a turbine-engined version, the 330.

■ ROBINSON R22 BETA: As one of the world's most popular basic training helicopters, the R22 is only occasionally used for spraying.

KAMOV

KA-27/29/32 'HELIX'

● Anti-submarine ● Assault/electronic warfare ● Civil transport

Using two rotors spinning in opposite directions the Soviet Kamov design bureau dispensed with the tail rotor normally used to give directional stability in helicopters. The design enabled shorter rotor blades to be used, which made it suitable for use aboard ships. The 'Helix' series of helicopters, which includes anti-submarine, assault transport and search-and-rescue versions, have served aboard a variety of Soviet warships.

▲ The Kamov Ka-27 'Helix' has progressively replaced the Ka-25 aboard ships of the Russian navy. The service now operates the Ka-27PL ASW helicopter, the Ka-27PS for SAR and utility duties, the Ka-29 naval assault variant and the Ka-31 for electronic warfare duties.

KAMOV KA-27/29/32 'HELIX'

▼ Export utility helicopter
The Ka-32T is a simplified utility helicopter for the transport of passengers/freight for civilian operators. The 32T lacks radar and other avionics of the 32S.

Inside the 'Helix' ▲
The naval Ka-27 family carry a crew of three: a pilot, tactical co-ordinator and ASW systems operator (PL model) or winch operator (PS model).

◄ Co-axial transport
Three major civil variants of the 'Helix' exist, and are used in Russia and abroad. Aeroflot operates approximately 150 Ka-32s including 32K cranes.

▼ Assault helicopter
The Ka-29 'Helix-B' is a heavily armed dedicated naval assault transport.

Search and rescue ▲
The Russian navy operates the Ka-27PS for air-sea rescue, utility and guard aboard aircraft-carriers.

FACTS AND FIGURES

➤ Russian navy Ka-27PLs carry Kh-35 anti-ship missiles, the heaviest to be carried by any naval helicopter.

➤ Ka-32s are operated by Swiss mountain rescue teams.

➤ Kamov is the world's only firm to have ever mass-produced co-axial helicopters.

➤ When flown by a single crewmember the Ka-32 can be left on autopilot while the pilot operates a winch from the cabin.

➤ The Ka-32K is a special version with a crane under the fuselage.

➤ In New Zealand Ka-32s are used for logging in remote hill areas.

PROFILE

Kamov's multi-mission wonder

First flown in 1974, the Ka-27PL 'Helix-A' anti-submarine helicopter carries dipping sonar and sonobuoys to locate submarines by their noise and has a radar under the nose.

The Ka-27PS 'Helix-D' is the search-and-rescue version. It is equipped with a rescue winch and floodlights instead of the sonar equipment.

An export version, designated Ka-28, is used by the Indian and Yugoslav navies. The Ka-29 'Helix-D' is an assault transport designed to ferry troops ashore during amphibious landings. It has a new fuselage and is armed with rocket launchers on the wings, plus a retractable nose gun. There is also a civil transport version, the Ka-32 'Helix-C'.

The Ka-32T is a basic load-carrier and is able to carry a payload of 4000 kg (8,800 lb.) internally or 5000 kg (11,000 lb.) externally. The Ka-32S is equipped with a radar and was designed to operate from ice-breakers and over barren terrain. It is used for such tasks as ice patrol, oilrig support and maritime search and rescue in Russia's icy seas.

The flight deck of the Russian carrier Kuznetsov accommodates (left to right) a Yak-38 strike fighter, Ka-27PL ASW helicopter, Ka-29 assault transport and an electronic warfare Ka-31.

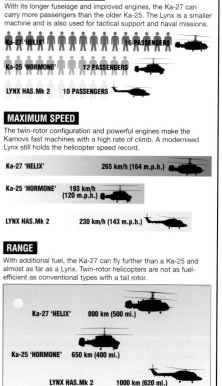

Ka-29 'Helix-B'

Type: maritime assault transport

Powerplant: two 1660-kW (2,225-hp.) Isotov TV3-117VK turboshaft engines

Maximum speed: 265 km/h (164 m.p.h.)

Maximum climb rate: 12.09 m/sec (40 f.p.s.) (inclined)

Combat radius: ferry range 800 km (500 mi.) with auxiliary fuel

Service ceiling: 4300 m (14,100 ft.)

Armament: one YakB-12 four-barrel 12.7-mm (.50-ca,.) machine-gun; one fuselage-mounted 30-mm 2A42 cannon; four pylons for gun pods, ASMs, rockets, fuel tanks or bombs

Dimensions:
rotor diameter	15.9 m (52 ft. 2 in.)
length	11.3 m (37 ft. 1 in.)
height	5.4 m (17 ft. 9 in.)
rotor disc area	198.60 m² (2,137 sq. ft.)

KA-29 'HELIX-B'

Shown here is one of the pre-production Ka-29s known as the Ka-27TB. The aircraft carries a non-standard flight instrumentation boom. Number 25 also lacks the fuselage mounted 30-mm gun.

The cabin door on the right of the Ka-29 does not slide as on other models, but hinges open rapidly for the 16 fully armed troops to disembark as quickly as possible. On the left side of the cabin there is now a sliding window where a light gun could be mounted.

The Ka-29 carries rocket pods, gun pods or guided missiles on its fuselage pylons.

The Ka-29 introduces a three-man side-by-side cockpit with a wider fuselage body as a result. The three flat front windscreen panels are bullet proof, and the cockpit is substantially armoured.

The two hydromechanically controlled Isotov turboshafts are uprated and heavily armoured to prevent any damage from enemy gunfire.

The nose contains retractable landing lamps, low-light television equipment, forward-looking infra-red and millimetric radar for use with anti-tank missiles.

Fixed armament on the Ka-29 consists of a four barrel 12.7-mm (.50-cal.) rotary machine-gun behind an articulated hatch inside the nose, and a starboard outrigger-mounted 30-mm single barrel cannon, with ammunition feed from the cabin.

Further protection is provided by flare and chaff cartridge launchers and the infra-red jammer above the fuselage. Production machines are likely to carry engine inlet filters and infra-red suppressors.

COMBAT DATA

MAXIMUM PASSENGERS

With its longer fuselage and improved engines, the Ka-27 can carry more passengers than the older Ka-25. The Lynx is a smaller machine and is also used for tactical support and naval missions.

Ka-27 'HELIX'	16 PASSENGERS
Ka-25 'HORMONE'	12 PASSENGERS
LYNX HAS.Mk 2	10 PASSENGERS

MAXIMUM SPEED

The twin-rotor configuration and powerful engines make the Kamovs fast machines with a high rate of climb. A modernised Lynx still holds the helicopter speed record.

Ka-27 'HELIX'	265 km/h (164 m.p.h.)
Ka-25 'HORMONE'	193 km/h (120 m.p.h.)
LYNX HAS.Mk 2	230 km/h (143 m.p.h.)

RANGE

With additional fuel, the Ka-27 can fly further than a Ka-25 and almost as far as a Lynx. Twin-rotor helicopters are not as fuel-efficient as conventional types with a tail rotor.

Ka-27 'HELIX'	800 km (500 mi.)
Ka-25 'HORMONE'	650 km (400 mi.)
LYNX HAS.Mk 2	1000 km (620 mi.)

Versatile 'Helix'

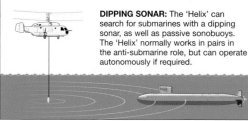

DIPPING SONAR: The 'Helix' can search for submarines with a dipping sonar, as well as passive sonobuoys. The 'Helix' normally works in pairs in the anti-submarine role, but can operate autonomously if required.

LOGGING MISSION: A Ka-32 is used by a New Zealand timber company for hauling tree trunks from remote mountain sides. Operators are impressed with the aircraft's reliability.

AIR-SEA RESCUE: Ka-27 'Helixes' are used to rescue survivors of shipwrecks. The helicopter can drop a dinghy pack to survivors in the water as well as carry out a conventional rescue with a winch.

LOCKHEED

AH-56 CHEYENNE

● High-speed gunship ● Two-seat aircraft ● Cancelled after 375 ordered

▲ The specifically designed gunship helicopter was a novel idea in the 1960s. With the end of the Cheyenne programme, the US Army was forced to wait more than 10 years for the AH-64 Apache.

Helicopters proved their worth once-and-for-all during the Vietnam War as troop carriers without equal. However, a pressing need for a specialised escort helicopter was soon apparent. Armed UH-1 'Hueys' were used in the meantime and Bell's AH-1 provided another interim solution, but the answer lay in the Cheyenne. However, this high-speed, heavily-armed weapons system was plagued by problems.

▲ **STOL take-off**
Intended to make short rolling take-offs when loaded, the AH-56 had a wheeled undercarriage.

▲ **Ahead of its time**
The cancellation of the Cheyenne forced the US Army to soldier on with the 'interim' Bell AH-1 HueyCobra for many years. The purpose-built AH-64 Apache was finally ordered in 1982.

▲ **Ground clearance**
To provide sufficient ground clearance for the ventral gun pack, tall landing gear was used.

▲ **Pusher rotor and wings**
For high-speed flight small wings produced most of the lift, while much of the engine power went to the pusher propeller and provided forward thrust.

Gunship layout ▶
Lockheed set the now-established formula for gunship helicopters. The gunner sat forward, taking responsibility for the weapons systems.

FACTS AND FIGURES

➤ Since the Cheyenne project, Lockheed has not put a military or civil helicopter into production.

➤ Power of the T64 engine was increased to 2927 kW (3,922 hp.) during testing.

➤ Cancellation, in May 1969, came just six months before production began.

➤ In common with other US Army helicopters, the Cheyenne was named after a native American tribe.

➤ The highly manoeuvrable AH-56 was found to be a stable weapons platform.

➤ The other short-listed AAFSS prototype was the Sikorsky S-66.

PROFILE

Fast and formidable

A top speed of 407 km/h (252 m.p.h.), a 4650-km (2,883-mi.) ferry range and good hover performance in hot-and-high conditions were among the US Army's Advanced Aerial Fire Support System's (AAFSS) requirements.

Twelve companies submitted proposals, with Lockheed being chosen to build 10 prototypes of their CL-840 compound helicopter. The first example flew on 21 September 1967. Initial testing was promising and the Army ordered 375 AH-56As.

On 7 January 1968 the US Department of Defense ordered 375 AH-56As for the US Army. In May 1969 the order was cancelled, although testing continued until 1972.

Then disaster struck. High-speed flight (over 320 km/h/200 m.p.h.) revealed stability problems. A cure was difficult to find; when a Cheyenne crashed in 1969 the rest were grounded and the production order was cancelled. Despite further testing and promising weapons trials, the controversy surrounding the project and the strain placed on the defence budget by the Vietnam War saw all development cease in 1972.

Production Cheyennes would have had six underwing attachment points for missiles and rockets. The inboard pair were able to carry fuel tanks.

Cockpit systems included a weapon sighting system with night-vision equipment and a helmet-mounted gunsight.

The small, low-set cantilever wings, which have no control surfaces, almost entirely 'offload' the main rotor (provide lift) during high-speed flight. Two pylons are provided under each one.

During high-speed flight most of the engine output is directed to the tail-mounted propeller, with only 223 kW (300 hp.) for the feathered main rotor. This prevents drag induced by 'windmilling'.

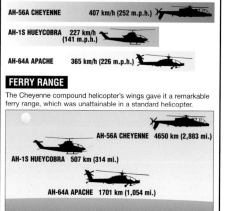

AH-56A Cheyenne

Type: two-seat all-weather compound combat helicopter

Powerplant: one 2561-kW (7,354-hp.) Pratt & Whitney T64-GE-16 turboshaft

Max speed: 407 km/h (252 m.p.h.) at sea level

Range: 1400 km (868 mi.) at maximum take-off weight with external fuel

Service ceiling: 7925 m (26,000 ft.)

Weights: empty 5320 kg (11,704 lb.); design take-off 7710 kg (16,962 lb.)

Armament: in nose turret, either one XM129 40-mm grenade-launcher or one 7.62-mm Minigun; in belly turret, XM140 30-mm cannon; two pylons under each wing for TOW anti-tank missiles or 70-mm rocket pods

Dimensions:
main rotor diameter	15.36 m (50 ft.)
length	18.31 m (60 ft.)
height	4.18 m (14 ft.)
rotor disc area	12.07 m² (130 sq ft.)

COMBAT DATA

MAXIMUM SPEED
Speed was an important consideration in the Cheyenne's design. The AH-56 was almost twice as fast as the contemporary AH-1.

AH-56A CHEYENNE — 407 km/h (252 m.p.h.)
AH-1S HUEYCOBRA — 227 km/h (141 m.p.h.)
AH-64A APACHE — 365 km/h (226 m.p.h.)

FERRY RANGE
The Cheyenne compound helicopter's wings gave it a remarkable ferry range, which was unattainable in a standard helicopter.

AH-56A CHEYENNE 4650 km (2,883 mi.)
AH-1S HUEYCOBRA 507 km (314 mi.)
AH-64A APACHE 1701 km (1,054 mi.)

AH-56A CHEYENNE

66-8827 was the second prototype to be built. Two were destroyed in accidents and one (66-8830) has survived to be displayed at the US Army Aviation Museum at Fort Rucker.

The first Cheyenne crash on 12 March 1969 was a result of the main rotor hitting the aft fuselage during high-speed flight. A second aircraft was badly damaged in similar circumstances in a NASA wind tunnel in September of that year.

Pratt & Whitney's T64 turboshaft engine also powered Sikorsky's S-65 heavylift helicopter which entered US Marine Corps service as the CH-53 in mid-1966.

Unlike more modern combat helicopters, the AH-56 was a dual-control machine. The pilot was in the rear position with the gunner/co-pilot in the front on a seat able to swivel through 360°.

The main undercarriage retracted rearwards into wingroot fairings. The rear of the helicopter was supported by a wheel in the ventral fin. Two turrets were to be fitted to service aircraft: one in the nose able to swing through 180° and another (detachable) under the fuselage.

The Cheyenne/TOW weapon system

TOW MISSILES: Hughes' Tube-launched, Optically-tracked, Wire-guided (TOW) missile was to be a key element of the Cheyenne 'weapon system'. This sequence shows a TOW launch at the Yuma missile test site in Arizona in 1970.

TANK KILLER: Designed to destroy tanks and ground fortifications, the TOW missile has a nose-mounted camera which relays an image to a screen in the gunner's cockpit. This allows him to steer the missile with a small joystick.

WIRE-GUIDED: A wire trailed behind the missile carries control commands from the helicopter's gunner. Cruciform 'pop-out' fins on the missile guide it to the target. TOW is powered by a small solid propellant rocket motor.

WARHEAD: The first Hughes BGM-71A TOW missiles (operational from 1975 aboard AH-1s) had a shaped-charge warhead (seen here destroying an old M4 tank hull) and a range of 4 km (2.5 mi.).

MBB EUROCOPTER

BO 105

● Utility helicopter ● Tank-destroyer ● Rescue helicopter

▲ The BO 105
has been a great success with
emergency services all over the world, especially
with police forces, air ambulance units and
rescue squadrons.

A dept at carrying people and cargo over medium distances the BO 105 is a marvellous light helicopter. A German design sold in several countries by Eurocopter, it is a hard worker and a reliable performer. The BO 105's rigid rotor system makes it very precise in flight. This makes it rather expensive for an aircraft of its class, but pilots and owners feel that it offers tremendous value.

MBB (EUROCOPTER) BO 105

▲ **Flying truck**
Rear doors give the BO 105 a useful capability as a cargo carrier. This kind of work is very common in Russia, where remote areas cannot be reached by road.

▲ **Dangling load**
Carrying an underslung load means a pilot must be very careful. In an emergency, the pilot can jettison the load by pressing a button in the cockpit.

◄ **Tank killer**
Armed with six HOT missiles, a BO 105 lies behind an obstacle waiting to ambush a tank group, its roof-mounted sight the only thing exposed to view.

◄ **Pulling a loop**
Few helicopters can match the spectacular agility of the BO 105. The strong rotor head allows it to loop and roll, unlike other types.

View down below ►
The cockpit of a BO 105 has excellent downward visibility, one reason why so many emergency services like to operate it.

FACTS AND FIGURES

➤ Unlike most helicopters, the BO 105 is fully aerobatic and very manoeuvrable.

➤ The medical evacuation version of this helicopter carries a pilot, two medical attendants and two patients.

➤ The 178 BO 105s in service in North America have flown 1,220,000 hours.

➤ The BO 105 combines three features – rigid rotor, twin engines and compact size – into an ideal light helicopter.

➤ More than 1,500 BO 105s are on order or are in use in 40 countries.

➤ The rear doors of the BO 105 offer straight-in loading capability.

PROFILE

Multi-role versatility

The BO 105's small size and good performance mean that it can land in places other helicopters would find impossible.

MBB's small yet capable BO 105 has won a well-deserved reputation for performance and reliability since it first flew over 30 years ago. Today this adaptable craft is in worldwide military and civilian service.

To the pilot, the BO 105 is a delight to fly, offering good flying characteristics with great agility thanks to its rigid rotors. The current BO 105 with seating

for six in an extended fuselage is regarded as one of the most sensible and effective light helicopters in the world, offering a superb view from its rounded contour nose.

Rescue versions of the BO 105 have saved thousands of people in life-threatening situations. It has made a great impact in construction, ambulance and police work, as well as forming the basis for

one of the most capable tank-destroyers currently in military service.

Now being marketed by the multinational Eurocopter concern, the BO 105 is a classic design which copes admirably with every task to which it has been assigned.

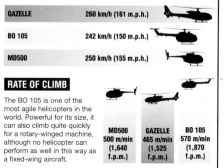

The tough and reliable BO 105 has found a ready market with law enforcement agencies. This comprehensively-equipped example is flown by the Bavarian State Police.

BO 105 CB

Type: light general-purpose helicopter

Powerplant: two 313-kW (419-hp.) Allison 250-C20B turboshaft engines

Maximum speed: 242 km/h (150 m.p.h.) at sea level

Rate of climb: 570 m/min (1,870 f.p.m.) at sea level

Range: 585 km (363 mi.) at sea level

Weights: empty 1277 kg (2815 lb.); loaded 2500 kg (5,511 lb.)

Accommodation: one pilot and four to six passengers or 870 kg (1,918 lb.) of cargo

Dimensions: rotor span 9.82 m (32 ft 2 in.)
length 11.84 m (38 ft. 9 in.)
height 2.98 m (9 ft 9 in.)

BO 105 PAH-1

The Heeresflieger has acquired more than 300 BO 105s, two-thirds being the heavily-armed PAH-1 anti-tank variant.

Roof-mounted infra-red sights allow the crew to carry out attacks at night and in bad weather. Some BO 105s also have high-magnification devices, and police and emergency versions usually have spotlights and cameras.

The BO 105 has an excellent cockpit, with clearly laid out instruments and full controls and with exceptional visibility. In anti-armour form it is flown by a crew of two.

Most light helicopters have only one engine; the BO 105 is unusual in having two. This is an important advantage in a helicopter; if one engine fails, the machine can get home on the other.

To provide lateral stability, the PAH-1, like most BO 105 derivatives, is fitted with a simple two-bladed semi-rigid tail rotor.

The Euromissile HOT system is a long-range wire-guided anti-tank missile. It is guided by the aircraft commander, who occupies the left seat in the front of the cockpit.

The tailboom of the BO 105 is of light alloy, and houses the drive shaft for the tail rotor. In military variants, the two small stabilising fins carry AM/FM radio antennas.

ACTION DATA

MAXIMUM SPEED

The bluff, rounded shape of the BO 105 is not conducive to great speed, but it is almost as fast as more streamlined helicopters like the Eurocopter Gazelle and the McDonnell Douglas MD 500. It is also much more agile.

GAZELLE	260 km/h (161 m.p.h.)
BO 105	242 km/h (150 m.p.h.)
MD500	250 km/h (155 m.p.h.)

RATE OF CLIMB

The BO 105 is one of the most agile helicopters in the world. Powerful for its size, it can also climb quite quickly for a rotary-winged machine, although no helicopter can perform as well in this way as a fixed-wing aircraft.

MD500 500 m/min (1,640 f.p.m.)
GAZELLE 465 m/min (1,525 f.p.m.)
BO 105 570 m/min (1,870 f.p.m.)

The many missions of the BO 105

MULTI-MISSION: Sweden took delivery of 24 BO 105s in the late 1980s. Most were anti-tank variants, but a number were configured for bad weather and Arctic search and rescue.

OBSERVATION AND LIAISON: The excellent visibility from the BO 105 makes it suitable for both military and civil observation duties. Heeresflieger BO 105s are also used as light transports.

MARITIME SEARCH AND RESCUE: The BO 105's small size makes it suitable for operations from light vessels, and several South American countries, including Chile, use the type at sea.

MBB EUROCOPTER
BO 105 AIR AMBULANCE

● Specialised emergency work ● Agile performance

MBB (EUROCOPTER) BO 105

▲ Health service helicopters
Despite being expensive to run, the air ambulance is so vital in many regions of the UK that funding has been made available for it.

▲ Quick load
The interior of the BO 105 can hold two stretcher cases along with two medical attendants.

▼ Dual role
Used for both medical and police work, this BO 105DBS/4 can be fitted with a powerful searchlight and infra-red imaging equipment.

▲ Mountain rescue
Swiss Air Rescue operate the BO 105CBS for mountain work. These aircraft are often used to rescue injured skiers or stranded hikers.

Far East connection ▶
Some Japanese operators fitted winches to their BO 105s giving them added rescue capabilities.

T he MBB BO 105 light-utility helicopter is a masterpiece of simple but effective design that has won an excellent worldwide reputation. This fine helicopter is a veritable 'jack of all trades', suitable for a wide variety of civil and military duties. Well known in Europe as a military aircraft armed with a variety of weapons, the BO 105 is equally visible in America as a means of transporting casualties to hospital.

▲ Rearwards opening clamshell doors enable easy access for a casualty on a stretcher. The quick transfer from incident to hospital allowed by ambulance helicopters has saved hundreds of lives.

FACTS AND FIGURES

➤ Military BO 105s are valuable because they can fly nap-of-the-earth missions below treetop level.

➤ The prototype for the BO 105 series first flew on 16 February 1967.

➤ To date, 1,300 BO 105s have been delivered and 3,400,000 hours flown.

➤ Police/Medical Aviation Services Ltd currently operate five specially-equipped BO 105s in the emergency services role.

➤ Eurocopter claims that the BO 105 was the world's first light twin-engined helicopter.

➤ Sweden operates an unarmed SAR version known as the HR 9B.

PROFILE

Saving lives by air ambulance

The manufacturer's brochures for the MBB BO 105 helicopter call it a 'reliable, hard-working aircraft with multi-mission capabilities'. Several versions of this attractive and versatile helicopter are flown in many parts of the world. The BO 105 has been a popular choice in a variety of locations and is rugged enough to operate in almost any climate. The manufacturer boasts that it has "outstanding hot environment, high-altitude performance".

Such a versatile airframe has proved no less adaptable to the role of air ambulance. Clamshell doors at the rear of the cabin make loading stretchers a simple task, while winches can be fitted to permit airborne rescues.

Design work on the BO 105 began in 1962. The German government was eager to support early testing of this design and to encourage its entry into service. Full production was well underway by 1971, with an improved version coming out of the factory by 1975. Civil BO 105s (as well as military versions) sold well, with air ambulance variants seeing service in the northern and southern hemispheres.

Above: The medical attendants, winchmen and pilots who operate ambulance helicopters have to undergo intensive training for their highly specialised duties.

Right: The helicopter is a vital tool for ambulance and rescue work. Not only can it reach areas inaccessible by road, it can also transport critical cases far more quickly, giving victims a better chance of survival.

BO 105CB

Type: five-seat light-utility helicopter

Powerplant: two 313-kW (420-hp.) Allison 250-C20B turboshaft engines

Max speed: 270 km/h (167 m.p.h.) at sea level

Range: 658 km (408 mi.) flying at 1525 m (5,000 ft.)

Operating ceiling: 5180 m (17,000 ft.)

Weights: empty 1256 kg (2,763 lb.); maximum take-off 2400 kg (5,280 lb.)

Armament: military versions carry up to eight Hughes TOW anti-armour missiles, or up to 38 air-to-ground rocket projectiles, or (typically) two 7.62-mm machine-guns; civil versions can carry 2800 kg (6,173 lb.) of cargo

Dimensions:
main rotor diameter	9.84 m (32 ft. 3 in.)
length	11.86 m (38 ft. 11 in.)
height	3 m (9 ft. 10 in.)
main rotor disc area	76.05 m² (818 sq. ft.)

The pilot and co-pilot or passenger have an excellent view in all directions. Extra equipment can include searchlights, doppler radar, infra-red imaging cameras or loudspeakers.

The BO 105's excellent agility is provided by the rigid titanium rotor head. Each of the four rotor blades is fitted with an anti-erosion strip and a vibration damper.

The twin-bladed, semi-rigid tail rotor unit is made from glassfibre reinforced plastic. Extra stability is provided by a horizontal stabiliser of light alloy construction with small endplate fins.

G-CDBS

BO 105DBS/4

G-CDBS is operated by Bond Helicopters on behalf of the Cornwall Ambulance Service in England. This vital service is entirely funded by donations from the people of Cornwall.

The landing gear is of skid type, designed with cross-tubes for energy absorption by plastic deformation in the event of a heavy landing. Inflatable emergency floats are fitted to this machine which can be removed. Entrance to the cabin is via side doors or the large rear-opening clamshell doors.

The fuselage is of the conventional pod and boom type and is constructed of light alloy metals. Two stretchers can be accommodated side-by-side in air ambulance configuration.

ACTION DATA

MAXIMUM POWER

All three of these types are currently used for mountain rescue in Europe. The added power of the A 109K2 is useful when lifting loads at altitude. The BO 105 has a good power-to-weight ratio, allowing it to winch casualties safely. All three types are fitted with twin-engines for safety and the added power they provide.

BO 105CB	626 kW (840 hp.)
AS 355 ECUREUIL 2	604 kW (810 hp.)
A 109K2	942 kW (1,263 hp.)

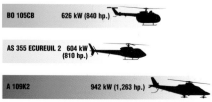

Air ambulances around the world

SA 365N DAUPHIN 2: Operated by the privately-funded company AirEvac, the Dauphin is used in major cities for medical evacuation.

AS 350B ECUREUIL: This AS 350 is seen operating for medevac company SAMU in France. The French police also use the Ecureuil.

BK 117: Operated by Life Flight on behalf of Stamford University Hospital, Connecticut, this BK 117 is specially equipped for medical duties.

A 109K2: Equipped with a rescue winch and skis, this A 109K2 is ideally suited to its mountain rescue duties in the Italian Alps.

McDONNELL DOUGLAS
MD 520

● Advanced design ● No tail rotor ● Increased safety

▲ Removing the tail rotor helps the NOTAR helicopter to operate from confined spaces. This has proved to be very convenient for commercial flight operations within large cities.

With its sleek shape and peppy performance, the McDonnell Douglas MD 520N is excellent for civil, commercial and police duties. The MD 520N combines a helicopter design from the 1960s (originally built for the military) with an evolving aerodynamic concept (the manufacturer's NOTAR, or 'no tail rotor' configuration) to produce the MD 520N, the helicopter everybody wants. As of 1996, McDonnell Douglas had sold 80 of the type.

McDONNELL DOUGLAS MD 520

Silent star ▶
The unique looks and performance of the MD 520 have meant that the helicopter has made numerous appearances in films and television programmes.

◀ Increased performance
Pilots have found adapting to the new helicopter's flying characteristics was easily accomplished without the need for extensive training.

▲ Staying afloat
Proving just as reliable as its earlier cousins, this MD 520N is equipped with two large floats.

▲ Police chase
Operating alongside a patrol boat, this MD 520N flies with a local sheriff's department in the USA.

◀ Proven design
Only minor modifications were required to install the NOTAR system on an existing helicopter's fuselage.

FACTS AND FIGURES

➤ In 1991 the Arizona Police Department, based in Phoenix, became the first operator of the MD 520N.

➤ This fine helicopter draws its basic design from the Vietnam-era Hughes OH-6.

➤ In September 1993, an MD 520N set a new Paris to London record of 1 hr 22 min.

➤ The NOTAR, or 'no tail rotor' concept is also used on the larger MD 630N and MD 900 Explorer helicopters.

➤ An MD 520N rescued four climbers from an 1800-m (5,600-ft.) mountain in Hawaii.

➤ Over 1,000 hours of testing was done before the MD 520N became operational.

Flying without a tail rotor

Pilots are delighted by the MD 520N, which springs aloft with a feisty enthusiasm. This is one helicopter that has plenty of power and carrying capacity, and it offers a quick response to the controls along with other excellent flying qualities.

Built in Mesa, Arizona, where McDonnell Douglas' helicopter division (originally the Hughes company) has decades of experience, the MD 520N is versatile and simply one of the world's best helicopters in the mid-sized class. It has proven popular with law enforcement officers, who value its agility and handling. The MD 520N can be equipped to carry a fascinating variety of police equipment, including searchlights and listening devices. Some police departments give the MD 520N a double-duty assignment, using it to stalk law-breakers but also to carry ambulance stretcher cases.

The MD 520N is a civilian spin-off of the military's OH-6 Cayuse (which differs in using a tail rotor, rather than the NOTAR blown-air system). A few military Cayuses have

Left: High speed and the added safety of removing the tail rotor, suggest that the NOTAR type of helicopter will have a bright future ahead of it. Users of the MD 520 would agree.

Right: Heavily marketed as a potential replacement military helicopter, the MD 530N has undertaken various combat evaluations without success.

been converted to the NOTAR configuration, but only for America's special operations forces. It is rumoured that these helicopters have been utilised for recent covert operations around the world.

MD 520N

Type: five-seat civil helicopter

Powerplant: one 317-kW (425-hp.) Allison 250-C30 turboshaft engine

Max speed: 281 km/h (174 m.p.h.) at sea level

Cruising speed: 249 km/h (154 m.p.h.)

Initial climb rate: 564 m/min (1,850 f.p.m.)

Hover ceiling: 2753 m (9,030 ft.)

Range: 402 km (249 mi.) at sea level

Service ceiling: 4320 m (14,170 ft.)

Weights: empty 742 kg (1,632 lb.); maximum take-off 1519 kg (3,342 lb.)

Dimensions:
rotor diameter	8.3 m (27 ft. 3 in.)
length	9.8 m (23 ft. 2 in.)
height	3.01 m (9 ft. 10 in.)
rotor disc area	54.47 m² (586 sq. ft.)

The heavily glazed cockpit offers the crew excellent visibility in all directions. For certain operations the doors can be removed allowing a rapid exit in an emergency.

A searchlight on the underside of the fuselage is now standard equipment on police helicopters. Protruding from the front is a cable cutter for protection during low level flying.

Skids are the standard landing equipment. These can be increased in length if required. Wheels can also be added for better ground handling.

MD 520N

Quickly adopted by America's law enforcement agencies, the MD 520N is proving to be a highly capable helicopter, offering exceptional manoeuvrability with increased safety.

Two upward-hinging doors are located on the rear of the fuselage allowing easy access to the engine. The exhaust is at the rear of the main body.

The nozzle for the NOTAR system is positioned at the rear of the tail boom. The pilot operates it with foot pedals, which give excellent and precise handling qualities.

ACTION DATA

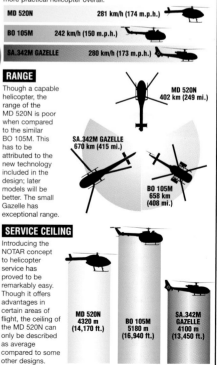

MAXIMUM SPEED

The deletion of the tail rotor allows the MD 520N to have a high maximum speed compared to some other helicopters in its class. The lightweight Gazelle is as fast, but the MD 520N is a much more practical helicopter overall.

MD 520N	281 km/h (174 m.p.h.)
BO 105M	242 km/h (150 m.p.h.)
SA.342M GAZELLE	280 km/h (173 m.p.h.)

RANGE

Though a capable helicopter, the range of the MD 520N is poor when compared to the similar BO 105M. This has to be attributed to the new technology included in the design; later models will be better. The small Gazelle has exceptional range.

MD 520N 402 km (249 mi.)

SA.342M GAZELLE 670 km (415 mi.)

BO 105M 658 km (408 mi.)

SERVICE CEILING

Introducing the NOTAR concept to helicopter service has proved to be remarkably easy. Though it offers advantages in certain areas of flight, the ceiling of the MD 520N can only be described as average compared to some other designs.

MD 520N	BO 105M	SA.342M GAZELLE
4320 m (14,170 ft.)	5180 m (16,940 ft.)	4100 m (13,450 ft.)

The flying bugs

■ **HUGHES 500:** Originally developed by Hughes helicopters, this remarkable helicopter has seen numerous civil applications.

■ **OH-6 LOACH:** Having seen extensive use in Vietnam as a reconnaissance helicopter, the OH-6 continues in widespread service.

■ **MD 500E:** Developed for the executive helicopter market, this design has received numerous orders from across the world.

■ **500MD TOW DEFENDER:** A cheaper alternative to the AH-64 Apache, this helicopter is proving to be a highly capable attack platform.

McDonnell Douglas

AH-64 Apache

● Combat proven ● All-weather capability ● Advanced weapons systems

Hughes developed the AH-64 Apache in response to the Warsaw Pact's massive armoured strength. Produced by McDonnell Douglas, the AH-64 can engage tanks, often at a safe distance, even at night and in bad weather. The Apache uses advanced sensors to detect enemy vehicles. It then stalks them, using natural cover as a shield, before rising above the treeline to launch laser-guided Hellfire missiles.

▲ Apache crews
go into battle confident that they have one of the world's most capable anti-armour weapons, especially when it is flown alongside the Bell OH-58D Kiowa Warrior scout and target designation helicopter.

McDonnell Douglas AH-64 Apache

Apache agility ▶
Although the AH-64 often attacks from cover, high speed and manoeuvrability are important factors for survival.

▲ **Hellfire launch**
An AGM-114 Hellfire missile is fired by an Apache during tests. The missile homes in on a laser-designated target, which has been marked by another aircraft, ground forces or the AH-64 itself.

▲ **Purposeful appearance**
Hughes designed the AH-64 for maximum survivability and effectiveness – not good looks.

▼ **Hidden danger**
In a classic example of terrain masking, this Apache demonstrates the aircraft's ability to use natural cover while preparing to attack.

▲ **Rocket fire**
Rocket pods are an important back-up to the Apache's Hellfire armament. Unguided rockets are extremely effective against soft targets and are essential in the fire support role.

FACTS AND FIGURES

➤ An Apache battalion consists of 18 AH-64s and 13 OH-58 scout helicopters for target spotting and designation.

➤ AH-64s escorted MH-53J helicopters in the first mission of Desert Storm.

➤ More than 500 Iraqi tanks were destroyed by US Army Apaches.

➤ Apaches of the 101st Aviation Regiment fired the first Allied shots of the Gulf War against Iraqi radar installations.

➤ Leased US Army AH-64As were delivered to the Netherlands army in 1996.

➤ New developments have led to the advanced AH-64D Longbow Apache.

PROFILE

At war with the Apache

Apaches performed with devastating effect during the Gulf War, with crews finding and destroying targets even in thick smoke when visibility was often down to 200 metres (600 ft.).

To defend against an armoured thrust into Western Europe, especially Germany, where 40,000 Warsaw Pact tanks once threatened NATO, the US Army developed an anti-tank strategy which hinged on the McDonnell Douglas AH-64 Apache.

One of the leading battlefield helicopters in the world, the tandem-seat AH-64, which has the gunner forward and pilot aft, uses high-tech sensors, a Chain Gun cannon and far-reaching Hellfire missiles to destroy tanks and other key targets. At night or in bad weather – even in dust storms as during Operation Desert Storm – the Apache crew can monitor enemy tank movements, using the PNVS (Pilot's Night-Vision System) and TADS (Target Acquisition and Designation System) to pinpoint and fire at targets. In the Gulf, these sensors and weapons also enabled Apaches to attack Iraqi air defence radar sites.

During war, the Apache crew is constantly challenged by the cat-and-mouse contest waged against enemy tank commanders. Flying low over the modern battlefield is extremely dangerous, but the Apache has all of the qualities needed for its tank-destroying mission.

A maximum load of 76 folding-fin rockets may be carried, although the configuration shown is almost standard.

Armour protects key engine components, and the upper parts of each engine cowling fold down to form maintenance platforms. Engines were uprated to 1409 kW (1,900 hp.) from the 604th aircraft.

Hellfire has been steadily improved and can home automatically on to a ground target. Video footage taken during the Gulf War demonstrated the missile's deadly accuracy.

AH-64A Apache

Type: two-seat all-weather attack helicopter

Powerplant: two 1265-kW (1,700-hp.) General Electric T700-GE-701 turboshaft engines

Maximum speed: 293 km/h (182 m.p.h.)

Range: 428 km (265 mi.)

Service ceiling: 6400 m (21,000 ft.)

Weights: empty 5165 kg (11,363 lb.); maximum take-off 9525 kg (20,995 lb.)

Armament: one 30-mm M230 Chain Gun cannon with 1,200 rounds of US, ADEN or DEFA ammunition, up to 16 AGM-114 Hellfire laser-guided missiles or up to 76 folding-fin rockets; various other combinations of rocket projectiles, guns and missiles

Dimensions:
main rotor diameter	14.63 m (48 ft.)
fuselage length	14.97 m (49 ft. 2 in.)
height	4.66 m (15 ft. 4 in.)
main rotor disc area	168.11 m² (1,809 sq. ft.)

A centre fuselage ammunition drum holds a maximum of 1,200 rounds of 30-mm ammunition. The McDonnell Douglas M230 Chain Gun fires at a maximum of 625 rounds per minute.

Constructed of glass-fibre, stainless steel and composites, the main rotor blades are proof against hits by 23-mm cannon shells. They have swept tips for increased performance.

Apache crewmembers sit on lightweight Kevlar seats and are protected by boron cockpit armour.

Should the powered flight control system fail, a Honeywell secondary fly-by-wire system is activated, allowing full control of both rotors and the tailplane.

Unusually, the AH-64's tailrotor consists of two twin-bladed units mounted at 55° to each other. This arrangement keeps noise to a minimum.

AH-64A APACHE

This early production aircraft carries standard US Army markings and paint scheme. In service the aircraft rarely sports any form of individual or unit marking.

23259

UNITED STATES ARMY

U.S. ARMY

Lockheed Martin builds the AN/AAQ-11 TADS/PNVS system which is turret mounted in the extreme nose.

The energy absorbing main landing gear combines with crash-resistant seat and airframe design to give the crew a 95 per cent chance of surviving a 12.8 m per second (42 f.p.s.) ground impact.

The tailplane incidence is controlled automatically by a Hamilton Standard flight control system. This allows it to hold the aircraft in an optimum position in all flight phases.

COMBAT DATA

MAXIMUM CRUISING SPEED

The Apache is the fastest of the helicopters shown here. This was a great asset on the long-range, covert missions into enemy-held territory during the Gulf War.

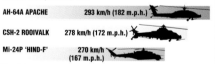

AH-64A APACHE	293 km/h (182 m.p.h.)
CSH-2 ROOIVALK	278 km/h (172 m.p.h.)
Mi-24P 'HIND-F'	270 km/h (167 m.p.h.)

WEAPON LOAD

The 'Hind-F' is a developed version of the earlier 'Hind' gunships. The armed assault role has been largely abandoned, with the aircraft carrying spare ammunition and a heavy weapon load instead of troops. The Apache carries fewer weapons and relies on accuracy.

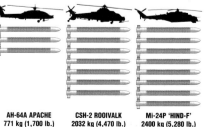

AH-64A APACHE	CSH-2 ROOIVALK	Mi-24P 'HIND-F'
771 kg (1,700 lb.)	2032 kg (4,470 lb.)	2400 kg (5,280 lb.)

Apache attack profiles

LASER GUIDANCE: The Apache is capable of designating its own targets, which means the Hellfire missile can be used in autonomous mode.

KIOWA WARRIOR: Other aircraft, primarily the OH-58D with its more powerful laser, can also designate targets for the Apache.

APACHE STAND-OFF: As it is a high-value target itself, the Apache often stands off at a safe distance and launches Hellfires at targets that are not visible.

KIOWA IN THE TREES: Small and agile, the OH-58D can often get closer to the enemy, and provides a 'cone' of reflected laser energy for the AH-64's missiles.

McDONNELL DOUGLAS

AH-64 APACHE

● Armoured gunship ● Tank destroyer ● Infantry close-support

▲ Designed to fly and fight in the hostile airspace over a modern battlefield, the AH-64 is a potent weapons platform.

Equipped with video-type electronic aiming devices, Hellfire missiles and rapid-fire cannon, the AH-64 Apache is a new kind of warrior bringing a powerful punch to the battlefield. When a ground commander wants support he summons the Apache, a miracle helicopter which can rush into the fray in any weather, day or night, to pin down the foe and help friendly troops to fight and win.

McDONNELL DOUGLAS **AH-64** APACHE

Tank ▶ killer
The Apache's primary weapon is the laser-guided Hellfire missile. It can destroy any known tank.

Combat ▶ reliability
Apaches are complex machines, but they are designed to be serviced easily in the field.

▲ **All-weather attacker**
Fast, agile and very tough, the AH-64 uses its advanced sensors to fly and fight in all conditions.

▲ **Chain Gun**
The helicopter's powerful 30-mm cannon is linked to the crew's helmets, aiming where the pilot or gunner is looking.

◀ **See through fog**
The Longbow Apache is equipped with millimetric radar which can see through rain, fog and snow.

▼ **Into action**
The Apache was one of the stars in the Gulf War, its high-tech weaponry proving lethal to a wide range of Iraqi targets.

FACTS AND FIGURES

➤ The Apache is designed to survive hits from 23-mm cannon, and the cockpit to withstand hitting the ground at 13 m (42 ft.) per second.

➤ The Apache uses a super-heated ceramic block to deceive heat-seeking missiles.

➤ Apache operators include Egypt, Greece, Israel, Saudi Arabia, the UAE and the USA.

➤ The Apache's 16 laser-guided Hellfire missiles can destroy a tank 20 km away.

➤ The Apache uses digital technology to pinpoint targets for commanders, other helicopters, tanks and vehicles.

➤ The Apache's Chain Gun weighs 56 kg (123 lb.) and fires 625 rounds per minute.

Battlefield destroyer

When a battle is unfolding, it is important to hit hard and disrupt the enemy's forces. The helicopter is the new knight in shining armour to ground troops, who need the flexibility and striking power of their own aircraft overhead, and the AH-64 Apache is the undisputed champion of battlefield helicopters.

The Apache uses electronic wizardry to find its way and to aim its hi-tech missiles and cannon. The two pilots of the slender, mantis-like Apache can

hug the earth when they need to, or navigate through smoke and rough weather to seek out enemy troops and tanks using night-vision equipment and hi-tech sensors.

Assisted by observation helicopters and staying in close contact with troops on the ground, the Apache can shoot with remarkable accuracy from a greater distance than most

In high-threat environments Apaches operate at low level, usually attacking from among the trees.

other combat helicopters. With its speed, durability, and accuracy, the Apache brings a new dimension to the ground commander's task of outsmarting and outfighting his adversary.

Communications and avionics systems are carried in armoured fairings on each side of the fuselage.

Power is provided by a pair of 1265-kW (1696 hp.) General Electric engines. Key propulsion components are armour-protected.

The four-bladed main rotor is of laminated steel, glass-reinforced plastic and composite construction.

AH-64A Apache

Type: two-seat all-weather attack helicopter

Powerplant: two 1265-kW (1696-hp.) General Electric T700-GE-701 turboshaft engines

Maximum speed: never-exceed speed 365 km/h (227 m.p.h.); maximum cruise speed 297 km/h (185 m.p.h.)

Initial climb rate: 428 km (266 mi.)

Weights: empty 5165 kg (11,400 lb.); normal mission weight 8000 kg (17,637 lb.); maximum take-off 9525 kg (21,000 lb.); maximum internal fuel weight 1157 kg (2,551 lb.)

Armament: one 30-mm M230 Chain Gun cannon with 1,200 rounds, up to 16 AGM-114 Hellfire laser-guided missiles or up to 76 folding-fin rockets

Dimensions: rotor diameter   19.55 m (64 ft.)
                 fuselage length 14.97 m (49 ft. 1 in.)
                 height   4.66 m (15 ft. 4 in.)
                 rotor area 168.11 m² (1,809 sq. ft.)

AH-64A APACHE

Israel's Defence Force was the first organisation to acquire the Apache after the US Army.

The Israelis have a wealth of combat experience with gunships, and consider the AH-64 the best of its kind. It has the standard gunship layout of gunner in front and pilot behind.

Passive Night Vision (PNV) sensors in the nose include infra-red and TV cameras and a laser designation system.

The engines are fitted with 'Black Hole' infra-red suppression systems as protection against heat-seeking missiles.

The two-tail rotor blades cross at 55°, which reduces the amount of noise they generate.

Apaches carry up to 1,200 rounds of 30-mm ammunition for the Chain Gun. It can fire at up to 625 rounds per minute.

Stub wings carry up to 16 missiles or four pods containing 76 folding-fin 70-mm high-explosive rockets.

The structure of the AH-64 is designed to allow it to withstand hits from high-explosive rounds of up to 23-mm calibre.

COMBAT DATA

HOVER CEILING

Both the Apache and the Havoc have more power than the Tiger, and can hover a kilometre higher than the Franco-German machine. This is not the absolute ceiling: sometimes, the terrain and air temperature bounce the air from the rotors straight back up in what is called ground effect, and the extra air cushion can add one or two thousand metres (3–6,000 ft.) to the hover limits.

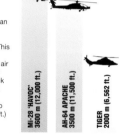

Mi-28 'HAVOC' 3600 m (12,000 ft.)	AH-64 APACHE 3500 m (11,500 ft.)	TIGER 2000 m (6,562 ft.)

MAXIMUM SPEED

All three helicopters have a good turn of speed, with the Mil Mi-28 having a very slight edge.

Mi-28 'HAVOC'	300 km/h (186 m.p.h.)
AH-64 APACHE	297 km/h (184 m.p.h.)
TIGER	280 km/h (174 m.p.h.)

COMBAT RADIUS

Attack helicopters operate from forward bases close to the fighting, so they do not need long range. Fighting at close quarters means that being able to refuel and re-arm quickly is more important than being able to fly great distances.

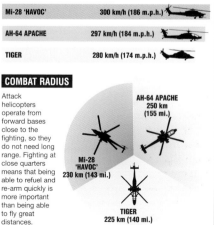

AH-64 APACHE 250 km (155 mi.)

Mi-28 'HAVOC' 230 km (143 mi.)

TIGER 225 km (140 mi.)

First Gulf War attack

1 TEMPORARY BASES: Forward Air Refuelling Points, or FARPs, are established close behind the forward echelons. One of the three AH-64 companies uses it to re-arm.

2 WAITING FOR ACTION: The second Apache company loiters in the air at a holding point some 20 km (12 mi.) ahead of the FARP, waiting to replace the company in contact.

3 OPEN FIRE: As soon as an enemy column is located, the lead company moves forward to engage with guns, rockets and Hellfire missiles.

4 CONTINUED ATTACK: As each company exhausts its weapons, it moves back to the FARP and is replaced by the company at the holding point. The enemy is thus kept under continual fire.

McDonnell Douglas

AH-64D Longbow Apache

● Improved performance ● All-weather attack ● New avionics

Halting an enemy's advance has become increasingly more difficult during recent conflicts. The fluid nature of engagements has seen the attack helicopter play an ever more important role. The AH-64A proved its worth in the Gulf War, but the need to strike the enemy in all weather prompted McDonnell Douglas to produce the AH-64D Longbow Apache, the ultimate attack platform.

▲ With its fire control radar above the rotors, the Longbow can hide from view and attack enemy targets at will. This technique was not possible with the AH-64A.

AH-64D Longbow Apache

▼ **British Longbow**
With Starstreak missiles, this is how British Apaches will look upon entering service with the Army Air Corps.

◄ **Agile Apache**
Additional equipment has not affected the flight performance of the AH-64D.

▲ **Capable killer**
An improvement over its cousin, the Longbow has the ability to attack targets in all weather conditions.

▲ **Staying low, staying alive**
Despite all the advantages that the new AH-64D has brought to the battlefield, flying low to avoid enemy fire is still practiced.

The next generation ►
A complete rework of the Apache, the AH-64D has received considerable interest, and will become a superb attack platform.

FACTS AND FIGURES

➤ The AH-64D first entered service with the 1-227 Aviation Battalion, US Army at Fort Hood, Texas, in July 1998.

➤ Development of the AH-64D was initiated following experience in the Gulf War.

➤ Future operations will see the AH-64D operate alongside F-15E Eagles.

➤ Longbow is actually the name of the sophisticated radar system installed on the Apache.

➤ The six Longbow test Apaches have amassed over 5,000 flying hours.

➤ The first overseas deployment of US Longbows is likely to be in South Korea.

PROFILE

More deadly than ever

In 1997 the AH-64D became the second version of the US Army's principal attack helicopter to enter service. In 1992 McDonnell Douglas converted four AH-64As, equipped with Longbow millimetre-wave fire control radar in a mast-mounted sight and Hellfire missiles, to act as a proof-of-concept machine for the AH-64D.

Flying on 15 April, 1992 the developmental model featured numerous changes compared to its predecessor. Two uprated GE 701C turboshaft engines offered better performance during engagements. The most significant change was the installation of the longbow radar, allowing attack operations to be undertaken in fog. It can detect up to 12 targets, including fixed-wing aircraft, and can classify them according to priority. The AH-64D can accomplish this while remaining completely concealed, thanks to its high-mounted sight.

The first batch of AH-64Ds entered service with the Army in 1997. Service will follow with a number of European customers, including the British AAC, which will operate the helicopter with Starstreak air-to-air missiles.

Below: An AH-64A test helicopter was equipped with the Longbow radar to undertake flight handling characteristics tests.

Above: The AH-64D has a red instrumentation boom on its nose. The type had a long and relatively trouble-free development, although problems occurred with the targeting radar.

AH-64D Longbow Apache

Type: advanced battlefield attack helicopter

Powerplant: two 1409kW (1,723-hp.) General Electric T-700-GE-701C turboshaft engines

Maximum level speed: 295 km/h (162 m.p.h.)

Endurance: 3 hours 9 minutes

Initial climb rate: 942 m/min (3,090 f.p.m.)

Range: 482 km (252 mi.) on internal fuel

Hover ceiling: 4115 m (13,500 ft.)

Weights: empty 5352 kg (11,774 lb.); max take-off 9525 kg (22,235 lb.)

Armament: one 30-mm M230 Chain Gun cannon plus 16 Hellfire laser-guided missiles

Dimensions:
Main rotor diameter	14.63 m (64 ft. 2 in.)
Fuselage length	14.97 m (49 ft. 2 in.)
Height	4.95 m (16 ft. 3 in.)
Rotor disc area	168,11 m² (1,809 sq. ft.)

The crew is fully surrounded by ballistic armour, which offers a high degree of protection from enemy fire when operating at low level. In the event of crash, air bags have been installed in the cockpit to reduce the risk of injury.

The Longbow radar is housed in a sphere mounted above the rotor head. Capable of scanning through 369° in all weather, it offers a fire-and-forget mode.

AH-64D LONGBOW APACHE

Based on a proven design that saw extensive action in the Gulf War, the improved AH-64D offers the ability to strike multiple targets anywhere on the battlefield in all weather.

All US AH-64Ds have the more powerful General Electric T700C engines. British Longbows will be powered by Rolls-Royce Turboméca turboshafts, which will be linked to a digital management system; this will offer optimum engine performance during manoeuvres.

900423

UNITED STATES ARMY

A distinguishing feature of the new Apaches is the increased length of the forwards fuselage cheeks to accommodate avionics.

Mounted on the outer wings, the Stinger air-to-air missiles can be removed from the helicopter and fired from the shoulder if the need arises. British Longbows will fly with the Shorts Starstreak missile.

ACTION DATA

SPEED
With its improved engines and lighter avionics, the AH-64D has maintained a high top speed. However, compared to the Boeing/Sikorsky Comanche, which uses a blended body design, its performance is relatively poor.

AH-64D	295 km/h (162 m.p.h.)
RAH-66 COMANCHE	324 km/h (201 m.p.h.)
Mi-28 "HAVOC-A"	300 km/h (186 m.p.h.)

POWER
Current frontline attack helicopters are required to operate at low altitude over the battlefield. Because of this, most have similar engine power, despite the different approaches taken by their manufacturers. The Russian-designed Mil 'Havoc' is the most powerful. It is a possible replacement for the attack 'Hind'.

AH-64D LONGBOW APACHE	RAH-66 COMANCHE	Mi-28 "HAVOC-A"
2818 kW (3,446 hp.)	2136 kW (3,000 hp.)	3280 kW (4,318 hp.)

TAKE-OFF WEIGHT
With the need to carry a sizeable war load, battlefield helicopters show a diverse range in weight. Required to carry all of its attack missiles in the fuselage, the Commanche compares poorly to earlier designs, but has better hitting power.

AH-64D LONGBOW APACHE	RAH-66 COMANCHE	Mi-28 "HAVOC-A"
9525 kg (22,235 lb.)	7896 kg (17,371 lb.)	10400 kg (22,880 lb.)

Apache mock-ups and prototypes

■ **HUGHES MODEL 77:** The Model 77 mock-up was built in response to the requirement for a dedicated attack helicopter.

■ **HUGHES YAH-64:** The T-tail and contoured nose are indications of an early prototype Apache.

■ **McDD AH-64A:** Now built by McDonnell Douglas, the Apache emerged victorious from the Gulf War.

McDonnell Douglas
MD500

● Single-engined turbine helicopter ● Top seller ● Civil OH-6

T he McDonnell Douglas MD500 is a 'great' of helicopter aviation – renowned for its economy, reliability and performance. The manufacturer tells cost-conscious operators that this aircraft offers the highest productivity per unit of any machine in its class. Whether supplying offshore oil platforms, helping the police in law enforcement or evacuating the sick by air, the MD500 is a bargain for its owners and a joy for pilots to fly.

▲ The 500 family started out as the OH-6A Cayuse two-seat observation helicopter. The same US Army requirement also spawned the development of another very successful civil helicopter and one of the MD500's main competitors – Bell's Model 206 JetRanger.

McDonnell Douglas MD500

Five-blade rotor ▶
The Hughes 500D introduced a five-blade rotor of smaller diameter to absorb the increased engine power.

▼ Small cabin
The original OH-6A was intended to carry just two crew; the rear cargo bay had two folding seats. Therefore, 500Ds had a fairly small cabin.

▼ Police patroller
This MD500E belongs to the Washington DC Metropolitan Police. It carries a powerful searchlight and additional antennas for a comprehensive radio fit.

▲ V-tail Hughes 500C
Initial civil versions of the OH-6 were the Model 500 and 500C. These can be distinguished from later variants by their V-tail and larger diameter, four-blade main rotor.

◀ MD500E
The main customers for this variant have been law enforcement agencies and utility operators in over 60 nations. This one carries a US registration.

FACTS AND FIGURES

➤ MD500s were built by RACA (Argentina), Breda Nardi (Italy), Korean Air and Kawasaki (Japan).

➤ Hughes was taken over in 1984: Hughes 500s became MD500s in August 1985.

➤ The 500 was the basis for NOTAR, the first helicopter sold without a tail rotor.

➤ First flown in September 1966, the MD500 carries 240 l (62 gal.) fuel compared to 231 l (60 gal.) in the military OH-6.

➤ An MD500 has been used by NASA to perform tests in engine and rotor noise.

➤ A military version of the 500D called the 500MD Defender has been sold widely.

PROFILE

The top-selling 500 family

Developed by Hughes Helicopters, which was purchased by McDonnell Douglas in 1984, the MD500 is a popular civil development of the US Army's OH-6 Cayuse observation helicopter.

Flown initially in February 1963, over 1,400 OH-6As were built for the US Army, serving with distinction in Vietnam. A few still remain in Air National Guard service.

Production of a commercial and export model, called the Hughes 500, began in 1968 and was soon followed by the improved 500C. The 500D appeared in 1974 and had a more powerful engine, redesigned rotors and a T-shaped tail.

The last member of the family was the 500E, which had a reprofiled, pointed nose, replacing the familiar round cockpit allowing more cabin space. The 500th MD500E was delivered in April 1992.

Considered a very versatile helicopter, the MD500 has been popular with pilots as well as cost-conscious operators. The military version, the Defender, could be armed with Stinger or TOW missiles and a Minigun pod. The related MD 520/530 family remains in production in Arizona.

Below: A major user of the 500 family have been police forces. This MD500E belongs to Oakland, California's Police Department and carries a spotlight under the cabin and wire cutters above and below the windscreen. Military MD500s are used in Colombia, Japan, Kenya, the Philippines and South Korea.

Above: Another popular use is that of executive transport, like the rival Bell 206. This smartly painted MD500E has extra clearance 'tall' skids.

500C

Type: light utility helicopter

Powerplant: one 236-kW (316-hp.) Allison 250-C18A turboshaft engine

Max cruising speed: 244 km/h (151 m.p.h.) at 305 m (1,000 ft.)

Initial climb rate: 518 m/min (1,700 f.p.m.)

Range: 606 km (375 mi.)

Weights: empty 493 kg (1,085 lb.); maximum take-off 1361 kg (2,994 lb.)

Accommodation: two pilots and seven passengers or up to 800 kg (1,760 lb.) of freight

Dimensions:
main rotor diameter	8.03 m (26 ft. 4 in.)
length	9.24 m (30 ft. 4 in.)
height	2.48 m (8 ft. 2 in.)
main rotor disc area	50.60 m² (545 sq. ft.)

500D

This brightly decorated helicopter was a demonstrator for the British market. The MD 500 has gained a sound reputation for speed and lifting ability.

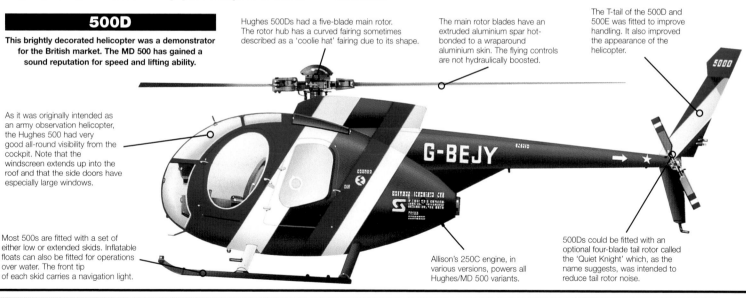

Hughes 500Ds had a five-blade main rotor. The rotor hub has a curved fairing sometimes described as a 'coolie hat' fairing due to its shape.

The main rotor blades have an extruded aluminium spar hot-bonded to a wraparound aluminium skin. The flying controls are not hydraulically boosted.

The T-tail of the 500D and 500E was fitted to improve handling. It also improved the appearance of the helicopter.

As it was originally intended as an army observation helicopter, the Hughes 500 had very good all-round visibility from the cockpit. Note that the windscreen extends up into the roof and that the side doors have especially large windows.

Most 500s are fitted with a set of either low or extended skids. Inflatable floats can also be fitted for operations over water. The front tip of each skid carries a navigation light.

Allison's 250C engine, in various versions, powers all Hughes/MD 500 variants.

500Ds could be fitted with an optional four-blade tail rotor called the 'Quiet Knight' which, as the name suggests, was intended to reduce tail rotor noise.

The Hughes helicopter family

■ **XH-17:** The largest helicopter in the world in the early-1950s, the XH-17's rotors were powered by jet nozzles on each blade tip.

■ **300C:** Another design originally built for the US Army, the TH-55 Osage was a pilot trainer and later a very successful civil type.

■ **AH-64 APACHE:** The AH-64 is one of the most lethal attack helicopters in service, especially the latest Longbow radar-equipped variant.

■ **MD520 NOTAR:** The first helicopter to use the revolutionary NOTAR tail, the MD520 is already demonstrating much lower noise levels.

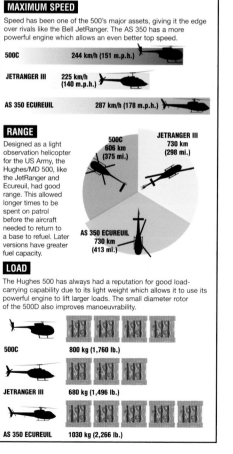

ACTION DATA

MAXIMUM SPEED

Speed has been one of the 500's major assets, giving it the edge over rivals like the Bell JetRanger. The AS 350 has a more powerful engine which allows an even better top speed.

500C	244 km/h (151 m.p.h.)
JETRANGER III	225 km/h (140 m.p.h.)
AS 350 ECUREUIL	287 km/h (178 m.p.h.)

RANGE

Designed as a light observation helicopter for the US Army, the Hughes/MD 500, like the JetRanger and Ecureuil, had good range. This allowed longer times to be spent on patrol before the aircraft needed to return to a base to refuel. Later versions have greater fuel capacity.

500C 606 km (375 mi.)
JETRANGER III 730 km (298 mi.)
AS 350 ECUREUIL 730 km (413 mi.)

LOAD

The Hughes 500 has always had a reputation for good load-carrying capability due to its light weight which allows it to use its powerful engine to lift larger loads. The small diameter rotor of the 500D also improves manoeuvrability.

500C	800 kg (1,760 lb.)
JETRANGER III	680 kg (1,496 lb.)
AS 350 ECUREUIL	1030 kg (2,266 lb.)

McDonnell Douglas

OH-6

● Equipped for night flying ● Light observation ● Police helicopter

▲ The OH-6 was used extensively by the US Army in Vietnam, armed with Miniguns and grenade-launchers. Many of the Border Patrol service's OH-6s are ex-Army machines in a new colour scheme.

Speeding along the border between Mexico and the United States at low level, the OH-6 Cayuse is exciting to fly. Hunting for illegal immigrants, the US Border Patrol service finds the OH-6 to be an ideal machine, fast and agile and providing a superb view of the terrain below from its bubble canopy. Patrolling the border in the agile and nippy OH-6 is a demanding task for these ex-Army pilots.

McDonnell Douglas OH-6

▼ **Latest of the breed**
The sharp-nosed MD 500E is the latest of a long line that began with the OH-6. This MD 500E has a nose-mounted searchlight, and wears the badge of the Orange County Sheriff's Department.

▲ **Italian patrol**
The Italian air force also uses the OH-6. This one has a bubble-type observation window on the port side.

Baywatch ►
Los Angeles County operates 10 MD 500s, which fly coastal patrols for smuggling ships and illegal immigration by sea.

▼ **Desert landing**
One of the less glamorous aspects of border patrolling is landing on empty stretches of desert to look for signs of life. Many OH-6s have the doors removed for cooling.

▲ **Highway patrol**
California's Police Highway Patrol department also uses the OH-6 (in its more modern MD 500 shape), to give warning of congestion on the freeways.

FACTS AND FIGURES

➤ The Hughes MD 500 Defender is an uprated version of the OH-6 airframe armed with TOW anti-tank missiles.

➤ The Model 500C could carry up to seven passengers or 776 kg (1,700 lb.) of cargo.

➤ The OH-6 was fitted with a new tail section and powerplant and became the MD 500.

➤ Hughes also developed a five-bladed OH-6 known as the 'quiet one' with a five-bladed main rotor.

➤ Hughes OH-6s and MD 500s were used by Argentina, Denmark, Mexico and Spain.

➤ Licence manufacture of the MD 500 was also undertaken by Kawasaki in Japan.

Patrolling with the Cayuse

First produced in response to a US Army request for a light observation helicopter (LOH), the Hughes OH-6 went to war in Vietnam soon after its introduction. It has also been sold to many civil users, but was overshadowed in the civil market by the Bell 206.

The OH-6 Cayuse really made its mark with the Border Patrol service in the United States. Flying in hot-and-high conditions along the desert border with Mexico, the Cayuse has the resilience to operate day after day in sand and heat. It offers an observer a superb view of the terrain below. The Border Patrol pilots are usually ex-Army, many of them having flown the OH-6 in Vietnam (where it was known as the 'loach', from the LOH designation).

A typical mission begins with a take-off from a small airfield only 15 km from the border, and check-in on the radio with a ground station. The pilot is alerted of unusual activity, and the OH-6 uses its spotlight to check out the border. There is no hiding from the 'flying eye', able to react at a moment's notice.

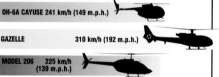

The Hughes OH-6 and MD 500 remain firm favourites with pilots for their superb handling. The classic egg-shaped fuselage remains in use on the new MDH NOTAR helicopters.

Government standard OH-6s are fitted with ARC-54 radios and the ASN-43 heading reference system.

The undercarriage is a simple, tubular steel skid, with integral shock absorbers.

The OH-6 has a side-by-side seating arrangement with full dual controls and two seats in the rear.

Clamshell rear doors provide access to the engine for maintenance.

The OH-6 uses a four-bladed main rotor and the main spar is hot-bonded to an aluminium skin. A trim tab is fitted to the end of each blade.

The fuselage of the OH-6 is of light alloy construction with the egg-shaped main cabin of semi-monocoque type. The shape gives good survivability in a crash as it tends to roll easily.

N67BP

The OH-6 has a chin-mounted wire-cutter spike, potentially a life-saving piece of equipment for a helicopter that must fly at low level at night.

The OH-6 is powered by an Allison T63-A-5A turboshaft engine.

Yaw control is effected through a simple two-bladed tail rotor. This OH-6 has a V-shaped tailfin, unlike the T-tail fitted to later models and MD 500s.

For night observation duty a powerful spotlight is fitted on the port fuselage.

OH-6A CAYUSE

The Border Patrol service operated four OH-6 helicopters, part of a mixed fleet of fixed- and rotary-wing aircraft responsible for assisting ground patrols in the border area with Mexico.

OH-6A Cayuse

Type: five-seat light multi-purpose helicopter

Powerplant: one Allison T63-A-5A turboshaft rated at 236 kW (315 hp.) peak power

Maximum speed: 241 km/h (149 m.p.h.)

Initial climb rate: 560 m/min (1,837 f.p.m.)

Combat radius: 611 km (379 mi.) at 1500 m (4,900 ft.)

Service ceiling: 2225 metres (7,300 ft.)

Weights: empty 520 kg (1,144 lb.); loaded 1090 kg (2,398 lb.)

Armament: provision for 7.62-mm Minigun or XM-75 grenade launcher on port fuselage

Dimensions:
rotor diameter	8.03 m (26 ft.)
length	9.24 m (30 ft.)
height	2.48 m (8 ft.)
rotor disc	50.6 m² (544 sq. ft.)

ACTION DATA

MAXIMUM SPEED

The OH-6 was one of the fastest light helicopters of its day, and could outrun the rival Bell 206. It was not as fast as the Aérospatiale Gazelle, which held several helicopter speed records for a short time in the early 1970s. All-out speed was not of primary importance to the designers of these helicopters.

OH-6A CAYUSE 241 km/h (149 m.p.h.)

GAZELLE 310 km/h (192 m.p.h.)

MODEL 206 225 km/h (139 m.p.h.)

RANGE

Range is an important consideration in light helicopters; all these machines were far superior to the older piston-powered aircraft. As all three were used by civil operators as well as the military, range meant potentially greater sales appeal. But despite its lack of range, the Bell 206 outsold its rivals in thousands.

GAZELLE 755 km (468 mi.)

OH-6A CAYUSE 611 km (379 mi.)

MODEL 206 549 km (340 mi.)

HOVER CEILING (IGE)

The hover ceiling is a product of the helicopter's weight and generated lift. Helicopters seldom ever fly at high level, and rarely ever reach their design ceiling after being test flown. Hover ceiling is measured both in and out of ground effect (the additional effect of sitting on a cushion of air that a helicopter experiences when near the ground).

MODEL 206 3900 m (12,800 ft.)

GAZELLE 3650 m (12,000 ft.)

OH-6A CAYUSE 3595 m (11,800 ft.)

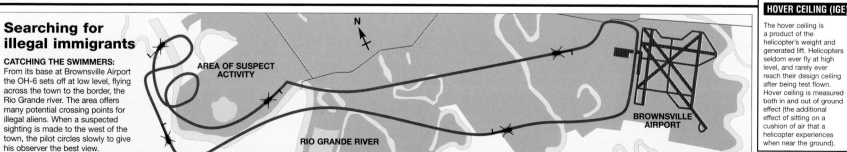

Searching for illegal immigrants

CATCHING THE SWIMMERS: From its base at Brownsville Airport the OH-6 sets off at low level, flying across the town to the border, the Rio Grande river. The area offers many potential crossing points for illegal aliens. When a suspected sighting is made to the west of the town, the pilot circles slowly to give his observer the best view.

N

AREA OF SUSPECT ACTIVITY

BROWNSVILLE AIRPORT

RIO GRANDE RIVER

McDonnell Douglas

EXPLORER

● NOTAR design ● Multi-role helicopter ● Police patrol

▲ *The NOTAR concept removes one of the most troublesome parts of the helicopter, the tail rotor, which causes a great deal of noise, is very vulnerable to damage and needs extra maintenance.*

The basic design of helicopters has changed remarkably little since the first practical machines flew in the 1940s. But McDonnell Douglas has taken a giant step in making rotary-winged flight both safer and quieter with its revolutionary NOTAR, or 'no tail rotor' concept. It was first used in the MD 520N and is now seen on the advanced composite construction Explorer. The NOTAR can even be reversed into trees or water and will still remain functioning.

PHOTO FILE

McDonnell Douglas EXPLORER

▼ NOTAR family
McDonnell Douglas' NOTAR family has so far applied only to light helicopters, but this technology could also be relevant to much larger models.

▲ Tank killer
One possible role for the Explorer is anti-armour, which requires flying at tree-top height. Tail rotors can become entangled in trees, but the NOTAR system is much safer.

▼ Police squad
Law enforcement agencies operate the MD 520N with great success, with the low noise emitted by the NOTAR system being a great advantage.

▲ Safe and simple
It may seem strange for a helicopter not to have a tail rotor, but the NOTAR system uses almost no new materials or high technology, and is very simple.

▲ Rescue
NOTAR is useful for sea rescue missions, as it can operate even when immersed in water. Emergency floats can be fitted as optional extras for over-water operations.

FACTS AND FIGURES

➤ McDonnell Douglas estimates a worldwide demand for up to 1,000 NOTAR machines in the decade to 2005.

➤ The first NOTAR was declared ready after over 1,000 hours of test flying.

➤ By 1993 over 100 operators had taken out options on over 250 MD Explorers.

➤ In September 1993, an MD 520N flew the 215-km (130-mile) trip from Paris to London in a class record of 1 hour 22 minutes and 29 seconds.

➤ The first user of a NOTAR helicopter was the Phoenix Police Department, Arizona.

Goodbye to the tail rotor

Most of the noise and vibration generated by a conventional helicopter is produced by the tail rotor, which is designed to counteract the torque or twisting force caused by the main rotor.

The NOTAR, or NO TAil Rotor, system was developed in the early 1980s by McDonnell Douglas. It manages to dispense with the noise and complications by using an ingenious combination of aerodynamics and an air jet

produced by a fan buried in the root of the tailboom to provide directional stability and control. As well as being much quieter, NOTAR helicopters are safer: there is no risk of the tail rotor strikes that are the cause of many helicopter accidents.

The five-seat MD 520N, a derivative of the US Army's Vietnam-era Hughes OH-6 light observation helicopter, first flew in 1990 and most of the 70 examples delivered by

1995 have been sold to police departments and other law enforcement agencies.

McDonnell Douglas has also launched an advanced new NOTAR light-utility helicopter called the Explorer. Made largely from carbon fibre and composites, it first flew in 1992.

Military interest in the NOTAR system remains limited. However, the US Army conducted experiments with the concept for special operations, where its low noise was a useful asset.

MD 520N

The McDonnell Douglas Helicopters 520N is now in use with several private operators and police forces, and has proven the superiority of the NOTAR concept.

MD 520N

Type: eight-seat civil helicopter

Powerplant: two Pratt & Whitney Canada PW206B turboshafts delivering 469-kW (629-hp.) take-off power

Max cruising speed: 249 km/h (155 m.p.h.)

Initial climb rate: 853 m/min (2,800 f.p.m.)

Range: 600 km (373 mi.) at 1500 m (4,300 ft.)

Service ceiling: 5485 m (18,000 ft.)

Hovering ceiling: 3960 m (13,000 ft.) with ground effect

Weights: empty 1458 kg (3,214 lb.); maximum take-off 3035 kg (6,700 lb.)

Dimensions:
rotor diameter	10.31 m (33 ft. 10 in.)
fuselage length	9.7 m (31 ft. 9 in.)
height	3.66 m (12 ft.)
width	2.79 m (9 ft 2 in.)
rotor disc area	83.52 m² (900 sq. ft.)

The main rotor system is a conventional five-bladed rotor with composite blades and an articulating hinged rotor head.

The fan is driven by a driveshaft via a secondary reduction gearbox, in a similar manner to a conventional tail-rotor driveshaft.

The flight controls of a NOTAR helicopter are identical to those of a conventional tail rotor craft. The one main difference is that the yaw control from the pilot's pedals is even more crisp and responsive than usual.

The port tail rotor fin moves to give directional control in autorotation, when power to the NOTAR fan is lost.

The engine exhausts through the rear fuselage, below the tailboom; this is to avoid interference of the hot engine gases with the NOTAR duct.

Yet another advantage of NOTAR is that the tailboom is slightly shorter than in a conventional helicopter. This makes it easier to manoeuvre the aircraft in confined spaces. The boom can even be reversed into foliage with care.

The MD 520 retains a conventional skid undercarriage similar to its distant ancestor, the Hughes 500. It is constructed of simple alloy tubing.

ACTION DATA

MAXIMUM CRUISING SPEED

The efficient shape of the Explorer gives it a high cruise speed. The lack of a tail rotor also helps to reduce drag and wasted energy, as anti-torque force is produced by the fin in the cruise.

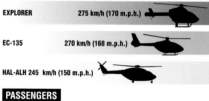

EXPLORER	275 km/h (170 m.p.h.)
EC-135	270 km/h (168 m.p.h.)
HAL-ALH	245 km/h (150 m.p.h.)

PASSENGERS

Both the Explorer and EC-135 are designed to be small multi-role machines, used for tasks such as city transport and police work, unlike the military ALH.

EXPLORER 7 people

EC-135 6 people

HAL-ALH 10 people

NOISE

The NOTAR system removes a major cause of noise, the conflicting airflow between a tail rotor and the main rotor. The EC-135 has a fan-in-fin, or fenestron, to help reduce this noise.

EXPLORER MIN

EC-135 MID

HAL-ALH MAX

How NOTAR works

THE COANDA EFFECT: NOTAR works by utilising the Coanda effect. This is the tendency for air flowing over a curved area to follow the path of that surface. With the NOTAR concept the tail rotor boom is the curved surface. NOTAR uses a fan to produce low-pressure air and a sleeve to control the airflow around the tailboom. This generates the anti-torque force. Instead of flowing evenly over the tailboom, it tends to flow towards the exiting air from the fan.

ROTATING SLEEVE: The air bleeds out through one side of a rotating sleeve. It then follows the profile of the tailboom, drawing more of the main rotor downwash over the slotted side than the unslotted side. This generates a force towards the slotted side, which opposes the rotor torque force.

TAIL CONE: Yaw control is generated by the rotating tail cone, which releases more air from the fan. This acts as a simple direct jet, and does not rely on the Coanda effect. In forward flight, most of the anti-torque is produced by the tail fins.

AIR INTAKE: Air is drawn in through a duct and blown by a simple fan.

MIL

MI-4 'HOUND'

● 1950s military and civil design ● Widely used ● S-55 lookalike

W ith its uncanny and possibly less than coincidental resemblance to the Sikorsky S-55, the Mi-4 appeared in 1952. Taking barely a year to reach flying status from initial design, the 'Hound,' as NATO codenamed it, became widely used at home and overseas. In some respects, though, it reflected the technology gap between the West and the Soviet Union—early Mi-4s had bakelite-and-wood rotor blades.

▲ First and foremost a military helicopter, the Mi-4 also had a civil role and was adapted for agricultural jobs and as a firefighter. Soviet production ended in 1964 when over 3,200 had been produced.

MIL MI-4 'HOUND'

▼ Sputnik capsule in suspension
Carrying the re-entry capsule from a returned Sputnik mission, this Mi-4 demonstrates its lifting capacity of around 1297 kg (2,860 lb.). Internally, 1,736 kg (3,828 lb.) can be carried in the transport role.

▲ Sniffing out submarines
Mi-4PL was the main anti-submarine warfare naval version. It featured radar, a towed MAD (magnetic anomaly detector) and sonobuoys. Four bombs could also be carried.

Indian 'Hound' ▶
India has been a major user of the Mi-4, though the type has been phased out in recent years. Much of their flying was at high altitudes.

▲ Clamshell doors
The rear clamshell doors, designed to ease loading of bulky items, could easily be removed, making troop exits quicker during an airborne assault.

Spatted wheels ▶
This Mi-4P in Aeroflot service shows the spatted wheels with which these aircraft were originally equipped.

FACTS AND FIGURES

➤ At least one Z-5 was re-engined with a Pratt & Whitney PT6T-6 Turbo Twin-Pac turboshaft engine and flew in 1979.

➤ Mi-4M was a tactical variant with a gun turret and air-to-surface rockets.

➤ The Mi-4 prototype used alcohol de-icing for the windscreens and rotor blades.

➤ After ground runs, the first flight of the prototype was delayed because of main rotor blade flutter problems.

➤ Most current users of the Mi-4 are small Middle Eastern and Asian countries.

➤ Harbin built 545 of their Z-5 variant in China, beginning in 1959.

PROFILE

Stalin's 'sudden, great advance'

Design of the Mi-4 transport helicopter began in 1951, at the insistence of Stalin, who was anxious to see a 'sudden, great advance in Soviet helicopters.' Mil was given one year to build a single-engine, 12-seat machine. The first such example flew in May 1952.

The main production variant was the military Mi-4T, which was able to carry 14 fully equipped troops and 3,520 pounds of stores. This was followed in 1954 by the civil Mi-4P for Aeroflot. It held 10 passengers each with 20 kg (44 lb.) of baggage.

Known as 'Hound' to NATO, the Mi-4's basic configuration mirrored that of the Sikorsky

S-55 (though the Mi-4 was larger) using a scaled-up Mi-1 rotor with four bakelite-and-plywood blades. The tried-and-tested Shvetsov ASh-82V 14-cylinder radial engine provided power. Improved versions followed, including anti-submarine warfare and assault variants (with appropriate armament), a supercharged high-altitude model in 1965, and an electronic warfare platform.

While Mi-4 production ceased in 1964 at about 3,200. In China, the license-built Harbin Z-5 was built for 20 years, until 1979. Several third-world air forces still operate the Mi-4 in limited numbers.

Above: The principal military role for the Mi-4 in the Soviet armed forces was initially as troop transport. This is an Mi-4T.

Above: For high altitudes, as here in a mountainous part of the USSR, a two-speed supercharged variant was built.

The position of the cockpit and engine are design features typical of the early 1950s. The heavy piston engines used in larger helicopters were positioned near the aircraft's center of gravity to maintain stability.

In general, the layout of the Mi-4 had features of a scaled-up Mi-1 or Mi-2, but with the engine in the nose of the aircraft and a much larger cabin, similar to the S-55.

It was not until 1954 that Mil was able to increase main rotor blade life to above 300 hours. From 1960, metal blades were fitted to production aircraft, in place of the early bakelite and wood examples.

Among improvements to the Mi-4 (that included dural metal blades from 1960) were magnesium fuselage skins (instead of aluminum), better flight controls and more advanced avionics.

Mi-4A 'Hound'

Type: Military transport helicopter

Powerplant: One 1268 kW (1,700-hp.) Shvetsov ASh-82V radial piston engine

Maximum speed: 200 km/h (124 m.p.h.) at 1000 m (3,300 ft.)

Service ceiling: 5486 m (18,000 ft.)

Accommodation: 14 fully equipped troops or 1736 kg (3,828 lb.) of cargo

Weapons: One 12.7-mm (.50 cal.) cannon in ventral gondola

Weights: Empty 6626 kg (14,608 lb.) max take-off 7534 kg (16,610 lb.)

Dimensions: Rotor diameter 2.3 m (68 ft. 10 in.)
Length (rotors turning) 25 m (82 ft. 1 in.)
Height 4.4 m (14 ft. 5 in.)
Rotor disc area 349 m² (3,760 sq. ft.)

MI-4A 'HOUND'

Mi-4T was the initial military 'Hound' variant, Mi-4As following on as an armed assault variant. Yellow 36 is an early example of later Soviet markings.

Shvetsov's reliable ASh-82V 14-cylinder radial engine powered the Mi-4, in a similar layout to the Sikorsky S-55. The ASh-82V was developed from the ASh-62, itself derived from the American Wright Cyclone.

The military variants had a ventral gondola, which was fitted with a 12.7-mm (.50 caliber) cannon and 200 rounds of ammunition.

In the anti-submarine warfare (ASW) role, the 'Hound' carried a towed magnetic anomaly detector (MAD) at the rear and could drop sonobuoys from an external rack.

Depending upon configuration, the Mi-4 was capable of carrying between 10 and 14 people, or eight stretcher cases (plus attendant) in the air ambulance role. The rear clamshell doors allowed the easy loading of the latter and other cargo. A VIP passenger variant (Mi-4L) had only six seats.

ACTION DATA

ACCOMMODATION

While the 'Hound' shared the basic layout of the S-55, it was a significantly larger aircraft and was therefore able to hold a bigger personnel load. Compared to the Sikorsky design, the Mi-4 also had the advantage of large rear doors to make the loading and unloading of troops and/or cargo easier.

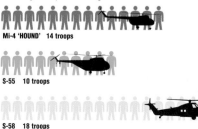

Mi-4 'HOUND' 14 troops

S-55 10 troops

S-58 18 troops

Early troop-carrying helicopters

■ SIKORSKY S-55: Serving with the USAF as the H-19 and the USN as the HO4S and HRS, the radial-engine S-55 first flew in 1949.

■ WESTLAND WHIRLWIND: Search-and-rescue and anti-submarine were typical roles for Westland-built S-55s in the British forces.

■ SIKORSKY S-58: Known as the HSS Seabat and HUS Seahorse in the U.S. Navy and H-34 Choctaw in the USAF, the first S-58 flew in 1954.

■ WESTLAND WESSEX: Westland improved the S-58 by installing a turboshaft engine, for the Royal Navy at first. RAF variants are still in use.

MIL

MI-6 'HOOK'

● Heavylift helicopter ● Speed record holder ● Heli-liner

▲ Mil's monster Mi-6 not only
made every previous helicopter look minute,
but it also proved a very viable and useful
aircraft, unlike the later Mi-10 and Mi-12.
Hence, it was exported widely and a handful
are still flying.

S etting a trend for enormous gas
turbine helicopters with massive
load-carrying capability, the Soviet
Union introduced the Mi-6 as a combined
military/civil project in 1954. Intended
primarily as a support vehicle for the air
force's huge An-12 transport, the Mi-6
needed just two 'lifts' to equal the payload of
the transport. Most Mi-6s were grounded in
1992, after a long service including wartime
operations in Afghanistan and Africa.

MIL MI-6 'HOOK'

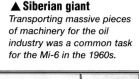

▲ Siberian giant
Transporting massive pieces
of machinery for the oil
industry was a common task
for the Mi-6 in the 1960s.

▲ Long service
About 800 Mi-6s were built between 1957 and 1980. During
the aircraft's busy life it ferried millions of passengers
around the remotest regions of the USSR.

Troop truck ▶
With extra seating the Mi-6 could carry up to 90 troops, but it
was rarely used in a tactical role as size made it vulnerable.

▼ Unique shape
The Mi-6 looked unique. It is an
indication of the success of the
design that the later Mi-26 has a
similar configuration, but with no
wings and an increased number
of rotor blades.

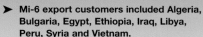

▲ Spacecraft recovery
Only the Mi-6 was big enough to carry the crew
capsule from the Vostok space launchers. The wing
was mounted at 15° to the fuselage and provided
about 20 per cent of the lift when cruising. The
wings could be removed for the 'flying crane' role.

FACTS AND FIGURES

➤ In 1961 the Mi-6 lifted 20117 kg to a
height of 2738 metres and flew at
340.15 km/h over a 100-km circuit.

➤ The Mi-6P was a firefighting version with a
water tank, but it did not have stub wings.

➤ By 1990 Aeroflot Mi-6s had carried
15 million tonnes and 12 million people.

➤ Mi-6 export customers included Algeria,
Bulgaria, Egypt, Ethiopia, Iraq, Libya,
Peru, Syria and Vietnam.

➤ The Mi-6R was a radio command post
containing eight tonnes of equipment.

➤ The Mi-6's main rotor revolved clockwise
at 120 rpm.

Mil's muscular 'Shestyorka'

During the 1950s the Soviets had industrial and military projects scattered across the country and the authorities faced huge problems in supplying them. It was for this reason that a fleet of large transport helicopters became necessary. The Mi-6 met the requirement from 1958.

Everything about the Mi-6 was large. Its engines were a giant leap in gas turbine technology as applied to heavylift 'flying crane' helicopters. It pioneered the use of supplementary wings for added lift and achieved an incredible performance for a machine in its weight class. Basically a freight carrier, military versions dominated the 800-plus production run which ended in 1981.

To cope with adverse weather conditions the Mi-6 had its own rotorblade de-icing system and an auxiliary power unit. The aircraft was known as 'Shestyorka' ('little six') by its crews. Variants included firefighters, military jammers, civil heli-liners and medevac aircraft. Military versions carried a machine-gun in the nose.

First flown in 1960, the Mi-10 was a developed 'flying crane'

Below: The Mi-6 carried loads such as oil drilling equipment, bulldozers, tractors and light artillery pieces.

Above: Although later Mils like the Mi-26 could lift more, they were not built in such large numbers as the versatile Mi-6.

version of the Mi-6, including the engines, gearboxes and stretched undercarriage. Not only was the Mi-6 the biggest helicopter in the world, it was also the fastest and had outstanding range.

Mi-6 'Hook'

Type: heavy-lift transport helicopter

Powerplant: two 4101-kW (5,495-hp.) Soloviev D-25V free-turboshaft engines

Maximum speed: 300 km/h (186 m.p.h.)

Range: 620 km (384 mi.)

Service ceiling: 4500 m (14,750 ft.)

Weights: empty 27,240 kg (59,928 lb.); loaded 42500 kg (93,700 lb.)

Armament: one (optional) 12.7-mm machine-gun in nose

Accommodation: flight crew of five and up to 90 troops or 41 stretcher cases

Dimensions:
main rotor span	35 m (115 ft.)
length	33.18 m (109 ft.)
height	9.86 m (32 ft.)
wing area	35 m² (377 sq. ft.)

ACTION DATA

INTERNAL PAYLOAD

For sheer lifting capacity nothing could match an Mi-6. The Rotodyne also relied on wings, which limited its carrying capacity when taking off. The CH-47 had a smaller internal volume.

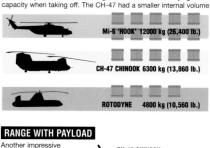

Mi-6 'HOOK' 12000 kg (26,400 lb.)

CH-47 CHINOOK 6300 kg (13,860 lb.)

ROTODYNE 4800 kg (10,560 lb.)

RANGE WITH PAYLOAD

Another impressive feature of the Mi-6 was its range, a necessity in the vast expanses of the former Soviet Union. The Rotodyne was also very long ranged, but could not carry as much as the Mi-6. The Chinook was designed for shorter range operations.

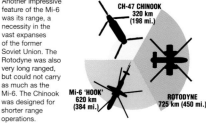

CH-47 CHINOOK 320 km (198 mi.)

Mi-6 'HOOK' 620 km (384 mi.)

ROTODYNE 725 km (450 mi.)

MAXIMUM SPEED

These helicopters were all very fast, with the Rotodyne benefiting from extra engines and wings. The CH-47's twin rotors produced a large amount of thrust, whereas the Mi-6 relied on brute power.

Mi-6 'HOOK'	300 km/h (186 m.p.h.)
CH-47 CHINOOK	298 km/h (185 m.p.h.)
ROTODYNE	307 km/h (190 m.p.h.)

Mi-6 'Hook'

Mi-6s were widely used in the Middle East, but almost all have now been retired. This helicopter was used by the Egyptian air force, which suffered from a lack of spares after the Soviets were expelled from the country.

For a helicopter the Mi-6 had an unprecedented equipment fit, including an autopilot. The flight deck had jettisonable doors on either side for the pilots and flight engineer. A navigator sat in the glazed nose and a radio operator was sometimes carried.

The massive gearbox weighed no less than 3200 kg (7,040 lb.). It also drove two 90-kVA alternators to feed the heavy load of electro-thermal de-icing systems and radios.

The five-bladed main rotor was based on an extruded steel main spar, with screwed-on aerofoil sections of duralumin. The blades were electro-thermally de-iced, and were connected to the head by conventional hinges and bearings.

Large clamshell doors made loading and unloading very easy. The main hold was 12 metres (39 ft.) long, had a volume of 80 m³ (61 cu. yds.) and included its own electric winch.

The tail rotor was a four-bladed AV-63B type with a steel spar and a Bakelite ply outer. Early versions had electro-thermal de-icing, which was replaced by alcohol in later models.

Big lifters in the West

■ **AÉROSPATIALE SA 321F:** The civil variant of the Super Frelon, the SA 321 is no longer in service. The military version is still used by France.

■ **SIKORSKY CH-53:** Still the biggest rotary machine built in the West, the CH-53 was a great success and is still in service in Germany.

■ **SIKORSKY S-64:** The West's answer to the Mi-10, the Skycrane was used extensively in Vietnam to recover shot-down UH-1s.

■ **WESTLAND WESTMINSTER:** Only two of these aircraft were ever built. It was cancelled in favour of the larger Fairey Rotodyne.

MIL
MI-8 'HIP'

● Assault transport ● Civil helicopter ● Gunship

A tough and resilient combat veteran, the Mil Mi-8 'Hip', and the closely related Mi-17, stands tall in its reputation as one of the most versatile helicopters in the world. The Mi-8 is the most widely used helicopter in service, and is cheap to run, easy to maintain and powerful. The 'Hip' is primarily a troop carrier and civil transport. Other roles include helicopter gunship, airborne command post, search and rescue and even communications jamming.

▲ One of the most enduring rotary designs ever, the Mi-8 has all the typical attributes of a Mil machine, combining strength and simplicity in a well-proven low-cost airframe.

MIL MI-8 'HIP'

▼ Shooting from the hip
The 'Hip-E' gunship version is one of the world's most heavily armed helicopters, and has been used extensively in Chechnya.

▲ Santa's sleigh
Even Santa Claus used the Mi-8 when travelling in distant areas of the Soviet Union. The Mi-8 was also vital to the Soviet oil industry, which explored in very remote areas.

Tourist flyer ▶
This Mi-8, belonging to Avialini Baltiski, flies tourists over St Petersburg on short pleasure flights in the summer.

▼ Assault transport
This Mi-8 of the Indian air force is landing troops close to the front. Soviet Mi-8s made thousands of air assaults in Afghanistan, and large numbers were shot down.

▲ KGB transport
Guarding the huge borders of the Soviet Union, the KGB needed a large number of Mi-8s to transport dog teams.

FACTS AND FIGURES

➤ More than 10,000 Mi-8s and Mi-17s have been built, with many hundreds being exported to more than 40 operators.

➤ The Mil Mi-17 is basically a Mi-8 with more power and a new tail rotor.

➤ The rare Mi-8PPA is a special communications jammer variant.

➤ The Mi-8 has fought in Afghanistan, Angola, Chechnya, Egypt, Mozambique and Nicaragua.

➤ The Czech Republic, Hungary and Russia use the 'Hip-G' command post version.

➤ The Mil Mi-14 'Haze' anti-submarine helicopter is derived from the Mi-8.

Helicopter workhorse to the world

Design of the Mi-8 'Hip' began in 1960. Unlike the earlier Mi-4 'Hound' which had its engine mounted in the nose, the Mi-8 has a more efficient shape with the turboshaft powerplant above the fuselage leaving maximum space for payload. Except on specialised models, large clamshell doors swing open at the rear fuselage.

Nearly a dozen versions of the Mi-8 and its upgraded Mi-17 derivative were used by Soviet forces and exported to Moscow's allies, and thousands of examples remain in service in Russia and around the world. Despite the age of the basic design, the type remains in production and sales continue. From the Arctic tundra of Finland to the tropical jungles of Peru, the 'Hip' is always a formidable performer, whether dropping into a landing zone with a load of troops or flying scheduled airline or cargo services to remote settlements.

Military Mi-8s are often equipped to a high specification, including additional cockpit armour, infra-red jammers, chaff and flare dispensers

Mi-8s belonging to Interflug, former state airline of the DDR, have now all been retired.

and exhaust gas diffusers. The Mi-17 improved upon the original Mi-8 by introducing a titanium rotor head for greater strength, improved efficiency engines and a new gearbox.

MI-8T 'HIP-C'

The Mi-8 remains in service in very large numbers with Aeroflot's successor airlines in the former USSR, such as Baltiski, Baikal Avia, Orbi, Tajik Air and Tatarstan, as well as with many military air arms.

The Mi-8 was cheap enough to produce in thousands, giving the Red Army mass airlift capability.

The Mi-8 has a traditional rotor head with flapping hinges and bearings. The improved titanium rotor head of the Mi-17 needs less maintenance and is more bullet resistant.

Although slightly redesigned, the Mi-8's large five-bladed main rotor was also used by the later Mi-24 gunship. Like all Mil designs, it rotates clockwise when viewed from above. The rotors have an automatic ice detection and thermal de-icing system, essential for operations in Russian conditions.

In the Mi-8 the tail rotor is on the starboard side of the tail, but on the port side of the Mi-17.

The Isotov TV-2 engines of the Mi-8 are very similar to the TV-3 engines in the Mi-24 and Mi-17. The TV-3 proved more reliable and economical and dramatically improved performance in 'hot-and-high' conditions.

АЭРОФЛОТ 367Н   CCCP-25852

The Mi-8 cockpit is surprisingly large. Israeli pilots flying captured examples in 1973 found that the machine had a totally different feel in flight to Western helicopters, and could easily outrun many of them.

Loading a Mi-8 is easy, thanks to the clamshell doors at the rear which can accommodate wide cargoes and allow infantry to exit very swiftly in an assault.

ACTION DATA

MAXIMUM SPEED

Typical top speeds for this type and size of helicopter tend to be around 250 km/h (155 m.p.h.). The Puma had a marginal edge in this respect, with a better power-to-weight ratio.

Mi-8T 'HIP-C'	250km/h (155 m.p.h.)
SA 330H PUMA	280km/h (174 m.p.h.)
COMMANDO Mk 2	226 km/h (143 m.p.h.)

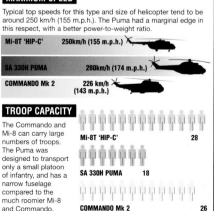

TROOP CAPACITY

The Commando and Mi-8 can carry large numbers of troops. The Puma was designed to transport only a small platoon of infantry, and has a narrow fuselage compared to the much roomier Mi-8 and Commando.

Mi-8T 'HIP-C'	28
SA 330H PUMA	18
COMMANDO Mk 2	26

Mil's multi-role 'Hip'

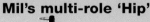

Mi-8 'HIP-A': The first Mi-8 was the single-engined prototype that lacked power and only had a four-bladed main rotor.

Mi-8 'HIP-C': With two engines and five main rotor blades, the Mi-8 'Hip-C' became the main assault helicopter of the USSR.

Mi-8 'HIP-E': Probably the most heavily armed helicopter in service, the 'Hip-E' carried up to six pods of 32 rockets.

Mi-17 'HIP-H': The Mi-17 featured new engines, gearbox and rotor shaft and was a lot more powerful and economical than the Mi-8.

AWACS HIP: The Mi-17 was even converted to act as an airborne early warning and control machine with side-mounted radar aerials.

MIL

MI-14 'HAZE'

● Twin-engined shore-based ASW/SAR helicopter ● Exports

MIL MI-14 'HAZE'

◀ **Export potential**
This Mi-14P was displayed at the Mosaero air show in 1995. It has a new nose radome in place of the undernose fairing and a searchlight.

▼ **Amphibious 'Haze' at sea**
The boat hull shape of the Mi-14's lower fuselage is supplemented by floating bags, which are useful when retrieving personnel in the SAR role or if the aircraft is forced to ditch.

▼ **Upgraded Mi-14 demonstrator**
To 'drum up' business, the Russian aviation industry is offering upgrades for existing airframes.

▼ **Land based**
As featured on other maritime helicopters like the Sikorsky Sea King, the Mi-14 has a shaped hull to provide an amphibious capability.

▲ **'Haze' underside**
This view of an Mi-14's underside shows the large weapons bay doors open and the MAD 'bird' deployed. Other apertures in the rear of the fuselage house dipping sonar and include parachutes for sonobuoys and flares.

Based on the Mi-8 'Hip', the Mi-14 was developed as a land-based anti-submarine helicopter in the early-1970s. A boat hull and retractable landing gear were used to make it suitable for amphibious operations, with more powerful engines compensating for the additional weight. Flight tests started in September 1969. Specialised versions for minesweeping and search and rescue operations have also been produced.

▲ *Entering production in 1978, more than 240 Mi-14 'Haze-As' were built. The 'Haze' family have been the Soviet Bloc's principal shore-based ASW and SAR helicopters.*

FACTS AND FIGURES

➤ The Mi-14PL 'Haze-A' entered service in 1976, the Mi-14BT 'Haze-B' followed in 1986 and the Mi-14PS 'Haze-C' in 1992.

➤ Poland was the only export customer for the search-and-rescue Mi-14PS.

➤ East German Mi-14s were retired after the German reunification.

➤ The engine and gearbox from the Mi-17, itself developed from the Mi-8, was installed in the Mi-14.

➤ The SAR 'Haze-B' carries ten 20-place liferafts and can tow these when filled.

➤ Mi-14PLs carry four crew: two pilots, a flight engineer and a systems operator.

Soviet ASW and SAR patroller

Below: The 'Haze' usually carries a flight crew of three, although the anti-submarine variants also have a systems operator for the sonar equipment and weapons.

Equipped with a search radar, dipping sonar, dispensers for sonobuoys and flares and a towed magnetic anomaly detector (MAD), the original anti-submarine version of the 'Haze' was the Mi-14PL. The Mi-14PLM is a later variant with an improved engine and has the search radar moved to the bottom rear end of the fuselage.

For minesweeping, the Mi-14BT 'Haze-B' has a mine-activating sled in place of the MAD. Towed behind the helicopter, it carries either

electrical cables or noise generators to detonate magnetic or acoustic mines. A searchlight on the tailboom enables the sled to be launched and recovered at night. The BT variant was used by the former East German navy, as well as the Soviet naval air arm, although only about 25 were built. The Luftwaffe did not keep the East German navy's six Mi-14BTs after reunification. Some have been converted to water bombers for use in civilian fire-fighting operations.

Above: Mi-14PL export markets included Bulgaria, Cuba, East Germany, Libya, North Korea, Poland, Syria and Yugoslavia.

The search-and-rescue version is known as the Mi-14PS 'Haze-C'. It has a more powerful winch and a wider main door, and is fitted with searchlights in the nose. The only users of the 'Haze-C' are Russia and Poland.

Mi-14PL 'Haze-A'

Type: land-based anti-submarine helicopter

Powerplant: two 1434-kW (1,925-hp.) Klimov (Isotov) TV3-117MT turboshafts

Max speed: 230 km/h (143 m.p.h.) at sea level

Climb rate: 468 m/min (1,535 f.p.m.) at sea level

Endurance: 5 hours 55 min

Range: 1135 km (704 mi.) with maximum fuel

Weights: empty 8902 kg (19,584 lb.); loaded 13000 kg (28,600 lb.); maximum take-off 14000 kg (30,800 lb.)

Armament: torpedoes and depth charges, as well as sonobuoys/smoke/flare floats

Dimensions:
main rotor diameter	21.29 m (69 ft. 10 in.)
length	18.37 m (60 ft. 3 in.)
height	9.63 m (31 ft. 7 in.)
rotor disc area	362 m² (3,895 sq. ft.)

MI-14PL 'HAZE-A'

This Mi-14PL serves with the Polish navy, which also operates an Mi-14PX in the SAR training role and a small number of Mi-14PS 'Haze-C' dedicated SAR machines.

The underfuselage radome contains a Type 12-M search radar. A watertight weapons bay on the centreline can carry depth charges and torpedoes.

In common with the Mi-8 'Hip' from which it was developed, the Mi-14 has a five-blade main rotor. A three-blade tail rotor is fitted on the left side of the tail boom, as on the improved Mi-17.

This aircraft wears a commonly used low-visibility grey colour scheme. East German examples were painted in a dark shade of blue.

To assist during personnel recovery, a 150-kg (300-lb.) hoist is fitted above the main cabin door.

The MAD 'bird' stowed behind the rear fuselage is used to detect submarines. Magnetic anomalies may be caused by the presence of a large metallic mass, like a submarine.

The fuselage sponsons and tail float both contain flotation gear for use if the helicopter ditches at sea. The tail float prevents the tail rotor touching the water during an on-water landing.

COMBAT DATA

MAXIMUM SPEED

Aircraft like the Mi-14 were not intended to be high-speed machines, range and endurance were more important factors. All three types are capable of speeds in the 250 km/h (150 m.p.h.) band.

Mi-14PL 'HAZE-A'	230 km/h (143 m.p.h.)	
SA 321G SUPER FRELON	275 km/h (171 m.p.h.)	
Ka-27PL 'HELIX-A'	250 km/h (155 m.p.h.)	

ENDURANCE

The land-based Mi-14 has the best endurance of these representative types. 'Helix' is a smaller carrier-based machine, and the Super Frelon has three engines and a higher fuel consumption.

Mi-14PL 'HAZE-A'	SA 321G SUPER FRELON	Ka-27PL 'HELIX-A'
5 hours 55 min	4 hours	4 hours 30 min

FERRY RANGE

The endurance of each type is reflected by the range figure. The values quoted are for ferry range with a maximum fuel load and no weapons or other equipment on board. Range performance is particularly important for carrier-based aircraft.

Mi-14PL 'HAZE-A' 1135 km (704 mi.)

SA 321G SUPER FRELON 1020 km (630 mi.)

Ka-27PL 'HELIX-A' 900 km (558 mi.)

Anti-submarine helicopter designs

■ **AÉROSPATIALE SA 321 SUPER FRELON:** The SA 321G ASW variant of this three-engined machine entered Aéronavale service in 1965.

■ **KAMAN SH-2 SEASPRITE:** Derived from the UH-2, this ASW variant appeared in 1970 and remains in use with the US Navy.

■ **WESTLAND LYNX:** The first naval version of the Lynx did not fly until 1976. Widely exported, it is the Royal Navy's principal ASW machine.

■ **SIKORSKY SH-3 SEA KING:** Sikorsky's very successful S-61 design flew in 1959 and has been developed by Westland and Agusta.

MIL

V-12

● Twin rotor ● Heavylift helicopter ● Unbroken records

▲ Mikhail Mil, son of a mining engineer, was perhaps the best helicopter designer ever. The V-12 was his greatest creation, but only two machines were produced.

Everything about the V-12 was enormous. The twin-rotor giant shattered every record for helicopter payload, and made every previous rotary-wing machine seem like a toy. But the problems of operating such a machine were also enormous and, despite the ingenuity of the design, it was not really a viable machine for commercial use. After a memorable appearance at the Paris Air Show, the V-12 rarely flew again.

PHOTO FILE

MIL V-12

'Hook' power ▶
The engines, gearbox and rotors were all taken from the Mi-6 'Hook', albeit with some changes; rotor rpm was reduced to 112.

▼ Big wing
A large wing helped to offload the main rotors in forward flight. Its trailing-edge flaps were fixed after early trials.

▲ Loading ramp
Practical touches like the rear clamshell doors and loading ramp showed that the V-12 was not just a record breaker. The fuselage interior also had four cargo winches and a reinforced floor structure.

▼ Paris performance
The Paris Air Show was the V-12's greatest moment, attracting enormous attention. But there was little interest in the machine from foreign customers.

▲ Room at the top
The immense cockpit held a pilot, co-pilot, electronics operator and engineer, with the navigator and radio operator seated above.

FACTS AND FIGURES

➤ The enormous D-25 turboshaft engines were also used in other very large Mil helicopters like the Mi-6 and Mi-10.

➤ The one remaining V-12 can be seen at the Monino air force museum in Moscow.

➤ The V-12 had hydraulic flight controls, but it could also be flown manually.

➤ Fully loaded, the V-12 was as heavy as nine Mi-24 'Hind' gunships, or more than twice as heavy as an Mi-6.

➤ The main cabin of the V-12 was 28.15 m (93 ft.) long and 4.4 m (47 ft.) square.

➤ Optional ferry tanks could be carried inside the V-12 for maximum range.

Hundred-tonne helicopter

Produced by the man who had built the world's previous largest helicopter, Mikhail Leontyevich Mil, the V-12 was a giant. With a maximum take-off weight of over 100 tonnes, it was bigger than many transport aircraft.

Developed with the engines, transmission and rotors of the Mi-6, but in double pods outboard of a long reverse-taper wing, the V-12 had a huge fuselage space that contained one-tonne cargo hoists and seats could be fitted for more

than 100 passengers. The V-12 even had a split-level flight deck, with pilots and flight engineer below and navigator and radio operator above.

The first V-12 was damaged in a crash in 1967, caused by resonance and control system problems. The second appeared at the Paris Air Show, and went on to break many helicopter payload records, most of which remain to this day. But despite its stunning performance and size, the V-12 was not really economical to use, and Mil

decided to develop the Mi-26 for heavy cargo work instead, leaving the V-12 in a museum.

Below: The Soviet obsession with having the biggest and fastest of everything was manifest in the V-12. Mil turned his attentions to the more successful Mi-26 after the problems with the V-12 became apparent.

Above: Twin-rotor power was a new concept for the Mil company. Despite overcoming many of the technical difficulties, the V-12 was plagued by problems with resonance.

V-12

Type: twin-rotor heavy transport helicopter

Powerplant: four 4847-kW (6,495-hp.) D-25V turboshafts driving in pairs with transverse shafting

Maximum speed: 260 km/h (161 m.p.h.)

Cruising speed: 240 km/h (149 m.p.h.)

Range: 500 km (310 mi.) with maximum payload

Weights: empty not disclosed; maximum payload 25 tonnes; vertical take-off 30 tonnes; maximum take-off 105 tonnes

Armament: none

Dimensions:
span	19.55 m	(64 ft.)
length	19.1 m	(63 ft.)
height	4.88 m	(16 ft.)
wing area	52.49 m²	(565 sq. ft.)

V-12

■ Number '21142' was the second Mil V-12 twin-rotor helicopter. In 1969, carrying a payload of 40204 kg (88,448 lb.), it was flown to 2255 m (11,224 ft.) by V. P. Koloshchyenko.

The pilot flew the V-12 with the aid of an autostabilisation system. A ground-mapping radar was fitted under the nose.

The podded engines had access panels on their undersides to allow easy maintenance. The whole engine assembly was mounted at a 4° nose down angle. Fuel was carried in the outer wing section.

The large central tailfin gave the V-12 some much needed stability in forward flight, supplemented by auxiliary tailfins outboard.

Fuel was carried in two external tanks as well as the outer wing structure.

The engine and wing were suspended with complex bracing. Vibration of the rotors through this bracing to the undercarriage caused many of the V-12's problems.

Light vehicles could be loaded through its rear doors, and a side door allowed access to passengers.

АЭРОФЛОТ МИ CCCP-21142

ACTION DATA

PAYLOAD

The V-12 could carry a huge load, even more with a running take-off in which it benefited from transition effect (like all helicopters). The Mi-26 carries almost as much using a single rotor and has trouble-free handling.

V-12
25000 kg (55,000 lb.)

CH-53E
16330 kg (35,926 lb.)

Mi-26 'HALO'
20000 kg (44,000 lb.)

POWER

Using four engines from the Mil-6, the V-12 had awesome power. The modern Mi-26 has almost the same power from two more modern engines, which drive through a less wasteful transmission. The CH-53E is driven by three relatively small engines.

V-12
4 x 4847 kW = 19388 kW
(4 X 6,495 hp. = 25,980 hp.)

CH-53E
3 x 3266 kW = 10798 kW
(3 X 4,376 hp. = 13,129 hp.)

Mi-26 'HALO'
2 x 8380 kW = 16760 kW
(2 X 11,229 hp. = 22,458 hp.)

MAXIMUM TAKE-OFF WEIGHT

The V-12 had a maximum take-off weight of 105 tonnes, or more than a loaded Vulcan bomber. The CH-53 is dwarfed by the much larger Mil helicopters, but is an impressive machine. The Mi-26 is almost as heavy as a fully loaded C-130 Hercules at maximum all-up weight.

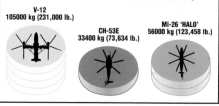

V-12
105000 kg (231,000 lb.)

CH-53E
33400 kg (73,634 lb.)

Mi-26 'HALO'
56000 kg (123,458 lb.)

Mil's family of helicopters

■ **Mi-4 'HOUND':** Still in service in some Third World countries, the Mi-4 can carry a 1300-kg (2,860-lb.) underslung load or an internal load of 1740 kg (3,820 lb.). Thousands of Mi-4s were built, including licence production in China.

■ **Mi-6 'HOOK':** Another Mil record breaker, the Mi-6 was the largest helicopter in the world for many years. It could carry 8 tonnes internally or 12 tonnes underslung. It used fixed wings to offload the rotors in forward flight.

■ **Mi-8 'HIP':** Using the same gearbox and rotors as the Mi-4, the Mi-8 has been produced in thousands and is the most widely used helicopter in the world. The Mi-8 could lift 4 tonnes internally or 4 tonnes externally.

■ **Mi-10 'HARKE':** Using the same engines as the Mi-6, the Mi-10 was developed as a flying crane with an extra long undercarriage for lifting bulky cargo. The Mi-10 could lift 15 tonnes internally or 8 tonnes underslung.

MIL

MI-24 'HIND-A'

● Soviet gunship/assault helicopter ● Exported ● Afghan action

▲ On its entry into Soviet service, the Mi-24 was unique. The West had no direct equivalent, which was considered disastrous at the time. The response was to develop the dedicated AH-64 Apache, a far more effective tank-killer.

Soviet helicopter pioneer Mikhail Mil's last helicopter design, the Mi-24, has been one of the most widely used military helicopters. The original Mi-24 prototype flew in 1970, and was used with two other prototypes to establish several speed, height and climb records. Initial production aircraft were given the NATO reporting name 'Hind-A', and were operated by a three-man crew, including a flight engineer as well as a co-pilot/gunner.

PHOTO FILE

MIL MI-24 'HIND-A'

▲ **Low-drag attributes**
Cockpit glazing was designed to reduce drag and contributed to the Mi-24's excellent performance.

▲ **Well armed**
A variety of weapons (anti-tank missiles, rockets and bombs) were carried on 'wings' attached behind the cabin. Each had a 250-kg (550-lb.) capacity. The Mi-24 saw its first action in Afghanistan.

▲ **Inspired by HueyCobra**
Mikhail Mil studied the American Bell 209 HueyCobra before proposing the Mi-24. The 'Hind' differed from the Cobra in having a troop carrying capability.

▲ **'Hinds' in action**
During the Soviet intervention in Afghanistan in the 1980s, 'Hind-As' and 'Hind-Ds' were used in the COIN role.

Museum piece ▶
Most early-model 'Hinds' are today relegated to the museums.

FACTS AND FIGURES

➤ Iraqi Mi-24s were credited with downing Iranian Cobra helicopters and even F-4 fighter-bombers during the Iran-Iraq War.

➤ An Mi-24 prototype flew for the first time in early 1970.

➤ A 'Hind-A' was modified to test systems for the later 'Hind-D'.

➤ Pre-production Mi-24s were known as 'Hind-B' in the West as they were not identified until after production 'Hind-As'.

➤ During the conflict in Afghanistan, Mi-24s were flown by Soviet and Afghan forces.

➤ As well as carrying weapons, the stub wings provide some lift.

PROFILE

Warsaw Pact armed assault chopper

Built to take troops to the thick of battlefield action, the Mi-24 gained from lessons learned by US forces in Vietnam. Big enough to carry eight troops, it was powerful and fast, and carried enough weapons to suppress hostile forces en route to the landing zone – a flying armoured personnel carrier.

Mil used the TV2-117 engines and dynamic system from the Mi-8 'Hip' so that design work could concentrate on the weapons installation. As a result,

the 'Hind-A' was in service with the Soviet forces in East Germany from 1973.

The TV2-117 engines were replaced by TV3-117s in later production aircraft, and the same powerplant was fitted to some earlier machines. 'Hind-As' with the later engine have the tail rotor repositioned on the left of the tail boom.

Though the 'Hind-A' was not exported as widely as some of the later gunship versions of the Mi-24, small numbers have served with the forces of

Afghanistan (where the type saw its first action, mainly in the counter-insurgency role), Algeria, Libya and Vietnam.

The 'Hind-C' (Mi-24U) was a dedicated training version of the 'Hind-A' with dual controls but stripped of armament. It was one of these aircraft (designated 'A-10') that was used in 1975 to set eight world marks, including a number of speed records, with a female aircrew. From the mid-1970s, the redesigned 'Hind-D' replaced the A model on the production line.

Straight wings without anhedral identify this Mi-24 as a 'Hind-B' from the first production series.

MI-24 'HIND-A'

Libya was among four Soviet allies to receive the 'Hind-A', the others being Algeria, Afghanistan and Vietnam. It is believed that few, if any, 'Hind-As' remain in service.

It is believed that from the outset the 'Hind' was expected to have a dual role as both a gunship and an assault helicopter (thus replacing the Mi-8 'Hip'). However, Mi-24s have never been able to carry a full weapons load while carrying troops, and the dual role abilities of the type are limited.

Twin 1434-kW Isotov TV-3 turboshafts powered most Mi-24s, though early production batches were fitted with smaller TV-2s as installed in the Mi-8, on which the Mi-24 design was based.

Shrouded in flat plate glazing, the cockpit of the 'Hind-A' had three seats. The crew consisted of a gunner seated in the centre front, a flight engineer/co-pilot behind him to the rear, and the pilot offset to the left rear, next to the co-pilot. In the lower nose a 12.7-mm (.50-cal.) machine-gun was fitted in a flexible mounting.

Unlike the extensively redesigned 'Hind-D', the 'Hind-A' was only lightly armoured.

While early production 'Hind-As' and some later 'Hind-Ds' had their tail rotors located on the starboard side of the tail fin, those on late 'Hind-As' were switched to the port side.

Each stub wing can carry two Falanga anti-tank missiles (known to NATO as AT-2 'Swatters') as well as four 32-round rocket pods. Various antennas on the aircraft were associated with radio equipment and defensive avionics, like IFF (identification friend or foe).

'Hinds' at home and abroad

■ **Mi-24 'HIND-A':** Algerian 'Hind-As' served alongside Mi-4s and Mi-8s. In 1996 the North African state continued to fly 'Hinds', though whether these were 'Hind-As' is unclear. Few export customers ordered the variant.

■ **Mi-24D 'HIND-D':** The 'Hind-D' was a major redesign of the Mi-24 intended to address the weaknesses of the 'Hind-A'. Early production examples of the new aircraft were delivered to Warsaw Pact countries, including East Germany.

■ **Mi-24P 'HIND-F':** Experience in Afghanistan led to the replacement of the 12.7-mm nose-mounted machine-gun with a twin-barrelled 30-mm cannon on the Mi-24P. The Soviet Union and GDR used this variant; the Mi-35P was an export derivative.

COMBAT DATA

MAXIMUM SPEED

As the 'Hind' was developed with new engines, a redesigned fuselage and more capable weapons, its top speed fluctuated. The first Mi-24Ds were marginally slower than the 'Hind-A', but by the time that the Mi-24P 'Hind-F' had appeared in service this had been addressed, the type having a small top speed margin over the Mi-24D 'Hind-D'.

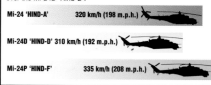

Mi-24 'HIND-A'	320 km/h (198 m.p.h.)
Mi-24D 'HIND-D'	310 km/h (192 m.p.h.)
Mi-24P 'HIND-F'	335 km/h (208 m.p.h.)

MIL

MI-24 'HIND'

● Gunship ● Tank-buster ● Afghan war veteran

▲ The 'Hind' was regarded with awe by NATO when it appeared in the 1970s. Now regarded as a simple machine by Western standards, it is respected for its speed, strength and massive firepower.

The Mil Mi-24 'Hind' is the hammer of the Russian army. A veteran of battles in Afghanistan and Angola, and most recently in Chechnya, the Mi-24 is a flying armoured personnel carrier, able to deliver a squad of soldiers and cover them with suppressive fire. Armed with a cannon and powerful laser-guided anti-armour missiles, and now fitted with the latest avionics and new engines, the 'Hind' is a highly potent attack helicopter.

PHOTO FILE

MIL MI-24 'HIND'

▲ Tank-buster
Standard armament in early 'Hinds' was UV-32 rocket pods and the AT-2 missile.

▲ Twin cannon
The 'Hind-F' replaced the nose turret machine-gun with a fixed twin-barrel 30-mm GSh cannon.

Battle wagon ▶
The 'Hind' proved its toughness in Afghanistan, where it often survived massive small-arms fire.

▲ German 'Hind'
The Luftwaffe has disposed of its Mi-24 fleet, acquired along with East Germany, mainly due to poor supplies of spares.

◀ Gunfighter
The 'Hind-D' carries the classic Mi-24 armament fit. A 12.7-mm multi-barrel gun turret shares the nose with an electro-optical guidance system to starboard and a missile guidance pod to port.

▲ Fast mover
The 'Hind' used its speed to advantage in attacks, acting much like a ground-attack jet fighter.

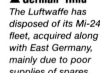

FACTS AND FIGURES

➤ The prototype for the Mi-24 series, fitted with a conventional cockpit, made its first flight in 1970.

➤ An Mi-24 set a helicopter world speed record of 368.4 km/h (229 m.p.h.).

➤ Mi-24s fought against South African troops during the Angolan war.

➤ Mujahideen guerrillas in Afghanistan shot down three Mi-24s at Jalalabad air base in five minutes using Stinger missiles.

➤ The 'Hind' is operated by more than two dozen countries.

➤ Two Mi-24s were flown to Pakistan by defecting Afghan air force pilots.

PROFILE

Russia's flying tank

First seen in the West in 1974, the 'Hind' was designed to carry eight men into front-line positions and support them with air-to-ground fire. The Mi-24 is very large and fast, but it is not as agile as Western battlefield helicopters. However, aircraft like the American AH-64 Apache are designed to engage tanks from hidden hovering positions, which calls for low-speed manoeuvrability. The 'Hind', by contrast, is a purely offensive weapon, heavily armed and armoured and designed to advance at high speed.

Most 'Hinds' are gunships, with a stepped tandem canopy housing a weapons operator in front and a pilot higher to the rear. Either can aim the gun with a magnifying sight in a bulge under the nose, which also contains a laser tracker for missiles.

After combat experience in Afghanistan, Mil introduced an improved 'Hind' with a twin-barrelled GSh-23L 30-mm cannon. This, together with its rockets and missiles, makes the 'Hind' very much a close-support weapon, with enormous firepower.

Like most Russian weapons the 'Hind' is a powerful machine, built to take battle damage and capable of operating in very harsh conditions. It will serve for many years yet, as the planned Mi-40 replacement has been cancelled.

The stub wings allow the 'Hind' to travel very fast by adding to the lift from the rotor, but by sticking out into the rotor downwash they inhibit low-speed and hovering handling.

Both cockpits have excellent armour protection and bulletproof glass canopies.

The five-bladed main rotor may be replaced by that of the more modern Mi-28 'Havoc', if the 'Hind' upgrade programme goes ahead.

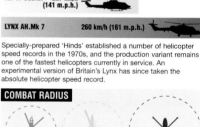

Mi-24D 'Hind-D'

Type: battlefield helicopter

Powerplant: two 1640-kW (1,500-hp.) Klimov (Isotov) TV3-117 Series III turboshafts

Maximum speed: 310 km/h (192 m.p.h.)

Max cruising speed: 260 km/h (161 m.p.h.)

Range: 750 km (465 mi.) with internal fuel

Service ceiling: 4500 m (14,760 ft.)

Weights: empty 8400 kg (18,400 lb.); loaded 12500 kg (27,500 lb.)

Armament: one four-barrel JakB 12.7-mm Gatling gun in chin turret; four S-8 80-mm rocket pods or up to 3460 kg (7,612 lb.) of rockets or missiles

Dimensions:
span	6.54 m (21 ft.)
main rotor diameter	17.3 m (57 ft.)
length	19.79 m (65 ft.)
height	6.5 m (21 ft.)

MI-24H 'HIND-E'

This Mi-24 'Hind-E' serves with the Polish air force's 56th squadron at Inowroclaw, armed with the 'Shturm' AT-6 laser-guided anti-tank missile.

All Mil helicopters have a clockwise rotating rotor. The rotor head was built to withstand heavy machine-gun fire.

Many 'Hinds' have an infra-red jammer fitted to counter shoulder-launched heat-seeking missiles such as Stinger and SA-14.

The original 'Hind-A' had its tail rotor on the starboard side of the tail boom, but it was switched to port soon after production had started.

The Isotov turboshafts are powerful engines, but they are getting old. They may be replaced by engines used in the Mi-28 if Russia can find the money to upgrade its 'Hinds'.

Large exhaust suppressors are fitted to some 'Hinds' to reduce infra-red signature.

Flare dispensers are often fitted to 'Hinds', usually on the tailboom. Lack of these units caused heavy losses to Stinger missiles in the Afghan war.

The tail rotor remains one of the weak points of the 'Hind'. The yellow warning strip has the Russian word for 'danger' painted on it, as ground crews often fail to spot it when it is rotating.

COMBAT DATA

MAXIMUM CRUISING SPEED

Mi-24D 'HIND-D'	260 km/h (161 m.p.h.)	
AH-1F COBRA	227 km/h (141 m.p.h.)	
LYNX AH.Mk 7	260 km/h (161 m.p.h.)	

Specially-prepared 'Hinds' established a number of helicopter speed records in the 1970s, and the production variant remains one of the fastest helicopters currently in service. An experimental version of Britain's Lynx has since taken the absolute helicopter speed record.

COMBAT RADIUS

Mi-24D 'HIND-D'	AH-1F COBRA	LYNX AH.Mk 7
160 km (100 mi.)	200 km (124 mi.)	270 km (167 mi.)

The Mi-24 is a big and heavy machine, and with a full combat load its range is noticeably shorter than those of its rivals, although it can double its range by carrying drop-tanks in place of weaponry. Since the 'Hind' is primarily a battlefield weapon, its lack of range is no real handicap.

ANTI-TANK WEAPONS

Mi-24D 'HIND-D'	AH-1F COBRA	LYNX AH.Mk 7
4 x AT-2 'Swatter' or AT-6 'Spiral' missiles	8 x TOW missiles	8 x TOW missiles

Although the 'Hind' carries fewer anti-tank weapons than its rivals, it should be remembered that it was not designed as an anti-tank platform. Its stub wings can be used to carry a much heavier weight of other weapons, including bombs, rockets, guns and even chemical weapons.

Gunship rivals

■ **BELL AH-1 COBRA:** This pioneering gunship helicopter introduced the now standard fighter-style cockpit, with a gunner in front and the pilot behind. Much smaller than the 'Hind', the Cobra is purely a fighting machine and has no passenger cabin.

■ **McDONNELL DOUGLAS AH-64 APACHE:** Much more manoeuvrable at low speeds than the 'Hind', the Apache is the West's premier gunship and anti-tank helicopter. Like the big Mil design, it is heavily armed and armoured.

■ **MIL Mi-28 'HAVOC':** Even more powerful than the 'Hind', the 'Havoc' dispenses with the earlier helicopter's passenger cabin. It is actively marketed by the Mil design bureau, but might not enter service with the financially-strained Russian military.

MIL

MI-26 'HALO'

● Largest production helicopter ● United Nations relief flights

▲ Once again, Mil has entered the record books with the superb Mi-26 'Halo'. It is currently both the largest and the most powerful helicopter of its type in service anywhere.

With the intention of surpassing the load-carrying capabilities of its mighty Mi-6 'Hook', Mil set about designing its Mi-26 'Halo' in the early 1970s. It was clear that the twin-rotor layout of the earlier V-12 had led to a developmental dead end, so Mil set out to produce a thoroughly conventional helicopter on a hugh scale, with a payload up to one and a half times greater than that of any previous rotary-winged type.

PHOTO FILE

MIL MI-26 'HALO'

◀ **Subcontinent service**
India has been the only export user and currently operates 10 examples, all with No. 26 Squadron.

▼ **Commercial Mil**
Mil has actively sought civilian customers; an Mi-26T variant is tailor-made for commercial use.

▼ **Enormous capacity**
The presence of these troops and a single jeep lend scale to the size of the Mi-26. The fuselage is as large as that of a C-130 Hercules and can accomodate up to 80 fully-equipped soldiers.

▼ **Special requirement**
A primary requirement prompting the design and development of this huge helicopter was for a machine able to carry substantial loads in vast, sparsely-populated areas, such as Siberia. The Mi-26 performs such tasks with ease.

◀ **Continuing production**
Although many Russian projects have fallen by the wayside due to a lack of funding, development of the 'Halo' continues, with new variants still emerging.

FACTS AND FIGURES

➤ Flown for the first time in a hover on 14 December 1977, the Mi-26 was initially designated the V-26.

➤ Machined from titanium, the main-rotor hub is the largest in the world.

➤ External steps and handholds allow access to the tailboom and rotor.

➤ Variants include the Mi-26TZ tanker, which can carry 14040 litres (3,709 gallons) of fuel dispensed on the ground using 10 hoses.

➤ In the firefighting role, the Mi-26 can drop 7500 litres (2,000 gallons) of fire retardant.

➤ A special variant, designated Mi-26MS, is a fully-equipped airborne hospital.

PROFILE

Heavyweight 'Halo'

Using the world's only operational eight-bladed rotor system, and having a cabin cross-section similar to that of the Il-76T 'Candid' four-turbofan airlifter, the Mi-26 is truly a machine of superlatives.

With its eight rotor blades, the Mi-26 is able to handle its two 7,460-kW (10,003-hp.) turbines, with a rotor of smaller diameter than that of the Mi-6. Power is transferred to the rotor shaft by a gearbox of unique design. It is smaller than that of the 'Hook', but weighs 3,500 kg (7,720 lb.).

Its strength allows it to control the huge 90,000-kg (20,000-lb.) maximum torque of the engines.

A hook beneath the fuselage is stressed for slung loads of up to 30,000 kg (66,000 lb.). The principal motivation for the Mi-26 programme was support for exploration work in the remotest areas of Siberia, and a hook of such capacity is vital if heavy items of equipment are to be positioned in otherwise inaccessible areas. Such locations also require the highest levels of reliability, and 'Halos' often

Above: When the 'Halo' made its debut at Paris in 1981, the French had an apt nickname for it: 'Le monstre'.

operate under harsh conditions for up to a week without proper engineering support. As well as its many civilian roles, the Mi-26 is also employed by the Indian, Russian and possibly Ukrainian military.

Above: Mi-26s have been actively used on United Nations humanitarian relief operations in recent years.

Mi-26 'Halo'

Type: heavylift civil/military transport helicopter

Powerplant: two 8,380-kW (11,237-hp.) ZMDB 'Progress' (Lotarev) D-136 turboshafts

Maximum speed: 295 km/h (183 m.p.h.)

Cruising speed: 255 km/h (158 m.p.h.)

Range: 2000 km (1,243 mi.) with auxiliary fuel; 800 km (497 mi.) with standard fuel

Service ceiling: 4600m (15,000 ft.)

Weight: empty 28200 kg (62,170 lb.); maximum take-off 56000 kg (12,350 lb.)

Payload: 20000 kg (44,100 lb.)

Dimensions:

main rotor diameter	32 m (105 ft.)
fuselage length	33.72 m (110 ft. 7 in.)
height	8.14 m (26 ft. 8 in.)
rotor disc area	804.25 m² (8,657 ft)

MI-26 'HALO'

This machine was one of the Soviet Frontal Aviation Mi-26s used during the clean-up of the Chernobyl nuclear power station in 1986. Later discovered to be radioactive, it was soon withdrawn from service.

At first glance, it would appear that the rotor design is very old fashioned and similar to that of its predecessor, the 1950s' vintage Mi-6 'Hook'. However, the head is extremely light and compact, and is the first in the world to carry eight rotor blades.

Unlike the main unit, the tail rotor unit was a completely new design and features five composite blades. The fin to which it is fitted incorporates a low-speed aerofoil section, which reduces load-bearing on the tail rotor, enabling better stability at cruising speed.

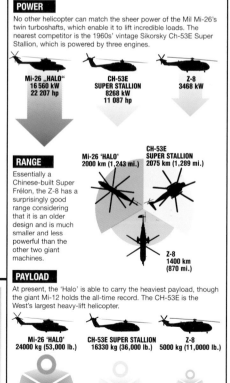

Rear access to the cavernous fuselage is provided by three clamshell doors: two hinge outwards, and the third incorporates a ramp, which can be lowered vertically.

At rest, the 'Halo' adopts a distinctive tail-heavy stance, similar to that of other Mil-designed helicopters. To protect the underside from damage when the helicopter is operating in 'hot-and-high' conditions, a heavy-duty tail skid is fitted.

ACTION DATA

POWER

No other helicopter can match the sheer power of the Mil Mi-26's twin turboshafts, which enable it to lift incredible loads. The nearest competitor is the 1960s' vintage Sikorsky Ch-53E Super Stallion, which is powered by three engines.

Mi-26 „HALO" 16 560 kW 22 207 hp	CH-53E SUPER STALLION 8268 kW 11 087 hp	Z-8 3468 kW

RANGE

Essentially a Chinese-built Super Frélon, the Z-8 has a surprisingly good range considering that it is an older design and is much smaller and less powerful than the other two giant machines.

Mi-26 'HALO' 2000 km (1,243 mi.)

CH-53E SUPER STALLION 2075 km (1,289 mi.)

Z-8 1400 km (870 mi.)

PAYLOAD

At present, the 'Halo' is able to carry the heaviest payload, though the giant Mi-12 holds the all-time record. The CH-53E is the West's largest heavy-lift helicopter.

Mi-26 'HALO' 24000 kg (53,000 lb.)	CH-53E SUPER STALLION 16330 kg (36,000 lb.)	Z-8 5000 kg (11,0000 lb.)

Mil's milestone helicopters

■ **MIL Mi-1:** This little machine has the distinction of being the first series production Soviet helicopter of conventional configuration. Now a museum piece, it was a milestone in Russian design.

■ **MIL Mi-8 'HIP':** Numerically the most important European helicopter ever built, some 8000 examples have entered service over the years, with a number of operators around the world. Many remain in use.

■ **MIL Mi-12 'HOMER':** Only two examples of this, the largest helicopter ever, were constructed. The Mi-12 (or V-12) was powered by four engines; however, technical difficulties halted development.

MIL

MI-26 'HALO'

● Heavylift helicopter ● Largest rotor craft in the world

▲ It is the world's biggest helicopter, the size of the Lockheed Hercules. Flown by the Russian air force, it has been used to open up the trackless wastes of Siberia.

The Mil Mi-26 brings size and brute force to the bold adventure of taming the wildest terrain on our planet. To permit humans to tap the wealthy resources of inhospitable Siberia, Mil engineers produced the largest helicopter being used anywhere. They made it a flying powerhouse, able to get in and out of tight places in fearsome winter climates while carrying cargoes of record-breaking size and weight.

MIL MI-26 'HALO'

▼ Damage control
In the first panicked response to the disaster at Chernobyl, Mi-26s were used to dump tons of sand to smother the fires in the out-of-control nuclear reactor.

▲ Western visitor
The first sight of the giant Mi-26 was at Western air shows, but Russian operators are now pushing hard to market its unmatched heavylift capacity as a commercial proposition.

▶ Multi-role
With such a huge cargo hold, the 'Halo' can carry a wide variety of loads. Its maximum payload is 20 tons, and it can carry light armoured vehicles, oilfield equipment or more than 100 passengers.

▼ Wide body
With a fuselage the size of a C-130 Hercules, the Mi-26 is capable of carrying internally large loads which most, if not all, other helicopters would have to hoist as a slung load from external cargo hooks.

◀ Crewing the giant
Unlike Western helicopters, which have highly automated cockpits, the Mi-26 has a full four-man flight crew of two pilots, navigator and engineer.

FACTS AND FIGURES

➤ The fuselage of the 'Halo' is twice the size of a Douglas DC-3 transport.

➤ India was the only overseas customer for the 'Halo', purchasing 10 aircraft.

➤ The Mi-26 is larger inside than a C-130 Hercules, and is the biggest helicopter ever put into production.

➤ To ease freight handling, there are two 2500-kg (5,511-lb.) winches in the cargo hold.

➤ The circle created by the Mi-26's rotor has four times the area of the VS-300, an early helicopter.

➤ 'Halo' carries 30 times the payload of a light helicopter like the Bell JetRanger.

The world's biggest rotor craft

It represents one of the greatest advances in rotary-wing aviation. The Mil Mi-26 'Halo', first flown in 1977, boasts unbelievable strength and lifting power.

The Mil engineering team, experts at big helicopter design, took Russia by storm when their Mil Mi-26 began airline and military duties. Then the 'Halo' went to work, exploiting forestry, minerals and hydro-electric power in the frozen expanse of Siberia. The Mi-26 is so huge that it surprised no one when it picked up and moved a four-bedroom house.

The Mi-26 is big, but it is also a beauty. Two incredibly powerful engines drive its eight-bladed main rotor. Pilots love this friendly giant: it has a spacious flight deck at floor level with large windows bulged to permit a look at underslung loads, and TV cameras augment the pilots' all-round view. With the benefit of this amazing visibility, the crew have little difficulty in carrying out major chores with the Mi-26. One amazing feat of the 'Halo' was to fly over the burning Chernobyl reactor, dropping chemicals and concrete to try and staunch the radioactive flow.

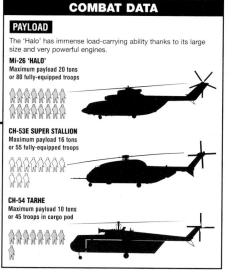

Above: The Mil design bureau has long specialised in heavylift helicopters. One of the first to be seen in the West was the Mi-10 'Harke' flying crane.

Although the main rotor of the 'Halo' is smaller than that of the preceding 'Hook', its advanced design generates more lift.

MI-26 'HALO'

This heavylift helicopter is in service with the Russian air force, Aeroflot, the Ukraine, and the Indian air force.

The Mil Mi-26 has been designed with the same internal cross-section as the Ilyushin Il-76 logistic freighter. At 3.2 metres square (34 sq. ft.), it can hold containers or medium-sized vehicles without any difficulty.

The eight-bladed rotor is of very advanced design and of lightweight but strong construction. It enables the Mi-26 to carry twice the load of its predecessors.

Two 8380-kW (11,203-hp.) Lotarev turboshaft engines power the Mi-26. These deliver over 50 per cent more power than the three engines of the American Sikorsky CH-53E Super Stallion.

Currently utilising aluminium–lithium alloy in its rotors, the 'Halo' will be fitted with composite blades in the future.

The 'Halo' is equipped with all the necessary systems to fly by day or by night, including a computerised flight/navigation system, automatic flight control and a weather radar in the hinged nosecone.

The 'Halo' can be quickly configured for passenger transport, freight, disaster relief or air ambulance duties. Access to the cabin is through a large pair of clamshell doors at the rear, with a lower door acting as a vehicle ramp.

CCCP-06141

H-351

АЭРОФЛОТ

Mi-26 'Halo'

Type: very large heavylift helicopter

Powerplant: two D-136 turboshaft engines each rated at 8,280-kW (11,103-hp.) and driving an eight-bladed rotor

Maximum speed: 295 km/h (183 m.p.h.) at 6096 m (20,000 ft.)

Range: 800 km (497 mi.) at economical cruising speed; 2000 km (1,243 mi.) with auxiliary fuel tank

Normal ceiling: 4600 m (16,000 ft.)

Weights: empty 28200 kg (62,170 lb.); loaded 56000 kg (12,346 lb.)

Dimensions:
rotor diameter	32 m (105 ft.)
fuselage length	33.73 m (110 ft. 8 in.)
height	8.14 m (26 ft. 8 in.)
rotor area:	804.25 m² (8,657 sq. ft.)

COMBAT DATA

PAYLOAD

The 'Halo' has immense load-carrying ability thanks to its large size and very powerful engines.

Mi-26 'HALO'
Maximum payload 20 tons or 80 fully-equipped troops

CH-53E SUPER STALLION
Maximum payload 16 tons or 55 fully-equipped troops

CH-54 TARHE
Maximum payload 10 tons or 45 troops in cargo pod

Mil's monsters

■ **MIL Mi-6 'HOOK':** First flown in 1957, the massive Mi-6 was for two decades the world's largest operational helicopter. Using stub wings to provide extra lift in forward flight, it could carry 65 passengers or up to 12 tons of cargo internally.

■ **MIL Mi-10 'HARKE':** Although the cabin of the Mi-6 was big, it still could not handle outsize loads. The Mi-10, which first flew in 1960, was a flying crane variant capable of hoisting loads the size of a bus and up to 14 tons in weight.

■ **MIL V-12 'HOMER':** This experimental aircraft is the largest rotary-winged machine ever flown. Powered by two sets of Mi-10 engines and rotors, it carried a load of 40 tons to 2000 m (6,500 ft.), but control problems meant that it never entered production.

MIL

MI-17 'HIP'

● Civilian and military use ● Many variants ● Flown worldwide

▲ Few aircraft
are as versatile or as rugged as the
Mi-17. New and improved variants are being
continuously developed for all types of
civilian, military and humanitarian missions.

Russia's powerful and versatile
Mil Mi-17, which was based on the
phenomenally successful Mi-8, is
a truly great design. The 'Hip-H' has much
greater power than the earlier machine,
producing huge improvements in both
hovering performance and single-engine
flight. The increased capabilities of
the Mi-17 make it even more versatile
than the Mi-8 and new versions continue
to be produced.

SAR 'Hip-H' ▶
Many 'Hip-H's are used in the
search-and-rescue role, with
a powerful winch fitted above the
cabin door on the left-hand side of
the fuselage. This Czech aircraft
does not carry the optional
emergency floatation equipment.

◀Long-distance operations
Used to fly to disaster areas where local medical
facilities have been destroyed, the Mi-17-1BA is
fully equipped with a modern operating theatre.

▼ Indian service
A number of 'Hip-Hs' are used by the Indian
air force as utility helicopters, and in service
are designated Mi-17s.

▼ Cabin heating
External fuel tanks are carried on either side of
the fuselage. The tank on the right, visible on this
Czech machine, is longer since the forward section
is occupied by a cabin heater.

Mi-17MD weapons ▶
A range of anti-tank and air-to-air missiles may be carried on the
strongly braced pylons of the Kazan-developed Mi-17-MD.

FACTS AND FIGURES

➤ Revealed to the world at the 1981 Paris
air show, the Mi-17 is known by the
Russian military as the Mi-8M.

➤ A new rotor hub of titanium alloy was
developed for the Mi-17.

➤ Export customers and Russian civilian
operators use the Mi-17 designation.

➤ Individual factories continue to develop
new Mi-17 variants, like the Mi-171
produced by the Ulan Ude factory.

➤ The Mi-17-1BA variant serves as a flying
operating theatre.

➤ Some Mi-17s may carry a nose-mounted
20-mm cannon.

Russia's trusty workhorse

Taking one of the most successful helicopters ever built and improving it produced the exceptional Mil Mi-17/Mi-8M series of civilian and military helicopters.

By replacing the 1044-kW (1,400-hp.) powerplant of the Mi-8 with two 1434-kW (1,923-hp.) Isotov TV3-117MT engines, designers gave the Mi-17 an improved cruising speed and hovering ceiling and an increased maximum take-off weight. The engines also dramatically reduced fuel consumption.

After the Mi-17's first flight in 1976, the first production aircraft

were delivered to Aeroflot. Passengers benefit from the airline-style seats of the 'Hip-H' compared to the folding, inwards-facing seats of the earlier Mi-8.

In Russian military service the Mi-8M flies as a utility and armed assault helicopter and in a wide variety of special mission configurations. The Hungarian air force uses the Mi-17P with large aerial arrays fixed to the rear-fuselage sides

in a communications jamming, and possibly electronic intelligence, role. A number of unusual modifications have also been noted on Czech aircraft.

Left: Kazan Helicopters build the standard Mi-17M. This one contains a weather radar in the nose.

Right: Many ex-WarPac nations, including the Slovak air force, have inherited Russian military hardware.

MI-17M 'HIP-H'

Czechoslovakian military aircraft were divided between the Czech Republic and Slovakia when these countries became independent nations. Most Czech Mi-17s are painted in this green/grey scheme.

Mi-17TB 'Hip-H'

Type: twin-turboshaft multi-purpose helicopter

Powerplant: two 1434-kW (1,923-hp.) Klimov TV3-117MT turboshafts

Maximum speed: 250 km/h (155 m.p.h.)

Range: 495 km (307 mi.) with maximum fuel

Hover ceiling: 1760 m (5,770 ft.) out of ground effect

Weights: empty equipped 7100 kg (15,620 lb.); maximum take-off weight 13000 kg (28,600 lb.)

Armament: up to six rocket pods, four AT-3 'Sagger' missiles and a 12.7-mm (.50 cal.) machine-gun

Dimensions:
main rotor diameter	21.29 m (69 ft. 10 in.)
length	25.35 m (83 ft. 2 in.)
height	4.76 m (15 ft. 7 in.)
main rotor disc area	356.00 m² (3,831 sq. ft.)

An all-new titanium rotor hub was designed for the Mi-17. The Mi-8 prototype had a four-bladed main rotor, as used on the Mi-4 'Hound', but all production aircraft, including Mi-17s, have been fitted with a five-bladed rotor. This larger rotor system is a scaled-down version of that used on the Mi-6 'Hook'.

Various weapons and equipment fits are seen on Mi-17s. This one combines a high-capacity rescue winch with a fuselage-mounted weapons pylons.

In the event of a single engine failure, the remaining engine automatically increases its power output from 1434 kW to 1637 kW (1,923 hp. to 2,195 hp.). This allows safe flight to continue. Filters are installed ahead of the engines to prevent the ingestion of debris, although they are rarely seen on Mi-8s.

One of the main recognition points distinguishing the Mi-17 from the Mi-8 is the repositioned tail rotor. This has been moved from the right side of the tailboom to the left.

0804

Troops, cargo and even small vehicles are easily loaded via the two clamshell doors at the rear of the fuselage. Hook-on ramps allow vehicles to drive straight into the cabin.

During very slow speed flight, especially sideways or backwards, normal means of measuring airspeed and altitude become unreliable. To solve this problem a Doppler radar, which provides precise flight data, is contained within this box.

All Mi-17s naturally adopt a tail-down attitude on the ground. This fixed tail bumper prevents damage to the tail rotor in the event of a heavy landing.

Mi-17 development

■ **Mi-17M:** This Ulan Ude-built 'Hip-H' is basically a standard Mi-17M. It appears to have been fitted with a radar and some type of targeting system under the nose.

■ **Mi-17Z-2:** The Slovak air force operates two of these AWACS-configured Mi-17s. They are thought to have a secondary Comint and jamming ability.

■ **DAEWOO HEAVY INDUSTRIES MK-30:** Using the upgraded Mi-17M/17Z from the Kazan plant as a basis, Daewoo planned to build the advanced MK-30. Little has been heard of the project.

ACTION DATA

MAXIMUM SPEED

Some experts have criticised the 'Hip' for its lack of speed and limited range, but these do not take into account the tactical nature of most of the aircraft's operations. The Mi-17 has a similar performance to the Kawasaki KV-107IIA, which has also undergone a continuous series of upgrades.

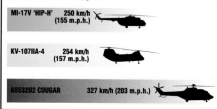

MI-17V 'HIP-H'	250 km/h (155 m.p.h.)
KV-107IIA-4	254 km/h (157 m.p.h.)
AS532U2 COUGAR	327 km/h (203 m.p.h.)

MIL

MI-28 'HAVOC'

● Anti-tank helicopter ● All-weather night attack version

MIL MI-28 'HAVOC'

▼ Anti-tank missions
For destroying enemy armour the Mi-28 can carry up to 16 Shturm (AT-6 'Spiral') anti-tank missiles and forty 80-mm rockets.

▲ Turret-mounted gun
The Mi-28's 30-mm NPPU-28 cannon has air-to-air capability and can fire up to 900 rounds per minute. Its ammunition is compatible with Russian armoured vehicle weapons.

▲ 'Havoc' for the 21st century
If funding permits, the Russian army would purchase the Mi-28N and the rival Ka-50/-52 combat helicopter.

▲ Production version
Mil upgraded the equipment fit of the Mi-28 to produce the much more capable Mi-28N. This has improved avionics and weaponry and an all-weather capability.

Combat rescue ▶
The 'Havoc' has a compartment in the rear fuselage for the rescue of combat personnel or for special forces insertion. For self-protection, composite armour and a combined chaff/flare and electronic warfare suite are fitted.

F lown for the first time in November 1982, the Mi-28 marked a change in the Soviet approach to battlefield helicopters. The earlier Mi-24 'Hind' was designed to be used like a dive-bomber rather than for attacking from concealed positions as Western helicopter gunships did. But the 'Havoc' is designed to be much better than the Mi-24 in low-speed and hovering flight, and gives its crews the option of either type of attack.

▲ Mil continues to develop the Mi-28 for the home market and actively promotes the aircraft abroad. It is likely that large-scale Russian procurement will concentrate on the night-attack Mi-28N.

FACTS AND FIGURES

➤ The Mi-28 'Havoc-A' prototype first flew on 10 November 1982 and appeared at the Paris air show in 1989.

➤ In emergencies an inflatable crew chute is deployed beneath the door sills.

➤ The fuel tanks of the 'Havoc' are self-sealing and fire retardant.

➤ Mil plans to develop the Mi-28N into the 8- to 10-seat Mi-40 infantry helicopter, which will replace the Mi-24 'Hind'.

➤ The Mi-28N can carry the Igla (SA-16 'Gimlet') AAM and new-generation ASMs.

➤ The Mi-28N rotorhead contains a 360° millimetre-wave radar system.

Eastern tank destroyer

Mil's 'Havoc' can carry an impressive weight of armament. The nose gun, with 300 rounds of ammunition, can be trained through 100° horizontally and from 13° upwards to 40° downwards. It fires at 300 rounds per minute against ground targets or at three times that rate against other aircraft. The Mi-28's stub wings have four pylons for anti-tank missiles, rockets, bombs, or air-to-air missiles.

Survivability was a key factor from the outset. The tandem seats and landing gear are designed to protect the crew in a crash landing at descent rates of up to 15 m (50 ft.) per second. In an emergency a survival system blasts the doors and wings away from the aircraft if the crew need to parachute.

Unlike its rival, the Kamov Ka-50 'Hokum', the Mi-28 has a conventional attack helicopter layout, with gunner/navigator seated in the nose and the pilot directly behind.

A night combat version of the 'Havoc' is designated the Mi-28N. It features infra-red and low-light television sensors in the nose, and has a laser rangefinder/designator, a missile guidance radar and a more modern range of ordnance.

Above: The Klimov TV3-117 turboshafts power a five-bladed composite main rotor and a scissor-type tail rotor. This system, and a fenestron tail rotor, were both first tested on an Mi-24 'Hind' development aircraft.

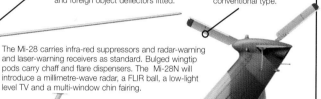

Above: For longer range missions the Mi-28 can carry up to four external fuel tanks. Designed to be capable of autonomous battlefield operations, it also has an internal weapons hoist.

Mi-28 'Havoc-A'

Type: helicopter gunship

Powerplant: two 1640-kW (2,200-hp.) Klimov TV3-117BMA turboshafts

Maximum speed: 300 km/h (186 m.p.h.)

Range: 470 km (290 mi.); ferry 1100 km (680 mi.)

Hover ceiling: 3600 m (11,800 ft.) out of ground effect

Weights: empty 8095 kg (17,809 lb.); maximum take-off 10400 kg (40,689 lb.)

Armament: one 30-mm cannon plus up to 16 9M114 (AT-6 'Spiral') anti-tank missiles, 40 80-mm or 130-mm rockets, bombs and two R-73 (AA-11 'Archer') air-to-air missiles

Dimensions: rotor diameter 17.2 m (56 ft. 5 in.)
length 16.85 m (55 ft. 3 in.)
height 3.82 m (12 ft. 3 in.)
rotor disc area 232.35 m²(2,316 sq. ft.)

MI-28 'HAVOC-A'

Yellow-022 was the second prototype Mi-28 and featured the late-model nose and gun installation. After the construction of a fifth prototype, it was decided that only a few more 'Havoc-A's would be built.

As well as having heavily armoured engines and fuel tanks, the Havoc has crew compartments which are protected by titanium and ceramic armour and the glass transparencies are also armoured. Fuel is held in multiple self-sealing tanks.

Power for the 'Havoc' is provided by two 1640-kW 2200 hp.) Klimov turboshafts with downward-deflected and shrouded exhaust nozzles. The air intakes have dust and foreign object deflectors fitted.

Later Mi-28 prototypes had a scissor-type, four-bladed tail rotor rather than this conventional type.

The Mi-28 carries infra-red suppressors and radar-warning and laser-warning receivers as standard. Bulged wingtip pods carry chaff and flare dispensers. The Mi-28N will introduce a millimetre-wave radar, a FLIR ball, a low-light level TV and a multi-window chin fairing.

The 30-mm NPPU-22 cannon traverses on both horizontal and vertical axes. A new specialised cannon is under development for the Mi-28N.

Mi-28 prototypes have been seen in the West only with B-8 20-round 80-mm rocket pods and Shturm (AT-6 'Spiral') missiles. The Mi-28 will probably carry newer Vikhr (AT-12) ASMs and Igla (SA-16) AAMs.

Mil's proposal for the Mi-40 utility helicopter will use the tailboom and rotor systems of the Mi-28.

The Mi-28 undercarriage comprises single-wheeled 720-mm x 320-mm (28 x 12 in.) main units and a castoring tailwheel. All are mounted on shock-absorbing assemblies.

COMBAT DATA

ENGINE POWER

Surprisingly, the Mi-24 'Hind-D' has the same engine power as its intended successor, the Mi-28. The Ka-50, the Mi-28's rival, has slightly greater engine power, which reflects its design brief for air combat superiority.

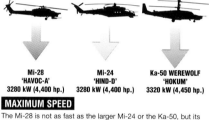

| Mi-28 'HAVOC-A' 3280 kW (4,400 hp.) | Mi-24 'HIND-D' 3280 kW (4,400 hp.) | Ka-50 WEREWOLF 'HOKUM' 3320 kW (4,450 hp.) |

MAXIMUM SPEED

The Mi-28 is not as fast as the larger Mi-24 or the Ka-50, but its maximum speed is adequate for the battlefield combat arena. The Mi-24 is optimised for high-speed assault and the Mi-28 for ground-attack and tank-busting duties.

Mi-28 'HAVOC-A' 300 km/h (186 m.p.h.)
Mi-24 'HIND-D' 310 km/h (192 m.p.h.)
Ka-50 WEREWOLF 'HOKUM' 350 km/h (217 m.p.h.)

COMBAT RADIUS

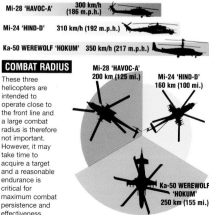

These three helicopters are intended to operate close to the front line and a large combat radius is therefore not important. However, it may take time to acquire a target and a reasonable endurance is critical for maximum combat persistence and effectiveness.

Mi-28 'HAVOC-A' 200 km (125 mi.)
Mi-24 'HIND-D' 160 km (100 mi.)
Ka-50 WEREWOLF 'HOKUM' 250 km (155 mi.)

'Havoc' over the battlefield

The Mi-28 gives Russian forces air-to-air, anti-tank, attack and combat search and rescue (CSAR) capabilities. It is one of the world's most versatile battlefield helicopters.

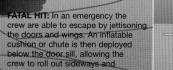

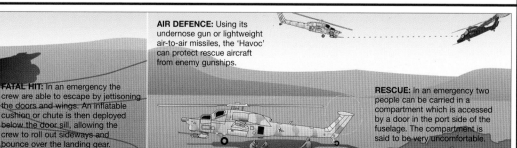

FATAL HIT: In an emergency the crew are able to escape by jettisoning the doors and wings. An inflatable cushion or chute is then deployed below the door sill, allowing the crew to roll out sideways and bounce over the landing gear.

AIR DEFENCE: Using its undernose gun or lightweight air-to-air missiles, the 'Havoc' can protect rescue aircraft from enemy gunships.

RESCUE: In an emergency two people can be carried in a compartment which is accessed by a door in the port side of the fuselage. The compartment is said to be very uncomfortable.

MIL

MI-34 'HERMIT'

● Military trainer ● Aerobatic ● Liaison aircraft

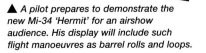

▲ *A pilot prepares to demonstrate the new Mi-34 'Hermit' for an airshow audience. His display will include such flight manoeuvres as barrel rolls and loops.*

First flown in 1986, the Mi-34 was designed as a replacement for the Mi-1 and Mi-2 helicopter trainers. It was also offered for the observation, liaison and border patrol roles. The Mi-34 can carry a maximum payload of 165 kilogrammes (360 lb.) of fuel over a distance of 160 kilometres (100 miles) and it fuel consumption is a modest 45 litres (12 gallons) per hour. A twin-engine version, flown for the first time iin 1993, has two VAZ-430 twin-chamber rotary engines.

MIL MI-34 'HERMIT'

▼ **Slim design**
Despite the compact layout of the Mi-34, the helicopter can accommodate two pilots and two passengers in the rear fuselage.

▲ **Mixed materials**
Although the Mi-34 relies heavily on conventional structures, the main rotor head and rear rotor blades are made of composite materials in an effort to save weight.

◄ **Overseas exhibition**
Mil has displayed the 'Hermit' at numerous airshows throughout the West as part of a sales drive.

▲ **Pilot trainer**
A military training variant has undergone flight testing with the Soviet armed forces as a possible replacement for the Mi-1/Mi-2.

◄ **Flight performance**
One of the latest helicopters developed in Russia, the 'Hermit' is sparsely equipped compared to its Western counterparts.

FACTS AND FIGURES

➤ The Mi-34 'Hermit' was designed as a replacement for the Mi-1/Mi-2 civil light helicopter and military trainer.

➤ 'Hermit' is the first Soviet helicopter capable of executing a loop.

➤ Composite materials are used for the main rotor and tail blades.

➤ Mil first flew the Mi-34 'Hermit' in 1986, using unboosted mechanical flight controls.

➤ A twin-engine version is built by the VAZ motor car works at Togliatigrad.

➤ The Mi-34VAZ features a totally new rotor head made from carbon fibre.

PROFIL

Russia's new lightweight

Using the same nine-cylinder piston engine as the Yak-52 trainer and Ka-26 helicopter, the Mi-34 has composite main and tail rotors attached to a straightforward light-alloy fuselage and non-retractable skids.

The 'Hermit' showed its competition-flying potential by becoming the first Soviet helicopter to perform loops and rolls. It can withstand loads of up to 2.5g for short periods at speeds of 50 to 150 km/h (30 to 93 m.p.h.), and can fly backwards at up to 130 km/h (81 m.p.h.).

As well as having a similar powerplant to other Soviet primary training aircraft – an important economical consideration – the Mi-34's reciprocating engine accelerates rapidly and is not distrubed by ingesting gases during acrobatic manoeuvres.

Although designed primarily for use as an aerobatic and training aricraft, the 'Hermit' offers scope for other duties, with space behind the dual-control flight deck for cargo or a bench seat for two passengers.

Left: After years of building military helicopters, the Mil design team is shifting its focus to the civilian helicopter market with the Mi-34

The twin engine Mi-34VAZ is built by the VAZ automobile factory. It has a new rotor head for enhanced control response, along with improved range, endurance and performance.

Above: The Mi-34 haas stunned airshow audiences with its flight demonstrations. An example is seen here about to enter a loop.

Mi-34 'Hermit'

Type: light military trainer/liaison helicopter

Powerplant: one 242.5-kW (325-hp.) VMKB M-14V-26 nine-cylinder air-cooled radial engine

Maximum speed: 210 km/h (130 m.p.h.)

Cruising speed: 180 km/h (112 m.p.h.)

Range: 450 km (280 mi.)

Hover ceiling: 1500 m (4,920 ft.)

Weight: Normal take-off 1080 kg (2,380 lb.)

Accommodation: two pilots and two passengers

Dimensions:
Span	10 m (39 ft. 7 in.)
Length	11.4 m (37 ft. 5 in.)
Height	2.8 m (9 ft. 2 in.)
Main rotor area	78,54 m² (845 sq. ft.)

Exceptional visibility is provided by the bubble canopy. This approach has been copied from Aérospatiale's Gazelle, which the Mi-34 closely resembles.

Later versions of the 'hermit' have two engines and offer increased range and speed.

Seating is provided for two pilots; the rear of the cockpit is devoted to cargo or an additional two passengers. Flight controls are unboosted mechanical controls requiring heavy inputs from the pilot during certain manoeuvres.

Composite structures are used throughout the helicopter, particularly in the main and tail rotor sections. This has reduced the overall weight and improved the safety of the design. Future Mil products will use more composite components.

All current production 'Hermits' have landing skids, although the design can be equipped with wheels if needed.

MI-34 'HERMIT'

The cancellation of a number of military contracts has caused many Russian aircraft manufacturers to turn their attention to the civil aviation field. Mil is now actively marketing the lightweight 'Hermit'.

ACTION DATA

SPEED

The 'Hermit' has a lower speed than its Western equivalents mainly beccause of is relatively poor quality engine. For sheer speed Aérospatiale's Gazelle is the fastest helicopter in its class.

Mi-34 'HERMIT'	210 km/h (130 m.p.h.)
SA 342M GAZELLE	310 km/h (192 m.p.h.)
F28F SHARK	180 km/h (115 m.p.h.)

HOVER CEILING

In this field, the Mi-34 shows a drastic reduction in performance. Compared to the lightweight civil F-28F Falcon, the Russian design has a very low ceiling. Its inability to reach a high hover ceiling will greatly affect future sales of Mil's helicopter.

Mi-34 'HERMIT' 1500 m (4,920 ft.)
SA 342M GAZELLE 2850 m (9,350 ft.)
F28F SHARK 2345 m (7,700 ft.)

RANGE

Mil gave the original 'Hermit' the ability to carry an additional fuel tank in the rear section of the fuselage to increase its poor range. Its range is reduced further when it is required to carry cargo. An improved 'Hermit' variant, with improved range, is now flying.

Mi-34 'HERMIT' 450 km (280 mi.)
SA 342M GAZELLE 670 km (415 mi.)
F28F SHARK 423 km (262 mi.)

Multiple Mils

■ **Mi-2 'HOPLITE':** Despite its small size, the Mi-2 is used for a variety of duties, including border patrols.

■ **Mi-6 'HOOK':** First of the heavyweight helicopters in service, the 'Hook' first flew in 1957 and remains in front-line service.

■ **Mi-17 'HIP':** Developed from the earlier Mi-8 in an effort to offer improved performance, the Mi-17 has seen widespread civilian service.

■ **Mi-35 'HIND-F':** Used as a battlefield attack helicopter, the 'Hind' has been constantly upgraded and has seen considerable combat.

NH INDUSTRIES

NH 90

● European partners ● Advanced design ● Utility helicopter

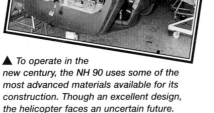

▲ To operate in the new century, the NH 90 uses some of the most advanced materials available for its construction. Though an excellent design, the helicopter faces an uncertain future.

T he NH 90 project began in 1985 as a co-operative project between European helicopter manufacturers for 'a NATO helicopter for the 1990s'. Today, the NH 90 partner nations – France, Italy, Germany and the Netherlands – operate a mix of helicopters as battlefield transports and shipboard ASW aircraft. Because of delays, the NH 90 is not now expected to enter service until 2003, with the first deliveries going to the Netherlands navy.

NH INDUSTRIES NH 90

▼ Difficult start
Britain was one of the original partners, but decided to drop out of the project at an early stage, in 1987.

▲ Future perfect
To help promote the aircraft, various artists' impressions of the NH 90 were distributed to the aviation press.

◀ Military mock-up
Future military customers were shown full-scale models of the NH 90 to illustrate the potential of the design. This example was displayed at Farnborough.

◀ Shipboard warrior
Most European clients are interested in replacing their ageing Sea King fleet with a specialised variant of the NH 90. This version will be equipped with anti-ship missiles and torpedoes.

Future saviour ▶
NH Industries has been quick to see the potential of the NH 90 as a rescue helicopter. Civilian operators have shown interest in the helicopter, although no orders have been forthcoming.

FACTS AND FIGURES

➤ Five European nations signed the memorandum in 1985 allowing the development of the NH 90.

➤ Two main versions (transport and naval) of the NH 90 are being developed.

➤ The naval version of the helicopter will be equipped with a search radar.

➤ The work is being shared by Eurocopter France (43%), Agusta (26%), Eurocopter Germany (24%) and Fokker (7%).

➤ Production of the NH 90 is expected to commence in 1999.

➤ The TTH version is expected to cost FF90 million; the NFH FF145 million.

PROFILE

A perfect partnership?

I n September 1985, the defence ministers of five European nations agreed to co-operate on a new multi-role helicopter for the armies and navies of NATO. The British government withdrew from the project in 1987 during the design phase, leaving Germany, France, the Netherlands and Italy in the project.

A combined organisation named NH Industries was formed in 1992 to manage the project, and is based at Aix-en-Provence in France.

In service, the TTH (Tactical Transport Helicopter) version of the NH 90 will fulfil various roles, including tactical army support, command post, search and rescue, and medical evacuation duties. The NFH (NATO Frigate Helicopter) will perform ASW (anti-submarine warfare), ASVW (anti-surface vessel warfare), SAR and transport missions. Helicopters that will be replaced by the NH 90 include French, German and Dutch Lynxes, French Super Frelons and Super Pumas, and Italian Sea Kings and Agusta-Bell 212s. So far, 647 NH 90s have been ordered; the biggest customer is Italy, with 224 examples. The first production example of the NH 90 flew in May 2004.

Below: The flying prototype of the NH 90 has exceeded all the performance levels required for the design. Pilots have praised the helicopter's handling.

NH 90 (provisional)

Type: transport/ASW helicopter

Powerplant: two 1599.5-kW (2,145-hp.) Rolls-Royce/Turboméca/MTU RTM 322-01/9 turboshaft engines

Maximum speed: 295 km/h (183 m.p.h.)

Endurance: 5 hr 30 min

Combat radius: 1110 km (688 mi.)

Hovering ceiling: 3500 m (3,500 ft.)

Weights: empty 5700 kg (12,540 lb.); maximum take-off 9100 kg (20,020 lb.)

Accommodation: three crew and 20 fully-equipped troops

Dimensions:

main rotor diameter	16.30 m (53 ft. 5 in.)
length	16.81 m (55 ft. 2 in.)
height	5.42 m (17 ft. 9 in.)
main rotor disc	213.82 m² (2,300 sq. ft.)

The NFH version will normally carry a flight crew of three, comprising a pilot, a co-pilot and one system operator in the cabin.

The titanium main rotor hub supports the four composite blades, which have advanced aerofoils and curved tips to reduce drag. The NFH version will have automatic folding of the main blades.

The four-bladed tail rotor is of composite construction and rotates at 1235.4 rpm. The whole tail pylon can fold for storage on the NFH version.

Made by a European consortium of Turboméca, Rolls-Royce, MTU, Piaggio and Topps, the twin RTM 322-01/9 engines are expected to achieve new levels of reliability.

MILITARY HELICOPTERS

MULTI-ROLE HELICOPTERS: European armies have long used the helicopter for combat operations. Whether flying troops low over a battlefield or searching for hostile submarines in the Atlantic, the capabilities of the helicopter are beyond doubt. Used as an aerial taxi for the French and British armies is the jointly developed Aérospatiale/Westland Puma (pictured below). The Puma will be replaced by the NH 90 in French army service.

For maritime operations the Sea King (below) has been a cornerstone of Western forces. A specialised variant of the NH 90 is in the process of being developed to replace the ageing Sea King in service. Italy, Germany and France have requested a variant equipped with a 360° search radar and hardpoints for anti-ship missiles and depth charges. The new helicopter was designed from the outset to be able to operate from small warships such as frigates and destroyers.

NH 90 **NH90** **F-ZWTI**

NH 90 PT2

PT2 is painted in naval-style light grey camouflage and is of basic configuration. As the second prototype to fly, on 19 March 1997, it also became the first example to operate with fly-by-wire controls.

The NH 90's fuselage is constructed in three countries. The front fuselage is built at Marignane, France; the centre at Ottobrunn Germany; the rear at Cascina Costa, Italy.

The landing gear is retractable and consists of a twin-wheel nose unit and single-wheel main units. Emergency floatation gear will also be available.

European rotorcraft projects

■ **EH INDUSTRIES EH101:** This Anglo-Italian multi-role helicopter has been ordered by Italy and the UK, and is being offered for export.

■ **EUROCOPTER EC 135:** This seven- or eight-seat, light, turbine-powered aircraft is projected to have achieved 700 sales by 2007.

■ **EUROCOPTER TIGRE:** Designed as an anti-tank and ground-support helicopter, the Tigre has orders for around 400 examples.

■ **EUROFAR:** Manufacturers from France, Germany and the UK are examining the possibility of building this twin-engined tilt-rotor aircraft.

PIASECKI

HUP RETRIEVER

● Single-engined, twin-rotor ● 'Planeguard' ● Utility helicopter

O ne of the first helicopters to serve aboard US Navy warships, the HUP Retriever was one of several tandem, twin-rotor helicopters designed by rotary-wing pioneer Frank Piasecki in the late-1940s and 1950s. Intended primarily for shore duty as a cargo hauler (in which role it also flew with the US Army), it is best remembered for its naval service and for rescuing many pilots who might otherwise have been lost at sea.

▲ Developed from the two XHJP-1 prototypes (Piasecki's Model PV-14), the HUP Retrievers earned their keep as 'planeguards' and rescue craft aboard the US Navy's carriers.

PHOTO FILE

PIASECKI HUP RETRIEVER

▲ Army Mule for casualty evacuation
The H-25A Army Mule was derived from the HUP-2. It had hydraulically-boosted controls, a stronger floor and enlarged cargo doors for stretcher cases.

▼ Winched aboard the Mule
In the rescue role the Retriever made use of a winch and an access hatch behind the cockpit.

▼ Army workhorse
The initial batch of 50 US Army H-25s also fulfilled a secondary utility transport role.

▲ Outrigger fins on the HUP-1
After trials with two XHJP-1s, the US Navy ordered 23 production HUP-1s, distinguished from later variants by their tail fins. Deliveries began in 1949.

In Canadian colours with VH-21 ▶
The Royal Canadian Navy received three HUP-3s from the US Navy which were operated by squadron VH-21. These were among 50 ex-US Army H-25As transferred as surplus to the Navy.

FACTS AND FIGURES

➤ The Piasecki Aircraft Corp. of Morton, Pennsylvania, evolved into today's Boeing Helicopter Company.

➤ The first US Navy HUPs were delivered to squadron HU-2 in February 1951.

➤ A Retriever could hover at 15 m (50 ft.) and lift an airman weighing 75 kg (165 lb.).

➤ After being transferred to reserve units, some HUPS were retained as rescue aircraft with an orange colour scheme.

➤ PV-18 production totalled 339, including 70 H-25s for the US Army.

➤ The Army's H-25s were procured by the USAF on the Army's behalf.

PROFILE

Twin-rotor US Navy rescuer

Designed to meet a US Navy need for a shipboard utility helicopter, the Piasecki Model PV-18, known in naval parlance as the HUP Retriever, first flew in 1948 and entered service three years later. Primitive by today's standards, the HUP was the finest helicopter in its class in the 1950s. It also served in the US Army as the H-25 Army Mule.

With a single engine driving twin rotors and with its functional but odd-looking 'tail-dragger' landing gear, the HUP was the kind of helicopter for which the Navy had been looking. The Navy's HUP lacked the hydraulically-boosted controls and strengthened cargo floor of the H-25, and was considered by some to be underpowered.

Though its primary mission was transport, the HUP also performed anti-submarine duties. Aboard aircraft-carriers, an important role was as 'planeguard', rescuing pilots if their aircraft was ditched on take-off or landing.

Above: Several US Navy HUP-2s had dunking sonar fitted for anti-submarine operations and were designated HUP-2S.

Below: Retrievers also served with the Marine Corps in transport and rescue roles from shore bases. The HUP was redesignated UH-25 in 1962.

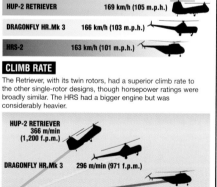

HUP-2 RETRIEVER

This HUP-2 carries the markings of Navy Utility Helicopter Squadron 1. This unit operated search-and-rescue HUPs from various aircraft-carriers during the Korean War.

The twin rotor layout was a trademark of Frank N. Piasecki's helicopter designs. This layout was perpetuated in later Vertol and Boeing-Vertol designs like the CH-46 Sea Knight and CH-47 Chinook.

HUP-3 Retriever

Type: single-engined, twin-rotor utility, cargo and rescue helicopter

Powerplant: one 410-kW (550-hp.) Continental R-975-46A radial engine

Maximum speed: 169 km/h (105 m.p.h.)

Maximum range: 547 km (340 m.p.h.)

Service ceiling: 3050 m (10,000 ft.)

Weights: empty 1782 kg (3,930 lb.); maximum take-off 2767 kg (6,100 lb.)

Accommodation: pilot, co-pilot and up to five passengers or three hospital stretchers with attendant

Dimensions:
main rotor diameter	10.67 m (35 ft.)
fuselage length	17.35 m (57 ft.)
height	3.81 m (12 ft. 6 in.)
rotor disc area	178.76 m² (1,924 sq. ft.)

Two three-bladed rotors lifted the HUP into the air. On the HUP-2 an auto-pilot served as the primary controller. This improved hover performance and allowed the removal of the tail fins fitted to the HUP-1.

A large loading door (larger still in the H-25A Army variant) and ample cabin dimensions allowed the carriage of a variety of cargoes.

The HUP had capacity for a crew of two and either four passengers or three stretcher cases. An internally-operated rescue hatch next to the pilot's seat was large enough to accommodate a loaded stretcher. A hydraulic hoist above the hatch was used to lift survivors aboard while hovering.

Unlike later twin-rotor designs, the HUP was a single-engined machine. A 410-kW Continental R-975-46 radial mounted in the rear fuselage provided the power.

'Midnight blue' was the name given to this dark shade which adorned almost all US Navy aircraft in the 1950s.

ACTION DATA

MAXIMUM SPEED

A maximum speed around 160 km/h (100 m.p.h.) was typical of these large helicopters. All were naval designs of American origin, the Dragonfly being a licence-built Westland version for the Royal Navy, fitted with a British engine.

HUP-2 RETRIEVER	169 km/h (105 m.p.h.)
DRAGONFLY HR.Mk 3	166 km/h (103 m.p.h.)
HRS-2	163 km/h (101 m.p.h.)

CLIMB RATE

The Retriever, with its twin rotors, had a superior climb rate to the other single-rotor designs, though horsepower ratings were broadly similar. The HRS had a bigger engine but was considerably heavier.

HUP-2 RETRIEVER	366 m/min (1,200 f.p.m.)
DRAGONFLY HR.Mk 3	296 m/min (971 f.p.m.)
HRS-2	213 m/min (699 f.p.m.)

ACCOMMODATION

The Retriever and Dragonfly both had limited load-carrying capacity. Even the larger HRS-2 was soon found to be too small for the US Navy's needs and was replaced by the HSS Seabat.

HUP-2 RETRIEVER
2 crew + 4 passengers

DRAGONFLY HR.Mk 3
2 crew + 2 passengers

HRS-2
1 crew + 8 passengers

US Navy carrier 'planeguards'

■ **SIKORSKY HO4S:** This naval version of the Sikorsky S-55 was primarily an anti-submarine and observation type, entering service in 1950.

■ **SIKORSKY HSS SEABAT:** Delivered in 1955, the first Seabats replaced the HO4S, which was short on range and load-capacity.

■ **SIKORSKY SH-3 SEA KING:** Purchased in large numbers by the Navy, the SH-3 has served for more than 30 years from 1961.

■ **SIKORSKY SH-60F SEAHAWK:** The carrier-borne version of the SH-60B, the F-model has a less comprehensive ASW suite.

PIASECKI/VERTOL

H-21

● Transport helicopter ● USAF's first twin rotor ● Vietnam action

▲ Frank Piasecki's
H-21/HRP made use of the designer's
well-known tandem rotor layout,
perpetuated in the later Vertol H-25/HUP,
H-46 and H-47 designs.

Developed for the USAF from the HRP
tandem-rotor designs, the H-21 made
its mark with the US Army, which
named its the Shawnee. After missing the
Korean War by just a year, the twin-rotor
H-21 Workhorse (its USAF name) entered
service with Army aviation units in the 1950s
and went to war briefly in Vietnam in the
1960s, the swansong of its career. A few
examples served with foreign forces, mainly
under the Military Assistance Program.

PIASECKI/VERTOL H-21

▼ Export Workhorse
Canada received six H-21As under
the Military Assistance Programme.

▲ Rescue colours
When operated by the USAF
Military Air Transport Service,
the aircrew rescue version
was known as the HH-21B.

▼ Shawnee in Vietnam
Operated by the 8th and 57th
Transportation Companies,
and armed with Browning
machine-guns, the CH-21C
served for just two years.

▲ Gallic 'flying banana'
Delivered in 1957, French army H-21Cs saw
service during the conflict in Algeria.

Border-to-border flight ▶
An Army H-21 Shawnee became the first helicopter
to fly non-stop from the US west coast to the east
coast. On the way it was refuelled by a de Havilland
Canada U-1A Otter via a rudimentary hose system.

FACTS AND FIGURES

➤ A few examples of the civil Piasecki
PD-22 (Vertol 44) served with New York
Airlines and other carriers.

➤ Two H-21Cs were re-engined with
turboshafts, as XH-21Ds.

➤ Foreign H-21 operators included West
Germany, France and Canada.

➤ Four US aviators killed in an H-21 in July
1962 are recognised by some sources as
the first American fatalities in Vietnam.

➤ The YH-21 prototype for this series made
its maiden flight on 11 April 1952.

➤ A total of 334 of these helicopters was
produced for the United States Army.

PROFILE

Frank Piasecki's 'flying banana'

S eeing the H-21's potential, the US Army awarded Piasecki a production contract in 1952. H-21s had extensive armour and the ability to carry two external fuel tanks, and introduced a 2-tonne hook.

In 1955, by the time helicopter pioneer Frank Piasecki was forced out of the firm which bore his name (the company became Vertol, later Boeing-Vertol), the US Army was the biggest user of this tandem, twin-rotor helicopter.

The H-21 was based on the US Navy's HRP-2, itself a development of the fabric-covered HRP-1, Piasecki's first successful tandem rotor design. Over 400 H-21s were built for the Army, mostly of the H-21C variant. One of these made the first non-stop helicopter flight from one coast of the US to the other, refuelled aloft by a de Havilland U-1A Otter. H-21s arrived in Vietnam in December 1961, during the early days of the US build-up.

H-21s were exported under MAP, and a civil version, the Model 44, saw limited service with the Swedish navy.

Until replaced by the Sikorsky H-3, some USAF H-21Bs saw service as drone retrieval aircraft. Here a Ryan Firebee remotely piloted vehicle (RPV) has been picked up after a mission.

Customers for the primarily passenger-configured Model 44 civilian variant of the Workhorse included the French government (Model 44Bs) and the Swedish navy, which adapted its examples to perform the anti-submarine warfare role.

H-21B Workhorse

Type: troop/cargo tandem rotor transport helicopter

Powerplant: one 1063-kW (1425-hp.) Wright R-1820-103 Cyclone radial piston engine

Maximum speed: 204 km/h (127 m.p.h.) at sea level

Cruising speed: 158 km/h (98 m.p.h.) at sea level

Range: 644 km (400 mi.)

Weights: empty 4060 kg (8,950 lb.), maximum take-off 6895 kg (15,200 lb.)

Accommodation: pilot, co-pilot, crew chief, and (in Vietnam) two gunners for door-mounted 12.7-mm M2 or 7.62-mm M60 machine-guns, plus 20 troops or 12 stretchers

Dimensions:

main rotor diameter	13.41 m (44 ft.)
fuselage length	16 m (52 ft. 6 in.)
height	4.8 m (15 ft. 9 in.)
rotor disc area	282.52 m² (3,041 sq. ft.)

MODEL 44A

Vertol produced a small number of Model 44s, which originated as the Piasecki PD-22, a civil version of the Workhorse. Belgium's flag carrier SABENA operated a single leased example during the 1958 World Fair.

Each of the two three-bladed main rotors was driven from a single main engine mounted behind the main cabin: a 1063-kW (1425-hp.) Wright Cyclone piston unit. Normal fuel capacity was 1136 litres (300 gallons).

N74057 SABENA *BELGIAN World AIRLINES* SABENA

Piasecki's Model 44 received its CAA Approved Type certificate in April 1957. It was intended for the Model 44 to be updated through the addition of two turboshaft engines instead of the single piston unit in order to increase performance.

Non-retractable tricycle landing gear was standard, but the Model 44/H-21 could also be equipped with inflatable pontoons, allowing operations from water.

Model 44A utility versions could carry 19 civilians, 12 stretcher patients and two attendants, or a 2.5-tonne cargo sling. The 44B, shown here, was an airliner with 15 seats and a mail and cargo compartment. The Model 44C was an executive transport with a range of custom-built interiors.

A door was provided for the passengers at either end of the 6.10 x 1.73 x 1.68-m (20 x 5 ft. 8 in x 5 ft. 6-in.) cabin. The rear door had built-in passenger steps and a handrail. The Model 44B featured larger oval observation windows than the other civilian Vertol Workhorse models.

Frank Piasecki's diverse designs

■ **MODEL PV-2:** Flown in April 1943, the single-seat, fabric-covered PV-2 was the second US-built helicopter flown publicly. In 1944 the Navy's HRP contract was awarded to Piasecki.

■ **MODEL 59/VZ-8:** Awarded a contract by the Army in 1957 to develop a 'flying jeep', Piasecki produced the Sky Car, powered by two piston or turbine engines driving ducted fans.

■ **MODEL 16H-1A PATHFINDER II:** A joint Army/Navy-funded programme to research compound helicopter designs led to the Pathfinder and Pathfinder II of the early-1960s.

■ **MODEL PV-15/H-16 TRANSPORTER:** At the time of its inception, the H-16 was the world's largest helicopter. Flown in 1953, it was judged unsuitable by the US Army.

COMBAT DATA

STRETCHERS

As a tandem rotor design, the H-21 was a large helicopter compared to other designs of the period. Its fuselage provided a sizeable troop and stretcher capacity, especially useful in Army use.

H-21A WORKHORSE	12
H-34A CHOCTAW	8
H-19B CHICKASAW	6

POWER

All three of these types used single radial piston engines, the Wright Cyclone in the H-21 having to power two main rotors. The Sikorsky H-34 and H-19 were conventional single main rotor designs, the former having the most powerful engine. Ultimately, turboshaft engines replaced radials in most helicopters, as they are lighter and more powerful than a piston engine of similar weight.

H-21A WORKHORSE 932 kW 1250 hp	H-34A CHOCTAW 1138 kW 1526 hp	H-19B CHICKASAW 597 kW 800 hp

MAXIMUM SPEED

The twin main rotors of the H-21 gave it a superior top speed to the smaller designs. Large transport helicopter speeds later peaked at around 250 km/h (in aircraft like the turboshaft-powered CH-47) as design limits were reached.

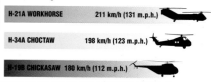

H-21A WORKHORSE	211 km/h (131 m.p.h.)
H-34A CHOCTAW	198 km/h (123 m.p.h.)
H-19B CHICKASAW	180 km/h (112 m.p.h.)

PZL SWIDNIK

W-3 SOKÓL

● **Twin-turboshaft transport helicopter** ● **Exports** ● **Multi-role**

In 1979, with nearly 20 years' experience of building Mil-designed helicopters behind it, Poland's PZL Swidnik flew the first prototype of a new design designated W-3 and named Sokól, or 'Falcon'. There was a long series of tethered tests and extensive design changes before the second prototype flew in May 1982, and it was another three years before production began. Since then, PZL has developed several specialised variants for military and civil applications.

▲ *PZL began its helicopter manufacture in the 1950s, license-building Soviet Mil designs. Today the company designs its own aircraft and sells them around the world.*

PZL SWIDNIK **W-3 SOKÓL**

Rescue Anakonda ▶
Bristling with equipment, this Polish navy W-3RM Anakonda is equipped for the search and rescue role. As well as flotation gear, the aircraft carries a hoist and life-saving equipment.

▲ Third prototype
SP-PSC, the third W-3 prototype, took to the air on 24 July 1984. Polish certification was granted in 1990; Russian in 1992.

▲ Naval service
The Polish navy operates W-3RMs alongside Russian-built Mil Mi-14s.

▲ Protracted development
PZL began W-3 design work in the mid-1970s, and the prototype flew in 1979.

First W-3A deliveries ▶
Saxony's police department took delivery of the first W-3A, equipped with Western avionics.

FACTS AND FIGURES

➤ Among proposed W-3 variants is an electronic reconnaissance and electronic countermeasures (ECM) aircraft

➤ By 1 January 1996, excluding prototypes, 85 W-3s had been built by PZL.

➤ At 1994 prices, a basic W-3A was available for US$2.5 million.

➤ Polish civil W-3 users include the Interior Ministry, a telephone company and a cardiac hospital.

➤ W-3 users include the air forces of the Czech Republic, Myanmar, and Nigeria.

➤ As well as the W-3, PZL has developed a light turboshaft-powered type, the W-4.

PROFILE

Poland's medium-weight Falcon

By 1996 PZL had completed more than 80 production W-3s, including 12 for Myanmar. Others were built for the Polish armed forces and government agencies, and included naval, fire-fighting and search and rescue (SAR) models.

Known as the Anakonda, the W-3RM is a rescue variant with flotation bags, a watertight cabin and a winch. The W-3U-1 Alligator was proposed for the anti-submarine role, but the planned W-3 Sokol-Long, with a stretched fuselage seating up to 14 fully armed troops, was discontinued in 1993.

W-3s have been fitted with several different weapons, including AT-6 'Spiral' anti-tank and SA-7 'Grail' anti-aircraft missiles, 20-mm and 23-mm cannon, and rocket launchers. At one stage, the manufacturer teamed with Kentron of South Africa to offer an export version with weapons systems similar to those of the Atlas Rooivalk, but the partnership failed in 1994.

In its basic transport form,

Below: Carrying its distinctive colour scheme, this Sokól demonstrates its abilities at an air show. PZL Swidnik has been keen to sell the aircraft in the West. Piasecki Aircraft Corporation markets the W-3A in the US and Pacific.

Above: With flotation gear inflated, this Anakonda demonstrates its amphibious abilities in the rescue role.

the W-3 has removable seats and can be used to carry cargo or casualties as an alternative to passengers. Only one example of the armed W-3 Huzar has been completed, but development is continuing.

W-3A Sokól

Type: medium multi-purpose helicopter

Powerplant: two 671-kW (900-hp.) WSK-PZL Rzeszów PZL-10W turboshafts

Maximum speed: 255 km/h at 500 m

Climb rate: 510 m/min at sea level

Range: 760 km

Service ceiling: 6000 m

Weights: empty 3300 kg; maximum take-off 6400 kg

Accommodation: (passenger configuration) two flight crew plus up to 12 passengers

Dimensions:
rotor diameter	15.7 m (51 ft 6 in.)
fuselage length	14.21 m (46 ft. 7 in.)
height	4.12 m (13 ft. 6 in.)
rotor disc area	193.6 m² (2,084 sq. ft.)

ACTION DATA

MAXIMUM CRUISING SPEED

The W-3A cruises significantly more slowly than similar modern Western types. Both the Sikorsky S-76B and the Eurocopter Dauphin are more streamlined designs.

W-3A SOKÓL	238 km/h (148 m.p.h.)
AS 365N2 DAUPHIN 2	285 km/h (177 m.p.h.)
S-76B SPIRIT	269 km/h (167 m.p.h.)

CLIMB RATE

Sokóls have a good climb rate performance, marginally better than that of the S-76 and considerably better than that of the Dauphin. This difference is a reflection of the type's power-to-weight ratio.

AS 365N2 DAUPHIN 2 420 m/min (1,378 f.p.m.)
S-76B SPIRIT 502 m/min (1,647 f.p.m.)
W-3A SOKÓL 510 m/min (1,673 f.p.m.)

W-3W SOKÓL

Derived from the W-3WB Huzar armed prototype (itself a version of the W-3A), the W-3W is an important type in Polish Air Cavalry Divisions. By January 1996, 22 had been delivered.

Two modern WSK-PZL Rzeszów PZL-10W turboshafts, each rated at 671 kW (900 hp.) for take-off, power the W-3W. They have a 30-minute emergency rating of 746 kW (1000 hp.).

US company Rockwell has proposed a 'Westernised' version of the W-3W, equipped with Hellfire anti-tank missiles, upgraded avionics, electronic warfare and targeting systems.

Early W-3s carried a three-person crew, including a pilot, co-pilot and flight engineer. W-3As, with improved avionics, can be flown by one pilot in VFR conditions.

On the starboard side of the aircraft a GSz-23 forward-firing 23-mm twin-barrelled cannon is fitted.

Standard fuselage configurations allow for 12 passengers. Anakonda SAR aircraft carry eight survivors and two attendants.

For its cavalry role, the W-3W has pylons fitted for rocket launchers, bomblet dispensers, mine-laying packs and six cabin-window-mounted AK 47 rifles or other guns.

Fuel is carried in four bladder fuel tanks beneath the cabin floor, the combined capacity of which is 1750 litres (462 gallons). An optional auxiliary tank of 1100 litres (290 gallons) may also be fitted.

Duralumin comprises most of the W-3A's fuselage structure and the tail rotor driveshaft. Glass-fibre-reinforced plastic (GFRP) is incorporated in the main and tail rotor blades, tailfin and horizontal stabiliser.

RANGE

Sokóls have a good range performance, better than that of the S-76, but not as good as that of the Dauphin. However, W-3As are able to carry larger loads, especially in their larger cabin areas. As many as 12 passengers may be accommodated.

AS 365N2 DAUPHIN 2 897 km (557 mi.)
W-3A SOKÓL 760 km (472 mi.)
S-76B 661 km (411 mi.)

Sokól's PZL-built predecessors

■ **SM-2:** PZL produced Mil's first helicopter design, the Mi-1, from the mid-1950s. Its own version, the SM-2 with an enlarged forward fuselage, was produced later.

■ **Mi-2 'HOPLITE':** Introduced in the late 1950s, the piston-engined Mi-2 was made exclusively in Poland from 1964. At least 5,000 have been built and production continued in the mid-1990s.

■ **KANIA:** In collaboration with US engine manufacturer Allison, PZL produced this updated Mi-2 variant powered by two Allison 250-C20B turboshafts.

PZL-SWIDNIK (MIL)

MI-2 'HOPLITE'

● Polish-built light helicopter ● Soviet design ● More than 5000 built

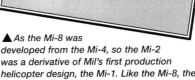

▲ As the Mi-8 was developed from the Mi-4, so the Mi-2 was a derivative of Mil's first production helicopter design, the Mi-1. Like the Mi-8, the 'Hoplite' was built in large numbers.

Designed in Russia by the Mil bureau but built in Poland by PZL at its Swidnik factory, the Mi-2 was the world's first light, twin-engined helicopter. The first prototype flew in September 1961, and since production started in 1965 more than 5000 have been delivered. They have been used for a range of missions by civil and military operators in many countries. As well as developing the Mi-2, PZL has also launched the improved W-3.

PZL-SWIDNIK (MIL) MI-2 'HOPLITE'

▼ Missile-toting Mi-2URP
The Mi-2URP, which dates from 1976, is among a number of armed 'Hoplite' variants. It may be fitted with up to four 9M14M Malyutka (known as AT-3 'Sagger' to NATO) air-to-surface missiles.

▲ Still in Russian use
Limited Mi-2 production continued into the 1990s. This gaudily painted 'Hoplite' was one of a number that remained in Russian service until 1991.

◄ Agricultural variant
Among the dozen Mi-2 variants was an agricultural version with externally-mounted hoppers and spray booms.

▼ External fuel tanks
All Mi-2 variants can be fitted with external fuel tanks, each of 250-l (66 gal.) capacity. Carrying a full load range is limited to 170 km (105 mi).

▲ Slovak veteran
The Slovak Republic inherited its modest fleet of Mi-2s from the former Czechoslovakia's Warsaw Pact forces.

FACTS AND FIGURES

➤ In the late-1970s PZL developed an export conversion of the Mi-2, called Kania (Kittyhawk), with two Allison engines.

➤ Mi-2s still serve with ex-Warsaw Pact countries, plus Nicaragua and Syria.

➤ Chronologically, the Mi-2 appeared in production after the Mi-4 and Mi-6.

➤ PZL's W-3 Sokół (Falcon), which flew in 1979, was based on the Mi-2 but had new engines, rotors and a larger cabin.

➤ East Germany used Mi-2s for artillery spotting and electronic warfare.

➤ Civil versions include air ambulance, TV relay, agricultural and survey models.

PROFILE

Soviet helicopter built in Poland

Originally designed to carry a load of 400 kg (880 lb.), the Mi-2 (codenamed 'Hoplite' by NATO) has been developed to carry twice that weight. This additional payload capability has enabled it to take on a variety of roles.

In its basic transport form the 'Hoplite' can carry up to eight passengers or 700 kg (1,540 lb.) of cargo; 1200 kg (2,640 lb.) may be carried externally. As an agricultural machine it can be fitted with two hoppers for spraying or dusting with

A rescue/ambulance version, designated Mi-2R, can carry four patients on stretchers, plus a doctor, equipment and a 120-kg (264-lb.) hoist.

Military Mi-2s can be fitted with fuselage-mounted 23-mm cannon and may carry machine-gun and rocket pods or anti-tank missiles on pylons. 'Hoplites' have been used by Iraq, Libya, North Korea and Syria, as well as by several former Warsaw Pact countries.

A Polish development of the original Mi-2, with more powerful

331-kW GTD-350P engines, is designated Mi-2M. It has been built in the same versions as the original helicopter and all may be fitted with either single or dual controls.

More than 5,400 Mi-2s have left PZL's Swidnik factory during 30 years of production.

Above: An Mi-8 and Mi-2 belonging to the Czech air force illustrate the family resemblance seen in the Mil bureau's designs.

Below: CCCP-06180 was the registration given to the Mi-2 prototype, V-2, which first flew in 1961. Externally, the design did not change significantly during production.

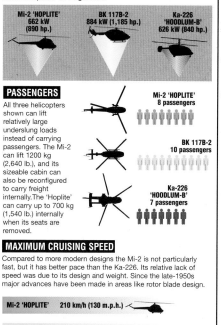

Mi-2 'Hoplite'

Type: twin-engined general-purpose light helicopter

Powerplant: two 331-kW (445-hp.) Isotov GTD-350P turboshafts

Max speed: 210 km/h (130 m.p.h.) at 500 m (1,640 ft.)

Maximum climb rate: 270 m/min (885 f.p.m.) at sea level

Range: 170 km (105 mi.) with maximum payload

Service ceiling: 4000 m (13,100 ft.)

Weights: empty 2402 kg (5,485 lb.); maximum take-off 3700 kg (8,140 lb.)

Dimensions:
main rotor diameter	14.56 m (47 ft. 9 in.)
fuselage length	11.94 m (39 ft. 2 in.)
height	3.75 m (12 ft. 4 in.)
rotor disc area	166.4 m² (1,790 sq. ft.)

ACTION DATA

POWER

One of the world's first twin-engined light helicopters, the Mi-2 had a relatively modest power output. Compared to more modern types like the BK 117 and Ka-226, the 'Hoplite' had an inferior power-to-weight ratio.

Mi-2 'HOPLITE' 662 kW (890 hp.)	BK 117B-2 884 kW (1,185 hp.)	Ka-226 'HOODLUM-B' 626 kW (840 hp.)

PASSENGERS

All three helicopters shown can lift relatively large underslung loads instead of carrying passengers. The Mi-2 can lift 1200 kg (2,640 lb.), and its sizeable cabin can also be reconfigured to carry freight internally. The 'Hoplite' can carry up to 700 kg (1,540 lb.) internally when its seats are removed.

Mi-2 'HOPLITE' 8 passengers

BK 117B-2 10 passengers

Ka-226 'HOODLUM-B' 7 passengers

MAXIMUM CRUISING SPEED

Compared to more modern designs the Mi-2 is not particularly fast, but it has better pace than the Ka-226. Its relative lack of speed was due to its design and weight. Since the late-1950s major advances have been made in areas like rotor blade design.

Mi-2 'HOPLITE'	210 km/h (130 m.p.h.)
BK 117B-2	247 km/h (153 m.p.h.)
Ka-226 'HOODLUM-B'	150 km/h (93 m.p.h.)

Although normally operated by one pilot, the Mi-2 may be fitted with dual controls for training missions.

The Mi-2 uses two 295-kW or 322-kW Isotov GTD-350 or 331-kW GTD-350P turboshaft engines built in Poland under licence by PZL. These are mounted in a nacelle above the cockpit and cabin.

The Mi-2 introduced a number of improvements over the Mi-1, including a bonded/welded fuselage and anti-icing equipment on the engine air intakes. The latter uses warm bleed air from the engine.

The tail rotor blades are of bonded-metal honeycomb construction. All blades have electro-thermal de-icing.

The eight seats in the main air-conditioned cabin can be removed to allow for up to 700 kg (1,540 lb.) of cargo to be carried. The large rear door makes loading and unloading easier.

Many military 'Hoplite' variants are fitted with an NS-23KM 23-mm cannon on the port side of the fuselage, below floor and door level, which is aimed by the pilot. This example carries two 57-mm Mars 2 rocket pods.

MI-2 'HOPLITE'

Until recently, Poland's army and navy operated more than 100 Mi-2s in a number of variants, including armed examples. A few remain in service and are used for transport and search-and-rescue duties.

Soviet designs in foreign production

■ **CAC F-7M AIRGUARD:** In 1961 China gained a licence to build the MiG-21F-13 and have since developed its own variants.

■ **HAL MiG-27L BAHADUR 'FLOGGER-J':** Since 1984, HAL in India has built more than 100 MiG-27 strike aircraft under licence.

■ **PZL-MIELEC An-2 'COLT':** PZL began licence-building the An-2 in 1960. China has also built An-2s as Y-5s.

■ **PZL-MIELEC An-28 'CASH':** Production of this Antonov An-14 derivative began in 1984. Most of these 17-seaters went to civil users.

ROBINSON

R22

● Two-seat light helicopter ● Cheap to own ● Private and business

▲ *Short of buying and building a kit helicopter, about the cheapest way to own and operate a helicopter is to opt for the R22. This has been the key to its sales success in several countries.*

For the beginner and the professional alike the Robinson R22 is the right helicopter. Since 1975, thousands of student pilots have earned their rotary-wing qualification flying the R22. Though it receives little publicity, the R22 is a popular, lightweight general aviation helicopter that is also economical. Few helicopters are tailored for people of modest means—but this aircraft is, making it the ideal training tool.

ROBINSON R22

▼ All tied up
Helicopter rotors can be surprisingly fragile. They must be carefully anchored to the fuselage to prevent windmilling on the ground.

▲ Simple controls
The R22 has a single cyclic stick connected by a cross bar with grips for each of the pilots.

▼ Crop duster
The R22 Agricultural is a version tailored for spraying pesticides and fertilizer. One person can install the spray equipment in five minutes without tools.

▲ Four-seat R44
The R44 is a four-seat version of the R22 incorporating many new features such as an automatic engine clutch and a rotor brake.

◀ R22 on floats
Another version of the R22 is the Mariner, which has inflatable floats and wheels for ground handling. The first examples delivered were used for fish spotting from tuna fishing boats off Mexico and Venezuela.

FACTS AND FIGURES

➤ It is estimated that over 13,000 student pilots have made their first helicopter solo in this aircraft.

➤ The first R22 prototype flew on August 28, 1975, and the second in 1977.

➤ Total production of the R22 had exceeded 2,500 aircraft by 1995.

➤ Despite the company's small size, Robinson achieved a production rate of about 30 R22s per month.

➤ The Turkish army is the only military user of the R22, as a basic flight trainer.

➤ Argentina's police forces are acquiring R22s fitted with both floats and wheels.

PROFILE

Popular light helicopter

It may sound like a lawn-mower flitting through the sky, but the Robinson R22 is actually a very efficient and pleasing lightweight helicopter.

This was also exactly what the world was waiting for. The manufacturer, which calls itself a small family in the California beach city of Torrance, recognized that there is a demand for a simple, easy-to-operate helicopter that can instruct students and perform basic missions.

Seeking to offer both simplicity and low cost, Robinson was so successful that in 1979, barely four years after starting flight tests, the company had already sold 524 of these fine aircraft.

With side-by-side seating and excellent vision through its rounded windshield, the Robinson R22 offers a superb ride for student and professional alike. Despite its small size, the R22 is basically but adequately equipped and carries

instruments and navigation gear for most kinds of routine flying. Pilots claim that the R22 is extremely stable and reliable, and that it will readily forgive mistakes.

Above: Brand new R22s awaiting their owners in the factory. The R22 continues to sell well.

Above: Helicopters have been operating over America's cities for many years. Only the safest and most reliable single-engine helicopters fly over the city.

R22 Beta

Type: Two-seat lightweight helicopter

Powerplant: One 119-kW (160-hp.) Lycoming O-320-B2C flat-four piston engine de-rated to 96-kW (130 hp.) for takeoff

Maximum speed: 180 km/h (112 m.p.h.)

Service ceiling: 4267 m (14,000 ft.)

Range: 595 km (370 mi.)

Hover ceiling: 2133 m (7,000 ft.)

Accommodation: 2 seats side by side in an enclosed cabin, dual controls optional.

Weights: Empty 346 kg (763 lb.); loaded 589 m (1,298 lb.)

Dimensions:
Rotor diameter	46.17 m² (25 ft. 2 in.)
Length	6.3 m (20 ft. 8 in.)
Height	2.6 m (8 ft. 9 in.)
Rotor disc area	46.2 m² (497 sq. ft.)

R22 BETA

This U.S.-registered R22 is typical of the many serving worldwide. The aircraft is popular for training and as a low-cost personal transport.

View from the cabin is excellent and the doors may be removed if desired. Police and observation models can be supplied with bubble door windows.

A tall rotor pylon holds the main rotor well clear of the upper fuselage. This distinctive feature of the R22 has also been adopted on the four-seat R44. A special system is installed to prevent the rotor blades hitting the tailboom when starting in windy conditions.

A bright-red beacon flashes to warn other aircraft to the presence of the R22. Much basic helicopter training occurs over the airfield.

For anti-torque control the R22 uses a small two-blade tail rotor. The blades have a stainless steel spar and leading edge with light alloy skins and honeycomb filling.

The Lycoming engine is mounted on the rear part of the cabin and has a prominent cooling fan. Fuel is carried in a 72.5-litre (19-gallon) tank in the upper left part of the fuselage.

Mounted below the vertical tail surface on the right-hand side is a small tailskid. This keeps the tail rotor clear of the ground in the event of a tail-low landing.

With a track of 1.9 m (6 ft. 4 in.), the skid undercarriage provides a stable landing platform. Combined float and skid landing gear is available on the R22 Mariner, but this requires an extra tailplane to be fitted.

N2276X

Helicopter lightweights

■ **ROTORWAY SCORPION TOO:** Designed by B. J. Schramm this aircraft is sold in kit form for assembly by amateur builders.

■ **BELL 47:** On 8 March, 1946, the American Bell 47 received the first ever Approved Type Certificate for a civilian helicopter.

■ **HUGHES 300:** Developed in the early 1960s, the Hughes 300 was also license-built in Italy and found favour with a range of operators.

■ **ENSTROM 280:** A more luxurious development of the F-28 of 1960, the 280 first flew in 1973 and remains a popular aircraft.

ACTION DATA

SPEED

Turbine power for the Schweizer 330 results in it having a higher maximum speed. Speed, however, is not always of great importance in the initial stages of flying training and the more docile characteristics of the R22 may benefit the student pilot.

R22 BETA	180 km/h (112 m.p.h.)
330	199 km/h (124 m.p.h.)
EXEC 162F	153 km/h (95 m.p.h.)

COST

For flying schools and private buyers alike, the purchase price is of great importance. If initial costs to a school are low then it can pass on these benefits by providing cheaper lessons and so attracting more pupils. The low price of the Exec 162F results from it being supplied as a kit for home assembly, while the 330 is a more complex aircraft with a price to match.

R22 BETA	EXEC 162F	330
$115,850	$56,000	$433,775

RANGE

All three of these small helicopters offer outstanding range due to their light weight and efficient engine design. The R22 is quite outstanding in this respect, providing novice pilots with the opportunity for long cross-country training flights.

R22 BETA	595 km (370 mi.)
330	495 km (308 mi.)
EXEC 162F	289 km (180 mi.)

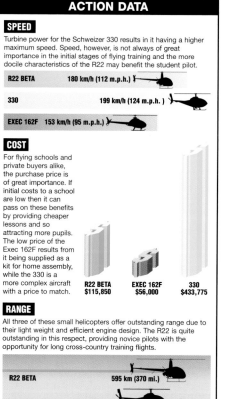

ROBINSON

R44

● Lightweight helicopter ● Proven design ● Brisk sales

Encouraged by the success of its two-seat light helicopter, the R22, the Robinson Helicopter Company of Torrance, California, created a slightly larger four-seater variant of the older machine for training and transport duties. Many proven features were retained in the interest of cost saving, simplicity and safety. The first R44 began flying in 1990, and by early 1994 around 300 R44s were in service around the world.

▲ *Robinson's R44 embodied many features of its predecessor. The simple controls kept the cost of the aircraft low, which is one of the reasons for the excellent sales figures.*

ROBINSON **R44**

▼ Value for money
At present, this little helicopter has a list price of just $265,000 in its home market, which makes it a very attractive buy.

▲ Trademark design
A distinctive feature of Robinson designs is the tall main rotor shaft. Many proprietary components are used on the rotor assembly.

Occupant protection ▶
Comfort and safety were prime aims for the R44, so an electronic throttle governor and safety restraints are standard.

▼ Popular in the US
Small helicopters have proved especially popular in the United States, and competition is fierce. The R44 has sold well.

Exceptional ▶ versatility
Base model R44s are known as Astros. They are also available for use as police helicopters, firebombers and for logging support.

FACTS AND FIGURES

➤ The first two R44s built accumulated more than 200 flying hours between 1990 and 1992.

➤ A total of $15,000 in deposits was taken on the first day of R44 sales.

➤ By January 1997, 308 R44s were operating in 38 different countries.

➤ The first R44 to reach 2,000 hours was the seventh production machine, which was returned for overhaul in mid-1996.

➤ The left-hand collective control lever and pedals can be removed if required.

➤ A float-equipped version, the Clipper, is available; it retails for $281,000.

PROFILE

Popular lightweight

Robinson's R44 has been an undisputed success story for the company. Since it was launched in the early 1990s, orders have continued to come in from customers in various parts of the world. A major reason for its popularity is the relatively low list price, which currently stands at around $265,000 in the USA.

Experience with the R22 resulted in the retention of the rotor design, which is unique in that it eliminates the need for the complicated hydraulic struts and shock absorbers found on most other rotary-winged craft. Other notable features include maintenance-free couplings in both the main and tail rotor drives, and spiral bevel gears.

Most R44s have been purchased for private use or as flying camera platforms by television news companies. Others have been bought by small police departments.

Above: N244H was the second R44 to fly and, like the first, was painted in this smart livery. It was later fitted with large floats in place of the skids and served as the demonstrator for the more upmarket R44 Clipper variant.

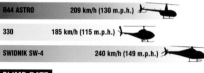

Below: R44s have enjoyed sales success outside the USA, too. This smart dark blue example is one of a number of machines currently registered in the United Kingdom.

R44 Astro

Type: four-seat general-purpose light helicopter

Powerplant: one 194-kW (260-hp.) Textron Lycoming O-540 horizontally opposed six-cylinder engine

Maximum speed: 209 km/h (130 m.p.h.)

Initial climb rate: 305 m/min (1,000 f.p.m.)

Range: 643 km (400 mi.)

Service ceiling: 4270 m (14,000 ft.)

Weights: empty 635 kg (1,397 lb.); loaded 1088 kg (2,394 lb.)

Accommodation: one pilot and up to three passengers

Dimensions:
tail rotor diameter	1.47 m (4 ft. 10 in.)
length	9.07 m (29 ft. 9 in.)
height	3.28 m (10 ft. 9 in.)
main rotor diameter	10.06 m² (108 sq. ft.)

Proven equipment on the R22 was retained for its larger sibling. In the cockpit, this includes the Robinson central cyclic stick plus an automatic throttle governor and rotor brake which help to reduce pilot workload.

An innovative feature of Robinson helicopters is the main rotor unit. It is triple-hinged, eliminating the need for lag hinges, shock absorbers and hydraulic struts, increasing reliability and reducing maintenance time.

A two-bladed main rotor is standard on the R44 and both blades are metal-bonded for maximum strength and durability. The leading edges are fabricated from steel.

In both the main and tail rotor drives, maintenance-free flexible couplings are used as is a special elastic teeter hinge. This prevents the main rotor blades from making contact with the tail unit.

G-NTEE

R44 Astro

Light alloy is primarily used on the fuselage, with the cabin section comprising a steel cage covered with lightweight metal and plastic skinning. Extensive use of sound deadening material results in a low level of cabin noise.

R44 Astro

This colourful British-registered example is typical of the many R44s currently in service around the world. Orders have been strong and production looks set to continue for many years to come.

ACTION DATA

CRUISING SPEED

Faster than the rival Schweizer 330, the R44 has excellent performance for a lightweight helicopter, a factor which has been instrumental in its popularity. The Polish Sw-4 features a much more powerful engine than the two American designs.

R44 ASTRO	209 km/h (130 m.p.h.)
330	185 km/h (115 m.p.h.)
SWIDNIK SW-4	240 km/h (149 m.p.h.)

CLIMB RATE

It may be faster than the 330 in a straight line, but the R44 cannot climb as quickly as the Schweizer machine. PZL's redesigned Swidnik Sw-4 can climb 600 m in just one minute, which is more than twice as quick as the Robinson helicopter.

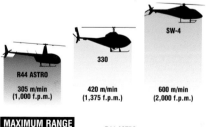

R44 ASTRO 305 m/min (1,000 f.p.m.)

330 420 m/min (1,375 f.p.m.)

SW-4 600 m/min (2,000 f.p.m.)

MAXIMUM RANGE

Depending on the role, range can have a varying degree of importance. The R44 has excellent endurance, a common characteristic of Robinson helicopters which makes it ideal for such tasks as crop-spraying. The Sw-4 is better still, capable of nearly 1000 km (560 miles) without being refuelled.

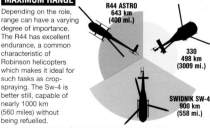

R44 ASTRO 643 km (400 mi.)

330 498 km (3009 mi.)

SWIDNIK SW-4 900 km (558 mi.)

Robinson helicopters at work

■ **FISHING SUPPORT:** Fitted with floats, these helicopters support large fishing fleets.

■ **COW HERDING:** Many large farms in the USA use helicopters for rounding up cattle.

■ **POLICE WORK:** R22s (shown) and R44s are employed by various police departments.

■ **CROP-SPRAYING:** Robinson helicopters are often used in the crop-dusting role.

SCHWEIZER

330

● American light helicopter ● Hughes ancestry ● Limited sales

▲ Looking similar to the larger Hughes/McDonnell Douglas Model 500 series of light helicopters, the Schweizer 300 first flew in June 1988, and went on sale during 1993.

Designed in the early 1980s to meet the US Army's requirement for a new flight training helicopter, the Schweizer 330 was produced with three sets of controls so that two students could be instructed simultaneously. It lost to the Bell TH-57 Creek in the military competition, but has been sold subsequently as a three- or four-seat light utility machine. It offers an attractive combination of low cost, high performance and mission flexibility.

SCHWEIZER 330

▼ **Common components**
In common with rival light helicopter designs, the 330 shares many components with another model, the Series 300. These include its basic fuselage structure and flying controls.

▲ **Army evaluation**
Schweizer's design was one of several tested for the US Army's New Training Helo requirement.

Sluggish sales ▶
Sales got off to a slow start, with only 12 Schweizer 330s being delivered by 1996.

▼ **First flight**
N330TT was the first 300 prototype and made its maiden flight on 14 June 1988.

Versatility ▶
The 330 was designed from the outset to fulfil a variety of roles, including fire fighting and law enforcement.

FACTS AND FIGURES

➤ Some design features of the 330 can be traced back to the Hughes 269, which first flew in 1956.

➤ The first Schweizer 330 in Europe was a demonstrator for Saab Helikopter.

➤ West Palm Beach Police Department in Florida operates a fleet of 330s.

➤ Main rivals in the US light helicopter market include the best-selling Robinson R44 and Enstrom 480 series.

➤ By January 1997 a total of 15 Schweizer 330 helicopters had been delivered.

➤ The Venezuelan army is one of the few military operators of the 330.

PROFILE

Lightweight performer

Schweizer's Model 330 is a turboshaft-powered development of the manufacturer's established Model 300. Originally a Hughes design, the Model 300 had been developed from the Model 269. Production was transferred to Schweizer in 1983.

The 330 was designed to combine safety and mission flexibility with outstanding performance. The unusual fuselage shape, combined with large stabilisers, make the 300 particularly stable, and the simple push-rod control system avoids the excessive weight and cost of hydraulic boost and stability augmentation devices. The fuselage also helps provide lift during forward flight and improves the flow of air to the main rotor.

Other safety features include a crash-resistant fuel bladder and a cabin floor and seat structure which has been specially designed to absorb sudden vertical impact during deceleration.

Left: An interesting and practical feature of the 330 is its ability to run on turbine fuel instead of Avgas if the operator wishes.

Right: This view of N330TT shows the similarity of the 330 to the elderly 300, especially the cockpit and doors.

330

Type: three-seat light utility helicopter

Powerplant: one 313.2-kW (420-hp.) Allison 250-C-20 turboshaft

Max cruising speed: 200 km/h (115 m.p.h.)

Range: 498 km (309 mi.)

Hover ceiling: 4300 m (14,100 ft.) in ground effect

Weights: empty 508 kg (1,117 lb.); loaded 1012 kg (2,226 lb.)

Fuel capacity: 227 litres (60 gal.)

Accommodation: one pilot and two passengers

Dimensions:
tailplane span	2.04 m (6 ft. 9 in.)
length	6.82 m (22 ft. 4 in.)
height	2.91 m (9 ft. 6 in.)
main rotor disc area	52.5 m² (565 sq. ft.)

Retaining many design features from the two-seat Series 300, the larger 330 offers an excellent view from the cockpit. The interior layout is flexible and three sets of full controls can be specified for student training.

Considerable attention was paid to ease of maintenance and this is reflected in the design of the rotor. Unlike the rival R44, the 330 features three blades and all are fully interchangeable. Elastometric dampers are incorporated.

On the original prototype, the tail boom was an open design, similar to that of the Series 300. The fuselage was later redesigned to produce an incredibly well streamlined integrated tail unit.

N330TT

A single Allison 250-C20 turboshaft powers the Schweizer 330. Flat-rated at just 175 kW (235 hp.), this engine has the ability to run on turbine fuel instead of Avgas and offers excellent hot-and-high performance.

330

Serialed N330TT, this particular machine was the first Schweizer 330 built and made its maiden flight on 14 June 1988. Originally painted white, it was subsequently modified with a more streamlined fuselage and repainted in this blue colour scheme.

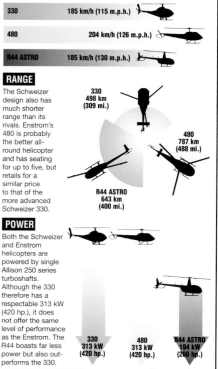

ACTION DATA

CRUISING SPEED

Two of the Schweizer 330's main rivals in the light helicopter market are the Enstrom 480 and Robinson R44. Both these machines have better all-round performance than the 330, which may be a reason for the Schweizer's relative unpopularity.

330	185 km/h (115 m.p.h.)
480	204 km/h (126 m.p.h.)
R44 ASTRO	185 km/h (130 m.p.h.)

RANGE

The Schweizer design also has much shorter range than its rivals. Enstrom's 480 is probably the better all-round helicopter and has seating for up to five, but retails for a similar price to that of the more advanced Schweizer 330.

330 498 km (309 mi.)
480 787 km (488 mi.)
R44 ASTRO 643 km (400 mi.)

POWER

Both the Schweizer and Enstrom helicopters are powered by single Allison 250 series turboshafts. Although the 330 therefore has a respectable 313 kW (420 hp.), it does not offer the same level of performance as the Enstrom. The R44 boasts far less power but also out-performs the 330.

330 313 kW (420 hp.)
480 313 kW (420 hp.)
R44 ASTRO 194 kW (260 hp.)

Proven utility helicopter designs

■ **AÉROSPATIALE ALOUETTE II:** Dating from the early 1950s, the Alouette was one of the first truly versatile light helicopters.

■ **AÉROSPATIALE GAZELLE:** Successor to the Alouette II, the Gazelle was also built under licence in the United Kingdom.

■ **BELL 206 JETRANGER:** One of the most successful helicopters in the world, the Jetranger is a familiar sight.

SIKORSKY

R-4/R-5

● First production helicopter ● Successful design ● Wartime service

Many people believe the role of the helicopter in World War II was restricted to experimental flights. The USAAC took it far beyond the test phase and Sikorsky's diminutive R-4 performed some of the most significant flights of the entire war. Pilots found themselves confronted with an entirely new era of flight, and the potential of the military helicopter was quickly seen. As a search and rescue platform, it was a life-saver.

▲ Sikorsky's R-4 can rightly be considered as the world's first true production helicopter. First flying in 1939, it entered service with the USAAF, the USN, the RAF and the Royal Navy.

SIKORSKY **R-4/R-5**

Natural progression ▶
Following on from the R-4 was a slightly larger machine, the R-5. It is seen here in early configuration with a tailwheel undercarriage.

◀ Production gets underway
With flight trials having been conducted successfully, the R-4 was put into production at Stratford, Connecticut in early 1942.

Workhorse forerunner ▶
Although the R-5 was successful, redesigning it resulted in the S-51, which did more to establish the concept of rotary-winged flight than any other helicopter.

◀ Distinctive looks
Compared to later designs, the R-4 was an ungainly machine featuring a boxed spar fuselage covered in fabric.

British helicopter evaluation ▶
After the R-4 had been ordered by the US armed services, a handful found their way overseas. The Royal Air Force and Fleet Air Arm evaluated the type during the closing months of World War II. In UK service, they were given the designation Hoverfly Mk I.

FACTS AND FIGURES

➤ On 21 April 1945 a single Canadian R-4 became the first helicopter to rescue a downed crew in the Arctic.

➤ Thirty production machines (YR-4As and YR-4Bs) were ordered in total.

➤ US Army Air Force R-4s were used to rescue downed crews in the Pacific.

➤ By the time production switched to the improved R-5/S-51 series, a total of 130 Sikorsky R-4s had been built.

➤ A Sikorsky R-4 was the first true helicopter to make a landing at sea.

➤ On 17 May 1942, the XR-4 flew a distance of 1224 km (760 mi.).

PROFILE

Rotary-winged warriors

Igor Sikorsky finally managed to fly his first successful rotary-winged craft in 1939. Known as the VS-300, it was instrumental in the development of the world's first true production helicopter, the amazing Sikorsky R-4. With the VS-300 flying at speeds of up to 113 km/h (70 m.p.h.) by 1941, it was obvious that a more practical machine was viable.

The resulting XR-4 featured an enclosed cockpit with dual, side-by-side seating and a single Warner R500 piston engine. After successful trials, an order for 30 production aircraft (three YR-4As and 27 YR-4Bs) was placed by the

United States Army Air Force. They were later augmented by 100 more R-4Bs which featured more powerful engines. R-4s were pioneers in the development of the helicopter and, on 6 May 1943, an early production machine became the first helicopter to land successfully aboard a ship, touching down on the aircraft carrier, USS *Bunker Hill*.

Using the R-4 as a basis, Sikorsky developed the larger R-5, which featured an all-metal fuselage and other improvements. It first flew in 1943, but did not enter service until after World War II. Nevertheless, it proved tremendously successful and

some 379 of these aircraft, later called S-51, were built.

Above: This photograph is unique, showing the Sikorsky R-4, R-5 and R-6 together. The evolution of the helicopter can already be seen.

Left: Col Frank Gregory, who helped to bring about the R-4, was the first person to land a helicopter on board ship.

R-4B

Type: experimental, training, search and rescue helicopter

Powerplant: one 138-kW (185-hp.) Warner R-550-3 Super Scarab piston engine

Maximum speed: 120 km/h (74 m.p.h.)

Endurance: 2 hours

Initial climb rate: 2440 m (8,000 ft.) in 45 min

Range: 209 km (130 mi.)

Service ceiling: 2440 m (8,000 ft.)

Weights: empty 913 kg (2,008 lb.); loaded 1153 kg (2,537 lb.)

Accommodation: two pilots, side by side

Dimensions:

rotor diameter	11.6 m (38 ft. 1 in.)
length	14.65 m (48 ft. 1 in.)
height	3.78 m (12 ft. 5 in.)
wing area	105.3 m² (1,133 sq. ft.)

Tests were conducted in which the tail rotor was mounted horizontally, with the hub pointing skyward. Although the aircraft could get airborne with few problems, stability and directional control were still difficult. The XR-4 reverted to the more familiar layout.

All R-4s were fitted with three-bladed main rotors. To reduce weight, they were constructed from spruce wood, which proved a problem during rescue operations in the Pacific theatre.

At the time, the cockpit of the R-4 was quite unusual for many pilots. The aircraft commander sat in the right-hand seat. It was not a difficult machine to fly and pilots could go solo in just a few hours.

The XR-4 was powered by a 123-kW Warner R-500 piston engine. From pre-production machines onward, this was substituted by a 138-kW (180-hp.) R-550.

Despite its appearance, the fuselage was extremely strong, with diagonally mounted spars increasing stiffness and strength. The rear section was uncovered.

Another feature pioneered by the R-4 was the interchangeable undercarriage. R-4Bs in service with the US Navy aboard ships were often fitted with floats.

Because of the extreme upward tapering of the fuselage, a very long tail wheel was necessary to keep the R-4 level while on the ground.

R-4

During initial trials the Sikorsky R-4 wore an overall silver dope scheme with full colour insignia. Wartime operations saw the adoption of a drab green colour scheme to offer some form of camouflage to the vulnerable R-4.

GETTING IT RIGHT

MULTIPLE ROTORS: Igor Sikorsky's most successful testbed before the R-4 was the VS-300. This strange-looking machine made its maiden flight on 14 September 1939. Sikorsky had been experimenting with the idea of rotary-winged aircraft for many years, but until the late 1930s the technology was not sufficient to warrant a full working example. This tri-rotored layout was just one configuration tested on the VS-300.

FURTHER IDEAS: After experimenting with many configurations, Sikorsky discovered that stability and directional control problems could be solved by adopting an anti-torque rotor on the tail. This configuration has been adopted by the vast majority of helicopters since; the design is similar to that which ultimately emerged on the R-4 itself.

Early Sikorsky helicopters

■ **SIKORSKY R-6:** Installing the R-4's engine and gearbox in a new, much more streamlined fuselage resulted in the R-6. They were delivered to the RAF as Hoverfly Mk IIs.

■ **SIKORSKY S-52:** This little helicopter has the distinction of being the first of its type to feature all-metal rotor blades. It also established national helicopter records for speed and altitude.

■ **SIKORSKY S-55:** Entering service in 1952, the S-55 served with the US Army and Air Force in large numbers as the H-19. It was built under licence in France and the United Kingdom.

SIKORSKY
R-4/R-6A

● Helicopter at war ● First in service ● Rescue role

▲ The father of modern helicopter design, Dr Igor Sikorsky (right), stands in front of a YR-4, which dictated the basic handling characteristics of helicopter flight for the next generation.

Igor Sikorsky flew the prototype of his first helicopter, the VS-300, in September 1939. By January 1942 his company had built and flown a more powerful derivative, the VS-316A and it was this model that the US Army Air Force bought for evaluation, as the XR-4. The USAAF went on to buy more than 100 R-4Bs. In October 1943 Sikorsky flew the XR-6, an improved variant with a more powerful engine and a more refined, streamlined fuselage.

SIKORSKY R-4/R-6A

▲ Merchant Navy
Sikorsky R-4B helicopters flew from merchant ships, acting as air observation posts.

▲ Warbird
Helicopters were employed during the war by both the US Navy and Army; one is seen lifting off on an early operational flight.

▲ Casualty evacuation
In addition to two crew members, two stretcher cases could be carried externally, enabling advanced area rescue.

▼ Tail rotor trials
A developmental model takes to the air, showing the early style auxiliary tail rotor.

▲ Precision flying
Bringing new dimensions of flight to the masses was part of the helicopter's early role, as in this display.

FACTS AND FIGURES

➤ Colonel Frank Gregory made the first helicopter landing aboard ship, on 7 May 1943 in Long Island Sound, USA.

➤ The first flight of the XR-4 was on 14 January 1942.

➤ Early XR-4s had a metal and fabric-covered fuselage.

➤ The US Navy established its first helicopter squadron, VX-3, at Floyd Bennett Field NAS.

➤ Three YR-6As made the first rescue mission in China during World War II.

➤ R-4Bs became the first production helicopters in the world.

PROFILE

The helicopter goes to war

Two batches totalling 41 YR-4Bs were used for trials by the USAAF and US Coast Guard, the latter using three examples designated HNS-1. Such was their success that a further 100 production R-4Bs were delivered. A number were diverted to the US Navy, while 45 others were passed to the RAF as Hoverfly Mk Is.

The R-4B was subsequently used operationally during World War II and achieved a number of notable firsts, including being the first helicopter to land on a ship at sea.

Sikorsky's VR-316B was the XR-6 – essentially a refinement of the R-4 featuring a vastly improved fuselage and a more powerful 179-kW (240-hp.) Franklin engine (in all but the prototype). Twenty-six pre-production YR-6s and 193 production R-6As were built, all by Nash-Kelvinator. Of these, 36 R-6As were used by the US Navy as the HOS-1 and another 40 were supplied to the RAF as

the Hoverfly Mk II.

After 1948, the R-4 and R-6 became known as the H-4 and H-6, respectively. Though they had relatively short careers, they paved the way for later developments. The helicopter configuration they pioneered remained essentially unchanged for more than 30 years.

Left: Single-engined and with a crew of two, YR-6As flew numerous missions involving spotting, reconnaissance and rescue over land and at sea.

Above: YR-4Bs gave bomber crews the chance of rescue, if needed; this one lifts off to search for a ditched aircraft.

R-4B

Type: experimental, training and rescue helicopter

Powerplant: one 138-kW (185-hp.) Warner R-550-1 or R-550-3 Super Scarab radial piston engine

Maximum level speed: 120 km/h (74 m.p.h.)

Endurance: approx 2 hr

Climb rate: 2440 m in 45 min

Range: 209 km (130 mi.)

Service ceiling: 2440 m (8005 ft.)

Weights: empty 913 kg (2,013 lb.); loaded 1153 kg (2,542 lb.)

Accommodation: two pilots seated side by side

Dimensions:
rotor diameter	11.6 m (38 ft.)
overall length	14.65 m (48 ft.)
height	3.78 m (12 ft. 9 in.)
rotor disc area	105.3 m² (1,133 sq. ft.)

The cockpit, with side-by-side seating, was fitted with instruments for both pilots. Glazing was extensive, giving excellent visibility in all directions.

The main rotor head was a simple and straightforward design consisting of various push rods all mounted on a metal pylon of four steel tubes. This proved effective and extremely versatile.

Three rotor blades were constructed from laminated spruce with balsa leading edges covered by fabric, an unusual construction method which proved extremely durable.

Mounted vertically directly behind the pilots, a Warner R-550-1 radial engine powered the R-4, driving both rotors through a complex series of transmission shafts.

The box-like fuselage consisted of heavy gauge steel tubing with welded joints and was covered in fabric to reduce drag.

346503

After numerous experimental trials the mounting of the tail rotor in the vertical position was found to give the best directional control.

Problems with landing resulted in the tail wheel being moved to the rear of the boom from its earlier central position, so allowing better handling.

R-4B

An example of a Sikorsky R-4B in US Army service with the Air Jungle Rescue Squadron, which was employed to retrieve wounded soldiers and aircrew from inaccessible areas.

COMBAT DATA

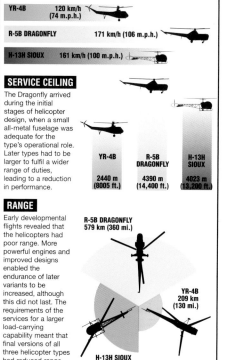

MAXIMUM SPEED

By obtaining sufficient knowledge with the YR-4B, Sikorsky developed in parallel the completely new tandem two-seat Dragonfly with increased performance. The addition of the medevac role saw the Sioux's speed reduced.

YR-4B	120 km/h (74 m.p.h.)
R-5B DRAGONFLY	171 km/h (106 m.p.h.)
H-13H SIOUX	161 km/h (100 m.p.h.)

SERVICE CEILING

The Dragonfly arrived during the initial stages of helicopter design, when a small all-metal fuselage was adequate for the type's operational role. Later types had to be larger to fulfil a wider range of duties, leading to a reduction in performance.

YR-4B	R-5B DRAGONFLY	H-13H SIOUX
2440 m (8005 ft.)	4390 m (14,400 ft.)	4023 m (13,200 ft.)

RANGE

Early developmental flights revealed that the helicopters had poor range. More powerful engines and improved designs enabled the endurance of later variants to be increased, although this did not last. The requirements of the services for a larger load-carrying capability meant that final versions of all three helicopter types had reduced range and speed.

R-5B DRAGONFLY 579 km (360 mi.)

YR-4B 209 km (130 mi.)

H-13H SIOUX 383 km (238 mi.)

Sikorsky's early years

■ **FIRST FLIGHT:** Igor Sikorsky made the first attempts to fly in the VS-300 on September 1939 at Stratford, Connecticut, in the USA.

■ **TAIL ROTORS:** Another variant of the VS-300 was constructed with additional tail rotors to improve the handling qualities.

■ **THREE TAILS:** Although the addition of tail rotors was thought to be the answer, eventually the single rotor was seen as most effective.

■ **BASIC DESIGN:** With the Sikorsky R-4 the basic principles of helicopter flight had been solved. This example is seen with floats.

SIKORSKY

S-51/R-5

● Rescue helicopter ● Amphibious design ● Mail service

▲ *This S-51 is rescuing a member of the Canadian Armed Forces from a platform during a demonstration. The Sikorsky displayed excellent handling qualities, which are vital for rescue work.*

After its success with the R-4, the USAAF issued a requirement for a larger machine which was able to carry out tasks such as observation duties. Vought-Sikorsky's Model 327 was designed to meet the new specification and shared the R-4's basic layout. However, it was an entirely new design and seated two crew in tandem in a more streamlined fuselage. Sikorsky went on to develop the S-51 civil helicopter from the R-5.

PHOTO FILE

SIKORSKY S-51/R-5

▼ **Airborne angel**
The Sikorsky S-51 saved lives by ensuring that casualties received medical attention quickly. This example carries two wounded men to a field hospital.

▲ **Early days**
With the fuselage panels removed for an engine test the small size of the R-5 is readily apparent.

Crop sprayer ▶
Seen displaying an unusual rig for spraying crops, the S-51 saw wide-spread civilian service as an air ambulance and work-horse.

▲ **Cross-deck operations**
Returning an admiral to his ship, an S-51 lands precariously on a gun turret.

Staying afloat ▶
A US Coast Guard H-5 sits on the water with emergency floatation bags inflated.

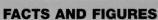

FACTS AND FIGURES

➤ Westland built the R-5 under licence in Britain as the WS.51 Dragonfly, for the RAF, Royal Navy and civil operators.

➤ Nine HO3S-1s were used by the US Coast Guard as HO3S-1Gs.

➤ HO3S-1s served with distinction in the Korean War with Squadron HU-1.

➤ In 1950 Sikorsky built and tested a single XHO3S-3 with a redesigned rotor head and blades.

➤ Two XR-5As were fitted with British instruments to an RAF requirement.

➤ The R-5B, R-5C and HO3S-2 were planned variants later cancelled.

PROFILE

The first rescue helicopter

Five prototypes were built under the designation XR-5, the first of which flew on 18 August 1943. Power was supplied by a fuselage-mounted 336-kW (450-hp.) Pratt & Whitney R-985 radial engine. These were followed by 26 YR-5A evaluation aircraft and 34 R-5A service aircraft, which could be fitted with stretcher carriers for casualty evacuation.

These R-5As were the first helicopters employed by the Air Rescue Service (ARS). Of these, 21 were converted to R-5D standard with a rescue hoist and an external fuel tank.

On 16 February 1946, the first S-51 took to the air. This model had a larger four-seater cabin, a nosewheel (the first R-5s had a tailwheel behind the cabin) and a higher gross weight. More than 200 were built, including a batch for the Royal Canadian Air Force. The USAF bought 11 examples, as R-5Fs, in 1947.

From June 1948 the R-5 family was redesignated H-5 and, later that year, the ARS added H-5Gs (based on the H-5F with a hoist and other equipment) to its inventory. The last H-5s built (in 1949) were 16 H-5Hs, which were equipped with combined wheel/pontoon landing gear.

The US Navy took delivery of three R-5As, designated HO2S-1s, in late 1945, and later ordered 88 HO3S-1s, equivalent to the H-5F. Although officially designated as observation aircraft, they performed a number of tasks.

Examples were also built under license by Westland in Britain and served with the Fleet Air Arm and the RAF. In Royal Navy service the helicopters operated as 'plane-guards' flying from aircraft-carriers.

Left: The H-5, seen here returning after a rescue, was the primary SAR helicopter for the USAF throughout the 1950s and rescued both servicemen and civilians.

Above: The first amphibious helicopter for US service, the new wheel/float combination of the Sikorsky design greatly improved its capabilities.

R-5B

Type: two-/four-seat rescue and utility helicopter

Powerplant: one 336-kW (450-hp.) Pratt & Whitney R-985-AN-5 radial piston engine

Maximum speed: 171 km/h (106 m.p.h.); cruising speed 137 km/h (85 m.p.h.)

Initial climb rate: 3048 m (1,000 ft.) in 15 min

Range: 579 km (360 mi.)

Service ceiling: 4390 m (14,400 ft.) with an operational load

Weights: empty 1715 kg (3,781 lb.); take-off 2189 kg (4,826 lb.)

Dimensions:
main rotor diameter	14.63 m (48 ft.)
length	17.4 m (57 ft.)
height	3.96 m (13 ft.)
rotor disc area	168.15 m² (1,810 sq. ft.)

ACTION DATA

MAXIMUM SPEED

Constructed under licence by Westland as the Dragonfly, the Sikorsky R-5 showed the rapid improvements that helicopters were making by its speed advantage over the Sikorsky R-4B a design which was produced just a few years before. This was repeated again in the Whirlwind which offered a larger cabin area.

DRAGONFLY HR.Mk 3	165 km/h (102 m.p.h.)
WHIRLWIND HAS.Mk 7	176 km/h (109 m.p.h.)
R-4B	120 km/h (74 m.p.h.)

SERVICE CEILING

Though smaller than the Whirlwind the Dragonfly enjoyed one of the highest operational ceilings of the early helicopters. But this was reduced in the Air Rescue role when the fuselage was fitted with a hoist and an auxiliary fuel tank.

DRAGONFLY HR.Mk 3	WHIRLWIND HAS.Mk 7	R-4B
4206 m (13,800 ft.)	2865 m (9,400 ft.)	2440 m (8,000 ft.)

WEIGHTS LOADED

The small fuselage of the Dragonfly restricted its capacity to lift any more than a minor load. The larger cabin area of the later Whirlwind proved to be far more practical, capable of carrying survivors, troops, and medical attendants.

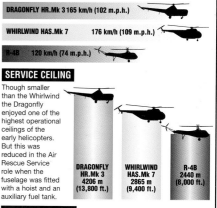

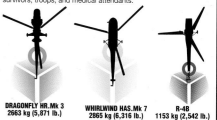

DRAGONFLY HR.Mk 3	WHIRLWIND HAS.Mk 7	R-4B
2663 kg (5,871 lb.)	2865 kg (6,316 lb.)	1153 kg (2,542 lb.)

The cockpit provided accommodation for two crew seated in tandem. Excellent visibility was afforded to the pilot which was ideal for search and rescue work.

To extend the capabilities of the design, a stretcher could be attached on each side of the helicopter to evacuate wounded personnel.

Three main rotor blades were fitted to the R-5 producing enough lift for the helicopter to have a surprisingly good performance.

A simple tail rotor allowed for excellent low speed handling particularly when manoeuvring in the hover, a fact that many downed crew came to appreciate.

The fuselage was of an all metal design which offered a major improvement over the earlier fabric covered Sikorsky R-4. The design was far more resistant to the elements, which was vital as the helicopter was soon operating in a war zone.

A standard tricycle undercarriage was installed on the helicopter to which floats could be attached for rescue work over water.

H-5

Displaying the title *Southern Comfort* on its nose, this example served with MAMs-33 in the Korean war. The helicopter patrolled the Sea of Japan retrieving downed pilots.

Sikorsky's rescue helicopters

■ **SIKORSKY HO5S-1:** Developed shortly after the S-51 the HO5S-1 offered a larger cabin area to accommodate more people. Used alongside the S-51 in the Korean War the type was used by both the US Navy and Marines. After Korea it was employed by the US Coast Guard.

■ **SIKORSKY H-19:** Continuous development of the helicopter fleet saw the H-19 become one of the most successful early designs. Constructed under licence by Westland in Britain the helicopter was often seen rescuing people from the sea, as illustrated here by this USAF example.

■ **SIKORSKY HU5-1A:** Operating over water, many helicopters were fitted with floats to allow landings on the sea. This proved invaluable during rescue work. Though highly effective, the use of floats resulted in a loss in performance and many operators did not use the extra capability.

SIKORSKY

S-55/H-19

● Korea veteran ● Pioneering troop-lifter ● Air-sea rescue

The S-55 was the first in a long line of successful large Sikorsky helicopters. Starting life as a piston-powered machine with a limited load-carrying capacity, the S-55 later received a turbine engine and considerably more capability. It could perform a variety of roles, including airlifting troops, air-sea rescue work, air taxiing, cargo-hauling and anti-submarine patrol. The S-55 took part in the Korean War, but was still providing useful service to military and civil users in the 1980s.

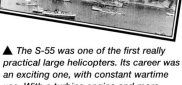

▲ The S-55 was one of the first really practical large helicopters. Its career was an exciting one, with constant wartime use. With a turbine engine and more power, it shone as a versatile machine.

SIKORSKY S-55/H-19

▼ **Piston power**
The large, bulky radial was faired under twin clamshell doors. Engineers loved this as it meant easy access to the engine. But the marriage of helicopters and large piston engines was never really successful.

▲ **At home on floats**
From the start, the helicopter's unique ability made it ideal for maritime use, and the float-equipped S-55 served as a rescue machine for many years.

Troop carrier ▶
The S-55's ability to carry up to 10 fully-equipped troops was used in the development of an entirely new kind of warfare known as helicopter assault. Troop-carrying S-55s saw action around the world, from Malaya to Algeria.

Load-lifter ▶
Hauling logs in the Rockies was another task that earlier helicopters were not capable of. The need for a powerful turbine engine was demonstrated vividly when carrying loads at high altitudes.

Sling load supplies ▶
The ability to get supplies to troops miles from any airfield was especially useful in Korea, where UN units were frequently bypassed and surrounded. The narrow fuselage profile made underslung load-carrying preferable to using the tight cabin space.

FACTS AND FIGURES

➤ The US Army version of the H-19 was known as the Chickasaw.

➤ The US Navy HOS-4 version was used for anti-submarine warfare duties.

➤ Westland-built S-55s were sometimes powered by the Alvis Leonides Major piston engine or Gnome turboshaft.

➤ French S-55s in Algeria used rockets and machine-guns in combat trials.

➤ The US Army was still using its last few H-19s in the early 1980s.

➤ In an air show stunt that went wrong, an RAF Whirlwind dragged a stuntman on a bicycle through trees.

PROFILE

First of the big Sikorskys

Helicopters really came of age after 1945, and the type owes much to the work of the great Igor Sikorsky. After the pioneering S-51, Sikorsky set about building a utility machine for the US Air Force, designated H-19. The first of these, known to the manufacturer as the S-55, flew in November 1949. It was powered by a Pratt & Whitney radial piston engine, similar to those in wartime fighters. The drive shaft ran under the cockpit to the high-mounted rotor. With a rear cabin that could carry 10 passengers, the S-55 was an instant success, and its combat debut came in Korea. It was licence-built by Westland in Britain, and served with the Royal Navy's 'Jungly' squadrons in Malaya, dropping commandos into the forest. French S-55s, built by SNCA, served in Algeria, pursuing the FNLA into the Atlas mountains. In numerous wars from the African desert to the jungles of Vietnam, S-55s carried out thousands of troop lifts and medevac (medical evacuation) missions. Later, when re-engined with a turboprop instead of the heavy piston engine, it gained a new lease of life and soldiered on into the 1990s.

The S-55 was very similar to its Soviet counterpart, the Mi-4. Both types provided valuable new experience of operating helicopters in unusual roles and conditions.

S-55 (H-19B)

Type: 10-passenger utility helicopter

Powerplant: one 522-kW (389-hp.) Wright R-1300-3 radial piston engine

Maximum speed: 180 km/h (112 m.p.h.); cruising speed 146 km/h (90 m.p.h.)

Range: 580 km (360 mi.)

Service ceiling: 3940 m (13,000 ft.)

Weights: empty 2381 kg (5,250 lb.); take-off 3583 kg (7,900 lb.)

Armament: none designed, but machine-guns and rockets were fitted in the field

Payload: 10 passengers or up to eight stretchers in ambulance role

Dimensions: rotor diameter 16.16 m (53 ft.)
length 12.85 m (12 ft. 2 in.)
height 4.07 m (13 ft. 3 in.)
rotor disc area 204.94 m² (2,206 sq. ft.)

H-19B

The US Air Force operated the S-55 as the H-19A and H-19B in the air-sea rescue role. The same version was known as the H-19C Chickasaw in US Army service.

The two-man cockpit had full dual controls. It was extemely noisy, especially in the radial-powered versions.

The engines of the S-55 were consistently uprated. The first H-19 had a Pratt & Whitney R-1340 radial, but the Wright 1820 of the HRS-4 had twice the power.

The main cabin accommodated up to 10 passengers, seated against the walls facing inwards; three on the front and rear walls, and two each side.

Search-and-rescue S-55s had a starboard-mounted winch.

The wide, stable undercarriage was essential as the S-55 was tall, although the engine weight was low down. Early helicopters often suffered 'ground resonance' due to their shape, which on occasion caused bad accidents.

The S-55 had an all-metal rotor, a great improvement on the wooden versions of early helicopters. The three-bladed rotor had conventional hinges.

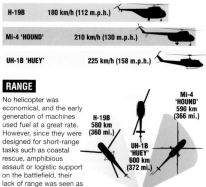

The main fuselage was of conventional aluminium and magnesium semi-monocoque construction, except for the chrome-molybdenum steel rotor pylon.

The tail rotor was a simple two-bladed unit, driven by a long shaft from the main transmission under the main rotor.

COMBAT DATA

MAXIMUM SPEED

The earliest helicopters were far from spritely machines. Although capable of 180 km/h (112 m.p.h.) the original S-55 cruised at 146 km/h (90 m.p.h.). The Soviet Mil came after the S-55. It looked similar but was a much larger and more powerful machine, with slightly better performance. The turbine-powered 'Huey' flew in the late 1950s, and was to replace the S-55 in many of its roles.

H-19B	180 km/h (112 m.p.h.)
Mi-4 'HOUND'	210 km/h (130 m.p.h.)
UH-1B 'HUEY'	225 km/h (158 m.p.h.)

RANGE

No helicopter was economical, and the early generation of machines used fuel at a great rate. However, since they were designed for short-range tasks such as coastal rescue, amphibious assault or logistic support on the battlefield, their lack of range was seen as no real handicap.

H-19B 580 km (360 mi.)
Mi-4 'HOUND' 590 km (366 mi.)
UH-1B 'HUEY' 600 km (372 mi.)

PAYLOAD

The helicopters which entered service at the end of World War II were pushed to carry two or three passengers as well as a pilot. So the S-55, which made its maiden flight in 1949, was a revelation. Capable of lifting 10 troops, it was easily the most capable helicopter of its time, only surpassed by the much bigger Mil Mi-4 in the early 1950s.

H-19B 10 troops
Mi-4 'HOUND' 12 troops
UH-1B 'HUEY' 6 troops

In service around the world

■ **US MILITARY S-55s:** Known as the H-19 (Air Force), H-19 Chickasaw (Army), HO4S (Navy) and HRS-3 (Marine Corps), the S-55 was the first helicopter to serve in large numbers.

■ **EXPORT SUCCESS:** The S-55's capabilities were so far in advance of any other Western helicopter that it sold widely abroad, to more than a dozen countries, including Canada.

■ **ROYAL HELICOPTER:** The most luxurious of all S-55 variants, the turbine-powered Westland Whirlwinds of Britain's Queen's Flight flew until the late 1960s.

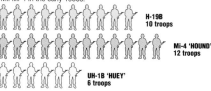

SIKORSKY

S-56/CH-37 MOJAVE

● US Army and Marines transport ● First twin-engined Sikorsky

▲ With experience
gained in designing the S-56, Sikorsky
went on to produce other large single-rotor
designs, like the S-64 Skycrane (CH-54 Tarhe)
and S-65 (CH-53 Sea Stallion).

For 10 years after its first flight the S-56 was the largest helicopter flying outside the Soviet Union and, until the end of 1961, it was the largest helicopter operated by the US military. Designed to meet a US Navy and Marine Corps requirement for an assault transport, it was also the first twin-engined Sikorsky design. Designated HR2S by the Navy, the S-56 flew in 1953. It served in larger numbers with the US Army as the H-37 Mojave.

PHOTO FILE

SIKORSKY S-56/CH-37 MOJAVE

▼ Retractable landing gear
Mojaves were not only novel in their engine arrangement; they also had a retractable undercarriage. The main gear assemblies retracted rearwards into the engine nacelle. Each leg was supported by twin wheels.

▲ Valuable heavy-lifter
H-37s provided US Army logistics personnel with a heavy-lift capability that they had never had before.

◀ On exercises in Puerto Rico
HR2S-1s of HMR-461 touch down at a marked landing area during exercises.

▼ YH-37 for the Army
In 1954, the US Army tested a pre-production XHR2S-1 as a YH-37.

◀ Early warning variant
Two HR2S-1Ws, with APS-20E radar scanners fitted, were evaluated by the US Navy. However, airframe vibration badly degraded radar performance.

FACTS AND FIGURES

➤ Mojaves were replaced by the CH-54 Tarhe, which weighed less but could lift five times as much cargo as the CH-37.

➤ In all, 150 S-56s were built; a prototype, 55 for the USMC and 94 for the Army.

➤ 1959 saw the first overseas H-37 deployment, by the Army to Germany.

➤ Army H-37As entered service with the 4th Medium Helicopter Transportation Company in February 1958.

➤ The H-37A had a fuselage capacity large enough to hold three Army jeeps.

➤ The Army briefly evaluated one of the two HR2S-1Ws in 'Arctic' colours.

PROFILE

First heavy-lift chopper for the Corps

Despite being piston-engined at a time when most new helicopter designs were powered by lightweight and powerful turboshafts, the CH-37 (as it was known to the US Army and Navy after 1962) proved its worth as a heavy-lift helicopter.

This was illustrated by the type's brief deployment by the Army in the Vietnam conflict. Four CH-37Bs recovered $7.5 million worth of downed aircraft during June 1963, many of them from otherwise inaccessible, enemy-dominated areas.

Sikorsky's S-56 was designed to meet a US Marine Corps requirement for an assault helicopter able to carry about 26 troops. The machine's unique configuration, with its engines in nacelles separate from the fuselage, left the latter clear for load-carrying. Large clam-shell doors in the nose allowed straight-in loading of up to 907 kg (2,000 lbs.) of cargo into the winch-equipped hold.

Fifty-five HR2S-1s were delivered to the US Marines; two were later modified for early warning duties by the Navy as HR2S-1Ws with a large radar scanner installed in a radome fitted under the chin.

After evaluating an XHR2S-1 (YH-37), the Army took delivery of 94 H-37As, all of which were delivered by June 1960. Most were later converted to H-37B standard with improved systems. The last CH-37s were retired in the late 1960s.

Above: A Marine Corps CH-37C and UH-34D return to MCAS El Toro, California, from an exercise.

Right: Distinctive 'eyes' painted on the front of the engine nacelles were a common feature of both Marine Corps and Army CH-37s.

CH-37B Mojave

Type: troop and supply transport helicopter

Powerplant: two 1566-kW (2,100-hp.) Pratt & Whitney R-2800-54 Double Wasp radials

Maximum speed: 200 km/h (124 m.p.h.)

Range: 233 km (145 mi.) with maximum payload

Weights: empty 9730 kg (21,450 lb.); maximum take-off 13608 kg (30,000 lb.)

Accommodation: two or three crew, plus up to 26 troops, 24 stretcher cases or three jeeps; underslung loads of up to 4536 kg (10,000 lb.) may be lifted

Dimensions:
main rotor diameter	21.95 m (72 ft.)
fuselage length	19.58 m (64 ft. 3 in.)
height	6.71 m (22 ft.)
rotor disc area	379.03 m² (4,080 sq. ft.)

CH-37C

Originally designated HRS-1 by the USMC, the S-56 became the CH-37C when US military designation systems were unified in 1962.

Pratt & Whitney's ever-reliable R-2800 Double Wasp (that powered such types as the Northrop P-61 Black Widow night-fighter and Douglas A-26 Invader bomber) found yet another application in the S-56.

Industry practice at the time of the S-56's design was to employ fore- and aft-mounted tandem rotors. Sikorsky broke with convention, using a single large, five-bladed main rotor with a four-bladed anti-torque rotor at the rear.

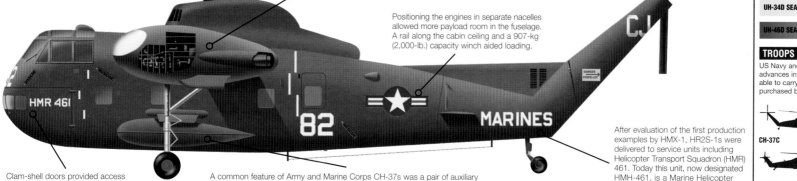

Positioning the engines in separate nacelles allowed more payload room in the fuselage. A rail along the cabin ceiling and a 907-kg (2,000-lb.) capacity winch aided loading.

Clam-shell doors provided access to the CH-37's hold. A ramp was fitted for vehicles.

A common feature of Army and Marine Corps CH-37s was a pair of auxiliary fuel tanks of 1136-litre (300-gallon) capacity, fixed to the fuselage inboard of the undercarriage. Fuel reached the engines direct via external pipes.

After evaluation of the first production examples by HMX-1, HR2S-1s were delivered to service units including Helicopter Transport Squadron (HMR) 461. Today this unit, now designated HMH-461, is a Marine Helicopter Squadron, Heavy and operates Sikorsky CH-53E Super Stallions.

COMBAT DATA

CRUISING SPEED

Marine Corps CH-37Cs (HR2S-1s) were marginally faster than the Sikorsky UH-34, which had been one of the Marines' larger helicopter types. The tandem-rotor Boeing-Vertol Sea Knight was a substantially faster aircraft.

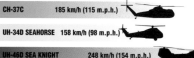

CH-37C	185 km/h (115 m.p.h.)
UH-34D SEAHORSE	158 km/h (98 m.p.h.)
UH-46D SEA KNIGHT	248 km/h (154 m.p.h.)

TROOPS

US Navy and Marine Corps H-34s, H-37s and H-46s represent advances in helicopter design and a trend toward larger machines able to carry more troops and cargo. The UH-46 was specifically purchased by the Navy for vertical replenishment (vertrep) duties.

CH-37C	20 troops
UH-34D SEAHORSE	18 troops
UH-46D SEA KNIGHT	25 troops

RANGE

Though able to lift heavy loads, the CH-37 was a little short on range compared to the Seahorse. In service with both the Marines and Army, the type was often fitted with extra external fuel tanks to boost range performance. Boeing-Vertol's Sea Knight took most performance standards to new heights on entering service in 1964.

CH-37C	UH-34D SEAHORSE	UH-46D SEA KNIGHT
233 km (148 mi.)	293 km (182 mi.)	370 km (230 mi.)

Marine Corps helicopters at war

■ **BELL UH-1E IROQUOIS:** First employed by the US Army in Vietnam in 1962, the 'Huey' was adopted by the Marines in UH-1E form and quickly deployed to Southeast Asia.

■ **SIKORSKY HRS-2 :** HRS-1s and HRS-2s equipped nine Marine transport (HMR) squadrons in Korea. Their main role was troop carrying, the type seating up to eight troops.

■ **SIKORSKY CH-53A SEA STALLION:** First deployed in Vietnam in January 1967, the CH-53 was specifically developed as a large assault type for the Marine Corps.

■ **SIKORSKY UH-34D (HUS-1) SEAHORSE:** The most widely used piston-engined helicopter of the war, the Seahorse was the USMC's main assault helicopter until the UH-1 entered service.

SIKORSKY

S-58/H-34 CHOCTAW

● ASW/utility helicopter ● US Army, Navy and Marines ● Piston engine

▲ *The military S-58 series was so successful that examples soon started to appear all over the world. VH-34Ds were used to support President Eisenhower on a visit to Spain.*

A new generation of helicopter design was ushered in by Sikorsky's S-58. Prior to its first flight in 1954, helicopters had been built for their unique capabilities, with little thought given to their role suitability. The S-58, operated by the US Navy, Marines and Army, was a highly versatile helicopter suited to a variety of roles. It went on to win many export orders in both military and commercial versions and a few still remain in service.

SIKORSKY S-58/H-34 CHOCTAW

▼ US Coast Guard rescue
Based on the Marines HUS-1A (CH-34E) version, six HUS-1G (HH-34F) helicopters, capable of operating on amphibious pontoons, were delivered to the Coast Guard.

▲ Japanese HSS-1
Japan obtained a large number of ex-US Navy HSS-1s (nicknamed the 'Hiss-1' in US service) and used them in the search-and-rescue role.

▼ Back to Earth
HUS-1 helicopters belonging to the Marines had the honour of recovering several astronauts and their capsules from the sea.

▲ Folded Choctaw
The US Army's CH-34A Choctaw retained the fuselage folding capabilities of its naval counterpart. Many Choctaws flew with US forces based in Germany.

◀ Bullpup shot
Several experiments were carried out with armed H-34s, but none entered service. This Marines HUS-1 makes an early test firing.

FACTS AND FIGURES

➤ When he checked in for a Sabena S-58 flight, Igor Sikorsky was asked if his name was spelt like the helicopter's.

➤ US military designation changes in 1962 led to the HSS-1 becoming the SH-34G.

➤ 'Doughnut' bags could be fixed to the S-58 undercarriage to make it amphibious.

➤ US Army CH-34s maintained a constant patrol along the border of West Germany with Czechoslovakia and East Germany.

➤ The US Army-Marines Executive Flight Detachment used VH-34D aircraft.

➤ A total of 603 S-58s were delivered to the US Marines.

PROFILE

Sikorsky's stunning S-58

When the Bell XHSL-1 anti-submarine warfare (ASW) helicopter proved disappointing, the US Navy was glad that it had ordered the Sikorsky XHSS-1 as a back-up. As the HSS-1 Seabat, the new helicopter entered US Navy service in August 1955, with aircraft often flying in hunter-killer pairs and later in close co-operation with ASW ships.

The HSS-1N version pioneered the use of the auto-hover facility. Shipboard stowage was made easier by folding the rear fuselage and tail rotor forwards, and the main rotor could also be folded. The US Marines used the 'stripped-out' HUS-1 Seahorse as a 12-seat utility transport.

The US Army, in a similar position to the Navy, was disappointed with the Piasecki H-21 and ordered the H-34A Choctaw straight off the production line in 1955. The 359 ordered by the Army could each carry 18 troops.

Civilian S-58B/Ds were used to carry cargo, while Sabena launched scheduled helicopter services with the 18-seat S-58C. Military S-58s were exported to many countries and a turbine engine conversion is available in the United States.

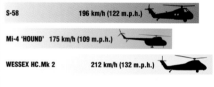

Left: Sabena, Belgium's national airline, was an early operator of passenger helicopters, flying S-55s. These were replaced by S-58s from 1956.

Above: The S-58T conversion is powered by a Pratt & Whitney Canada PT6T-3 Twin Pac coupled-turbine engine. Only a small number of customers have been found.

H-34A Choctaw

Type: piston-engined transport helicopter

Powerplant: one 1137-kW (1,524-hp.) Wright R-1820-84B/D Cyclone radial piston engine

Maximum speed: 196 km/h (122 m.p.h.) at sea level

Initial climb rate: 335 m/min (1,100 f.p.m.) at sea level

Range: 397 km (250 mi.) with standard fuel

Hover ceiling: 1490 m (4,900 ft.) in ground effect; 730 m (2,395 ft.) out of ground effect

Weights: empty equipped 3515 kg (7,749 lb.); maximum take-off 6350 kg (14,000 lb.)

Dimensions:

main rotor diameter	17.07 m (56 ft.)
length, rotors turning	17.27 m (56 ft. 7 in.)
height	4.85 m (15 ft. 10 in.)
main rotor disc area	228.81 m² (2,463 sq. ft.)

H-34G

Germany used its H-34s as utility transports supporting the army, and in the SAR role with a winch mounted above the cabin door. These SAR H-34s have now been replaced by Westland Sea King Mk 41s.

Pilots had an excellent view from the high-set cockpit and large cabin windows. These windows could be slid to the rear along rails, for cooling or a better view vertically downwards.

The main rotors and tail rotors were driven by a large gearbox in the upper-rear fuselage which received drive from a high-speed shaft that ran upwards from the engine between the crew seats.

All S-58s had a small horizontal stabiliser. Within the tailfin structure immediately below this, was the gearbox which linked the tail rotor driveshaft to a long shaft that carried drive from the main gearbox to the tail.

An R-1820 nine-cylinder diagonally-mounted engine drove the high-speed shaft to the main gearbox. Cooling air was drawn in through large grills around the upper nose. Complete engine access was provided by the clamshell doors which formed the nose.

The rugged, fixed undercarriage incorporated a rearwards-angled shock-absorber strut. Various flotation aids could be fitted.

Two windows were fitted in the left-hand side of the cabin, with a large sliding door on the opposite side providing access. A slung load of 2268 kg (5,000 lb.) or 18 troops could be carried.

Most S-58s retained the tail-folding of the original HSS-1. The tail folded along this hinge line to lie along the left fuselage side and was useful for transportation.

HEER QA 475

Sikorsky S-58 selection

■ **H-34A CHOCTAW:** H-34s became the standard US Army light transport helicopter. This helicopter has an unusual fin-mounted whip aerial and was later updated to H-34B standard.

■ **H-34A:** Sikorsky delivered 90 H-34As to the French army and Sud-Aviation built a further 166 under licence for army and navy use in the Algerian war.

■ **S-58T:** New York Helicopter received two of these turbine-engined conversions, which were fitted with a greater number of windows. S-58B/D models are the most popular for conversion.

COMBAT DATA

MAXIMUM SPEED

Westland in the UK developed the Wessex as a turbine-engined evolution of the S-58. Speed was increased by the new engine, but only slightly.

S-58	196 km/h (122 m.p.h.)
Mi-4 'HOUND'	175 km/h (109 m.p.h.)
WESSEX HC.Mk 2	212 km/h (132 m.p.h.)

HOVERING CEILING

Improved altitude performance was the principal benefit of turbine power. The Mi-4 'Hound' had poor performance compared to the S-58, with the Soviets trailing in helicopter technology in the 1950s.

WESSEX HC.Mk 2 1220 m (4,000 ft.)

S-58 730 m (2,395 ft.)

Mi-4 'HOUND' 700 m (2,300 ft.)

MAXIMUM TAKE-OFF WEIGHT

In the transport role maximum take-off weight reflects the load that an aircraft can lift. For the ASW role cabin space for avionics is important, and the S-58 strikes a balance between the two.

S-58	Mi-4 'HOUND'	WESSEX HC.Mk 2
6350 kg (14,000 lb.)	7550 kg (16,650 lb.)	6123 kg (13,500 lb.)

SIKORSKY
S-61

● Search and rescue ● Oilrig supply ● Passenger carrier

▲ *The rescue crews of S-61s carry out hundreds of dangerous missions every year, often at great risk. Search and rescue is a favourite job for aircrews.*

To an imperilled survivor of a sea disaster, no gift could seem more heavenly than an S-61 helicopter lowering its survival hoist. A quantum leap in helicopter design, the long-serving S-61 Sea King has been a diligent labourer at many civil and military tasks. But no-one appreciates this superb helicopter more than the thousands around the world who are alive today because of an S-61 rescue.

PHOTO FILE

SIKORSKY S-61

▲ Instruments
Flying rescues in all weathers needs a comprehensive instrument panel.

▲ Heli-liner
S-61s are very common in the North Sea area, operated by Dutch, Norwegian and British companies in the oil and gas sector. Its safety and size make it ideal in this role.

◀ Pilot rescue
The Belgian air force is one of many that uses the Sea King to snatch its downed pilots from the sea after they have ditched. Belgian Sea Kings are kept busy, working in the crowded Channel shipping lanes.

◀ Oilrig supply
The S-61 has been a very popular oilrig helicopter in the North Sea. Its twin engines and all-weather capability are essential in this work.

Load lifter ▶
Using an underslung net on its cargo hook, the S-61 can lift a wide variety of different cargoes of up to 3630 kg (8,000 lb.).

FACTS AND FIGURES

➤ The S-61L land-based prototype made its maiden flight on 6 December 1960.

➤ S-61Ls entered service with Los Angeles Airways on 1 March 1962.

➤ A heavylift version of this helicopter, nicknamed the 'Payloader', carried cargoes as heavy as 4990 kg (11,000 lb.).

➤ S-61 production by Sikorsky came to an end after two decades on 19 June 1980.

➤ Military S-61s served in 30 countries, plus with the US Air Force, Navy, Marine Corps and Coast Guard.

➤ S-61s were licence-built by Westland in Britain and Agusta in Italy.

PROFILE

Sikorsky to the rescue

Russian-born aviation pioneer Igor Sikorsky was one of the most important figures in rotary-wing aviation, and the 'angel of mercy' S-61 was one of his most remarkable achievements. Built in land-based and amphibious versions, the S-61 came into being partly because friendly nations needed it for military tasks, including anti-submarine and rescue work. However, civil S-61s became fantastic performers for Sikorsky, supplying offshore oilrigs,

helping construction projects, and shuttling airline passengers.

No role filled by the ubiquitous S-61 is more important than its continuing duty in offering salvation to those endangered by natural catastrophe, fire, ship-sinking, and other calamities. The S-61 offers the speed, range and lifting capability to fly quickly to a trouble spot, hover, and lift people to safety. It can carry a considerable amount of search gear, food and medicine.

The S-61R is a revised Sea King incorporating a rear ramp. As with most Sea Kings it can land on water, but this rarely happens: the high-mounted engines and gearbox make it top-heavy and vulnerable to swamping in all but the calmest of seas.

Bright yellow RAF Sea Kings are a common sight along the UK coastline in the summer months rescuing people stranded on cliffs or at sea. No-one knows the number of successful S-61 rescues, but the figure probably exceeds 10,000.

The front of the hull mounts two searchlights to floodlight the rescue scene. A winch is mounted above the port cabin doorway.

SEA KING HAR.MK 3

Built under licence by Westland, the Sea King performs a wide variety of military tasks with both the Royal Navy and the Royal Air Force. One of its most important roles is non-military, however, since it is Britain's most important search-and-rescue helicopter.

The windscreen can be jettisoned to allow the crew to escape in an emergency.

Sea Kings are usually flown by two pilots, but can be flown single-handed. Rescue crews generally include a winch operator and winchman.

Westland aircraft are powered by two Rolls-Royce Gnome turboshaft engines in place of the General Electric engines of the S-61.

The Sea King has a large six-bladed main rotor, giving it good hovering performance in adverse weather.

The main compartment of the Sea King can carry up to 22 survivors, or up to a dozen stretcher cases.

ROYAL AIR FORCE

RAF RESCUE

RESCUE

XZ597

DANGER

Westland's Sea King has a six-bladed tail rotor, compared to the five-bladed rotor of Sikorsky's original S-61.

Coast Guard rescue team

Maritime rescue is one of the most important tasks assigned to the United States Coast Guard. With more ships and aircraft than many national navies and air forces, the Coast Guard is well placed to perform its rescue mission along the thousands of miles of America's coasts. It is a mission upon which lives depend, and which calls for expert flying and seamanship on the part of the Coast Guard crews. It is a team effort, requiring expert co-ordination of search planes, helicopters and surface-cutters. Thousands of lives have been saved thanks to the brave S-61 crews.

■ **LOCATING SURVIVORS:** The Dassault Falcon can cover huge areas at great speed, and can drop rafts when survivors are found.

■ **MAKING THE PICK-UP:** Once survivors are found, their location is supplied to helicopters and fast surface craft, which make the rescue.

■ **REWARD:** Success to the Coast Guard is a scene like this: a mother and daughter safe in a rescue helicopter's cabin, having been plucked from a sinking yacht in storm-tossed waters.

S-61N

Type: all-weather helicopter transport and rescue aircraft

Powerplant: two 1119-kW (1,500-hp.) General Electric CT58-140-1/2 turboshafts

Maximum speed: 241 km/h (150 m.p.h.) at sea level

Range: 797 km (518 mi.), with 30-minute reserves

Service ceiling: 3810 m (12,500 ft.) with typical load

Weights: empty 5674 kg (12,340 lb.); loaded 9299 kg (19,000 lb.)

Dimensions:
rotor diameter	18.9 m (62 ft.)
length	22.2 m (72 ft. 10 in.)
height	5.32 m (17 ft. 6 in.)
rotor disc area	280.47 m² (3,020 sq. ft.)

ACTION DATA

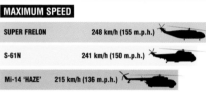

MAXIMUM SPEED

SUPER FRELON	248 km/h (155 m.p.h.)
S-61N	241 km/h (150 m.p.h.)
Mi-14 'HAZE'	215 km/h (136 m.p.h.)

Big helicopters carry much more powerful engines and larger rotor blades, generating more lift than smaller machines. As a result, they are generally among the fastest of all rotary-wing craft.

PAYLOAD

Standard Sea Kings can carry up to 22 passengers, but the civil versions have been stretched to give a greater carrying capacity. The original S-61L was a land-only version with a 30-passenger capacity, but the S-61N, which is used for oilrig support operations and for rescue work, is fully amphibious, giving added safety for over-water sorties.

SUPER FRELON 34 passengers

Mi-14 'HAZE' 28 passengers

S-61N 26 passengers

ENDURANCE

Endurance is a key quality in a rescue helicopter. Sea disasters can take place hundreds of miles from shore, and once there it can take several minutes to winch up one survivor. A full load can take hours to hoist, so good hovering ability is vital.

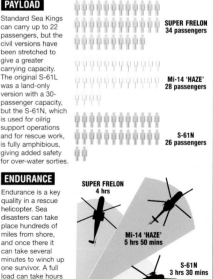

SUPER FRELON 4 hrs

Mi-14 'HAZE' 5 hrs 50 mins

S-61N 3 hrs 30 mins

SIKORSKY

S-61/SH-3 SEA KING

● Anti-submarine helicopter ● In service for 30 years

▲ One of the world's best known helicopters, the Sikorsky S-61 is also one of the longest-serving. Although now a rare sight in US Navy colours, the type continues to fly with other air arms.

A s a true rotorcraft pioneer, Sikorsky was quick to realise the potential of the helicopter for anti-submarine warfare (ASW) operations. With its HSS-1 Sea Bat already in service, Sikorsky designed the HSS-2 Sea King as its turbine-engined replacement. The company could not have realised that the Sea King would become one of the world's most important helicopters, in service with the US Navy (USN) and many export customers.

PHOTO FILE

SIKORSKY S-61/SH-3 SEA KING

▼ Topex
An SH-3H, belonging to HS-9 from Carrier Air Wing 8 aboard the USS Nimitz, flies in company with a Brazilian Navy machine during the annual 'Topex' anti-submarine warfare exercise in the Atlantic.

▲ Space rescue
Sea Kings were used for recovering astronauts after the Apollo lunar landings.

Dual-role helicopter ▶
In the early 1970s the USN needed a helicopter to perform both plane guard and ASW duties aboard its attack carriers and the SH-3 proved ideal.

▼ Enduring design
Despite being in service for nearly 40 years, the outward appearance of the S-61 has surprisingly changed very little, though the latest versions are considerably more capable than early variants.

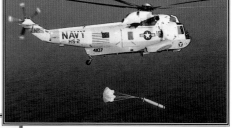

▼ Helicopters for the White House
Possibly the most glamourous of all S-61s are the VH-3Ds in use as VIP transports for the US president and government officials.

FACTS AND FIGURES

➤ Sea Kings were heavily involved in Vietnam, rescuing many downed USN pilots during the long conflict.

➤ A small number of RH-3A minesweeper variants entered service in 1964.

➤ The Royal Canadian Navy was the first export customer, ordering 41 of the type.

➤ Aeronautiche Giovanni Agusta acquired a licence to assemble Sea Kings for the Italian air force and navy.

➤ Argentina is unique in that it operates both Sikorsky and Agusta built examples.

➤ The SH-3 has been replaced by aboard USN carriers by the SH-60F Sea Hawk.

PROFILE

Backbone of the world's navies

Known by Sikorsky as the S-61 and by the US Navy as the SH-3, the Sea King serves into the late 1990s in considerable numbers, having flown for the first time on 11 March 1959.

Combining the roles of submarine hunter and killer thanks to its Bendix AQS-10 dipping sonar, Ryan APN-130 radar, and torpedo or depth bomb weapon load, the SH-3A was an instant success. The few

remaining USN Sea Kings have all been upgraded to SH-3H standard. The design has also formed the basis of the much-modified Westland Sea King.

In addition to its ASW machines, the USN also flew nine examples of the specialised RH-3A minesweeping version of the basic SH-3, while a number of combat search and rescue HH-3 aircraft, also based on the SH-3 airframe, were built for the US Air Force.

Export customers included Argentina, Brazil, Canada, Denmark, Iran, Italy, Japan, Malaysia, Peru, Spain, and the UK. Several of these deals have included production licences.

Above: SH-3s can actually be refuelled in flight, though the usual method is somewhat different from that shown here!

Below: In Italian naval service, the Agusta SH-3Ds wear this dark sea grey colour scheme with high visibility day-glo noses and tail bands.

SH-3H Sea King

Type: anti-submarine and plane guard shipboard helicopter

Powerplant: two 1044-kW (1,400-hp.) General Electric T58-GE-10 turboshafts

Maximum speed: 267 km/h (166 m.p.h.)

Cruising speed: 219 km/h (136 mi.)

Initial climb rate: 670 m/min (2,200 f.p.m.)

Range: 1005 km (624 mi.)

Service ceiling: 4480 m (14,700 ft.)

Weights: empty 4428 kg (9,762 lb.); loaded 9525 kg (21,000 lb.)

Accommodation: two pilots and two systems operators

Dimensions: rotor diameter 18.9 m (62 ft.)
length 22.15 m (72 ft. 8 in.)
height 5.13 m (16 ft. 9 in.)

SH-3H SEA KING

This SH-3H of HS-7 'Shamrocks' served aboard the USS *John F. Kennedy* (CV-67) during the carrier's 1983-84 Atlantic cruise.

Powering the SH-3H variant are two General Electric T58-GE-10 turboshafts. These provide impressive performance for a relatively large helicopter and allowing the aircraft to carry substantial underslung loads if so required.

All Sea Kings are fitted with five-blade main rotors. These can be folded aft and are interchangeable. They also feature the Sikorsky spar inspection system, which releases an inert gas if the blades are cracked, thus alerting maintenance staff to potential problems.

NAVY
615
HS-7
USS JOHN F KENNEDY
2112

All Sikorsky S-61s are amphibious and are capable of landing on water for brief periods if necessary. The underside of the fuselage is sculpted to act as a watertight hull.

Equipment unique to the USN 'H' variant includes an AQS-13B sonar, a Canadian Marconi surveillance radar, and towed magnetic anomaly detector for hunting submarines.

The anti-torque tail rotor is fitted on the port side and also features five blades. A single stabiliser is fitted on the opposite side. The entire tail section is moveable and can hinge to starboard for accessibility and stowage below carrier decks.

ACTION DATA

POWER

Even when it entered service, the Sikorsky Sea King was a powerful machine, able to lift substantial loads. In later years Westland built its own version with more powerful engines.

SH-3H SEA KING
2088 kW
(2800 hp)

SEA KING HAS.MK5
2476 kW
(3320 hp)

SA 321G SUPER
FRELON
3300 kW (4425 hp)

RANGE

When employed for plane guard or search and rescue duties the Sea King does not operate far afield. In the ASW role Sea Kings work with longer-ranged fixed wing aircraft. The bigger Aérospatiale Super Frelon is primarily a tactical transport helicopter.

SH-3H SEA KING
1005km (624 mi.)

SEA KING HAS.MK5
1230km (764 mi.)

SA 321G SUPER
FRELON
1020km (634 mi.)

CLIMB RATE

Despite being fitted with more powerful engines, the Westland Sea King performs less well than its slightly older Sikorsky cousin. The lumbering Super Frelon is very slow by comparison.

SH-3
SEA KING
670 m/min
(2,200 f.p.m.)

SEA KING
HAS.MK5
616 m/min
(2,020 f.p.m.)

SA 321G
SUPER FRELON
300 m/min
(984 f.p.m.)

Sea King goes foreign

■ **BRAZILIAN NAVY SH-3D:** A number of machines were delivered to the Brazilian Navy and operated by 1° Esquadro de Helicopteros Anti-submarinos from Sao Pedro de Aldeida.

■ **JMSDF HSS-2B:** Mitsubishi of Japan acquired a licence to build Sea Kings and Japan's Maritime Self-Defence Force uses the type for anti-submarine warfare and rescue duties.

■ **SPANISH SH-3D:** This smart example is one of a batch of ex-USN machines transferred to Spain. These have been upgraded to SH-3H standard and serve with Escuadrilla 001.

SIKORSKY

S-61R/CH-3

● USAF transport ● Combat search and rescue ● US Coast Guard

▲ Optimised for USAF use, the S-61R was built in four highly successful variants and under licence in Italy. Few aircraft can match the fame of the 'Jolly Green Giant'.

In 1962 the USAF borrowed three SH-3A helicopters from the US Navy. Used for transport as CH-3Bs, these aircraft from the Sikorsky S-61 series impressed the Air Force so much that it ordered a new version for its own use. Known as the S-61R, this transport helicopter went on to save many lives in the CSAR (combat search and rescue) role over Vietnam as the 'Jolly Green Giant' and, from 1968, with the US Coast Guard as the Pelican.

SIKORSKY S-61R/CH-3

▼ Italian navy SAR
Agusta built 20 HH-3Fs from 1973. These were similar to US Coast Guard aircraft.

▲ Inflight refuelling
In 1966 the USAF revealed a series of tests using a US Marine Corps KC-130F tanker. Ten contacts of up to five minutes duration were performed.

▼ Civilian model
Sikorsky's own S-61R hovers above the first USAF CH-3C. As the aircraft was designed around a USAF requirement, commercial buyers did not appear.

▲ Practice rescue
US Coast Guard machines used their search radar, hoist and amphibious capabilities to the full. The HH-3F was used to search coastlines and out at sea.

Test boom ▶
Carrying an air data boom for experimental and test purposes, the first CH-3C, in common with others of the model, was later upgraded to CH-3E standard.

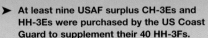

FACTS AND FIGURES

➤ Two HH-3Es made the first non-stop transatlantic helicopter flights in 1967, making nine tanker contacts each.

➤ The first S-61R flew on 17 June 1963, almost one month ahead of schedule.

➤ The CH-3E could seat up to 30 troops or carry 2270 kg (5,000 lb.) of cargo.

➤ At least nine USAF surplus CH-3Es and HH-3Es were purchased by the US Coast Guard to supplement their 40 HH-3Fs.

➤ In 1975 CH/HH-3Es became the first helicopters in the US Air National Guard.

➤ Variants of Sikorsky's S-70 have replaced S-61Rs in US service.

PROFILE

USAF's 'Jolly Green Giant'

In order to satisfy the USAF's requirements, Sikorsky found that a major redesign of the SH-3 anti-submarine variant of the S-61 was necessary. The company designated the new helicopter S-61R and four versions of the basic amphibious transport design were built.

Principal amongst the design changes were a tricycle nose-wheel undercarriage and a large rear loading ramp door. Of the initial CH-3C model, 41 were built before production of the

1119-kW T58-5 engined CH-3E began in 1966. Meanwhile, the USAF had an urgent need for a helicopter capable of rescuing downed aircrew in a hostile environment – Vietnam.

Optimised for CSAR, the HH-3E had armour, defensive machine-guns, jettisonable long-range fuel tanks and an in-flight refuelling (IFR) probe. Such was the ability of the HH-3E that it often rescued downed aircraft as well as aircrew and became known as the 'Jolly Green Giant'.

The last development was the

HH-3F Pelican for the US Coast Guard. Basically an HH-3E with military equipment removed, the aircraft gave superb service into the 1990s, flying long-range rescue and anti-drug missions.

Below: The rear loading ramp had upper and lower parts, allowing vehicles up to 2.21 metres (7 ft. 2 in.) tall to be loaded. Large sponsons on either side of the fuselage kept the aircraft stable on water and accommodated the main landing gear.

Above: CH-3Es also carried a winch above the starboard forward door, adding extra flexibility and giving the helicopter a secondary SAR role.

HH-3E

This is an Air Force Reserve squadron HH-3E in standard 'European One' camouflage. In 1990 the HH-60G Pave Hawk began replacing HH-3Es. The new helicopter retains all the best features of its ancestor, including jettisonable external tanks and an IFR probe.

HH-3E

Type: long-range combat search-and-rescue helicopter

Powerplant: two 1044-kW (1,400-hp.)General Electric T58-GE-10 turboshafts

Maximum speed: 261 km/h (162 m.p.h.)

Climb rate: 6.7 m/sec

Range: 1005 km (624 mi.)

Service ceiling: 3660 m (12,008 ft.)

Weights: maximum take-off 10002 kg (22,0466 lb.), usual gross 8165 kg (18,000 lb.)

Armament: at least two 7.62-mm or 12.7-mm machine-guns on flexible mounts, fired through the side doors

Dimensions:
main rotor diameter	18.9 m (62 ft.)
length	17.45 m (57 ft. 3 in.)
height	5.51 m (18 ft.)
rotor disc area	280.5 m² (3,020 sq. ft.)

The HH-3E provided its two-man flight crew with armour protection and a comprehensive radio and navigational avionics suite. Coast Guard HH-3Fs added search radar for maritime operations. Up to 15 stretcher patients could be accommodated in the square-section cabin.

Twin T58-GE-10 turboshafts gave the HH-3 good speed and climb performance. With the enemy closing in on a casualty, speed was essential for a successful rescue.

The main rotor did not retain the blade folding mechanisms of the naval SH-3. Vietnam pilots are rumoured to have used the rotor to trim branches from trees, allowing them to reach downed airmen.

A five-bladed aluminium tail rotor was adopted directly from the SH-3. A strut-braced tailplane was mounted opposite the rotor mounting. On the ground, the tail-low in-flight attitude was corrected by the length of the undercarriage.

HH-3Es were the first helicopters to carry in-flight refuelling booms. The probe was telescopic, extending to twice its retracted length in order to keep the HC-130's drogue and refuelling hose well clear of the rotor blades.

Hydraulically operated doors formed the rear loading ramp. The open upper section retracted into the upper fuselage, while the lower part hinged downwards to form the ramp. In combat, the partially open ramp often held an extra machine-gun.

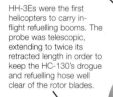

Multi-mission S-61R

US COAST GUARD SAR: Having located the survivor using search radar, locater beacons and distress flares the HH-3F crew pluck casualties to safety using the rescue winch.

USAF VIETNAM CSAR: While a Douglas AD-1 Skyraider provided cover, the HH-3E winched shot-down aircrew from the jungle. The helicopter's own machine-guns forced the enemy to remain undercover during the rescue.

USAF CH-3C DRONE RECOVERY: DC-130 Hercules released reconnaissance or target drones. After using up all their fuel these drones are recovered by the CH-3C and returned to base, where they may be prepared for re-use.

COMBAT DATA

RANGE

All three of these helicopters offer good long-range performance, essential in the SAR role. Although the HH-3E's range is shortest, when equipped with in-flight refuelling capability its range is limited only by the endurance of the crew and the durability of the airframe.

HH-3E	1005 km (624 mi.)
Mi-14PS 'HAZE-A'	1135 km (705 mi.)
SEA KING HAR.Mk 3	1230 km (764 mi.)

SIKORSKY

S-62/HH-52 SEAGUARD

● Search and rescue helicopter ● Turbine-powered ● Overlooked

▲ *Looking like a scaled-down version of the S-61 Sea King, the S-62 was not a great commercial success and only a handful were built. It served with the US Coast Guard and in Japan.*

Conceived in the mid-1950s, the S-62 incorporated several new features. The US Coast Guard was sufficiently interested to purchase the type as the HH-52A Seaguard. A single T-58 turbine, a relatively spacious fuselage and amphibious capability made the S-62 an ideal search and rescue helicopter, particularly for coastal areas. It was capable of operating from almost any surface in just about any weather.

SIKORSKY S-62/HH-52 SEAGUARD

◀ **On land and water**
One of the prototypes performs a 'power-off' landing. As an amphibious helicopter, the HH-52 proved ideal in the coastal SAR role.

▼ **Northern search and rescue**
HH-52s operating from ice-breakers received a bright orange scheme with a white stripe for greater conspicuity over the frozen sea.

▲ **Rig support**
First order for the S-62 came from Petroleum Helicopters, which purchased a single example for serving large offshore oil rigs located in the Gulf of Mexico.

Sikorsky on the silver screen ▶
This strange-looking machine is actually a South African example, modified to represent an 'enemy' gunship, possibly an Mi-24, for film purposes.

◀ **Special equipment**
As first delivered to the US Coast Guard, HH-52s featured automatic stabilisation, towing equipment and other features tailored for the rescue mission.

FACTS AND FIGURES

➤ HH-52s based at Houston, Texas, frequently practised recovery of the NASA Apollo astronauts.

➤ First flight of the Sikorsky S-62 took place on 22 May 1958.

➤ A small number of Seaguards were put on display in museums after retirement.

➤ Nine examples were built under licence for service with Japanese Maritime Self-Defence Force (JMSDF).

➤ One US Coast Guard machine was used in the film *Airport '77*.

➤ A civilian S-62B model was built, but it was not popular on the civil market.

PROFILE

Unsung rescue helicopters

In commercial aviation, Sikorsky's S-62 was overshadowed by other helicopters. The US Coast Guard liked it enough to use the type from 1963 to 1989 for short- to medium-range rescue work. The ability to land on water, not found in any of today's Coast Guard helicopters, helped the HH-52A Seaguard in its rescue duties.

The HH-52A also joined the Coast Guard ice patrol operations aboard powerful ice-breakers. Typical was Operation Deep Freeze, the exploration of the

Antarctic in 1973. The aim of this project was to improve ice-breaking services, thus assisting the movement of maritime traffic through icy waterways.

Coast Guard pilots and crewmen were quite fond of the HH-52A – especially its ability to operate in all weathers. Although most flying was conducted from shore bases, Coast Guard crewmen also serviced the HH-52A onboard ship, which often proved to be a demanding task. By the time the last examples retired during 1989, HH-52s had

Above: Toward the end of their service lives, HH-52s were upgraded with Northrop forward-looking infra-red sensors, mounted in a small turret on the nose.

Below: This rare machine is one of a very small number of S-62s sold to non-US operators. It flew with the Canadian Department of Transport.

gained distinction for rescuing more people than any other helicopter. They were replaced by Aérospatiale HH-65 Dolphins.

HH-52A SEAGUARD

Some 99 examples of the Sikorsky S-62 were delivered to the US Coast Guard. They flew search and rescue (SAR) duties for nearly 30 years.

HH-52A Seaguard

Type: US Coast Guard all-weather amphibious rescue helicopter

Powerplant: one 932-kW (1,249-hp.) General Electric T58-GE-8 turboshaft engine

Maximum speed: 175 km/h (109 m.p.h.)

Cruising speed: 144 km/h (89 m.p.h.)

Range: 762 km (473 mi.)

Hover ceiling: 526 m (1726 ft.)

Weights: empty 2224 kg (4,900 lb.); loaded 3765 kg (8,300 lb.)

Accommodation: two pilots sitting side-by-side and one loadmaster, plus seating for up to 11 fully equipped troops if required

Dimensions: rotor diameter 16.15 m (53 ft.)
length 13.79 m (45 ft. 3 in.)
height 4.39 m (14 ft. 5 in.)

In the late 1950s, the General Electric T-58 was one of the most advanced engines available for use in helicopters. It was light, powerful and efficient compared to piston engines of the period.

Although a considerable improvement over Sikorsky's S-55, the HH-52 did feature a sizeable number of components from the earlier machine, including the rotor blades, heads and gearbox.

The new all-metal fuselage was of aluminium construction. The aircraft was designed from the beginning to be able to operate from water, and the hull was fully watertight.

COAST GUARD

Like the main rotor, the tail rotor assembly was also from the S-55. Common components included the twin blades, the tail rotor head, auxiliary gearbox and shaft assembly. This permitted Sikorsky to save considerable time and reduce cost during manufacturing, and enabled the company to offer the S-62 at an attractive price.

Up to 11 troops or rescued personnel could be seated on fold-down seats in the spacious fuselage. Civilian S-62s had forward- and inward-facing seats for up to 10 passengers.

ACTION DATA

MAXIMUM SPEED

As one of the earliest turbine-powered helicopters, the HH-52 offered much better performance than several rival machines of the day. The 'Hormone' was twin-engined but was a relatively poor performer, unlike the single-engined Westland Wessex.

HH-52A	175 km/h (109 m.p.h.)
WESSEX Mk 1	212 km/h (132 m.p.h.)
Ka-25PS 'HORMONE-C'	209 km/h (130 m.p.h.)

SERVICE CEILING

Despite being single-engined, both the HH-52 Seaguard and the Wessex had impressive service ceilings, better than that of the twin-engined Ka-25 'Hormone'. The single-engined Wessex was essentially a licence-built, turbine-powered Sikorsky S-58.

HH-52A 3415 m (11,204 ft.)
WESSEX Mk 1 4298 m (14,101 ft.)
Ka-25PS 'HORMONE-C' 3350 m (10,990 ft.)

MAXIMUM TAKE-OFF WEIGHT

A light but strong all-metal fuselage, combined with the low weight of the turbine engine, permitted the HH-52 to carry a substantial payload if required. At maximum take-off weight the aircraft was much lighter than either the Wessex or 'Hormone'; the latter tipped the scales at almost 8000 kg fully laden.

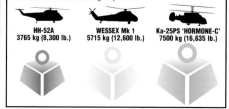

HH-52A 3765 kg (8,300 lb.)
WESSEX Mk 1 5715 kg (12,600 lb.)
Ka-25PS 'HORMONE-C' 7500 kg (16,635 lb.)

Sikorsky's amphibious family

■ **S-61 SEA KING:** Similar in appearance to the smaller S-62, the Sea King was one of the most successful helicopters built by Sikorsky. It was widely exported.

■ **S-61N:** Clearly resembling the military Sea King, the S-61N was developed as a civil passenger helicopter. It retained amphibious capability and entered service in 1964.

■ **S-61R:** Yet another derivative of the basic S-61 design, this variant had a completely redesigned fuselage with a rear loading ramp and a retractable tricycle undercarriage.

SIKORSKY

S-64 SKYCRANE

● Heavylift helicopter ● Flying crane ● Salvage and retrieval

This bizarre-looking but superbly performing machine has got real muscle. Called the CH-54 Tarhe – an American Indian name meaning 'crane' – by soldiers and the S-64 by its makers and by civilians, the big Sikorsky SkyCrane lifts, hauls and delivers almost any cargo on a sling or in a van under its fuselage. Used in combat in Vietnam, this veteran went on to serve on construction projects, oilfields and logging sites, where the SkyCrane works today as a heavylift champion of the skies.

▲ Groundcrew prepare the Tarhe to lift another massive load. A cargo net is used to gather lots of items together so that they can all be lifted at once.

SIKORSKY S-64 SKYCRANE

▼ **Flying crane**
The S-64 was little more than a rotor system with a cockpit on the front. The giant legs could straddle just about anything the helicopter could lift.

▲ **The office**
The front end of the Tarhe looks like that of any large helicopter, but it incorporates a position in the back so that the crew can watch the load underneath.

◀ **Rotor system**
The upper part of the Tarhe consisted of a propulsion system with two engines, and a slender boom to hold the tail rotor.

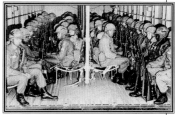

◀ **Troopship helicopter** ▲
To turn the S-64 into a troop assault helicopter, Sikorsky designed a special pod which could be clipped underneath the aircraft. This could accommodate a large number of fully-armed troops.

FACTS AND FIGURES

➤ CH-54 Tarhe helicopters in Vietnam retrieved 380 shot-down aircraft, saving $210 million.

➤ The S-64 made its first flight on 9 May 1962; about 20 are still flying today.

➤ The S-64's cargo pod is a box 8.36 x 2.69 x 1.98 m (approximately 27 x 9 x 6 ft.)

➤ When repairs were needed to the 11000-kg (24,250 lb.) statue atop Washington's Capitol dome, it was lifted away and then returned by a SkyCrane.

➤ This colossal 'derrick of the air' was patterned after Sikorsky's earlier S-60 heavy lifter.

PROFILE

Sikorsky's heavy lifter

Sikorsky's pioneering efforts with heavylift helicopters reached a peak at the start of the Vietnam War. The US Army used the CH-54 Tarhe to sling-lift such weighty cargoes as artillery pieces, armoured vehicles and recovered aircraft. In the Southeast Asia conflict SkyCrane's cargo pod proved amazingly useful, for it could carry 87 troops, a mobile hospital or a command post. In a less typical

mission, the SkyCrane carried a 4536-kg (10,000-lb.) bomb used to blast away trees to create a landing zone.

The improved CH-54B model set international payload and climb records which stood for years before bigger, Russian-built craft exceeded them. The newer Chinook and Stallion have replaced the SkyCrane in the Army, releasing many of these sturdy ships for private use.

Today the ageing SkyCrane has been retired from military service and is much missed by the US Army. Some still soldier on in civil hands, however, hauling logs and outsize cargoes that no other helicopter can touch.

A huge variety of missions can be flown by the Tarhe, from airlifting field hospitals (left) through the recovery of crashed aircraft (below). The aircraft shown left is fitted with skis to operate from snow, and carries extra fuel tanks on the inside of the undercarriage legs.

CH-54A Tarhe

Type: heavylift helicopter

Powerplant: two 3400-kW (4559-hp.) Pratt & Whitney T73-1 turboshafts

Cruising speed: 169 km/h (105 m.p.h.)

Range: 370 km (300 mi.)

Weights: empty 8724 kg (19,240 lb.); loaded 19050 kg (42,000 lb.)

Armament: none, but has been used to carry 4536-kg (10,000-lb.) bombs

Dimensions:
main rotor diameter	21.95 m (72 ft.)
length	26.97 m (88 ft. 6 in.)
height	5.67 m (18 ft. 7 in.)
main rotor disc area	378.1 m² (4,070 sq. ft.)

CH-54 TARHE

Now eclipsed by the CH-47 Chinook, the CH-54 was widely used by the US Army in a massive number of roles. If anything needed moving, then the Tarhe was called to move it. Those serving in Alaska became such a part of the local scenery that they made their way into traditional native art.

The Tarhe had two engines, which drove the main rotor through a central gearbox. The power from either engine could keep the CH-54 aloft in an emergency, but not while carrying a load.

Since the CH-54's job was to lift heavy loads rather than fly fast or fight, much of the rotor system was left uncovered, which made maintenance easier. Running along the top of the tailboom from the engines to the tail was the drive-shaft for the tail rotor.

The Tarhe's tail rotor was a conventional four-bladed unit related to that of the Sea King from which it was derived.

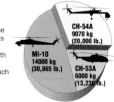

The CH-54 was one of the first modular aircraft. The cabin section, drive train and fuselage were interchangeable units which could be replaced with little effort in the field.

Designated S-64 by Sikorsky, the Tarhe used a modified version of the S-61 Sea King front end mated to a 'flying crane' type fuselage.

As well as conventional forward-facing positions, the cockpit of the Tarhe also had a rearward-facing station with a large glazed area. This allowed the crew to make delicate manoeuvres when picking up loads.

The undercarriage legs were made very wide and tall so that the Tarhe could straddle most loads. Attachment points on the central fuselage could hold pods designed specially for the Tarhe or slung loads carried on strops and cables. In Vietnam the CH-54 even functioned as a bomber, dropping giant weapons to clear vegetation for landing sites or artillery emplacements.

COMBAT DATA

PAYLOAD

Although the standard Tarhe could sling loads of up to nine tonnes, it was not so much its ability to hoist heavy weights but more its ability to deal with awkward or outsize loads which made the SkyCrane such a useful, and irreplaceable, workhorse.

CH-54A 9070 kg (20,000 lb.)
Mi-10 14000 kg (30,865 lb.)
CH-53A 6000 kg (13,236 lb.)

RANGE

Heavylift helicopters are generally called on to move their loads over relatively short distances, to where they can be trans-shipped to more conventional means of transportation. As a result, they do not need a long operating range.

CH-54A	370 km (230 mi.)
CH-53A	420 km (261 mi.)
Mi-10	600 km (373 mi.)

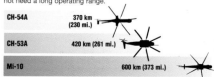

You call, Tarhe hauls

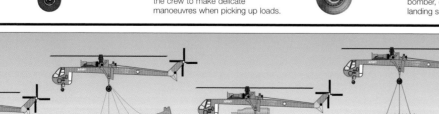

VEHICLE TRANSPORT: Many types of vehicle could be carried from the underfuselage attachment points.

AIRCRAFT RECOVERY: Tarhes regularly retrieved crashed or damaged aircraft.

MAKESHIFT BOMBER: In Vietnam CH-54s dropped the BLU-82 bomb to make clearings in the jungle.

OUTSIZE LOADS: A bewildering variety of loads has been carried by CH-54s, including boats.

PLACING ARTILLERY: The CH-54 was the principal means by which the US Army shifted its artillery around the battlefield.

SIKORSKY

S-65/HH-/MH-53

● Special forces helicopter ● Combat rescue ● Advanced sensors

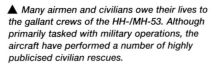

▲ Many airmen and civilians owe their lives to the gallant crews of the HH-/MH-53. Although primarily tasked with military operations, the aircraft have performed a number of highly publicised civilian rescues.

One of the biggest and most versatile combat helicopters ever developed in the West, Sikorsky's S-65 serves with the USAF as the HH-/MH-53. In the hands of skilled pilots, the S-65 can lift heavy cargoes, carry special forces troops far behind enemy lines, or successfully rescue downed airmen, using the latest technology. From Vietnam as the HH-53C to the Persian Gulf as the MH-53J, the S-65 has been a great success story.

SIKORSKY S-65/HH-/MH-53

▼ Jolly Green doorman
An MH-53J crewman leans through the open escape hatch. A window may be fitted in this position, but is often omitted.

▲ First of the eight Bs
As the first of eight HH-53Bs, this aircraft introduced the S-65 into regular CSAR service with the USAF over Vietnam.

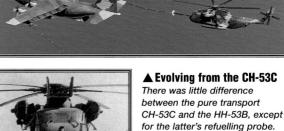

▼ Vietnam insertion
HH-53Bs were tasked with a number of covert missions in Vietnam. Troops were often dropped by rope to avoid the risk of landing in enemy territory.

▲ Evolving from the CH-53C
There was little difference between the pure transport CH-53C and the HH-53B, except for the latter's refuelling probe.

▼ Pave Low III
Although short-lived, the six HH-53H helicopters introduced the Pave Low III sensor package.

▲ Sensitive nose
All of the MH-53J's primary sensors are clustered around the nose. They include the AN/AAQ-10 FLIR below the in-flight refuelling probe on the starboard side.

FACTS AND FIGURES

➤ Having originally used the CH-53A in 1966/67, the USAF received a handful more in 1989 as TH-53A trainers.

➤ Sponson bracing struts allowed the HH-53B to carry 2460-l (650-gal.) drop-tanks.

➤ Two HH-53Cs flew 14500 km (9010 mi.) with only seven stops.

➤ Some CH-53C and HH-53B helicopters remained unmodified until the late 1980s, when they became MH-53Js.

➤ MH-53H and MH-53J Pave Low IIs were involved in the US invasion of Panama.

➤ MH-53 pilots receive special operations training on the TH-53A.

PROFILE

Enhancing the 'Super Jolly'

Although more than three decades old, the S-65 remains at the front line with the USAF. Special forces rely on it for daring missions, such as the raid to destroy President Noriega's personal jet during the US invasion of Panama in 1989.

In November 1966 the US Marine Corps loaned two CH-53A helicopters to the USAF. This led to an order for eight specialised HH-53B combat search-and-rescue (CSAR) aircraft to replace the HH-3E

then flying with great distinction in Vietnam.

Having replaced the 'Jolly Green Giant', the HH-53B became the 'Super Jolly'. One modified aircraft unsuccessfully tested an all-weather sensor system known as Pave (Precision Avionics Vectoring Equipment) Low I.

From August 1968 the USAF Aerospace Rescue and Recovery Service began receiving the HH-53C. With improved armour and a comprehensive radio fit, allowing better communications

between the helicopter and HC-130 in-flight refuelling tankers, the HH-53C served into the late 1980s. The last machine was then converted to MH-53J Pave Low III Enhanced standard.

Developed via the unsuccessful HH-53H Pave Low II, the MH-53J is likely to serve for many more years.

Left: This MH-53J carries a gun mount on its loading ramp. It can be easily removed and stowed in flight.

Above: With weapons fitted in all positions, this 'Super Jolly' shows a typical configuration for special forces operations. MH-53Js often fly alone on such missions.

MH-53J Pave Low III Enhanced

Type: twin-engined combat search and rescue and special operations helicopter

Powerplant: two 2935-kW (3,935-hp.) General Electric T64-GE-7A turboshaft engines

Maximum speed: 315 km/h (196 m.p.h.) at sea level

Initial climb rate: 631 m/min (2,070 f.p.m.) at sea level

Range: 868 km (540 mi.) with maximum auxiliary fuel

Weights: empty 10691 kg (23,570 lb.); mission take-off 17344 kg (38,240 lb.); maximum take-off 19051 kg (42,000 lb.)

Armament: up to three 7.62-mm Miniguns or three 12.7-mm machine-guns mounted in the side door, port side escape hatch and on the rear loading ramp

Dimensions:
main rotor diameter	22.02 m (17 ft. 3 in.)
fuselage length	20.47m (67 ft. 2 in.)
height	5.22 m (17 ft. 2 in.)
main rotor disc area	380.87 m² (4100 sq. ft.)

MH-53J PAVE LOW III

This aircraft is shown in the markings worn while based at RAF Woodbridge, Suffolk, with the USAF's 67th Aerospace Rescue and Recovery Wing. The Wing has since withdrawn from Britain.

A number of systems are employed to protect the helicopter from the enemy. They include powerful infra-red countermeasures devices mounted above each sponson.

For versatility, the MH-53J can be operated from a variety of bases, including aircraft-carrier decks. The rotor blades fold to conserve space.

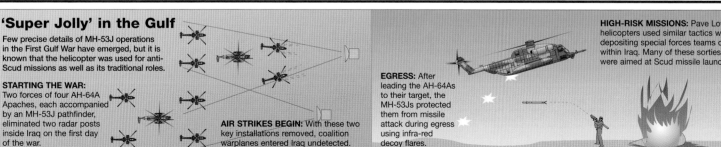

Most of the Pave Low III sensor package is clustered around the nose. The FLIR (forward looking infra-red) radome and the larger radome of the terrain-following radar have been removed from this aircraft.

Each of the sponson fuel tanks holds 1893 litres of fuel. The tanks are jettisonable in flight, but the MH-53J is rarely seen without them.

Although originally designed to allow the rapid handling of light vehicles, the main loading ramp also offers a quick method of entering or leaving the 'Super Jolly' in the heat of battle.

Secure communications facilities, a global positioning system and night-vision goggle compatibility enable the MH-53J to perform dangerous missions alone. The comprehensive avionics fit is indicated by the large number of antennas.

'Super Jolly' in the Gulf

Few precise details of MH-53J operations in the First Gulf War have emerged, but it is known that the helicopter was used for anti-Scud missions as well as its traditional roles.

STARTING THE WAR: Two forces of four AH-64A Apaches, each accompanied by an MH-53J pathfinder, eliminated two radar posts inside Iraq on the first day of the war.

AIR STRIKES BEGIN: With these two key installations removed, coalition warplanes entered Iraq undetected.

EGRESS: After leading the AH-64As to their target, the MH-53Js protected them from missile attack during egress using infra-red decoy flares.

HIGH-RISK MISSIONS: Pave Low III helicopters used similar tactics when depositing special forces teams deep within Iraq. Many of these sorties were aimed at Scud missile launchers.

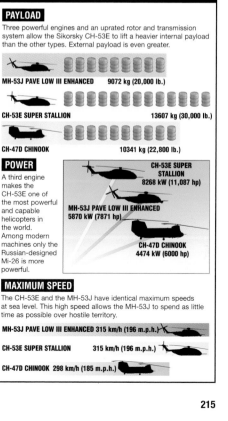

COMBAT DATA

PAYLOAD

Three powerful engines and an uprated rotor and transmission system allow the Sikorsky CH-53E to lift a heavier internal payload than the other types. External payload is even greater.

MH-53J PAVE LOW III ENHANCED	9072 kg (20,000 lb.)
CH-53E SUPER STALLION	13607 kg (30,000 lb.)
CH-47D CHINOOK	10341 kg (22,800 lb.)

POWER

A third engine makes the CH-53E one of the most powerful and capable helicopters in the world. Among modern machines only the Russian-designed Mi-26 is more powerful.

CH-53E SUPER STALLION	8268 kW (11,087 hp)
MH-53J PAVE LOW III ENHANCED	5870 kW (7871 hp)
CH-47D CHINOOK	4474 kW (6000 hp)

MAXIMUM SPEED

The CH-53E and the MH-53J have identical maximum speeds at sea level. This high speed allows the MH-53J to spend as little time as possible over hostile territory.

MH-53J PAVE LOW III ENHANCED	315 km/h (196 m.p.h.)
CH-53E SUPER STALLION	315 km/h (196 m.p.h.)
CH-47D CHINOOK	298 km/h (185 m.p.h.)

SIKORSKY

S-65/RH-53D

● Minesweeper ● Hostage rescue helicopter ● Heavy lift

From the 34th CH-53A Sea Stallion onwards, all examples of the type were fitted with hardpoints enabling them to deploy towed minesweeping equipment. The US Navy (USN) soon decided that a dedicated minesweeping helicopter was required, and 15 RH-53As were produced by modifying CH-53As with more powerful engines. These helicopters were the stopgap before the definitive RH-53D could be introduced.

▲ A deck crewman
signals to the crew of an RH-53D that is chained to the carrier's flight deck to begin pre-flight checks, at the start of another day's flying from USS Inchon.

SIKORSKY S-65/RH-53D

▼ **Rescue bid**
Lined up on the deck of USS Nimitz, three Sea Stallions are prepared for the covert rescue mission into Iran. The helicopters were painted in a sand scheme.

▲ Personnel transport
Navy crewmen exit from the rear loading ramp of this RH-53D, seen on the flight line at Ascension Island in the South Atlantic. The helicopter has proved very versatile.

Deck operations ▶
Crewmen cover an RH-53D to protect the helicopter from the corrosive marine environment.

▼ Agile performer
Despite its high weight and large size, the helicopter's manoeuvrability is exceptional.

Joint exercises ▶
Operating with the Spanish navy on joint minesweeping duties, these two examples are fitted with additional fuel tanks on pylons to increase their sweep area.

FACTS AND FIGURES

➤ RH-53Ds were deployed to the Persian Gulf for minesweeping operations in 1987, and in 1991 for Desert Storm.

➤ Minesweeping equipment is towed behind the helicopter on a trapeze.

➤ Towing equipment was installed from the 34th production aircraft onwards.

➤ Once brought to the surface, mines are detonated using two door-mounted machine-guns.

➤ Though a dedicated minesweeper, the helicopter also has a transport role.

➤ Eight RH-53Ds were used to fly into Iran during Operation Eagle Claw in 1980.

PROFILE

Sea-sweeping Stallion

Early experience with minesweeping helicopters such as the RH-3 Sea King had demonstrated that any rotary-winged type engaged in such work would require enormous power reserves so that it could overcome the drag of the towed mine sled as it moved through the water.

Powered by two 3266-kW (4379-hp.) T64-GE-415 turboshafts, the RH-53D proved to be an excellent aircraft for the role. In addition, the new machine has a number of features from the RH-53A. It also had provision for an in-flight refuelling probe and carried two 1893-litre (500-gal.) external fuel tanks.

Using Boeing Vertol Mk 103, American General Mk 104 and Edo Mk 105 systems to counteract contact, acoustic and magnetic mines, respectively, the RH-53D also employs the AN/SPU-1 Magnetic Orange Pipe system against shallow-water mines. Such mines are brought to the surface, where they are detonated by fire from the RH-53D's two swivel-mounted 12.7-mm machine-guns.

The RH-53D was disastrously and inappropriately used in the 1980 Eagle Claw operation.

Above: A minesweeping operation is performed in the Persian Gulf under the watchful eye of a UH-1N.

Above: Lifting off from the deck of USS Guadalcanal, an RH-53D sets out on another mission. The helicopters are normally assigned to amphibious assault ships.

RH-53D Sea Stallion

Type: minesweeping and transport helicopter

Powerplant: two 3266-kW (4,379-hp.) General Electric T64-GE-415 turboshafts

Maximum speed: 315 km/h (196 m.p.h.)

Endurance: 4 hr

Initial climb rate: 644 m/per minute (2,113 f.p.m.) at sea level

Range: 413 km (256 mi.)

Service ceiling: 6400 m (21,000 ft.)

Weights: empty 10180 kg (22,450 lb.); loaded 22680 kg (50,000 lb.)

Armament: two 12.7-mm machine-guns

Dimensions:
span (main rotor)	22.02 m (72 ft. 3 in.)
length	20.47 m (67 ft. 2 in.)
height	5.22 m (17 ft. 1 in.)
rotor disc area	380.87 m² (4,100 sq. ft.)

Side-by-side cockpit seating provides for good crew co-ordination. Positioned on the bottom of the fuselage are two large mirrors which allow the crew to observe operations to the rear of the helicopter; this is particularly useful when the trapeze is being towed.

Because of the increase in power required, the engines were replaced with the more powerful T-64-GE-415, which offered an improved safety margin for operations over water and when using the towed mine sled.

A large six bladed rotor gives the RH-53D a huge lifting ability which is vital for its role. Adopted from previous '53' models the design has proved to be extremely reliable.

A folding tail is fitted to the RH-53D, enabling the helicopter to use aircraft-carrier lifts. The large rear tail rotor gives the RH-53D excellent response to pilot inputs.

The attachment points for the towed trapeze used in mine clearing operations are located at the rear of the fuselage. The rear ramp is left down during such flights.

26 NAVY
HM-12

An optional refuelling probe can be attached to the RH-53D, for in-flight refuelling from a KC-130 Hercules tanker aircraft.

Additional fuel is carried in two large tanks positioned on either side of the fuselage. Their sponsons also provide extra lift during flight manoeuvres.

The rear loading ramp is retained on the RH-53D, giving the aircraft a secondary heavy transport role.

RH-53D

The RH-53D is steadily being removed from front-line service. This brightly coloured example belongs to HM-12 serving aboard the assault ship USS Inchon.

COMBAT DATA

MAXIMUM SPEED

Developed from the earlier CH-53 series, the RH-53D has superb performance for its size. The necessary increase in power for minesweeping operations offers a high top speed compared to that of the French Super Frelon.

RH-53D	315 km/h (196 m.p.h.)
HH-3E	261 km/h (162 m.p.h.)
SUPER FRELON	248 km/h (154 m.p.h.)

SERVICE CEILING

Despite the large size of the RH-53D, it can operate at high altitude through its increased engine power. The smaller HH-3E offers little in operational ceiling, although it is still superior to that of the Super Frelon. That type will be in operation well into the 1990s.

RH-53D 6400 m (21,000 ft.)
HH-3E 3660 m (12,008 ft.)
SUPER FRELON 3100 m (10,170 ft.)

RANGE

When compared to the Super Frelon and HH-3E, the operational range of the RH-53D is limited. However, with the addition of an IFR probe, the range of the helicopter can be greatly improved to give longer endurance and a greater operational search area.

SUPER FRELON 1020 km (634 mi.)
RH-53D 413 km (256 mi.)
HH-3E 1005 km (624 mi.)

Operation Eagle Claw

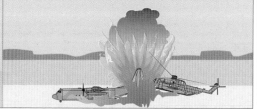

TEHRAN •
• Desert Two
Desert Three •
• Desert One

1 THE RESCUE PLAN: A plan was devised to rescue American civilians held hostage in the US Embassy in Tehran. The operation was divided into three stages. However, the catastrophe at Desert One meant that the mission was aborted at the first phase.

2 RESCUE BID: As dusk fell, eight pink-camouflaged RH-53Ds lifted off the deck of USS Nimitz and crossed the Iranian coast west of Chah Bahar, en route to Desert One to meet the six C-130s.

3 DESERT ONE DISASTER: As helicopter No. 3 lifted off it struck the fuselage of a waiting Hercules. Fire immediately broke out, killing eight soldiers, and the mission was aborted.

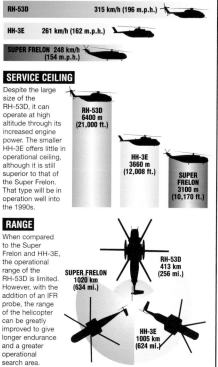

SIKORSKY

S-65/CH-53

● Heavylift transport helicopter ● Combat rescue ● Minesweeper

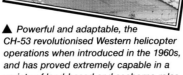

O ne of the rotary-wing marvels of the Vietnam era, the Sikorsky S-65 was the largest helicopter built outside the USSR. Its dynamic parts (rotor, gearboxes and control system) were developed from those of the earlier S-64 SkyCrane and made extensive use of titanium. Fitted with folding rotor blades for shipboard stowage and given the designation CH-53 Sea Stallion by the US Marines, the S-65 emerged as the world's most capable assault transport.

▲ Powerful and adaptable, the CH-53 revolutionised Western helicopter operations when introduced in the 1960s, and has proved extremely capable in a variety of land-based and seaborne roles.

SIKORSKY S-65/CH-53

◀ Grenada attack
The CH-53 saw action in the US invasion of Grenada, landing large numbers of Marines. The CH-53 fleet suffered no casualties in the operation, although UH-60s and AH-1s were shot down.

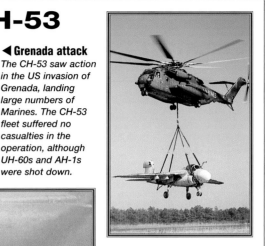

▲ Heavy lifter
The CH-53 was one of the few helicopters in Vietnam that could recover damaged aircraft, such as this Grumman A-6D.

▼ Soldiering on
Although succeeded in the 1980s by the more powerful CH-53E Super Stallion, the CH-53D remains in widespread service.

▲ Vietnam airlift
The CH-53 won its laurels in Southeast Asia, flying in difficult 'hot and high' conditions and constantly threatened by ground fire. It is seen here delivering Marines to the besieged base at Khe Sanh.

◀ Green Marine
In Marine Corps service, the CH-53 is based on 'Tarawa'-class assault ships. It is the largest troop lifting asset available to the USMC.

FACTS AND FIGURES

➤ US Air Force CH-53 cargo-haulers and HH-53B/C 'Super Jollies' began reaching Vietnam in 1967.

➤ The interior of the CH-53 is fitted with rollers for easy movement of cargo.

➤ Air Force special operations HH-53Hs and MH-53Js are rebuilds of HH-53B/Cs.

➤ Germany has the biggest fleet of S-65s outside the USA. VFW-Fokker licence-built 110 of the helicopters for the army.

➤ RH-53Ds were used as transports in the hostage rescue attempt in Iran in 1980.

➤ Marine pilots demonstrated that the S-65 could perform loops and rolls.

PROFILE

Sikorsky's strong lifter

The US Marine Corps had been strong believers in the value of the helicopter since Korea, and during the Vietnam War it was the Marines who were the inspiration for the largest and most powerful helicopter in the world outside the Soviet Union. From their earliest battles in 1965 they counted on the box-shaped, heavylift S-65 to haul ammunition, troops and supplies from logistics bases right out to the battle area. To the Marines who use air power as an adjunct to ground forces, the S-65 provided a new

standard of speed and mobility in battle.

The CH-53A was the only version of the Sikorsky S-65 for some time after the first flight on 11 October 1964. In time, however, others saw the value of the powerful machine. US Navy MH- and RH-53s were used to sweep mines at sea; the US Air Force's HH-53 'Super Jolly' is a dedicated combat rescue machine. Other important operators include Austria, Germany and Israel. The Marines' 'ultimate' twin-

engine S-65 was the CH-53D, which has since been supplanted by the much more powerful three-engined CH-53E, which is an entirely new machine.

The CH-53 is still used in the aircrew rescue role, and carried out a successful mission in Bosnia.

The MH-53J's rotor blades and tailboom have a power folding mechanism, which reduces the time needed to prepare the helicopter for air transport aboard the C-5 Galaxy.

An extensive avionics fit includes terrain-following radar and forward-looking infra-red sensors.

Special forces CH-53s have a crew of four: two pilots and two parajumpers, who act as loadmasters, winchmen, medics and gunners.

The tailboom folds to take up less space on confined carrier decks. The fixed tailplane acts as a stabiliser, providing improved pitch control.

Two external 1703-litre (450-gal.) drop-tanks more than double the MH-53's maximum range to nearly 900 km (1,060 mi.).

MH-53J 'PAVE LOW III'

The US Air Force has long used the H-53 as a rescue helicopter. The latest variant is the MH-53J, in service with the special operations squadrons of the US Air Force.

Twin General Electric T64 turboshafts are mounted in pods on each side of the central gearbox.

The MH-53J's engines can be fitted with sand filters over the inlets and infra-red suppressors over the jetpipes.

The long inflight-refuelling probe extends forward, well clear of the rotor blades, when in use.

The tail bumper is fully retractable and the four-bladed tail rotor is slightly canted to port.

Special operations MH-53s have mounts for heavy machine-guns or multi-barrel Miniguns in the side doors and on the rear ramp.

CH-53A

Type: twin-engine cargo helicopter

Powerplant: two 2127-kW (2,852-hp.) General Electric T64-GE-3, -6, -6B, or -12 turboshafts driving a six-bladed main rotor

Maximum speed: 305 km/h (189 m.p.h.) at sea level

Range: 870 km (540 mi.)

Weights: empty 10690 kg (23,567 lb.); loaded 18370 kg (40,500 lb.)

Accommodation: 55 troops, 24 stretchers and four attendants, or 3629 kg (8,000 lb.) of cargo loaded through full section rear ramp/doors; US Air Force rescue versions carry up to three 7.62-mm Miniguns

Dimensions:
main rotor diameter	22.02 m (72 ft. 3 in.)
length	20.47 m (67 ft. 2 in.)
height	7.6 m (24 ft. 11 in.)
rotor disc area	378.1 m² (4,070 sq. ft.)

COMBAT DATA

MAXIMUM SPEED

Big helicopters can be fitted with large rotor blades and powerful engines, and tend to be faster than their smaller brethren. The CH-53 is no exception. Even when carrying a heavy load, it remains one of the fastest helicopters in the world.

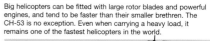

CH-53	305 km/h (189 m.p.h.)
Mi-26 'HALO'	295 km/h (183 m.p.h.)
SA 321 SUPER FRELON	248 km/h (154 m.p.h.)

RANGE

Although they cannot match the reach of fixed-wing machines, the CH-53 and its rivals have very long ranges for helicopters. Large size usually means the ability to carry large loads of fuel, which translates into the ability to fly quite long distances.

Mi-26 'HALO' 800 km (497 mi.)

CH-53 870 km (540 mi.)

SA 321 SUPER FRELON 1020 km (634 mi.)

PAYLOAD

Large helicopters are designed to carry heavy loads. The CH-53 was for many years the West's most powerful helicopter, only replaced by the much modified and more powerful CH-53E. Though it cannot match Russia's giants for sheer lifting ability, the CH-53 is better in a tactical situation, being more agile.

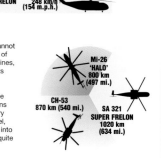

CH-53 6 tonnes or 55 troops

Mi-26 'HALO' 20 tonnes or 80 troops

SA 321 SUPER FRELON 5 tonnes or 28 troops

S-65s in service

■ **MARINE ASSAULT:** The CH-53 was designed primarily for the United States Marine Corps, which uses the type as its primary heavylift assault helicopter. Current versions can carry a 9-tonne payload.

■ **GERMAN LOAD-LIFTER:** The largest user of the big twin-engined Sikorsky outside the USA is the German army. The first of a fleet of 112 aircraft, all but two assembled or built by VFW-Fokker, entered service in March 1973.

■ **AIR FORCE RESCUE:** The Sikorsky's size and speed made it ideal for combat rescue, and as the HH-53 it entered service with the US Air Force in Vietnam. Current versions are among the most sophisticated helicopters now flying.

SIKORSKY
UH-60 BLACK HAWK

● Tactical assault helicopter ● Gulf War transporter

Sikorsky's UH-60 Black Hawk is one of the most important combat helicopters in service today. Replacing the famous Bell Huey as the US Army's workhorse, the UH-60 was designed to haul a squad of 11 fully-equipped infantrymen into battle. The same basic airframe has also been developed for special forces, combat rescue, air-sea rescue and anti-submarine operations.

▲ Carrying troops into battle demands a tough, fast helicopter. The UH-60 entered service in this role at the end of 1979, and has been a great success.

SIKORSKY UH-60 BLACK HAWK

▲ Squad carrier
The UH-60 can carry a larger squad of soldiers than the UH-1 it replaced, and in much greater comfort and protection.

Troops out ▶
The UH-60's doors are designed to allow an infantry squad to get into action in the minimum possible time.

▼ Weight lifter
Although designed as a troop carrier, the UH-60 can also carry a significant cargo load both internally and slung on hooks externally.

▲ Air assault
One of the conditions for the bulk of the equipment supplied to the Air Assault divisions of the US Army is that it should be Black Hawk-portable.

▼ Medical evacuation
A flying ambulance comes in to land at a desert airstrip, the soldier on the ground guiding the pilot through the fog of rotor-blown sand.

▲ Rope down
Special forces soldiers can abseil down from the UH-60 very quickly. This is useful in tight situations where the pilot cannot land safely.

FACTS AND FIGURES

➤ The original UH-60A prototype first flew on 17 October 1974.

➤ Black Hawks entered service with the 101st Airborne Division in 1979.

➤ Though the US Marine Corps has not adopted the UH-60, they fly nine VH-60N presidential transport helicopters.

➤ Black Hawks moved more than a million soldiers during the Gulf War.

➤ In a tragic 'friendly fire' mishap, F-15 fighters shot down two US Army UH-60s in Iraq on 14 April 1994, killing 26.

➤ The Army is developing a UH-60Q medical evacuation model of the Black Hawk.

PROFILE

Sikorsky's flying troop-truck

Known to the manufacturer as the Sikorsky S-70, the remarkable UH-60 Black Hawk provides soldiers with speed and mobility in the middle of the action, freeing them from terrain obstacles.

While combat troops enter and leave the battle zone aboard the UH-60, versions of the helicopter carry out electronic warfare duties, fight with Special Operations forces, or perform ambulance or VIP transport duties.

Pilots in the UH-60 have excellent visibility and armour protection as they fly in and out of landing zones. An exhaust suppression system reduces their vulnerability to heat-seeking battlefield missiles.

The UH-60 fought in Grenada, Panama and in both Gulf Wars, and appears little changed after two decades of Army duty. In fact, the UH-60 has been continuously upgraded with more powerful engines and other improvements. The latest UH-60L has the power to lift a military Hum-Vee tactical vehicle loaded with TOW anti-tank missiles.

The UH-60 was designed with all the years of experience of battle in Vietnam in mind. The low profile of the airframe makes it a difficult target, and safer if it crashes.

As a precaution against battle damage, the UH-60's engines are as widely spaced as possible.

The UH-6's rotor system features swept tips, giving enhanced performance and allowing heavy loads to be lifted in 'hot and high' conditions.

The fuselage plan is noticeably broad and long, giving a generous internal capacity while allowing a very flat profile.

UH-60A Black Hawk

Type: utility helicopter

Powerplant: two 1261-kW (1,690-hp.) General Electric T700-GE-700, -701 or -401 turboshafts

Maximum speed: 296 km/h (184 m.p.h.)

Range: 600 km (370 mi.)

Weights: (Army UH-60) empty 4819 kg (10,600 lb.); loaded 9185 kg (20,200 lb.) (Navy SH-60) empty 6191 kg (13,620 lb.); loaded 9926 kg (21,837 lb.)

Armament: usually two 7.62-mm door guns

Dimensions: rotor diameter 16.36 m (54 ft.)
length 19.76 m (65 ft.)
height 5.13 m (17 ft.)
rotor disc area 210.10 m² (2,261 sq. ft.)

UH-60A BLACK HAWK

The UH-60A, the first of many versions of the Black Hawk family, saw action during the invasion of Grenada in 1981. The Black Hawk has since been in action in Lebanon, Somalia and both Gulf wars.

The UH-60's rotor-head and blades were designed to withstand hits from large machine-gun rounds. The gearbox that drives it can run for half an hour after losing its entire oil supply.

The Black Hawk has an exhaust suppression system which dissipates hot engine gases. This makes the helicopter less of a target for heat-seeking infra-red missiles.

The transparent panels in the nose are essential for safe landing in confined spaces.

In an assault landing, the UH-60 comes in fast. Its undercarriage is designed to absorb vertical impacts of up to 45 km/h (28 m.p.h.)

Although the Black Hawk can carry armament, it is essentially a troop carrier. Its cabin and hatches are designed to allow a squad of infantry to get into action fast.

Sikorsky's designers intentionally built the tail rotor at an angle. This design feature means that lift is generated at the tail, allowing heavier loads at the rear of the cabin than would otherwise be possible.

COMBAT DATA

RANGE

PUMA 570 km (353 mi.)
UH-60A BLACK HAWK 600 km (370 mi.)
Mi-8 'HIP' 900 km (558 mi.)

The Mi-8's greater size and fuel-carrying capacity give it an advantage over the Black Hawk when operating on internal fuel only. But the UH-60 can be fitted with stub wings, onto which can be mounted weaponry or external fuel tanks. With four tanks fitted, the efficient Sikorsky helicopter has a ferry range of more than 2000 km (1,240 mi.).

MAXIMUM SPEED

The Black Hawk's powerful engines and slender aerodynamic cross-section make it one of the fastest helicopters around. It is quicker than most of its rivals, and this, allied to its great agility, makes it a superb platform for mounting helicopter assaults.

Mi-8 'HIP' 250 km/h (155 m.p.h.)
UH-60A BLACK HAWK 296 km/h (184 m.p.h.)
PUMA 271 km/h (168 m.p.h.)

PAYLOAD

Mi-8 'HIP' 28 troops or up to 4000 kg (8,800 lb.) of cargo
PUMA 15 troops or up to 3200 kg (7,040 lb.) of cargo
UH-60A BLACK HAWK 11 troops or up to 3700 kg (8,140 lb.) of cargo

Although the UH-60 is nominally an 11-seater, it can carry up to 20 troops in an emergency. The Black Hawk has enough power to lift the same kind of loads as its bigger Russian and European rivals, yet retains the agility of a much smaller machine.

Airborne helicopter assault in the Gulf wars

■ **DEPLOYMENT:** The Black Hawk was the most numerous helicopter in the Gulf in 1991, with over 350 serving with major US Army formations.

■ **LOW-LEVEL FLIGHT:** The biggest users of UH-60s were the 1st Cavalry Division and the 82nd and 101st Airborne Divisions.

■ **COALITION SPEARHEAD:** Black Hawks were at the forefront of the Coalition offensive in 1991, taking troops deep into Iraqi-held territory.

■ **SADDAM DEFEATED:** By attacking in helicopters, elite US Army airborne troops were able to outflank Iraq's battlefield defences.

SIKORSKY

SH-60B/F SEAHAWK

● Anti-submarine warfare ● Air-sea rescue ● Helicopter delivery

▲ Sikorsky's SH-60B
filled the US Navy's LAMPS (light airborne multi-purpose system) III requirement for a helicopter with over-the-horizon search-and-strike capability.

America's navy would not be able to function without the SH-60 Seahawk, the versatile Sikorsky helicopter which flies from frigates, destroyers and aircraft-carriers. The Seahawk has to operate at night, in heavy seas, from the deck of a ship swaying and pitching and bombarded by salt water. When airborne it must fulfil its assigned role, searching for hostile submarines and surface vessels that may pose a threat to the battle fleet.

PHOTO FILE

SIKORSKY SH-60B/F SEAHAWK

The mainstay of the US Navy ▶
The first SH-60B flew in 1983, with its initial shipboard deployment taking place in 1985. The first SH-60Fs were delivered in 1989.

▲ MAD bird
The red and yellow 'MAD bird', or towed Magnetic Anomaly Detector, helps to locate submarines by measuring changes in the earth's magnetic field.

▲ Spanish Armada
The Spanish navy has operated SH-60Bs under the designation HS.23 since 1988. Twelve are based at Rota and regularly deploy aboard 'Santa Maria'-class guided missile frigates. They differ from US Navy SH-60Bs in having a dipping sonar.

▲ Frigate based
Some of the US Navy's FFG-7 'Oliver Hazard Perry'-class guided missile frigates operate with one SH-60B.

Australian Hawks ▶
Exported examples of the Seahawk use Sikorsky's S-70 model designation. In the foreground is an RAAF S-70A-9 Black Hawk; behind is a naval S-70B-2.

FACTS AND FIGURES

➤ Taiwan operates the S-70C(M)-1, equipped with new radar and torpedoes, from 'Kwang Hua I'-class frigates.

➤ During the Gulf War two downed pilots were rescued by US Navy SH-60s.

➤ Door-mounted machine-gun armament is often carried by US Navy SH/HH-60s.

➤ A third version operated by the US Navy is the HH-60H (unofficially called 'Rescue Hawk') for the rescue of downed aircrew.

➤ The US Coast Guard flies the HH-60J Jayhawk in the search-and-rescue role.

➤ The only US Marine Corps H-60s are nine VH-60N 'Presidential Hawks' for VIPs.

Ocean-going sub-hunter

Left: The main anti-submarine sensor carried by US Navy SH-60Fs is the Bendix AN/AQS-13F dipping sonar, used to 'listen' for submarines.

Below: The Greek navy has five S-70B-6 aircraft based aboard frigates. These are armed with the Norwegian Penguin anti-ship missile.

With the proven airframe of the US Army's Black Hawk, the SH-60B Seahawk serves as the backbone of rotary aviation aboard the US Navy's surface vessels. The SH-60F (unofficially named 'Ocean Hawk') fulfils a similar role on aircraft-carrier decks.

The SH-60B operating from a frigate or destroyer and the SH-60F flying from a carrier both have a crew of three: pilot, airborne tactical officer/co-pilot and sensor operator. These are primarily anti-submarine helicopters and their search for submarines is aided by the parent vessel's combat information centre. The final location of the submarine and its subsequent attack, however, are the responsibility of the SH-60B crew.

While the SH-60B is an over-the-horizon weapon system, the SH-60F, obtained to replace the elderly Sikorsky SH-3H Sea King, performs the Navy's 'inner zone' ASW mission for the Carrier Battle Group, called 'CV-Helo'. The SH-60F also fills air-sea rescue 'plane guard' and utility transport roles.

SH-60F SEAHAWK

This Seahawk carries the markings of Helicopter Anti-submarine Squadron 3 'Tridents', the first SH-60F unit in the US Navy's Atlantic Fleet, when it was deployed aboard *Theodore Roosevelt*.

To take up the minimum amount of space on the aircraft-carrier, the SH-60F has a folding tail, tailplane and rotors. The main blades fold back to lie above the rear fuselage.

The four main rotor blades feature swept-back tips known as 'tip caps'. These improve speed and reduce rotor noise.

The General Electric T700 engines in the Seahawk have been modified for operation at sea. The SH-60 is able to hover on one engine if necessary.

The three crewmembers consist of pilot, air tactical officer and sensor operator.

The 'AJ' marking is that of the Carrier Air Group aboard the *Theodore Roosevelt* and is carried by all aircraft on the carrier.

Number 164099 carries the standard US Navy low-visibility grey colour scheme designed to make the helicopter difficult for potential enemies to spot.

Up to three torpedoes can be carried. Two may be fitted to the extended portside pylons, although the inboard of these usually carries a fuel tank.

NAVY 610 HS-3 SH-60F 164099

Submarine hunting in the Seahawk

SHIP CONTACT: If the captain of a destroyer thinks the sonar has acquired a possible contact, he will launch the SH-60 to investigate. The helicopter's data is sent back to the ship for processing.

1 A line of passive sonobuoys, released from the helicopter, provides an approximate location of the submarine.

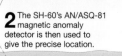

2 The SH-60's AN/ASQ-81 magnetic anomaly detector is then used to give the precise location.

3 Once located, the Seahawk launches a Mk 46 homing torpedo, which uses sonar to find its target.

ACTION DATA

MAXIMUM SPEED

Anti-submarine warfare equipment is heavy, and so are the weapons, fuel, extra crewmembers, dipping sonar and processing gear. Naval helicopter therefore tend to be slower than their battlefield equivalents: a land-based UH-60, for example, would easily outrun a Sea King Commando. Speed is largely irrelevant to naval helicopters, which mainly require range and endurance.

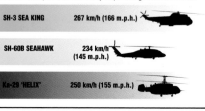

SH-3 SEA KING	267 km/h (166 m.p.h.)
SH-60B SEAHAWK	234 km/h (145 m.p.h.)
Ka-29 'HELIX'	250 km/h (155 m.p.h.)

SIKORSKY

HH-60

● Special Operations ● All weather ● Coast Guard rescue

The HH-60 is an angel of mercy. This helicopter flies from ships' decks and shore bases to bring salvation to those in peril. In disaster and in war, the Navy's HH-60H Rescue Hawk and the Coast Guard's HH-60J Jayhawk can mean the difference between life and death. Not surprisingly, HH-60 rescue flying is one of the most difficult missions pilots can undertake. A secondary role is supporting operations by the Special Forces.

▲ Designed to rescue troops from the battlefield, the HH-60 has enough space to allow stretcher patients to be given immediate medical attention, thus improving their chances of recovery.

SIKORSKY HH-60

▼ Extended range
The role of retrieving downed aircrew often involves flying long distances; the HH-60 is fitted with a refuelling boom, allowing contact with an HC-130 tanker.

▲ Coast Guard rescue
Operating from land bases around America's coasts, the Jayhawk is the civilian variant of the HH-60. It lacks any military equipment, although rescue in all weathers is still possible.

Credible Hawk ▶
One of the first developmental models of the project, a UH-60A is seen here testing the refuelling boom. Further modifications improved the variant.

◀ Anywhere, anytime
The rescue role has made the HH-60 an extremely adaptable platform. Even when in service with the US Air Force, missions often take place over water.

Dust off ▶
A derivative of the HH-60 is the UH-60Q, which is a specialised air ambulance version capable of accommodating nine stretchers and three medical attendants.

FACTS AND FIGURES

➤ USAF Pave Hawks fly rescue missions worldwide, and were used over Iraq and Kuwait during the Gulf War.

➤ Operations can be flown as low as 15 m (49 ft.) in all weathers.

➤ The helicopter can be fitted with skis to operate from snow-covered terrain.

➤ During in-flight refuelling, the HC-130 tanker has to maintain an airspeed only 10 kt higher than its stalling speed.

➤ Jayhawks are used in drug interdiction missions by the Coast Guard.

➤ The first Jayhawk flew on 8 August 1990 from Stratford, Connecticut.

PROFILE

Pave Hawk to the rescue

Left: Devoid of external tanks and refuelling boom, this early UH-60A is seen in flight prior to conversion to HH-60 standard.

Below: Based in Alaska, these HH-60Gs support rescue operations for NATO aircraft flying in the area.

In the technical alphabet of American helicopter designations, an 'H' prefix means that the aircraft has a rescue mission. The Navy's HH-60H and the Coast Guard's almost identical but simpler HH-60J are top-notch medium-range rescue craft. They were developed from the famous H-60 Black Hawk and have the same sprightly performance as that familiar army helicopter.

The Rescue Hawk operates from aircraft-carrier decks, while the Jayhawk flies primarily from land bases (though it has had modest success aboard Coast Guard cutters). Either way, these fine helicopters are a challenge to flight crews.

When a rescue is under way, the pilot must take off immediately and put together a flight plan under pressure while en route. The rescue swimmer may have to go into the water to pull out the people being rescued. In wartime, this act of salvation may be performed under enemy fire. Fortunately, HH-60 helicopters are durable and versatile, and have amassed a fine record of success.

Despite the rescue role of the helicopter, they are often armed with door-mounted Miniguns. Front-line units flying the helicopter are based as far afield as Iceland and Japan, providing rescue cover for all the US armed services.

HH-60G PAVE HAWK

Providing the rescue element for the USAF, Pave Hawks give downed aircrew the chance of rescue from behind enemy lines. They also extend the reach of the Special Forces on covert operations.

Expected to operate anywhere, the HH-60s have foldable rotors that allow rapid air transportation inside current US military transports. The rotors also incorporate de-icing, which means that the aircraft can operate in all climates with no reduction in flight performance.

To deflect heat-seeking missiles away from the exhaust, provision is made to attach HIRSS exhaust suppressors. They remove the infra-red signature from the engine, allowing for improved survivability. The engines are also uprated to meet the demanding operational requirements.

A well-equipped cockpit is installed in the Rescue Hawk. The pilots are seated side by side, allowing for excellent crew co-ordination.

The high-risk missions that the HH-60 is expected to undertake mean that defensive systems include chaff/flare dispensers and radar warning receivers located in various parts of the airframe.

The refuelling probe extends nearly to the point of clearing the rotor disc. The tanker aircraft are variants of the C-130 equipped with wing-mounted drogues that trail behind the aircraft.

The cabin area has room for stretcher cases and their attendants, or a rescue team of four who retrieve the downed aircrew if they are unable to reach the helicopter themselves through injury.

Most HH-60s have been modified from basic UH-60s. Improvements have made the helicopter far superior to standard Army models, it being able to operate in all weathers.

One of the design specifications for the HH-60 was that it could be deployed quickly to operational theatres. Its folding stabilators and rotors help it fit easily inside existing transport aircraft.

COMBAT DATA

RANGE

Because of the compact fuselage design of the HH-60, internal fuel load is small. This has the effect of reducing the range compared to larger types such as the Sea King, but the addition of an IFR boom extends it. Range is then dependent only on crew endurance.

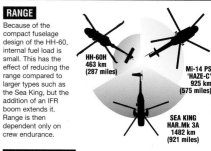

HH-60H
463 km
(287 miles)

Mi-14 PS
'HAZE-C'
925 km
(575 miles)

SEA KING
HAR.Mk 3A
1482 km
(921 miles)

MAXIMUM SPEED

Progression in helicopter design has seen a gradual increase in speed because of improved powerplants. Given the covert role that the HH-60 is expected to undertake, high performance is required. It is only slightly faster than the earlier Mi-14, however.

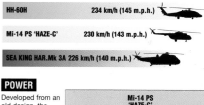

HH-60H	234 km/h (145 m.p.h.)
Mi-14 PS 'HAZE-C'	230 km/h (143 m.p.h.)
SEA KING HAR.Mk 3A	226 km/h (140 m.p.h.)

POWER

Developed from an old design, the Mi-14 'Haze' features a troop-carrying fuselage with added equipment and has two very powerful engines. The smaller Sea King and HH-60 feature less powerful engines but still have impressive performance.

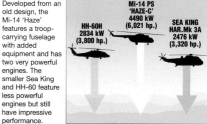

HH-60H
2834 kW
(3,800 hp.)

Mi-14 PS
'HAZE-C'
4490 kW
(6,021 hp.)

SEA KING
HAR.Mk 3A
2476 kW
(3,320 hp.)

US rescue helicopters

■ **HH-53C:** Tasked with rescuing downed aircrew in Vietnam, the 'Super Jolly Green Giant's range was improved by adding a refuelling probe to undertake operations in North Vietnam.

■ **MH-53E:** Developed for the US Navy, the Sea Dragon is designed for long-range maritime missions. The addition of large fuel tanks on the fuselage is supplemented by a refuelling boom.

■ **HH-3E:** The first of the long-range rescue helicopters, the HH-3E pioneered rescue missions in Vietnam and was used to develop the routine procedure of IFR for helicopters.

SIKORSKY

HH-60H RESCUE HAWK

● Strike rescue ● Gulf War participants ● US Coast Guard service

▲ Based upon the ASW SH-60B, the Rescue Hawk is a dedicated strike rescue variant. It has the ability to recover a four-man crew, such as that from an EA-6B Prowler or S-3 Viking.

Based upon the SH-60B Seahawk, the HH-60H is a specialised combat rescue variant. Entering service in 1990 it has proved highly effective, giving the US Navy a much-needed dedicated rescue helicopter. Two detachments from HCS-4 and -5 took part in Operations Desert Shield and Desert Storm, where the HH-60s flew a total of more than 750 mission hours. The US Coast Guard also took delivery of a rescue Seahawk, known as the HH-60J.

SIKORSKY HH-60H RESCUE HAWK

▼ Air force rescue
Like the Navy, the US Air Force also operates a fleet of rescue variants based on the UH-60 Black Hawk. These feature retractable refuelling probes.

▲ First 'Rescue Hawk'
Seen at the Stratford plant, the first HH-60H was rolled out in 1987. The aircraft is still known officially as a Seahawk.

▼ Close co-operation
Since 1991 Rescue Hawks have been deployed aboard carriers, alongside SH-60F Ocean Hawks providing additional and useful rescue capability.

▲ Coast guard variants
Besides the US Navy, the Coast Guard also operates a fleet of machines known as HH-60J Jayhawks. These have no armament.

◄ Unsung heroes
Although perhaps lacking the glamour of their naval counterparts, the Coast Guard Jayhawks have an important role and are often used on anti-drug smuggling missions off the south-eastern USA and around the Bahamas.

FACTS AND FIGURES

➤ During the Gulf War the two HH-60H detachments remained combat-ready 95 per cent of the time.

➤ Both the airframe and the engines are shared with the SH-60F Ocean Hawk.

➤ Surviving aircraft are being upgraded with defensive armament.

➤ First operational deployment of the HH-60H took place in 1990, when HS-2 took the type aboard USS Nimitz.

➤ US Coast Guard HH-60Js have greater endurance than their Navy counterparts.

➤ Forward looking infra-red turrets have been fitted to the HH-60s in recent years.

PROFILE

Combat rescue, Navy style

In the official terms used for American helicopters, an 'H' prefix tells us that the aircraft has a rescue mission. The US Navy's HH-60H and the Coast Guard's almost identical HH-60J fulfil the need for a dedicated rescue helicopter. Developed from the famous UH-60 Black Hawk, the naval variants – officially known as Seahawks – feature more powerful engines and specialist equipment.

HH-60s can operate from land, aircraft carriers and smaller

vessels such as frigates and destroyers. Coast Guard HH-60J Jayhawks are primarily land-based, but are sometimes deployed aboard cutters.

Experience with helicopter rescues in Vietnam confirmed the need for sturdier machines and the HH-60 features titanium rotors, capable of absorbing hits from large anti-aircraft shells, and considerable protection for both the pilots and cabin personnel.

Coast Guard aircraft lack the comprehensive avionics fit and

defensive armament of the naval machines, but do have a Bendix/King search radar. They are often deployed on drug traffic interdiction flights over the Bahamas.

Below: Purchased to replace ageing HH-3F Pelicans, the Jayhawks offered greater range, but the large cabin of the old helicopter is sorely missed.

Above: HH-60Js have somewhat larger sponson tanks because of their greater endurance requirements.

HH-60H Seahawk

Type: strike rescue/covert operations helicopter

Powerplant: two 1417-kW (1,900-hp.) General Electric T700-GE-401C turboshafts

Maximum speed: 296 km/h (184 m.p.h.)

Initial climb rate: 213 m/min (700 f.p.m.)

Combat radius: 463 km (287 mi.)

Range: 966 km (600 mi.)

Weights: empty 6114 kg (13,450 lb.); loaded 8334 kg (18,335 lb.)

Maximum payload: 3629 kg (7,984 lb.)

Dimensions:
main rotor diameter	16.36 m (53 ft. 8 in.)
tail rotor diameter	3.35 m (10 ft. 11 in.)
length	15.26 m (50 ft. 1 in.)
height	3.63 m (11 ft. 10 in.)
main rotor disc area	210.05 m² (2,260 sq. ft.)
tail rotor disc area	8.83 m² (95 sq. ft.)

HH-60H SEAHAWK

This HH-60H wears the markings of HS-3 'Tridents' which is shore-based at NAS Jacksonville in Florida. At present the unit operates a mixture of SH-60F and HH-60 variants and is assigned to Carrier Air Wing 3 and the USS *Theodore Roosevelt*.

Propelling the Seahawk through the air is a four-bladed main rotor. Experience gained during the Vietnam War resulted in very strong titanium blades being fitted which were designed to absorb hits from 23-mm shells. The rotor head employs just six elastomeric bearings as opposed to 18 on many other designs, resulting in greater reliability and less maintenance time.

Like the main rotor, the tail rotor is four-bladed and incorporates titanium blades. For stowage in tight confines aboard ship, the tail unit can be hinged to port and the hub can even be canted 20 degrees if required. A long span, fully moveable tailplane is fitted for greater stability and control.

Designed primarily for the combat rescue role, the HH-60F lacks the under-nose search radar and the data link equipment of the standard SH-60B Seahawk.

HH-60Hs feature the slightly more powerful 401C variant of the General Electric T700 turboshaft. These are immensely powerful and the aircraft is able to lift substantial loads if required.

For combat operations, the HH-60H can be armed with twin 7.62-mm (.30-cal.) machine guns mounted on posts in the main cabin.

Unlike the SH-60F Ocean Hawks, recovery assist and traverse (RAST) gear can be fitted for operations from smaller vessels such as destroyers or frigates.

For naval operations, the Seahawk features a relocated tailwheel with twin tyres which are stressed for lower crash impact.

Other features unique to the naval H-60 include a hovering in-flight refuelling capability, emergency floatation gear and extensive use of anti corrosion materials for extended use in a salt-water environment.

COMBAT DATA

MAXIMUM SPEED

Compared to its long-serving predecessor, the Sea King, the HH-60 is smaller, but faster and much easier to maintain. It has proved an ideal aircraft both with the US Navy and Coast Guard. The smaller Dolphin is one of the quickest helicopters in its class.

HH-60H RESCUE HAWK	296 km/h (184 m.p.h.)
SH-3H SEA KING	267 km/h (166 m.p.h.)
HH-65A DOLPHIN	257 km/h (159 m.p.h.)

RANGE

Theoretically not as far reaching as the Sea King, the HH-60s have still proved very suitable for long-range rescue and surveillance work, particularly with the US Coast Guard. The Dolphin has a reasonable radius for its size.

HH-60H RESCUE HAWK 966 km (600 mi.)

SH-3H SEA KING 1005 km (623 mi.)

HH-65A DOLPHIN 760 km (471 mi.)

POWER

Power is where the HH-60 really scores, the twin T700-410C engines putting out 2834 kW (3,800 hp.), a substantial amount more than those of its predecessor. The US Coast Guard has plans to re-engine its HH-65s with even more powerful engines.

HH-60H RESCUE HAWK 2834 kW (3,800 hp.)	SH-3H SEA KING 2088 kW (2,800 hp.)	HH-65A DOLPHIN 1014 kW (1,360 hp.)

Combat rescue support aircraft

■ **BOEING E-3A SENTRY:** Amongst the most sophisticated military aircraft in service, the Sentry, with its sophisticated AEW system, is able to track and identify activity over great distances.

■ **FAIRCHILD OA-10A THUNDERBOLT II:** Currently A-10s are employed as rescue support aircraft, clearing a path for the rescue helicopters. Some are also used for observation work.

■ **LOCKHEED HC-130P HERCULES:** These specially equipped variants of the ubiquitous C-130 are used primarily to support helicopters during rescue operations.

SIKORSKY
MH-60 PAVE HAWK

● Covert operations ● Combat search and rescue ● Combat-proven

▲ USAF MH-60Gs and their similar US Army counterparts, MH-60Ks, fly hazardous missions with minimal support, and are an increasingly important asset.

Sikorsky's familiar 'Hawk' series is the basis for the MH-60 Pave Hawk, the USAF's special operations helicopter, intended to support secret missions behind enemy lines. Equipped with advanced navigation equipment, defensive machine-guns and an in-flight refuelling probe, the MH-60 is establishing a fine reputation on long-range covert operations. The aircraft is designed to be easily transportable for worldwide deployment.

SIKORSKY MH-60 PAVE HAWK

▲ **Army special operations**
At least 22 MH-60K helicopters serve with the US Army's 160th Special Operations Aviation Regiment (SOAR).

▼ **Hawk over water**
Rescues at sea are also possible with the MH-60G, although it lacks the amphibious capabilities of the HH-3E it replaced.

▲ **Defence suppression**
With its door-mounted guns, the MH-60G is able to keep enemy heads down in the drop zone.

▼ **Special forces insertion**
It is often too hazardous for the MH-60G to land in a hostile drop zone, so troops use ladders or ropes to leave the aircraft.

◄ **MH-60K – enhanced army capability**
The US Army has not suffered the budget constraints of the USAF and has been able to fit extra items, such as terrain-following radar.

FACTS AND FIGURES

➤ Slightly more basic aircraft assigned solely to combat search-and-rescue (CSAR) duties are designated HH-60Gs.

➤ Up to four combat-ready MH-60Gs may be stowed in the hold of a C-5 Galaxy.

➤ MH-60 Pave Hawks saw combat in Operation Desert Storm.

➤ MH-60Gs carry a Bendix-King 1400C colour weather radar in a port-side nose 'thimble' radome.

➤ The first MH-60Gs were delivered to the 55th SOS in December 1987.

➤ HC-130 Combat Shadow aircraft support MH-60Gs on long-range missions.

Special forces Sikorsky

USAF sources are reluctant to reveal much about how the Sikorsky MH-60G is used. Basically, the MH-60G is a UH-60A, or more powerful UH-60L helicopter, modified with radar, defensive weapons, an in-flight refuelling probe, options for external fuel-tank pylons, and additional cabin fuel tanks.

Pave Hawk helicopters are expected to go into combat deep behind enemy lines, operating at great distances from home, in support of special forces troops.

A primary requirement of the Pave Hawk programme was that the aircraft should be rapidly air transportable to any part of the world at a moment's notice. This capability was proven in 1989, when MH-60Gs were deployed to Ethiopia within 14 hours of the news of the loss of Congressman Mickey Lelands in an air crash.

Supported by warplanes such as the A-10, the MH-60G is also expected to insert itself into a 'hot' zone to rescue downed pilots. Several rescue missions were flown during the Gulf War and continuing upgrades will ensure that the MH-60 remains highly effective in the future.

Some criticism has been made of the lack of cabin space in the MH-60, compared to the HH-3E. The new helicopter is fully air transportable, however.

All MH-60Gs are fitted with HIRSS (Hover Infra-Red Suppressor Subsystem). This reduces the aircraft's vulnerability to heat-seeking missiles.

To enhance survivability at low level, most military S-70s, including the MH-60G, have sets of cable-cutters fitted above and below the fuselage.

A programme is currently underway to equip the MH-60G with an AA/AAQ-16 forward looking infra-red (FLIR) turret, which will be fitted in the lower nose. The HH-60G fleet will not receive the system.

Because it lacks terrain-following radar and some other advanced systems, the MH-60G has to use its colour weather radar to avoid the worst conditions. This is not ideal for a special forces aircraft.

MH-60G Pave Hawk

Type: special operations warfare helicopter

Powerplant: two 1210-kW (1,622-hp.) General Electric T700-GE-700 turboshaft engines

Maximum speed: 296 km/h (476 m.p.h.)

Vertical climb rate: more than 137 m/min (449 f.p.m.) at sea level

Operational radius: about 964 km (600 mi.) with two 1703-litre (450-gal.) drop tanks

Service ceiling: 5790 m (19,000 ft.)

Weights: empty 6114 kg (13,480 lb.); maximum take-off 9979 kg (22,000 lb.)

Armament: a range of external stores including Hellfire missiles and cannon or rocket pods may be carried, but usually two pintle-mounted 12.7-mm machine-guns

Dimensions:

main rotor diameter	16.36 m (53 ft. 8 in.)
fuselage length	17.38 m (57 ft.)
height	5.13 m (16 ft. 9 in.)
main rotor disc area	210.05 m² (2,164 sq. ft.)

MH-60G PAVE HAWK

Normally based at Hurlburt Field, the USAF's 55th Special Operations Squadron was deployed to Al Jouf in Saudi Arabia during the 1991 Gulf War.

From the outset, the S-70 series was developed for maximum survivability. The fin area is sufficient to allow a controlled crash-landing following loss of the tail rotor at low altitude.

Sikorsky used a one-piece forged titanium rotor head on the S-70. In addition to this advanced feature, the titanium and composite main rotor blades can withstand hits by 23-mm ammunition.

USAF

Fuselage attitude is adjusted using the powerful, electrically operated tailplane. The surface is automatic and moves between +34° in the controlled hover and -6° during autorotation.

Several MH-53Js and MH-60Gs wore white identification stripes over rapidly applied desert camouflage during the Gulf War.

In addition to the normal door-mounted weapons, in this case 7.62-mm miniguns, this aircraft also has a 12.7-mm machine-gun mounted in the cabin.

In its retracted state, the MH-60G's refuelling probe is almost long enough to clear the rotor disc. In operation it extends telescopically to keep the refuelling hose clear of the rotor.

Pave Hawk in action

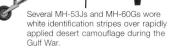

COVERT INSERTION: With the MH-60G hovering just centimetres from the ground, troops are able to jump from the cabin as the door gunners lay down suppressive fire.

TERRAIN-FOLLOWING RADAR (TFR): Currently unique to US Army MH-60Ks is the nose-mounted Texas Instruments' AN/AFQ-174A TFR. This allows much safer low-level flight.

AIR-TO-AIR REFUELLING (AAR): US Forces pioneered helicopter AAR in order to extend the range of CSAR helicopters. Army and Air Force MH-60s regularly practise the technique.

COMBAT DATA

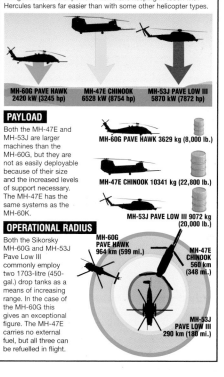

POWER

Although it has less power than the other principal US special forces helicopters, the MH-60G is much lighter. Pilots find that it has good reserves of power which make keeping in touch with Hercules tankers far easier than with some other helicopter types.

MH-60G PAVE HAWK 2420 kW (3245 hp)	MH-47E CHINOOK 6528 kW (8754 hp)	MH-53J PAVE LOW III 5870 kW (7872 hp)

PAYLOAD

Both the MH-47E and MH-53J are larger machines than the MH-60G, but they are not as easily deployable because of their size and the increased levels of support necessary. The MH-47E has the same systems as the MH-60K.

MH-60G PAVE HAWK 3629 kg (8,000 lb.)

MH-47E CHINOOK 10341 kg (22,800 lb.)

MH-53J PAVE LOW III 9072 kg (20,000 lb.)

OPERATIONAL RADIUS

Both the Sikorsky MH-60G and MH-53J Pave Low III commonly employ two 1703-litre (450-gal.) drop tanks as a means of increasing range. In the case of the MH-60G this gives an exceptional figure. The MH-47E carries no external fuel, but all three can be refuelled in flight.

MH-60G PAVE HAWK 964 km (599 mi.)

MH-47E CHINOOK 560 km (348 mi.)

MH-53J PAVE LOW III 290 km (180 mi.)

SIKORSKY

S-76 SPIRIT

● Multi-role helicopter ● Army scout ● Passenger transport

▲ With the worldwide demand for oil rig support and business transport helicopters in the 1980s, Sikorsky pitched its S-76 against Bell's Model 222 and the excellent Agusta A 109. It did not gain much penetration in the military market despite its success in civil sales.

One of the family of highly successful Sikorsky rotorcraft of recent times, the S-76 is the first type since the S-62 designed by the company purely for the civil market. The main customer area was seen to be the offshore oil support industry, with the S-76 offering 12 passenger seats in standard form with IFR equipment and other navigational aids for all-weather operation. Among the 'optional extras' are long-range fuel tanks and air-conditioning.

SIKORSKY S-76 SPIRIT

◄ New York bird
This Heli Union S-76C is powered by Turboméca Arriel turboshafts. The S-76C first flew in 1990, and has also been sold to the Spanish air force.

▲ Screaming Eagle
Armed with rocket pods or guns, the S-76 was offered on the military market as the 'Eagle'. But it had to compete with the successful Agusta A 109.

▲ Passenger comfort
Compared to the A 109 and Bell Model 222, the S-76 was a much roomier machine, and the executive version could carry eight people in luxury.

▼ Spirit in action
Known as the 'Spirit' to civil operators, the S-76 soon demonstrated impressive performance compared to its smaller rivals.

▲ Sikorsky at sea
Operating from oil platforms was an important source of business for the S-76, with companies like Bond Helicopters in Scotland. Sikorsky had already cornered much of the market with the larger Sikorsky S-61 series helicopter.

FACTS AND FIGURES

➤ When configured for full day and night, all-weather offshore flying, the S-76 generally carries up to 12 passengers.

➤ Sikorsky sold 428 S-76s to customers in Canada, Mexico, the UK and the US.

➤ A harmonic control system tested on an S-76 reduced vibration by 90 per cent.

➤ The S-76 Shadow had a nose radar housing and fly-by-wire controls grafted onto the front section.

➤ The S-76B is operated in China, Germany, Japan, Korea and the Netherlands.

➤ The first S-76 prototypes flew in 1977 and deliveries began in 1979.

PROFILE

Sikorsky's middle weight

Having flown for the first time in 1978, the S-76 soon had a full order book and by the following spring over 200 had been ordered. The first production example, which in the meantime had been named 'Spirit', was delivered to Offshore Logistics of Louisiana in February 1979. Other early customers included Evergreen Helicopters Inc. based in Oregon, who ordered 20 Spirits in 1980.

The first British operator

of the Spirit was Bristow Helicopters, which took delivery of the first two helicopters in November 1979. This and other sales reflected the boom in oil business at that time – one that did not last, and adversely affected requirements for new helicopters intended for offshore work.

Bristow soon demonstrated the speed which could be attained by a helicopter with fully retractable landing gear, by setting a new London to Paris

record of one hour 15 minutes at a speed of 272.75 km/h. (171 m.p.h.). This bettered the previous record by some 26 minutes. On the return trip, the Spirit clipped another four minutes off its own record.

Sikorsky's development programme bore further fruit in 1985 when, on 24 June, it flew the first privately-funded S-76 Shadow. This acronym stood for Sikorsky Helicopter Advanced Demonstrator of Operator Workload.

Above: This 'fantail' variant was fitted with a fenestron-type tail rotor in trials for the Light Helicopter Experimental programme.

Left: With the space to accommodate a high standard of luxury features, the S-76 offered the ultimate in executive transport with its low-noise interior and high speed.

S-76 Spirit

Type: medium-capacity helicopter

Powerplant: two Allison 250-C30 turboshaft engines each rated at 484.7-kW (649-hp.)

Maximum speed: 289 km/h (180 m.p.h.)

Normal cruising speed: 269 km/h (167 m.p.h.)

Range: 1100 km (683 mi.)

Service ceiling: 1555 m (5,100 ft.)

Weights: empty 2241 kg (4,940 lb.); loaded 4400 kg (9,700 lb.); maximum take-off weight 5171 kg (11,400 lb.)

Dimensions:
rotor diameter	13.41 m	(44 ft.)
length	16 m	(52 ft. 6 in.)
height	4.41 m	(14 ft. 5 in.)

S-76 SPIRIT

First flown in 1979, the S-76 has sold widely in the North American market despite competition from the Bell Model 222 and Agusta A 109. The latest version is the S-76C with Ariel turboshaft engines.

To reduce vibration, the S-76 has bifilar vibration absorbers above the rotor head. The blades rotate on elastomeric bearings, with damping provided by hydraulic drag dampers.

The tail rotor is a conventional four-bladed type mounted on the port side.

Power is transferred from the engines to the tail rotor and main rotor through a gearbox, which also drives the twin hydraulic pumps and 200A DC generators. The engines have an automatic fire detection and suppression system.

S-76s are fitted with a high standard of cockpit controls, with full instrument flight rules equipment fitted and optional 'EFIS' and weather radar.

The fuselage contains many composite and honeycomb structural components to reduce weight.

The main cabin can accommodate 12 or 13 passengers in an economy-type seating arrangement or can be configured in a four-seat flying office arrangement with additional soundproofing.

The main undercarriage retracts under hydraulic power into the fuselage to reduce drag. The wheel brakes are also hydraulically powered.

A baggage hold is located aft of the cabin with an external door on each side of the fuselage. The tail rotor was reconfigured in the S-76B to reduce weight.

The many faces of the Spirit

■ **BATTLEFIELD EAGLE:** Fast and agile, the Eagle military transport could carry a squad-sized unit of 10 troops, as well as providing its own firepower with rocket and gun pods.

■ **FLYING AMBULANCE:** Equipped with full emergency medical service equipment, the S.76 air ambulance can provide full patient care en route to hospital.

■ **RESCUE MISSION:** The S-76 is used by the Government Air Service in Hong Kong as a search and rescue aircraft in the dangerous waters of the South China Sea.

■ **SHADOW:** A technology demonstrator for advanced cockpit instrumentation layouts, the Shadow paved the way for the advanced Boeing-Sikorsky LHX helicopter.

ACTION DATA

ACCOMMODATION

The S-76 was aimed at a gap in the market between helicopters like the Mi 8 and Bell 212, which were slower and bigger, and the Bell 222 and A 109, which were as fast as the S-76 but smaller.

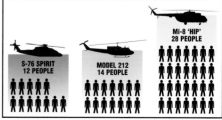

SIKORSKY

S-80/CH-/MH-53E

● Heavy-lifter ● Minesweeper ● Three-engined variant of CH-53

▲ *The CH-53E is currently the West's most powerful helicopter. Like the world-beating Mi-26, it is a single-rotor type and can lift heavier loads than the twin-rotor Boeing-Vertol CH-47 Chinook.*

Worldwide attention was focused on the US Marine CH-53E when helicopters from the assault ship *Kearsarge* landed a TRAP (Tactical Recovery of Aircrew Personnel) team to rescue an American pilot in Bosnia in 1995. Second-generation Sikorsky S-80s differ from the earlier S-65s in having three engines, expanded capacity and improved performance. They undertake heavy-lifting, rescue and minesweeping duties.

SIKORSKY **S-80/CH-/MH-53E**

▼ **US Navy CH-53Es**
The Navy's interest in the Sea Stallion was as a supply helicopter for use between shore bases and naval vessels. Three Navy squadrons operate the CH-53E.

▲ **Marine Corps heavy-lifter**
The USMC has the largest CH-53E fleet, with six squadrons including a training unit. Their main role is in support of amphibious assaults.

Export model ▶
Japan has been the only export customer for the three-engined CH-53; its S-80M-1 is similar to the MH-53E.

▼ **Refuelling in the air**
An important feature of many H-53Es is their ability to refuel in the air, greatly enhancing their flexibility. The US Marine Corps use KC-130 Hercules aircraft for the air-to-air tanker role.

◀ **Minehunter**
A cable with a tension of up to 13 tonnes is used to tow a hydrofoil sled, which skims through the water seeking out mines. This device is too large to be stowed aboard the helicopter.

FACTS AND FIGURES

➤ Overall production of the US Marine Corps and Navy Super Stallions is projected to reach 177 aircraft, MH-53Es about 50.

➤ The first S-80/CH-53E was a test aircraft and made its first flight on 1 March 1974.

➤ The H-53 family contains the most powerful helicopters used by US forces.

➤ The first MH-53E minesweeper, which flew in 1983, was not fitted with large sponsons; deliveries began in 1986.

➤ The first prototype of this series was tragically lost in a ground mishap.

➤ A CH-53E can lift 16 tonnes – 6 tonnes more than the twin-rotor CH-47 Chinook.

PROFILE

Super Stallion and Sea Dragon

Marine Corps' CH-53Es are well-known as the heavylift and rescue helicopters of the US fleet. The MH-53E minesweeper, also known as the Sea Dragon, uses the airframe of the CH-53E but carries extra fuel and equipment, allowing it to sweep for mines for up to four hours while operating 30 minutes from its base.

The MH-53E has a new acoustic countermeasures system and the ALQ-166 mine countermeasures sled. The sled is towed by the helicopter to neutralise mines, but as it is too bulky to be taken aboard, it is towed throughout the mission. In April 1987 the first MH-53Es joined MH-12 Squadron at Norfolk, Virginia. Japan has also purchased the minesweeper as the S-80M-1.

Both the CH-53E and MH-53E are developments of the proven twin-engined CH-53 Sea Stallion, itself a large helicopter. The Marines, however, wanted something even bigger. Sikorsky produced the S-80 model, which had an extra T64 engine fitted and a new main rotor.

The main external features of the MH-53E are readily apparent: the seven-blade rotor, larger sponsons, a third engine and redesigned tail assembly.

Rear-view mirrors are used by the crew to monitor the magnetic minesweeping sled towed behind the helicopter. An inflight-refuelling boom is also fitted to the nose. Japanese S-80M-1s lack this feature.

The tail of the H-53E is unusually canted to port and has a large, four-blade rotor. To offset this the tailplane has a gull-wing configuration.

To absorb the power of the third engine, the H-53E has an extra blade on its main rotor. Its diameter and blade chord are also increased.

CH-53E Super Stallion

Type: three-engined heavy-lift, assault and rescue helicopter

Powerplant: three 2756-kW (3,695-hp.) (continuous rating) General Electric T64-GE-416 engines

Maximum speed: 315 km/h (196 m.p.h.) 'clean'

Ferry range: 2075 km (1,289 mi.)

Service ceiling: 5640 m (18,504 ft.)

Weights: empty 15072 kg (33,228 lb.); maximum take-off 31640 kg (69,754 lb.) with internal load or 33340 kg (73,502 lb.) with external load

Accommodation: two flight crew and up to 55 troops or 13607 kg (30,000 lb.) of cargo internally

Dimensions: main rotor diameter 24.08 m (79 ft.)
length 30.19 m (99 ft.)
height 8.97 m (29 ft. 5 in.)
rotor disc area 455.38 m² (4,901 sq. ft.)

MH-53E SEA DRAGON

Helicopter Mine Countermeasures Squadron HM-14 operated this MH-53E from Naval Air Station Norfolk, Virginia, attached to the Atlantic Fleet. During the Gulf War HM-14 neutralised over 1,000 Iraqi mines.

MH-53Es have a flight crew of three and three to five enlisted crew to operate the mine-hunting equipment and man the two 12.7-mm machine-guns used to explode surfaced mines.

The key feature of the H-53E is the third General Electric T64 turboshaft engine which has been accommodated with comparatively little change to the basic H-53 airframe. Total power output is close to the equivalent of two twin-engined CH-53s.

This aircraft carries a dark-grey version of the standard low-visibility markings now carried by US Navy helicopters.

Formerly equipped with the RH-53D, the HM-14 squadron is known as the 'Sea Stallions'; its aircraft carry a stallion's head on the sponson.

The enlarged sponsons of the MH-53E contain fuel, raising internal capacity from 3850 litres to 12,100 litres (1,017–3,196 gal.)

Moored mines are detached using an internal pod system. An ALQ-160 acoustic countermeasures system forms part of this equipment.

Fitted with a 13600-kg (30,000-lb) tension tow boom and a hydraulic winch with 140 metres (460 ft.) of cable, the MH-53E can tow various types of ALQ-166 minesweeping sled.

COMBAT DATA

MAXIMUM SPEED

The three-engined Super Stallion has a slight edge in straight-line speed, although 300 km/h is about the norm for this type of helicopter. Speeds are drastically reduced when a helicopter is fully loaded.

CH-53E SUPER STALLION	315 km\h (196 m.p.h.)
Mi-26 'HALO'	295 km\h (183 m.p.h.)
CH-47D CHINOOK	298 km\h (185 m.p.h.)

FERRY RANGE

A ferry range of 2000 km (1,243 mi.) is average for this class of aircraft. In the case of the CH-53E and some versions of the Chinook, range can be increased by air-to-air refuelling.

CH-53E SUPER STALLION	2075 km (1,289 mi.)
Mi-26 'HALO'	2000 km (1,243 mi.)
CH-47D CHINOOK	2026 km (1,259 mi.)

PAYLOAD

The Mi-26 is currently the world's most powerful helicopter, with the capability to lift 20 tonnes. The three-engined CH-53E carries much more than the twin-rotor Chinook.

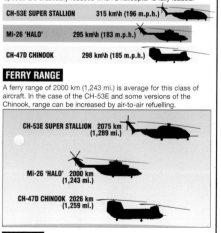

CH-53E SUPER STALLION 16338 kg (36,019 lb.)

Mi-26 'HALO' 20000 kg (44,092 lb.)

CH-47D CHINOOK 10341 kg (22,800 lb.)

USMC helicopters past and present

BELL AH-1 SEACOBRA: A twin-engined development of the HueyCobra, the SeaCobra serves aboard US Navy assault ships.

BOEING-VERTOL CH-46 SEA KNIGHT: Still in use after 30 years, the CH-46 remains the mainstay of USMC transport aviation.

SIKORSKY HR2S: Predecessor of the CH-53D , this troop-carrying assault helicopter was powered by two Pratt & Whitney radial engines.

SIKORSKY HUS SEAHORSE: Sikorsky's highly successful S-58 entered service with the USMC in the support role in 1957.

SIKORSKY

MH-53J

● Combat rescue ● Covert operations ● Behind the lines

SIKORSKY MH-53J

▼ Gulf veteran
Desert Storm proved that the helicopter could undertake high-risk covert operations behind enemy lines and survive.

▲ Missile defense
Sophisticated jamming devices are located on either side of the MH-53J. These prevent any SAMs from locking on and destroying the helicopter.

Tanker support ▶
The MH-53J has an inflight-refuelling boom, which allows it to fly deep behind enemy lines. Specially equipped C-130 Hercules tankers support the MH-153J for the mission.

◀ Pick-up point
The Pave Low is extremely vulnerable in the hover and the recovery phase of the operation. Two of the helicopter's crew keep the enemy's heads down with suppressive fire from the door-mounted mini-guns.

▲ Sting in the tail
The rear-loading ramp is retained from earlier models. For combat rescue operations, a rearwards-firing machine gun is mounted on the ramp, allowing the helicopter's crew to cover their exit from a landing zone.

To a pilot downed deep behind enemy lines, the lumbering shape of the MH-53J Pave Low III is a welcome sight. This rescue helicopter was developed following experiences in Vietnam and played a vital role in the Gulf War, ranging into enemy territory and snatching aircrews from the hans of the Iraqis. The Pave Low is also used by the US Special Forces, but how they deploy the helicopter remains secret.

▲ *Though not as glamourous as the F117 Nighthawk or F-15 Eagle, the MH-53J Pave Low III played a role in the Gulf War, rescuing downed American pilots.*

FACTS AND FIGURES

➤ The Pave Low is equipped with a multi-mode radar for terrain-following and FLR for night operations.

➤ Titanium armor plating is used to protect the engines and fuel tanks.

➤ Pave Low is the largest and most powerful helicopter used by the USAF.

➤ Special Operations Forces who use the Pave Low include the SEALS, the Delta Force and US Army Rangers.

➤ Pave Lows were used on the very first mission of the Gulf War.

➤ If funding is available, the V-22 Osprey will replace the Pave Low in service.

PROFILE

Warrior of the night

Black operations, covert insertions and combat rescue: the Sikorsky MH-53J Pave Low is America's true warrior of the night.

Developed from the Super Jolly Green Giant transport helicopter, the Pave Low III is a far more capable model, tailored for the rescue role and able to operate at night in all weather and at long range.

Entering service in 1988, the Pave Low could operate from ship decks and refuel in flight. The helicopter played a key role during the invasion of Panama, delivering a commando team to Panama's main airport to destroy Noriega's Learjet, which might otherwise have been used in an escape attempt.

A few years later, the helicopter was in the heat of battle again, this time in the Persian Gulf. Crossing the Iraqi border on the first night of the war – in company with AH-64 Apache armed attack helicopters – the Pave Low acted as a pathfinder, allowing the Apaches to locate and neutralize a radar listening post.

Other roles for the helicopter remain highly classified, but are known to involve the elite of

Below: Special Forces troops demonstrate how to leave a Pave Low during an exercise. In wartime, this could take place under fire at night.

Above: The transport lineage of the Pave Low is apparent in this low-angle view of this grey example.

America's fighting troops on worldwide covert operations.

Despite its capabilities, the helicopter is nearing replacement, with Boeing's V-22 Osprey being a possible candidate in the role.

MH-53J Pave Low III

Type: Combat rescue/special operations helicopter

Powerplant: two 2935-kW (4,380-hp.) General Electric T64-GE-415 turboshaft engines

Maximum speed: 315 km/h (195 m.p.h.) at sea level

Range: 870 km (538 mi.) with auxiliary fuel

Hover ceiling: 1980 m (6,500 ft.) out of ground effect

Weights: empty 10,690 kg (23,518 lb.); maximum 19,051 kg (41,912 lb.)

Armament: three 7.62-mm (.30-cal.) mini-guns mounted in door positions

Dimensions:
Length	20.47 m (67 ft. 2 in.)
Height	7.6 m (24 ft. 11 in.)
Rotor disc area	378.10 m² (4,068 sq. ft.)

MH-53J Pave Low III

Wearing a hastily applied desert camouflage, the MH-53J Pave Low IIIs were some of the first aircraft deployed to the Gulf following Iraq's invasion of Kuwait. Operated mainly at night, the helicopters undertook some of the most dangerous missions of the war.

The flight crew of three is protected by titanium armour plating and is able to use sophisticated avionics such as terrain-following radar and Forward-Looking Infrared (FLIR).

Already capable of operating at great distances, the Pave Low can be equipped with external fuel tanks. These can be jettisoned to increase the speed of the helicopter.

The large tail rotor is canted at 20 degrees to port to offset the power of the main rotors.

A large flexible skid protrudes from the rear of the tailboom. This is designed to protect the tail rotor from striking the ground during take-offs. To facilitate operations from ships, the tailboom can be folded to reduce the overall length of the helicopter.

A loading ramp on the rear of the fuselage is often flown in the down position during combat operations. A machine gun can be mounted here if required.

ACTION DATA

AIR SUPPORT: Because Pave Lows operate deep behind enemy lines, support for their missions has to be provided from the air. If the rescue mission requires artillery support, it is provided by the large AC-130H Spectre (pictured below). The Spectre flies a circular orbit around the rescue site firing its mini-guns and cannon at any threat to the helicopter. During the Gulf War, the combination of Pave Low and Spectre proved highly advantageous, resulting in many successful covert operations.

ARMED RECONNAISSANCE: Though not as capable as the Pave Low, the small lightweight OH/AH-6 Night Fox (pictured below) is used in the reconnaissance and scouting roles. Continually upgraded in recent years, the type got its first taste of combat during the 'oil tanker war', which saw Western ships come under fire from both Iraq and Iran. Operated in complete secrecy, the helicopters were used to destroy a number of oil installations that were being used as gun emplacements. Following this successful deployment, the Night Fox has seen combat in South America on anti-drug operations. One of its most unusual roles is as a sniping platform for Delta Force.

Down in Iraq

1 PROWLER ESCORT: on 21 January. 1991, a Tomcat from VF-103 'Sluggers' squadron was assigned to provide escort for a group of Grumman Prowlers. During the mission, the Tomcat was hit by an SA-2 surface-to-air missile.

2 ALONE IN THE DESERT: Ejecting from the Tomcat, the RIO was quickly captured, while the pilot managed to escape and hide. Prior to the rescue, A-10s strafed an advancing Iraqi army lorry

3 THE PICK-UP: Flying in at low altitude in daylight, the Pave Low quickly landed and sent a crew member to collect the pilot. Although under fire from Iraqi troops, the crew completed its mission successfully.

WALLIS

AUTOGYROS

● 1950s design ● Many world records ● Film star

Wing Commander K.H. Wallis is the most famous name in post-war autogyro design. After his distinguished career in the RAF, his first machine took to the air in 1961. Since then his revolutionary designs have broken almost every autogyro world record. Trials were also carried out on a military reconnaissance version, but the aircraft which achieved the greatest fame was 'Little Nellie' in the 1967 James Bond film *You Only Live Twice*.

▲ Ken Wallis broke the world autogyro records for speed in a straight line (1986) and distance over a closed circuit (1988) flying this WA-116/F/S machine.

WALLIS AUTOGYROS

Record breaker ▶
Seen with its designer and pilot Ken Wallis, this WA-116/F broke an impressive nine world records.

▲ Army evaluation
The Beagle company helped produce early WA-116s, three of which were evaluated by the British Army.

First to fly ▶
After Wallis started design work in 1958, the first WA-116 was constructed by Beagle and flew in 1961. It had a 54-kW (72-hp.) McCulloch engine.

▼ Hand control
To keep the rotor blades steady when taxiing, the pilot can reach above his head to control them.

▲ 'Little Nellie'
For its starring role, 'Little Nellie' was armed with dummy air-to-air missiles, 44-mm rockets, rearward-firing 'flame-throwers' and two machine-guns.

FACTS AND FIGURES

➤ As well as the Bond movie, a Wallis design also appeared in and was used as a camera ship in *The Martian Chronicles*.

➤ A version built in conjunction with Vinten was designed for aerial photography.

➤ The WA-116 uses 27.5 metres (90 ft.) of runway during its take-off run.

➤ The Wallis WA-122 can be easily transported in a container thanks to its folding rotors and landing gear legs.

➤ The prototype WA-116 was flown by Wallis for the first time on 2 August 1961.

➤ The WA-119 Imp was powered by an engine from the Hillman Imp motor car.

Record-breaking autogyros

In 1908 Ken Wallis' father and uncle, H.S. and P.V. Wallis, designed and built the first aeroplane which employed steel tubing: the Wallbro monoplane. The family's position as revolutionary aviation designers continues 90 years on with the series of Wallis autogyros.

After constructing high-speed watercraft in the 1930s and a long career as a pilot in the RAF, including two operational bombing tours over Germany, Ken Wallis pursued a personal ambition of designing and building autogyros. The original design was the WA-116, which introduced many patented features, including a new rotor head design, a high-speed rotor shaft and a novel safe starting arrangement.

Three examples, built by Beagle, were evaluated by the British Army but never entered service. In 1967 G-ARZB 'Little Nellie' appeared alongside Sean Connery in *You Only Live Twice* and has since been displayed at air shows around the world.

Various versions of the basic WA-116 design have taken almost every autogyro world record, piloted by the original designer Ken Wallis.

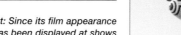

Right: Since its film appearance G-ARZB has been displayed at shows as far away as Australia. The aircraft can be flown 'hands-off'.

Left: The WA-122 was a two-seat design with dual controls, making it suitable as a trainer. It is powered by a larger Rolls-Royce Continental 119-kW (160-hp.) flat-four engine.

WA-116/W

Type: single-seat general-purpose or reconnaissance autogyro

Powerplant: one 56-kW (75-hp.) Weslake 65/75 flat-twin engine driving a two-blade pusher propeller

Max cruising speed: 185 km/h (115 m.p.h.)

Loiter speed: 65 km/h (40 m.p.h.)

Endurance: 4 hours

Initial climb rate: 365 m/min (1,200 f.p.m.)

Range: 483 km (300 mi.)

Service ceiling: 4570 m (15,000 ft.)

Weights: empty 140.5 kg (309 lb.)

Dimensions: rotor diameter 6.15 m (20 ft. 2 in.)
length 3.38 m (11 ft. 1 in.)
height 1.85 m (6 ft. 1 in.)

WA-116/Mc

This is the aircraft which appeared in the film *You Only Live Twice*. When it appears at air displays around the UK it is still fitted with the original dummy weapons.

This Wa-116 is powered by a 67-kW (90-hp.) McCulloch Model 4318A four-cylinder, air-cooled, two-stroke engine mounted aft of the rotor pylon. It drives a two-bladed propeller.

Constructed of wood, the two-bladed teetering autorotative rotor has metal reinforcements and internal mass balances. The initial rotor spin-up is achieved via a flexible shaft and engine clutch. A rotor brake is also fitted.

The dummy armament fitted to the modified WA-116 'Little Nellie' consisted of four jettisonable rearward-firing 'flame-throwers', fourteen 44-mm rockets, two air-to-air missiles, two nose-mounted machine-guns and 50 air mines deployed on parachutes.

A large fin and rudder, attached to the end of a short boom, help to control the aircraft in forward flight. They are constructed of hollow plywood and finished in Madapolam.

ACTION DATA

ENDURANCE

Powered by a very economical piston engine, the Wallis design has an excellent endurance for a craft of its size. This feature made it attractive to armed forces as a reconnaissance platform. The R22HP helicopter and Shadow microlight have lower endurance.

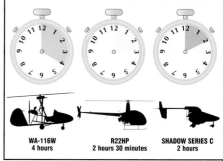

WA-116W	R22HP	SHADOW SERIES C
4 hours	2 hours 30 minutes	2 hours

Bond film aircraft stars

THUNDERBALL: Emile Largo was foiled by James Bond in his attempt to threaten the world with nuclear weapons obtained from RAF Vulcans that had ditched in the Caribbean Sea.

THE MAN WITH THE GOLDEN GUN: James Bond flew the Republic Seabee to Scaramanga's island in the South China Sea for a final showdown with the assassin.

GOLDFINGER: Pussy Galore's Flying Circus flew Piper Cherokees carrying nerve gas to disable US Army soldiers guarding the US Gold Reserves at Fort Knox, Kentucky.

THUNDERBALL: In the dramatic opening sequence of this film, James Bond fights and kills a SPECTRE secret agent at a chateau in France. Bond then makes his escape using mounted jet pack which enables him to fly over the castle's walls. A modified version of the jet pack was used during the opening ceremony of the 1984 Olympic Games.

WESTLAND

WHIRLWIND

● American design ● Piston and turbine variants ● Military service

▲ A licence-built
Sikorsky design, the WS-55/Whirlwind
served the British armed forces for many
years, mainly in transport, anti-submarine
warfare and rescue roles.

Early Whirlwinds were licence-built Sikorsky S-55s, with Pratt & Whitney Wasp or Wright Cyclone piston engines. Westland soon replaced the US engines with the more powerful Alvis Leonides Major, a two-row radial which gave improved performance. Then, in 1958, Westland decided to build a version using the Gnome, a licence-built version of the General Electric T58 turboshaft. The result was a much more capable machine.

WESTLAND WHIRLWIND

Popular in export markets ▶
This WS-55 Series 3 was among a number of Whirlwinds exported to both civil and military users. Ghana's air force was among military customers who also included Austria, Canada, France, Jordan, Spain and Yugoslavia.

▲ Navy ASW
Royal Navy HAS.Mk 7s were the first British helicopters used for front-line anti-submarine work.

▲ Army transport
In addition to SAR, RAF Whirlwinds were tasked with light transport duties in support of the British Army. This role took the type into action in the Far East.

▲ Search and rescue
In RAF and Royal Navy service, SAR was a major Whirlwind role. The type often co-operated with RAF rescue motor launches.

◀ WS-55 Series 3
Some examples of this civil version of the turbine-powered WS-55 were, like this aircraft, converted from piston-engined aircraft.

FACTS AND FIGURES

➤ Westland built a total of 364 S-55s under licence between 1953 and 1966, including 68 WS-55 civil aircraft.

➤ Bristow Helicopters' Series 1s were used for 'flying crane' and oil rig support duties.

➤ British airline BEA used WS-55s between central London and Heathrow airport.

➤ Most turbine-powered WS-55 Series 3s were converted from piston-engined Series 1s and 2s.

➤ WS-55s were used from the 1950s in the Falkland Islands for whaling operations.

➤ In 1955 a Whirlwind on delivery was flown 5000 km (3,100 miles) to the Persian Gulf.

PROFILE

First British ASW helicopter

Flown for the first time in November 1952, Westland's initial version of the Whirlwind was delivered to the Royal Navy as the HAR.Mk 1 and to the RAF as the HAR.Mk 2, both marks filling the rescue and transport role.

The HAR.Mk 3 was a Wright Cyclone-powered version for the navy, and the HAR.Mk 4 was an RAF variant with more powerful Pratt & Whitney Wasp engines for tropical operations. It was used for rescue and transport missions

during the counter-insurgency campaign in Malaya.

Leonides-powered variants were the naval HAR.Mk 5 transport and the HAS.Mk 7, the latter a dedicated anti-submarine aircraft with radar, a dipping sonar and the ability to launch homing torpedoes. It was the first British helicopter designed for front-line ASW use. Most of the 120 delivered from June 1957 were re-engined with the lighter and more powerful Gnome as HAS.Mk 9s in the mid-1960s. They were finally replaced by the Wessex in 1977.

The RAF's HAR.Mk 10 and HC.Mk 10 had introduced the

Gnome engine in 1959. The latter variant could be armed with four AS11 anti-tank missiles and carried eight passengers in addition to a three-man crew. The HAR.Mk 10 was the RAF's standard rescue helicopter for many years; from 1968 it served with the UN peace-keeping force in Cyprus.

Left: XJ398 was one of three Whirlwind Mk 3s used by Westland to develop a turboshaft-powered WS-55 with considerably improved performance.

With the exception of a redesigned main rotor gearbox, Westland's WS-55 embodied all the Sikorsky S-55's design features, including its Pratt & Whitney radial engine.

The WS-55's three-bladed main rotor featured offset flapping hinges with hydraulic damping about the drag hinges. The two-bladed tail rotor was driven by a shaft running along the top of the tailboom.

A turboshaft engine replaced the radial piston engine in the Whirlwind from the Mk 9 onwards. Bristol Siddeley's 783-kW (1,050-hp.) Gnome H.1000 was installed in the Mks 9, 10 and 12, offering increased power but only one-third of the radial's total weight.

Whirlwind HAR.Mk 10

Type: single-engined military rescue helicopter

Powerplant: one 783-kW (1,050-hp.) Bristol Siddeley Gnome H.1000 turboshaft

Maximum speed: 177 km/h (110 m.p.h.)

Cruising speed: 170 km/h (105 m.p.h.)

Initial climb rate: 366 m/min (1,200 f.p.m.) at sea level

Service ceiling: 5060 m (16,600 ft.)

Weights: empty 2159 kg (4,750 lb.); normal loaded 3538 kg (7,784 lb.)

Dimensions:
main rotor diameter	16.15 m (53 ft.)
fuselage length	13.46 m (44 ft. 2 in.)
height	4.76 m (15 ft. 7 in.)

A rectangular, light alloy semi-monocoque structure, the fuselage had a rear cone-shaped extension carrying the tail rotor pylon. A triangular fin filled the step between the two.

Accommodation for eight passengers, 10 fully-armed troops or six stretchers was available in the S-55/Whirlwind's 9.63-m³ (340 cubic-foot) cabin interior.

To accommodate its turbine engine, the fuselage was lengthened by 76.2 cm. The gearbox and transmission remained unchanged.

WHIRLWIND HCC.MK 12

XR486 was the first of two Mk 12s delivered to the Queen's Flight in early 1964. Although the second aircraft was destroyed in a fatal accident, '486 continued to transport Royal Family members until replaced by the Wessex.

Whirlwind HCC.Mk 12s were a specially furnished and equipped variant of the HAR.Mk 10 search-and-rescue type used by the RAF from 1962 until 1978.

Westland helicopters of Sikorsky design

DRAGONFLY: Sikorsky's S-51 was the basis for the first helicopter built in Britain to enter service with the RAF. Westland acquired rights to the design in 1947, repowering it with a British Alvis Leonides radial.

WESSEX: After the success of WS-55 production, Westland built this turbine-powered version of the S-58, with either a single Napier Gazelle or two coupled Gnome engines. Small numbers remain in RAF use.

SEA KING: In 1959 Westland signed a licence agreement for the S-61, developing the type for a naval anti-submarine role. Two Gnome engines were fitted. Many were built for the Royal Navy, the RAF and export.

COMBAT DATA

TROOPS

Successive developments in helicopter design allowed greater carrying capacity, largely because of the increased engine power available. The Westland Wessex and Sikorsky H-34 were both developed from the S-58, the Wessex having a turbine engine.

WHIRLWIND HC.Mk 10	8
WESSEX HC.Mk 2	16
H-34A CHOCTAW	18

CRUISING SPEED

Twin turboshaft engines gave both the Whirlwind Mk 10 and Wessex Mk 2 a considerable speed advantage over the H-34. Turbines are also considerably lighter and more economical than the equivalent piston engine.

WHIRLWIND HC.Mk 10	167 km/h (105 m.p.h.)
WESSEX HC.Mk 2	195 km/h (121 m.p.h.)
H-34A CHOCTAW	158 km/h (98 m.p.h.)

INITIAL CLIMB RATE

Among the performance parameters improved by the introduction of turboshaft engines was climb rate. The Wessex's rate of climb is considerably better than that of both the Whirlwind and piston-engined H-34. Gas turbine engines also provide improved general performance at altitude, where even supercharged internal combustion engines are less efficient because of oxygen deficiency.

WESSEX HC.Mk 2 503 m/min (1,650 f.p.m.)

WHIRLWIND HC.Mk 10 366 m/min (1,200 f.p.m.)

H-34A CHOCTAW 335 m/min (1,100 f.p.m.)

WESTLAND

WESSEX

● Anti-submarine ● Tactical airlift ● Search and rescue

Westland's Wessex performs solidly in every task a helicopter can undertake. The popular British-built version of the Sikorsky S-58 entered service in 1961 and since then has appeared on ship decks, on battlefields and in many countries and climates. With its stalky fuselage and jutting nose, the turbine-powered Wessex is easy to recognise. This ageing machine remains in operation as a tactical support helicopter.

▲ In the 1960s the Wessex seemed to get everywhere, fighting in numerous British colonial wars from naval Commando carriers and developing vital new helicopter tactics for Britain's forces.

WESTLAND WESSEX

▲ Australian Wessex
The Royal Australian Navy used the Wessex in the anti-submarine role. This one has the radar removed, but the fairing remains in place.

◀ 22 rescue you ▶
Serving in the search-and-rescue role with No. 22 and No. 202 Squadrons, the Wessex has rescued hundreds around the British coastline.

▲ RAF support role
In support of the army, the RAF still uses the Wessex in the tactical support role. It will be replaced by the EH.101 Merlin in 1998.

◀ Navy gunship
One in four Wessex HU.Mk 5s was configured as a gunship with rocket pods and missiles.

▲ Heli-liner
Although it was noisy and had a narrow fuselage, Bristow Helicopters used the Wessex 60 to transport oil workers to rigs off the coast.

FACTS AND FIGURES

➤ Australia's navy flew 27 Wessex helicopters on anti-submarine duties starting in August 1962.

➤ Westland's first prototype, a rebuilt Sikorsky S-58, flew on 17 May 1957.

➤ Users of the versatile Wessex include Australia, Brunei, Ghana and Iraq.

➤ The Wessex had top priority and in 1960 Westland halted work on a larger 'heavylift' helicopter.

➤ A Wessex fired AS.12 missiles at an Argentine commander in the Falklands.

➤ Australia's Wessexes used Gazelle engines instead of coupled Gnomes.

PROFILE

Westland's 'old faithful'

The Wessex was based upon the Sikorsky H-34. It was intended to have a traditional piston engine, but Westland introduced the gas turbine Gazelle engine which enhanced both performance and economy.

The first Wessex was the anti-submarine HAS.Mk 1, which was fitted with advanced equipment, including dipping sonar and radar. The Royal Navy's Wessex HU.Mk 5s, flying in the tactical airlift role for the support of the Royal Marines, were deployed to Borneo and Oman to support the soldiers of 22 SAS Regiment.

The HC.Mk 2, produced for the Royal Air Force, was ordered in substantial numbers and saw active service in Aden, Cyprus and Northern Ireland. But the Wessex's finest hour was in the Falklands War. Naval HAS.Mk 3s carried out rescue and anti-submarine missions and fired AS.12 missiles.

The Royal Navy retired its last Wessex in the early-1980s, but the RAF continued to operate it in the tactical airlift role.

The RAF's Royal Flight used the Wessex for transporting the Royal Family, including their visits to Northern Ireland. Reliability has always been a great strength of the Wessex despite its age.

The Wessex rotor head was an old-style conventional type with dragging and flapping hinges. The blade pitch was altered by control rods attached to rotating and non-rotating swash plates.

Wessex HC.Mk 2

Type: tactical transport/ground assault helicopter

Powerplant: two coupled 1007-kW (1,350-hp.) Bristol Siddeley Gnome Mk 110 and Mk 111 turboshaft engines

Maximum speed: 212 km/h (132 m.p.h.) at sea level

Range: 769 km (477 mi.)

Weights: empty 3767 kg (8,287 lb.); maximum take-off 6123 kg (13,470 lb.)

Armament: provision for 7.62-mm GPMGs, rocket pods or SS.11 or AS.12 missiles; naval versions carry two Mk 44 torpedoes or Mk 11 depth charges

Dimensions:
main rotor diameter	17.07 m (56 ft.)
length, rotors turning	20.04 m (65 ft. 9 in.)
height	4.93 m (15 ft. 3 in.)
main rotor disc area	228.81 m² (2,462 sq. ft.)

WESSEX HAS.MK 3

This Wessex was nicknamed 'Humphrey'. It flew from the destroyer HMS *Antrim* when serving with the British taskforce in South Georgia and rescued an SAS patrol.

The Wessex Mk 3 had four all-metal main rotor blades driven by a Napier Gazelle rather than the twin Gnomes of the Wessex Mk 2.

The Wessex HAS.Mk 3 had accommodation for 12 to 16 troops or eight stretchers. An external winch could carry an additional 1800 kg (4,000 lb.) weight. The Royal Flight's HCC.Mk 4 is a specialised VIP version with soundproofing, flare-launchers and a luxury interior layout.

Emergency flotation bags triggered by contact with water were fitted to the wheels. They had a reputation for unreliability, failing to work during ditchings and being affected by rain.

Two pilots sat side-by-side in a high-mounted cockpit, with access via steps from the rear bay.

The Wessex HAS.Mk 3's main sensor for surface ship attack and diesel submarines was its radar set. This was operated by the observer.

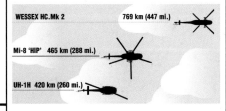

ROYAL NAVY

The Gazelle engine was reached through a hinging front door.

Weapons for the HAS.Mk 3 included 7.62-mm general-purchase machine-guns, Mk 46 torpedoes and Mk 11 depth charges.

Royal Navy Wessexes featured hinged rear fuselages for ease of stowage on ships.

Falklands operations

MISSILE ATTACK: Wessex HAS.Mk 3s armed with Mk 46 torpedoes and depth charges attacked the Argentinian submarine *Santa Fe* near Grytviken harbour and caused serious damage.

GLACIER RESCUE: A Wessex HU.Mk 5 crashed in whiteout conditions on Fortuna Glacier, South Georgia. After the attempted rescue of stranded SAS troops, casualties were eventually picked up by another Wessex HAS.Mk 3, called 'Humphrey'.

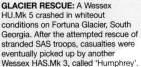

LIFE SAVER: A Wessex rescued sailors of the stricken HMS *Ardent* after the ship had been bombed by Argentine A-4Q Skyhawks and Daggers at Falkland Sound in 1982.

COMBAT DATA

MAXIMUM SPEED

Mil's helicopters are well known for their high speed, and Israeli pilots flying captured examples found that few other helicopters could keep up with them. The Wessex and UH-1 were much slower.

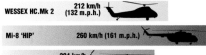

WESSEX HC.Mk 2	212 km/h (132 m.p.h.)
Mi-8 'HIP'	260 km/h (161 m.p.h.)
UH-1H	204 km/h (126 m.p.h.)

RANGE

One great strength of the Wessex was its range. The original H-34 had much shorter range because its piston engines were so much less efficient for the same weight. Range is more important at sea; on land a helicopter can refuel in the field.

WESSEX HC.Mk 2	769 km (447 mi.)
Mi-8 'HIP'	465 km (288 mi.)
UH-1H	420 km (260 mi.)

TROOP LOAD

Using the narrow fuselage from the original piston-engined H-34, the Wessex was limited in carrying capacity. The Mi-8 has a much wider fuselage and can carry much wider loads as well as more troops. The UH-1 is smaller than both these types.

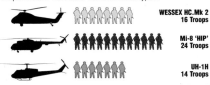

WESSEX HC.Mk 2	16 Troops
Mi-8 'HIP'	24 Troops
UH-1H	14 Troops

WESTLAND

WASP

● Anti-submarine ● Missile equipped ● Rescue

S aunders-Roe's P.531 not only evolved into the excellent Scout but also the redoubtable Wasp anti-submarine helicopter. Still in service with minor navies, the Wasp has proved to be adaptable to many roles including sub-hunting, rescue, fire bombing and even crop-dusting. Armed with missiles or torpedoes, the Wasp was a familiar sight on the decks of Royal Navy frigates and destroyers until the mid-1980s.

▲ The Wasp served with the Royal Navy for more than 20 years operating from frigates and destroyers. New Zealand, Indonesia and Malaysia still operate the Wasp.

WESTLAND WASP

▼ Projecting power
During the 1960s the Royal Navy was tasked with protecting British interests around the globe. The Wasp could be seen from Norway to the Antarctic.

▲ Fleet defender
The primary job of the Wasp was to protect British shipping from attack by submarine. By 1968 21 frigates were operating Small Ship Wasp Flights.

Stung by the ▶ Wasp
For anti-submarine missions the Wasp carried two Mk 44 torpedoes. For surface targets these were replaced by the AS.12 missile, as seen here.

◀ Up and away
Flying from a small helipad on a rolling ship is hazardous, and pilots were aided by deck crew with flags.

To the rescue ▶
In the medevac and rescue role the Wasp can winch help to casualties or pick up stretchers.

FACTS AND FIGURES

➤ Wasp deliveries began in 1963 after more than 200 test deck landings had been completed.

➤ The Royal Navy received a total of 98 Wasps; the last was retired in 1988.

➤ The second crewman acted as navigator, gunner, missile operator and winchman.

➤ Wasps were ordered by the navies of Brazil, South Africa, New Zealand and the Netherlands.

➤ Nine ships operated Wasps during the Falklands War of 1982.

➤ Wasps flew in support of British expeditions in Antarctica.

PROFILE

Lightweight sub-hunter

During a long and distinguished career in the Royal Navy, Wasps served around the world from the decks of warships. Developed from the Saro P.531, which first flew in 1958, the Wasp was a lightweight and adaptable anti-surface vessel and anti-submarine helicopter.

To counter the threat of enemy submarines the Wasp could be airborne within seconds, and with the aid of its mother ship's sonar it could attack with torpedoes or depth charges.

The 1982 Falklands War saw the Wasp operating in anger. Flying from survey ships, patrol ships, warships and hospital ships, as well as merchant vessels, Task Force Wasps completed 727 sorties, making 3,333 deck landings on tasks such as gunnery spotting, casualty evacuation and armed escort. In the most famous Wasp action aircraft from *Plymouth* and *Contender Bezant* attacked the Argentine submarine *Santa Fé*, and were instrumental in its destruction.

Although finally retired from Royal Navy service in the late-1980s, the Wasp, despite its antiquated equipment and appearance, continues to provide valuable service for the navies of New Zealand, Indonesia and Malaysia.

Above: The Netherlands navy was the second largest export operator and flew ship-based AH-12A Wasps until 1983.

Below: The three P.531s were pre-production Scout and Wasp trial aircraft and, unlike production Wasps, had skid landing gear. Tests were conducted on the frigate Nubian.

Wasp HAS.Mk 1

Type: anti-submarine and general-purpose naval helicopter

Powerplant: one 783-kW (1,050-hp.) Rolls-Royce Nimbus 103 turboshaft derated to 529 kW (710 hp.)

Maximum speed: 193 km/h (120 m.p.h.)

Initial climb rate: 439 m/min (1,560 f.p.m.)

Range: 435 km (270 mi.)

Service ceiling: 3810 m (12,500 ft.)

Weights: empty 1566 kg (3,445 lb.); maximum take-off 2495 kg (5,489 lb.)

Armament: two Mk 44 or Mk 46 torpedoes, or two depth charges, or two AS.11 or AS.12 air-to-surface missiles

Dimensions:
main rotor diameter	9.83 m (32 ft. 3 in.)
length	12.29 m (40 ft. 4 in.)
height	3.56 m (11 ft. 8 in.)
main rotor disc area	75.90 m² (817 sq. ft.)

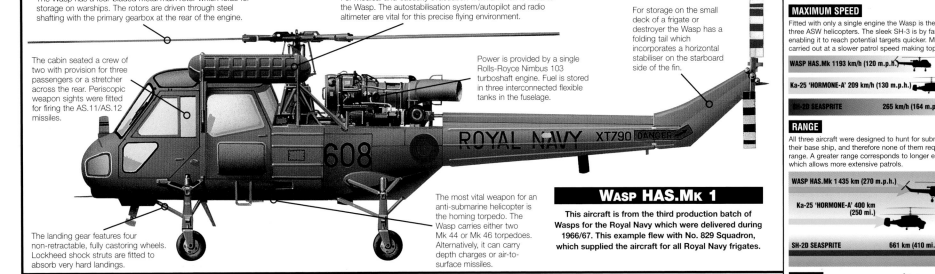

The Wasp has a four-bladed metal main rotor which folds for storage on warships. The rotors are driven through steel shafting with the primary gearbox at the rear of the engine.

For medical and casualty evacuation work a winch is fitted to the Wasp. The autostabilisation system/autopilot and radio altimeter are vital for this precise flying environment.

For storage on the small deck of a frigate or destroyer the Wasp has a folding tail which incorporates a horizontal stabiliser on the starboard side of the fin.

The cabin seated a crew of two with provision for three passengers or a stretcher across the rear. Periscopic weapon sights were fitted for firing the AS.11/AS.12 missiles.

Power is provided by a single Rolls-Royce Nimbus 103 turboshaft engine. Fuel is stored in three interconnected flexible tanks in the fuselage.

The landing gear features four non-retractable, fully castoring wheels. Lockheed shock struts are fitted to absorb very hard landings.

The most vital weapon for an anti-submarine helicopter is the homing torpedo. The Wasp carries either two Mk 44 or Mk 46 torpedoes. Alternatively, it can carry depth charges or air-to-surface missiles.

WASP HAS.MK 1

This aircraft is from the third production batch of Wasps for the Royal Navy which were delivered during 1966/67. This example flew with No. 829 Squadron, which supplied the aircraft for all Royal Navy frigates.

ACTION DATA

MAXIMUM SPEED

Fitted with only a single engine the Wasp is the slowest of these three ASW helicopters. The sleek SH-3 is by far the fastest, enabling it to reach potential targets quicker. Most ASW work is carried out at a slower patrol speed making top speed irrelevant.

WASP HAS.Mk 1 193 km/h (120 m.p.h.)
Ka-25 'HORMONE-A' 209 km/h (130 m.p.h.)
SH-2D SEASPRITE 265 km/h (164 m.p.h.)

RANGE

All three aircraft were designed to hunt for submarines close to their base ship, and therefore none of them requires extensive range. A greater range corresponds to longer endurance, however, which allows more extensive patrols.

WASP HAS.Mk 1 435 km (270 m.p.h.)
Ka-25 'HORMONE-A' 400 km (250 mi.)
SH-2D SEASPRITE 661 km (410 mi.)

POWER

Both the Seasprite and Ka-25 are twin-engined and can therefore lift a heavier weapons load. Two engines also offer safer over-water operations. The Wasp's single engine was always one of the design's major weaknesses, greatly limiting range and load.

SH-2D SEASPRITE 1864 kW (2,500 hp.)
Ka-25 'HORMONE-A' 1342 kW (1,800 hp.)
WASP HAS.Mk 1 529 kW (710 hp.)

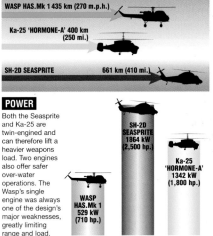

ASW helicopters of the Royal Navy

 **WHIRLWIND HAS.Mk 7:** As the Royal Navy's first ASW helicopter, the HAS.Mk 7 was fitted with radar and a torpedo.

 **WESSEX HAS.Mk 1:** This Westland-built version of the Sikorsky S-58 entered service aboard HMS Ark Royal in September 1961.

 **SEA KING HAS.Mk 1:** Again adapted from a Sikorsky design, the Sea King has been the Royal Navy's primary ASW platform for 20 years.

 **LYNX HAS.Mk 2:** Lethal against submarines or surface vessels, the Lynx currently serves aboard Royal Navy frigates and destroyers.

WESTLAND

SCOUT

● Anti-tank ● Casualty evacuation ● Battlefield liaison

estland's Scout was a versatile and reliable helicopter which was retired from the British Army in 1994. Serving in the anti-armour and scout helicopter role, it was similar to the naval Wasp. Despite being a rather limited machine built using old technology, the Scout was very popular. During the Falklands War, Scouts rescued injured soldiers while under fire, and fired wire-guided missiles at enemy strongpoints.

▲ The British Army typically flew its Scouts from remote bases with minimal support. Simple and easy to operate, the Scout helped the Army to develop the use of light helicopters.

WESTLAND SCOUT

▼ Wet feet
During the Falklands War a Scout suffered a main gearbox failure while hovering over a lake to avoid Argentine fighters. The pilot had to ditch the helicopter.

▲ Rocket launcher
A Scout gunner was required to steer the SS.11 missile to its target through thin command wires. The SS.11 was a powerful weapon, but the wires often snagged and broke in flight.

▼ Army trials
XP190 was the Army's first pre-production aircraft fitted with power controls. The Scout entered service in 1963, and was finally retired in 1994. By then only about 30 of the 150 originally in service were still operating.

▼ Bucket balancing
It was a test of skill to fly the Scout well, but the Army Air Corp's finest pilots could carry a bucket through a series of posts as part of the British Helicopter Championships.

▲ Checkpoint lifter
Dropping troops, often Special Forces soldiers, into surprise vehicle checkpoints in Ulster was a common Scout task.

◄ Naked engine
The Scout was designed in the days before heat-seeking, shoulder-launched missiles, and its engine was not shrouded to reduce heat signature.

FACTS AND FIGURES

➤ A Scout pilot won the Distinguished Flying Cross in the Falklands for flying under fire to rescue a severely injured soldier.

➤ Total production of the Westland Scout numbered 150 aircraft.

➤ King Hussein of Jordan had a Scout for his own personal use.

➤ The Empire Test Pilot School at Boscombe Down flew a Scout in their 'raspberry ripple' colour scheme.

➤ Two Scouts were operated from survey ships by the Royal Australian Navy.

➤ A Scout still flies with the British Army's historic flight at Middle Wallop.

Britain's flying jeep

The Westland Scout evokes vivid memories for British Army veterans, none stronger than the drama of Scouts during the 1982 Falklands War flitting to and from the front line, bringing in ammunition and carrying back casualties. This was highly dangerous: early in the conflict Argentine Pucarás shot down a Scout, killing its pilot and wounding the gunner.

Throughout much of the Cold War, the helicopter laboured at less violent but vitally important military duties.

The Scout was developed from the Saunders-Roe P.531, a design of the mid-1950s. The first examples to reach the Army in 1960 were, in fact, known as P.531 Mk 1s.

Renamed the Scout, this craft became a kind of flying jeep for hard-working soldiers. Some were fitted with roof-mounted sights and SS.11 missiles for use in the anti-tank role. This weapon was used in the Falklands War.

To its pilot, the Scout was a delight; a quick-responding helicopter able to pop in and

out of tight places. Scouts were very busy in Northern Ireland, used as a high-flying surveillance platform over the border and for moving troops to checkpoints.

Below: Formations of Scouts over the British Army's training area on Salisbury Plain were a common sight when the craft was based at the camp at Middle Wallop.

Above: The Scout and SS.11 was one of the first helicopter-missile combinations, and was reasonably successful.

SCOUT AH.MK 1

Serving in United Nations colours, the Scout was used in peacekeeping operations in Cyprus with the British Army during the 1960s.

Scout AH.Mk 1

Type: five-seat light utility helicopter

Powerplant: one 511-kW (685-hp.) Rolls-Royce (Bristol Siddeley) Nimbus Mk 101 or Mk 102 free-turbine turboshaft engine

Maximum speed: 212 km/h (131 m.p.h.)

Rate of climb: 155 m/min (508 f.p.m.)

Range: 510 km (316 mi.)

Service ceiling: 4085 m (13,400 ft.)

Weights: empty 1465 kg (3,223 lb.); loaded 2405 kg (5,291 lb.)

Armament: various options including manually aimed guns of up to 20-mm calibre; fixed 7.62-mm machine-gun installations, rocket pods or four SS.11 missiles

Dimensions:
main rotor diameter	9.83 m (32 ft. 3 in.)
length (rotors turning)	12.2 m (40 ft.)
height (rotors turning)	3.56 m (11 ft. 8 in.)
rotor disc area	75.89 m² (817 sq. ft.)

The main rotor had four blades of all-metal construction. The fully articulated hub had flapping and dragging hinges.

The cockpit of the Scout was very spartan. An autopilot/autostabiliser system could be fitted.

The pilot sat in the right seat, with the observer/missile aimer in the left seat.

Built initially as the Blackburn-Turboméca Turmo, the engine eventually became the Rolls-Royce Nimbus Mk 102 when Blackburn was taken over. The Scout showed its age in having an unshrouded engine.

The tail rotor was a simple, two-bladed metal type with a central flapping hinge.

For UN operations, the Scout traded in its national markings for the famous blue insignia.

The fuselage structure was all-metal semi-monocoque. The tail rotor driveshaft ran along the top of the tailboom.

Unlike its naval counterpart, the Wasp, the Scout had a small horizontal stabiliser under the rear of the tailboom.

ARMY   XP890   DANGER
UN

COMBAT DATA

OPERATIONAL SPEED

Battlefield helicopters fly at fairly low speed except when flying casualty evacuation or evading fighters. Anti-tank missions require short bursts of speed.

SCOUT AH.Mk 1	196 km/h (122 m.p.h.)
OH-58A	196 km/h (122 m.p.h.)
ALOUETTE II	180 km/h (112 m.p.h.)

RANGE

Scouts normally operated close to the front line, so their relatively short range was not a problem providing that there were convenient fuel supplies close at hand.

ALOUETTE II 720 km (446 mi.)
OH-58A 481 km (298 mi.)
SCOUT AH.Mk 1 510 km (316 mi.)

SS.11 missile attack

MISSILE LAUNCH: The SS.11 had a maximum range of just 3 km (1.8 mi.), so the Scout usually fired from a concealed position.

MANUAL GUIDANCE: Keeping the missile on track was the gunner's role. He looked through the site, keeping the target in the centre of the crosshairs and making any adjustments to the course with a small joystick.

HEAT WARHEAD: The conical cavity of the explosive turned the metal liner of the warhead into a super-heated gas, which was able to blast a hole through thick steel. The SS.11 could pierce 600 mm (24 in.) of armour.

WESTLAND

SEA KING

● Anti-ship and anti-submarine ● British built ● Search and rescue

▲ Originally designed to fulfil the anti-submarine warfare (ASW) mission with the Royal Navy, the Sea King now serves in a variety of roles with air arms around the world.

I n the UK a modified version of the Sikorsky S-61 Sea King, with Rolls-Royce Gnome engines replacing the original General Electric T58s, is built under licence by Westland. The first Westland-built aircraft flew in May 1969. Since then, the helicopter has been produced in several variants for a variety of roles. Typical anti-submarine equipment includes radar, dipping sonar and torpedoes. Sea Kings are also used in SAR and anti-shipping roles.

WESTLAND SEA KING

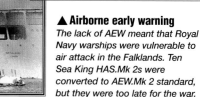

▲ Airborne early warning
The lack of AEW meant that Royal Navy warships were vulnerable to air attack in the Falklands. Ten Sea King HAS.Mk 2s were converted to AEW.Mk 2 standard, but they were too late for the war.

▲ Anti-submarine SAR
When ships were hit during the Falklands conflict every available helicopter flew rescue missions.

Advanced Sea King ▶
In this developed form the Sea King is a formidable weapon, especially when armed with the lethal Sea Eagle missile.

◀ Norwegian Mk 43B
All of Norway's surviving Sea Kings have been upgraded to Mk 43B standard with nose-mounted search radar and forward-looking infra-red (FLIR). They fly in the search-and-rescue role from bases located along Norway's long, dangerous coastline.

▲ RAF rescue
RAF search-and-rescue units fly the Sea King HAR.Mk 3, which was specially built for the role. An even more advanced HAR.Mk 3A has entered service despite problems with the auto-hover system.

FACTS AND FIGURES

➤ Westland had to fight off stiff competition from the Sikorsky Sea King to gain Royal Navy orders.

➤ Rolls-Royce based its Gnome turboshaft on the T58 of the Sikorsky helicopter.

➤ Sea King AEW.Mk 2s are known to their crews as 'bags'.

➤ Only the airframe shape and rotorhead of the Sikorsky Sea King remained unchanged.

➤ British ASW and assault Sea Kings served during the Gulf War.

➤ Searchwater radar used by the AEW.Mk 2 is similar to that fitted to RAF Nimrods.

Westland's king of the sea

Britain's Royal Navy bought a total of 152 Mk 1, 2, 5 and 6 Sea Kings, most of them as anti-submarine aircraft. Ten of the helicopters have been modified with side-mounted radomes to act as airborne early-warning (AEW) aircraft, a conversion which was introduced as a result of experience gained during the Falklands War.

The RAF uses the Mk 3 for air-sea rescue, and more than 140 Sea Kings have been delivered to export customers, including the Australian and German navies.

The Advanced Sea King introduced more powerful Gnome engines and composite rotor blades. India was the first customer for this model. Many older Sea Kings have also been fitted with the composite rotor blades, which reduce fuel consumption. Mission equipment has also been dramatically improved since the type first entered service, with current aircraft compatible with a range of modern weapons, including the Sea Eagle anti-ship missile.

Above: The primary role of Royal Navy Sea Kings is ASW. However, some HAS.Mk 5s have been converted to SAR HAR.Mk 5s by the removal of anti-submarine equipment.

Below: A specialised SAR variant, based on the HAS.Mk 1, was delivered to the West German Marineflieger in 1973/74. In the late-1980s any surviving machines were modified and upgraded by MBB to give them an anti-ship capability.

Sea King Mk 42B

Type: naval helicopter

Powerplant: two 1092-kW (1,465-hp.) Rolls-Royce Gnome H.1400-1T turboshafts

Maximum speed: 226 km/h (140 m.p.h.) at sea level

Climb rate: 619 m/min (2,030 f.p.m.) maximum at sea level

Range: 1482 km (920 mi.) with standard fuel

Weights: empty 5393 kg (11,865 lb.); maximum take-off 9752 kg (21,454 lb.)

Armament: four torpedoes or depth charges, or Sea Skua, Sea Eagle or Exocet anti-ship missiles

Dimensions:
rotor diameter	18.9 m (62 ft.)
length	22.15 m (72 ft. 8 in.)
height	5.13 m (16 ft. 10 in.)
main rotor disc area	280.47 m² (3,018 sq. ft.)

SEA KING MK 48

Belgium received five Sea Kings which were roughly equivalent to German and Norwegian SAR specialised aircraft.

During the mid-1980s Belgian Sea Kings received their first major upgrade. This included new, composite main rotor blades and the installation of advanced navigation systems.

The MEL ARI.5995 search radar is housed in this spine-mounted radome. In an ongoing upgrade programme this system is being replaced by a Bendix RDR1500B radar in an enlarged radome.

Having been designed to operate from the confines of a ship, the Sea King was given a folding tail. Although rarely used on land-based aircraft, the tail folds along this prominent hinge line.

RS02 DANGER→

Crew entrance is via this two-part door on the left-hand side of the fuselage. A large sliding door allows cabin access from the opposite side.

With its boat-shaped hull and fuselage-mounted sponsons the Sea King is capable of amphibious operations. Helicopters are naturally top-heavy, however, and the best a ditched crew might hope for is to escape before the aircraft turns over and sinks.

A fixed tailwheel protrudes from the rear of the Sea King's boat-like hull. Operations from water are rare and the fixed tailwheel does not hinder normal service alterations.

Many early Sea Kings were fitted with five-bladed tail rotors. A six-bladed unit has now replaced the older rotor in most cases, usually as part of an upgrade programme.

ACTION DATA

MAXIMUM SPEED

With its aerodynamically cleaner airframe and slightly lower maximum take-off weight, the Sikorsky SH-3H is faster than the Westland Sea King. The 'Haze-A' closely matches the British machine.

SEA KING Mk 42B 226 km/h (140 m.p.h.)
Mi-14PL 'HAZE-A' 230 km/h (143 m.p.h.)
SH-3H SEA KING 267 km/h (166 m.p.h.)

INITIAL CLIMB RATE

Again the lighter, less well-equipped SH-3H has a better climb rate than the Sea King Mk 42B. The Mi-14PL lags considerably behind and has proved less versatile in service.

SEA KING Mk 42B 619 m/min (2,030 f.p.m.)
SH-3H SEA KING 670 m/min (2,200 f.p.m.)
Mi-14PL 'HAZE-A' 468 m/min (1,535 f.p.m.)

RANGE

For long anti-submarine patrols and SAR missions, range is an important factor. The Westland helicopter outperforms its American cousin because of its more advanced engines and engine control systems. The Mi-14PL is again left trailing.

SEA KING Mk 42B 1482 km (920 mi.)
Mi-14PL 'HAZE-A' 925 km (575 mi.)
SH-3H SEA KING 1005 km (625 mi.)

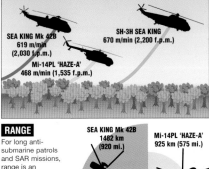

Sea King operations

In Royal Navy service most Sea Kings fly as ASW or ASV (anti-surface vessel) platforms. RAF Sea Kings are used exclusively in the search-and-rescue role.

ANTI-SUBMARINE WARFARE: Using its dipping sonar in combination with dropped sonobuoys, the Sea King is able to detect a submarine from the acoustic echoes it produces.

AIRBORNE EARLY WARNING AND CONTROL: As well as providing advanced warning of an attack, the AEW.Mk 2 is capable of controlling the air war.

SEARCH AND RESCUE: Not all rescues are made at sea. RAF and Royal Navy helicopters are busy, especially during the winter months, in the mountains of Wales and the Scottish Highlands.

WESTLAND

LYNX (ARMY)

● Anti-tank ● Tactical transport ● Gulf War veteran

▲ Although built in reasonably modest numbers for the British Army, the Army Lynx has become an invaluable Army Air Corps asset in the battlefield transport and anti-tank roles.

Westland and Aérospatiale produced the Lynx, together with the Puma and Gazelle, under the Anglo-French helicopter agreement of 1967. The first of 13 prototypes flew in March 1971, and subsequent production includes both army and navy versions. Unlike its naval counterpart, the Army Lynx has not attracted export orders, but it has been developed into the British Army's main battlefield helicopter.

PHOTO FILE

WESTLAND LYNX (ARMY)

▲ **Combat ready**
Infra-red exhaust suppressors, a roof-mounted sight and TOW missiles make the Lynx AH.Mk 7 a formidable weapon system.

▲ **Humanitarian Lynx**
Britain's army, like many European forces, has dedicated a number of aircraft to United Nations' support missions.

▼ **Looking for exports**
Lynx 3 was a bold attempt by Westland to win export orders and was marketed several times.

▲ **TOW attack**
Using natural cover as its only defence, a Lynx AH.Mk 1 unleashes a TOW missile at an unsuspecting tank. The missile's guide wires can just be seen at the mouth of the launch tube.

Lynx in yellow ▶
XW835 was the first Lynx prototype and was known as the WG.13. It later became G-BEAD for tests with two Pratt & Whitney PT6B-34 turboshafts. These engines made the helicopter underpowered.

FACTS AND FIGURES

➤ Westland planned to build 16 WG.13 prototypes because it considered the programme so technically demanding.

➤ Modified Scout helicopters were used to test the Lynx's main rotor system.

➤ An Army Lynx was rolled out publicly for the first time at Farnborough in 1972.

➤ During 1977 the Army Air Corps received its first production Lynx; the aircraft became operational in 1978.

➤ Lynx AH.Mk 1s were converted to AH.Mk 7 standard by the Royal Navy.

➤ Several features of the Lynx 3 were incorporated into the AH.Mk 9.

PROFILE

Claws of the Army Air Corps

Designated AH.Mk 1, the first Army Lynxes were delivered in 1977. They could carry nine troops, over 1350 kg (3,000 lb.) of external cargo or eight TOW (Tube-launched, Optically-tracked, Wire-guided) missiles, aimed using a sight on the cabin roof.

More powerful Gem 41 engines were introduced in the AH.Mk 7, in addition to improved avionics and a more powerful tail rotor. This enabled the helicopter to remain in the hover when carrying the heavy loads involved in anti-armour operations.

The final Army Air Corps version was the AH.Mk 9, which has wheels instead of skids and diffusers to reduce the infra-red signature of the exhaust. It serves with the two squadrons formed to support the rapid intervention 24th Armoured Brigade.

One-off experimental and trials versions of the Army Lynx include a fly-by-wire conversion of an AH.Mk 7 and a single AH.Mk 5X with Gem 41 engines.

A few other AH.Mk 5s were built, and although most were completed as AH.Mk 7s, one of the development aircraft was used for night-flying trials using a helmet-mounted display.

Above: Currently, the Lynx AH.Mk 9 has no TOW compatibility. If funding permits this could be added later, but the capability seems irrelevant following the recent purchase of the AAC Apache.

Above: XX153 was the first Lynx to be completed as a 'utility variant'. It set a world speed record on 29 June 1972, achieving 321.7 km/h (199.5 m.p.h.) over a 15/25-km (9.3/15/5-mile) course.

LYNX AH.MK 1

Seen in service with No. 1 Wing, British Army of the Rhine, XZ669 has been converted to AH.Mk 7 standard and is now based at Wattisham, Suffolk, with No. 669 Squadron of No. 4 Regiment, Army Air Corps.

Lynx AH.Mk 7

Type: multi-role battlefield helicopter

Powerplant: two 835-kW (1,120-hp.) Rolls-Royce Gem 42-1 turboshaft engines

Maximum cruising speed: 259 km/h (161 m.p.h.)

Initial climb rate: 756 m/min (2,480 f.p.m.) at sea level

Range: 630 km (390 mi.) with standard fuel

Weights: operating empty 2787 kg (6,130 lb.); maximum take-off 4354 kg (9,580 lb.)

Armament: two GIAT 20-mm cannon pods and one 7.62-mm (.30-cal.) machine-gun, rocket or gun pods, HOT, TOW or Hellfire anti-tank missiles

Dimensions:
main rotor diameter	12.8 m (42 ft.)
fuselage length	12.06 m (39 ft. 7 in.)
height	3.66 m (12 ft.)

Up to nine soldiers could be carried in the main cabin of the AH.Mk 1, or six with full combat equipment. A common transport mission for the Lynx is the forward movement and insertion of Milan-armed anti-tank teams.

Westland introduced a semi-rigid main rotor head on the Lynx. This system was far less bulky and complex than previous systems, and it improved performance and handling significantly.

British Aerospace, under licence from Hughes, built the Lynx roof-mounted sight. It allows missile guidance at ranges of up to 3750 metres.

Originally fitted with Gem 41-1 engines, from 1987 the Lynx's powerplant was upgraded to Gem 42-1 standard in the AH.Mk 7. These aircraft also have composite rotor blades.

A skid undercarriage allows the helicopter to operate from a variety of surfaces without the risk of sinking into soft ground.

Hughes manufactured the TOW missiles which are the Lynx's principal anti-tank armament. Optional weapons include air-to-air missiles and gun or rocket pods.

The AH.Mk 1 featured a counter-clockwise-rotating tail rotor. On the upgraded AH.Mk 7 it has been replaced by a more powerful clockwise-rotating unit made from composite materials, which gives better control in the hover.

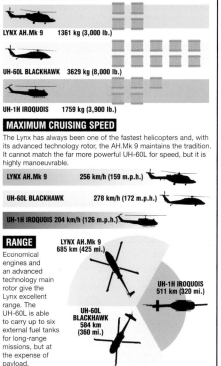

ACTION DATA

MAXIMUM PAYLOAD

With an increased maximum take-off weight, the Lynx AH.Mk 9 can carry a greater payload than previous Army Lynxes. It does not have the capacity of contemporary US Army battlefield transport helicopters, however.

LYNX AH.Mk 9	1361 kg (3,000 lb.)
UH-60L BLACKHAWK	3629 kg (8,000 lb.)
UH-1H IROQUOIS	1759 kg (3,900 lb.)

MAXIMUM CRUISING SPEED

The Lynx has always been one of the fastest helicopters and, with its advanced technology rotor, the AH.Mk 9 maintains the tradition. It cannot match the far more powerful UH-60L for speed, but it is highly manoeuvrable.

LYNX AH.Mk 9	256 km/h (159 m.p.h.)
UH-60L BLACKHAWK	278 km/h (172 m.p.h.)
UH-1H IROQUOIS	204 km/h (126 m.p.h.)

RANGE

Economical engines and an advanced technology main rotor give the Lynx excellent range. The UH-60L is able to carry up to six external fuel tanks for long-range missions, but at the expense of payload.

LYNX AH.Mk 9 685 km (425 mi.)
UH-1H IROQUOIS 511 km (320 mi.)
UH-60L BLACKHAWK 584 km (360 mi.)

Westland and the British Army

■ **WAPITI:** Using components from the DH.9A, Westland built the Wapiti as a specialised army co-operation aircraft for the RAF.

■ **LYSANDER:** Designed to fulfil the same role as the Wapiti, the Lysander was flown by the RAF in close co-operation with the Army.

■ **SCOUT:** Also built as the naval Wasp, the Scout was the AAC's primary observation and attack helicopter before the Lynx and Gazelle.

■ **GAZELLE:** Co-produced with Aérospatiale, the Gazelle took over the battlefield observation role from the Scout.

WESTLAND

LYNX (NAVY)

- ● Anti-submarine helicopter ● Missile-armed anti-ship strike

▲ *The Lynx has been a very successful light shipboard helicopter, outselling most of its competitors due to its excellent handling, good weapons fit and all-round versatility.*

Naval helicopters have added a new dimension to naval warfare. Blooded in the Falklands and used to deadly effect in the Gulf, the Westland Lynx, flown by the Royal Navy and other maritime services, is one of the most capable and versatile of the breed. In addition to hunting for submarines and attacking with torpedoes, depth charges or mines, it can track down even the fastest of surface vessels with onboard radar, striking with highly accurate air-to-surface missiles.

PHOTO FILE

WESTLAND LYNX (NAVY)

▼ Rolling deck
Royal Navy Lynx decks have a special grid fitted to them. After landing, the pilot lowers a 'harpoon' hook through it, which secures the Lynx to the deck even in very violent sea conditions such as this.

Super Lynx▶
The very latest Lynx variants have a 360° radar capability, passive infra-red sensors and inertial and satellite navigation systems.

▲ Marineflieger
The German Marineflieger operates its Sea Lynx helicopters from 'Bremen'-class frigates in the anti-submarine role. Unlike British Lynxes, the Marineflieger versions have a dipping sonar fitted. The unit, MFG 3, is based at Nordholz when it is not deployed at sea.

▲ War veteran
Britain's Fleet Air Arm has used the Lynx to devastating effect in modern maritime confrontations. It made its name launching Sea Skua missiles against Argentine craft.

▲ Rescue Lynx
While it was not specifically built for rescue missions, all Lynxes are capable of this, and most end up doing a rescue at some stage. Dutch navy Lynxes are also equipped with dunking sonar.

FACTS AND FIGURES

- ➤ The first Lynx prototype made its initial flight on 21 March 1971.

- ➤ The naval Lynx made its maiden flight on 10 February 1976.

- ➤ Most export Lynxes, like the nine used by the Brazilian navy, are based on Britain's HAS.Mk 2.

- ➤ Britain's first naval Lynx unit was No. 702 Squadron, Royal Navy, at Yeovilton, formed in December 1977.

- ➤ The Norwegian air force uses the naval Lynx for unarmed rescue missions.

- ➤ A modified Lynx holds the helicopter world speed record.

PROFILE

Westland's king of the waves

Originating in the Anglo-French helicopter agreement of 1967, the Westland Lynx is one of the most advanced medium shipborne helicopters in the world. The Royal Navy and French Aéronavale were the first users of the type, but it has since been ordered by eight other navies.

Although with a crew of two or three its maximum weight is only 4600 kg (10,120 lb.), the Lynx can perform a wide variety of naval tasks. Its primary function is anti-submarine

warfare, but it can also perform reconnaissance, anti-shipping search-and-strike, search-and-rescue, fire support, liaison and vertical replenishment missions, and as an attack transport it can carry 10 fully-equipped Marines.

Among many naval Lynx weapons is the highly accurate Sea Skua missile, which, like the helicopter, made its combat debut in the Falklands War of 1982. The war made it necessary to fly helicopters at double the most intensive normal flying rate, often in blizzard conditions, where the

Lynx proved not only its potency but also its resilience. Later in the Gulf War, using the same weapon, Royal Navy Lynxes ripped the heart out of Iraq's force of fast-attack craft picking off their targets with impunity.

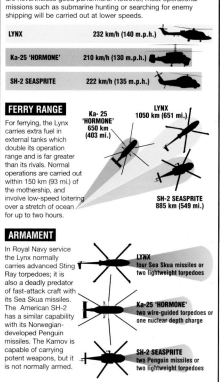

The Lynx has been the most successful small shipboard helicopter of the post-war period. It combines small size and high performance with excellent handling at sea, advanced-technology sonar and weapons, and unmatched multi-role capability.

The Lynx is an extremely agile machine, thanks to its high-technology rigid rotor head and advanced rotor blades.

The Lynx crew consists of a pilot and observer (tactical systems operator) sitting side by side in the cockpit. Some users also have a crewman in the rear cabin, for sonar-operating or rescue work.

Lynx HAS.Mk 2 (FN)

Type: shipboard anti-submarine, anti-ship, and rescue helicopter

Powerplant: two 836-kW (1,120-hp.) Rolls-Royce Gem 41-1 turboshaft engines

Max speed: 322 km/h (200 m.p.h.)

Max cruising speed: 232 km/h (140 m.p.h.)

Range: (typical) 590 km (365 mi.)

Weights: empty 3030 kg (6,670 lb.); max loaded 4763 kg (10,479 lb.)

Armament: twin Mk 44, Mk 46 or Sting Ray ASW torpedoes or Mk II depth charges plus anti-submarine sensor systems, or four Sea Skua or similar anti-ship missiles; provision for 1361-kg (2,995-lb.) slung cargo

Dimensions:
main rotor diameter	12.8 m (42 ft.)
length	11.93 m (39 ft.)
height	3.6 m (12 ft.)

LYNX HAS.MK 2 (FN)

The Aéronavale operates the Lynx in the anti-submarine and anti-surface roles. It will soon be replaced by the new Eurocopter NH 90.

The nose contains the advanced Seaspray radar for surface search. British Lynxes use it to guide the Sea Skua anti-ship missile.

If dipping sonar is fitted, the sonar body and its winch and cable unit are located in the rear cabin.

French Lynxes of the Aéronavale mount a winch on the starboard fuselage.

Naval Lynxes are easily identifiable from their land-based counterparts by their wheeled undercarriages. Most military variants are equipped with landing skids.

269 MARINE

DANGER →

269

The Lynx can carry depth charges or lightweight torpedoes. Most nations use the American Mk 44/46.

The wheels of the Lynx can move through 360˚, to allow it to manoeuvre safely on small flight decks.

Aéronavale Lynxes have a small tail-guard fitted to prevent the tailboom striking the deck when landing in rough weather conditions.

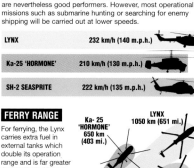

COMBAT DATA

MAXIMUM CRUISING SPEED

A specially-prepared variant of the Lynx broke the world helicopter speed record in the 1980s. Operational aircraft are not as fast, but are nevertheless good performers. However, most operational missions such as submarine hunting or searching for enemy shipping will be carried out at lower speeds.

LYNX	232 km/h (140 m.p.h.)	
Ka-25 'HORMONE'	210 km/h (130 m.p.h.)	
SH-2 SEASPRITE	222 km/h (135 m.p.h.)	

FERRY RANGE

For ferrying, the Lynx carries extra fuel in external tanks which double its operation range and is far greater than its rivals. Normal operations are carried out within 150 km (93 mi.) of the mothership, and involve low-speed loitering over a stretch of ocean for up to two hours.

Ka-25 'HORMONE' 650 km (403 mi.)

LYNX 1050 km (651 mi.)

SH-2 SEASPRITE 885 km (549 mi.)

ARMAMENT

In Royal Navy service the Lynx normally carries advanced Sting Ray torpedoes; it is also a deadly predator of fast-attack craft with its Sea Skua missiles. The American SH-2 has a similar capability with its Norwegian-developed Penguin missiles. The Kamov is capable of carrying potent weapons, but it is not normally armed.

LYNX four Sea Skua missiles or two lightweight torpedoes

Ka-25 'HORMONE' two wire-guided torpedoes or one nuclear depth charge

SH-2 SEASPRITE two Penguin missiles or two lightweight torpedoes

Lynx Sea Skua attack

■ **SOLID FUEL:** The Sea Skua is powered by a solid rocket, and can be handled and stored like ammunition.

■ **FAST TARGETS:** Sea Skua was designed to engage small missile-armed attack craft travelling at speeds of 75 km/h (46 m.p.h.).

■ **LAUNCH:** The Lynx detects targets with its radar. It will launch its attack when within missile range, which at low level is between 15–20 km (9–12 mi.).

■ **SEA SKIMMER:** To avoid detection on enemy radar, the 1000-km/h (600-m.p.h.) Sea Skua is programmed to fly just above the surface of the water.

■ **TARGET DESTROYED:** A blazing Iraqi patrol boat proves the devastating effect of the Sea Skua's 20-kg (44-lb.) armour-piercing warhead.

WESTLAND
COMMANDO

● Middle Eastern favourite ● Combat proven ● Assault transport

A tactical transport helicopter based on the anti-submarine Sea King, the Commando dispenses with the naval equipment to make room for troops, cargo or casualties. Operated in various versions as troop and VIP transport, electronic warfare platform and anti-ship helicopter by several overseas air arms, as well as the Royal Navy, it has seen service in the Falkland Islands, the Persian Gulf and Bosnia.

▲ Having operated in some of the world's harshest environments, including the Arctic Circle and Arabian desert, the Commando is regarded as a fine assault helicopter.

WESTLAND COMMANDO

▼ Commando production
Wearing a 'class B' registration, this Commando is undergoing pre-delivery test flying. The aircraft has been produced in some numbers for export.

▲ Sponsors gone
Neither the Commando Mk 2 nor the Sea King HC.Mk 4 have the distinctive undercarriage sponsons of the Sea King.

Egyptian assault ▶
Having used the early Commando Mk 1, Egypt later purchased the Mk 2. The aircraft are often flown without sand filters.

◀ VIPs on the Mk 2B
Egypt's Mk 2Bs have air-conditioning and a thoroughly soundproofed cabin.

Qatari ship killers ▶
Qatar may have added upgraded Commando Mk 2As to its fleet of Mk 3s. The latter aircraft represent a powerful maritime strike effort.

FACTS AND FIGURES

➤ The Commando Mk 1 is also known as the Sea King Mk 70 and is basically a stripped-out Sea King HAS.Mk 1.

➤ No customer has ever specified the Mk 2's optional underwing hardpoints.

➤ Westland flew the first commando Mk 2 on 16 January 1975.

➤ An idea to fit the Commando Mk 2 with 26 inflatable cabin seats was abandoned at an early stage.

➤ Commando Mk 2Bs have extra seats for two flight attendants.

➤ Qatar's Mk 3s have Sea King-like undercarriage sponsons.

Sea King assault version

Based on the Sea King Mk 41, the original Commando Mk 1 was developed by Westland in the hope that it might be ordered to replace the Royal Navy's Wessex Commando helicopters. In the event, no initial British interest was expressed and the Egyptian air force placed the first order.

The Mk 1 had minimal modifications, but the Mk 2 has a fixed undercarriage, an Advanced Sea King tail unit and composite rotor blades. Egypt acquired 17 standard Mk 2s, plus two Mk 2B VIP transport versions and four Mk 2E electronic warfare variants,

with Italian systems.

When armed, most Commandos carry a cabin-mounted 7.62-mm (.30-cal.) machine-gun, and the eight Mk 3s delivered to Qatar have provision for Exocet anti-ship missiles as well as rocket and machine-gun pods.

The biggest customer for the Commando is the Royal Navy, whose 41 Sea King HC.Mk 4s replaced the Wessexes used to transport Royal Marine Commandos. They carry the Sea King name despite being based closely on the Commando Mk 2.

Other operators include the

Royal Aerospace Establishment, which uses two Sea King Mk 4Xs to test various equipment, including rotors and avionics.

Above: Qatari Commando Mk 2As wear a two-tone desert camouflage scheme.

Right: Royal Navy Sea King HC.Mk 4s flew in support of British forces during the Gulf War. They also flew intensively during the Falklands conflict.

Commando Mk 2

Type: tactical military helicopter

Powerplant: two 1238-kW (1,660-hp.) Rolls-Royce Gnome H.1400-1T turboshafts

Maximum cruising speed: 204 km/h (126 m.p.h.) at sea level

Range: 396 km (245 mi.) with maximum payload; 1482 km (920 mi.) with standard fuel

Hover ceiling: 1980 m (6,500 ft.) in ground effect

Weights: empty operating 5620 kg (12,364 lb.); maximum take-off 9752 kg (21,455 lb.)

Accommodation: two crew plus up to 28 troops

Dimensions:

main rotor diameter	18.9 m (62 ft.)
fuselage length	17.02 m (55 ft. 10 in.)
height	4.72 m (15 ft. 6 in.)
main rotor disc area	280.47 m² (3,018 sq. ft.)

COMMANDO MK 2

Egypt received 19 Commando Mk 2s. Two are flown as VIP aircraft (Mk 2Bs), one of which wears a smart dark green and white colour scheme.

All operators of the Commando frequently use their aircraft in harsh, sandy environments. Sand filters for the engine intakes are therefore a useful option.

Removing the hydraulic blade-folding system of the naval Sea King gave the Commando a 91-kg (200-lb.) weight saving in this area alone. Simplification of the undercarriage and the removal of heavy naval avionics improved payload even further.

Westland lengthened the cabin of the Commando, although external dimensions are unaltered. To achieve this, the rear bulkhead was moved aft by 1.7 metres (5 ft. 7 in.).

Although it retained the boat-shaped hull of the Sea King, the Commando dispensed with the retractable main wheels and the sponsons with their associated flotation equipment. The simple stub wing-mounted undercarriage saves weight and increases weapons-carrying ability, and may be fitted with removable emergency flotation packs.

ACTION DATA

RANGE

With its extensive range, the Commando is able to transport troops over long distances. Alternatively, it has long endurance for multiple missions over a small radius, such as moving supplies and equipment between ships.

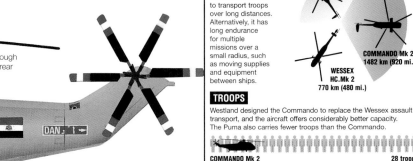

PUMA HC.Mk 1 572 km (355 mi.)

COMMANDO Mk 2 1482 km (920 mi.)

WESSEX HC.Mk 2 770 km (480 mi.)

TROOPS

Westland designed the Commando to replace the Wessex assault transport, and the aircraft offers considerably better capacity. The Puma also carries fewer troops than the Commando.

COMMANDO Mk 2 — 28 troops

WESSEX HC.Mk 2 — 16 troops

PUMA HC.Mk 1 — 15 troops

INITIAL CLIMB RATE

With its powerful Gnome turboshafts, the Commando offers good performance. This is reflected in its initial climb rate, especially when compared to the older Wessex and the RAF's Puma HC.Mk 1.

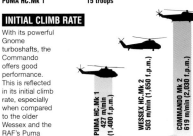

PUMA HC.Mk 1 427 m/min (1,400 f.p.m.)

WESSEX HC.Mk 2 503 m/min (1,650 f.p.m.)

COMMANDO Mk 2 619 m/min (2,030 f.p.m.)

Royal Navy Commandos in the Falklands

TAKING THE *NARWAL*: Following a Sea Harrier attack on the Argentine spy trawler *Narwal*, two Sea King HC.Mk 4s and an HAS.Mk 5 took the crew prisoner.

SKYHAWK ATTACK: After delivering a cargo of 105-mm artillery shells to a forward location, ZA298, a Sea King HC.Mk 4 of No. 846 Naval Air Squadron, was attacked by an A-4B Skyhawk. The main rotor was hit by 20-mm cannon fire, but, despite the pilot's evasion tactics, a replacement blade was flown in and the helicopter was repaired in the field.

INDEX